Dear Martin,

A gift for you to mark our many years of warm friendship. I hope you will enjoy reading it. I wish you all the best for the future!

Amitiés!

[illegible]

Shafi Fazaluddin

Conciliation in the Qur'an

Islam – Thought, Culture, and Society

Volume 9

Shafi Fazaluddin

Conciliation in the Qur'an

The Qur'anic Ethics of Conflict Resolution

DE GRUYTER

ISBN 978-3-11-074720-1
e-ISBN (PDF) 978-3-11-074734-8
e-ISBN (EPUB) 978-3-11-074746-1
ISSN 2628-4286

Library of Congress Control Number: 2021946830

Bibliographic information published by the Deutsche Nationalbibliothek
The Deutsche Nationalbibliothek lists this publication in the Deutsche Nationalbibliografie; detailed bibliographic data are available on the Internet at http://dnb.dnb.de.

Cover image: Calligraphy by Osman Özçay. With friendly permission.
Typesetting: Integra Software Services Pvt. Ltd.
Printing and binding: CPI books GmbH, Leck

MIX
Papier aus verantwortungsvollen Quellen
FSC www.fsc.org
FSC® C083411

www.degruyter.com

This book is dedicated to the memory of my late parents, Mr. M. Fazaluddin and Mrs. S. Fazaluddin, who first encouraged me towards the pursuit of knowledge, particularly in the field of Qur'anic Studies. A special mention should also be given to their notable teacher and renowned exegete of the Qur'an, the late Professor Abdul Qadeer Siddiqui, the first Dean of the Faculty of Theology at the Osmania University, Hyderabad, India.

Acknowledgements

I would like to express my appreciation for the support and encouragement of Professor M. A. S. Abdel Haleem and Professor A. H. I. Al-Matroudi of SOAS, University of London. Both were inspirational teachers during my academic venture into Qur'anic Studies, and later became guiding mentors and supportive supervisors of my doctoral thesis, on which this book is based. Mr. I. D. Edge at SOAS acted as a third supervisor of the doctoral thesis, providing a valuable legal perspective on the research. Also at SOAS, Dr. Yenn Lee provided motivation and helpful suggestions as the research progressed, and Mr. Ahmed Al-Khashem was consulted in respect of some Arabic terms.

Professor Ian Netton of Exeter University and Dr. Salwa El-Awa of Swansea University both offered their advice and kind encouragement with regard to the publication of this work, and Dr. El-Awa in particular provided detailed suggestions for its development.

I would like to thank the whole team at De Gruyter for their efforts in the editing and publication of this work, with special thanks to Dr. Sophie Wagenhofer and Katrin Mittmann for their valuable suggestions, and their pleasant and efficient handling of the entire process to publication.

I would also like to thank my family and friends for their support throughout. My children Habeeb, Kareem, Raheem and Hakeem provided enthusiastic encouragement together with their mother Dr. U. Hussain who also kindly reviewed some of the drafts and provided editing suggestions.

https://doi.org/10.1515/9783110747348-202

Contents

Notes

The doctoral thesis on which this book is based was completed at SOAS, University of London, in September 2019 and the doctorate degree was awarded in July 2020.

Chapter 2 of this book has previously been published as an article in adapted form (Fazaluddin S., 'Conciliation and Conflict in the Meccan and Medinan Qur'an: A Thematic Study of Suras 6 to 9', *Journal of Qur'anic Studies*, October 2020, vol. 22, Issue 3, pp. 63–101).

https://doi.org/10.1515/9783110747348-204

Introduction

Despite its nature as a historical, religious text, different interpretations of the Qur'an's social message regarding intra-community and inter-community relations can have significant contemporary implications. A balanced understanding of this important aspect of the Qur'an's discourse is therefore crucial, particularly in light of increasing diversity resulting from global migration. An over-riding focus on conflict in the Qur'an by historical and contemporary commentators has, however, obscured the subject of Conciliation in the Qur'an, which remains an under-researched field of study. This study aims to analyse, and evaluate the importance of, Conciliation in the Qur'an to provide a more balanced and complete understanding of the Qur'an's perspective on social relations.

Traditional Islamic authorship on the subject of Conciliation in the Qur'an, such as Muṣṭafā (2007), has also been unduly restrictive, often content to cite repetitively a small number of Qur'anic verses such as Q.4:35 and Q.4:128 which deal with marriage disputes and Q.49:9–10 which deal with group disputes. More academic literature has sufficed with an examination of Conciliation as an Alternative Dispute Resolution process in isolated social contexts such as Employment or Islamic Finance (see Hassan, 2006; Rasyid, 2013). Two important studies in the Arabic language by ʿAbd Al-Quddūs (1999) and Ṭāhā (2009) provide more in-depth examination but their relatively descriptive approach and restricted linguistic emphasis on the Arabic terms *ṣulḥ* (reconciliation, settlement) and *iṣlāḥ* (reconciliation, reform/order, proper conduct) have also resulted in a fragmented consideration of the subject. In particular, the context of suras such as Q.12 (the story of Joseph) and Q.48 (regarding Ṣulḥ Al-Ḥudaybiya) relates almost entirely to Conciliation, despite not mentioning *ṣulḥ*. In addition to a handful of Arabic language academic papers which largely reproduce classical legal theory of *ṣulḥ* in specific contexts such as criminal law, there are Arabic works on the important historical events of Ṣulḥ Al-Ḥudaybiya, such as Ḥijāzī (1986).

Whilst much has been written about Conciliation in Western literature, there is a dearth of material on the subject in relation to the Qur'an. In my previously published research on 'Conciliation Ethics in the Qur'an' (Fazaluddin, 2016, pp.336–39), I included a review of literature regarding the importance and application of *ṣulḥ*, and discussed some Western Conciliation theories which I also reference in this work. The same paper deals extensively with Conciliation in the context of marriage by reference to Q.4:35 and Q.4:128, mentioned above, and other verses. I will therefore not address this subject matter again in this research but provide a brief summary of the key points arising from the earlier analysis in Chapter 1.

https://doi.org/10.1515/9783110747348-001

Scope of Research and Research Questions

This research aims to redress the fragmented approach of existing research, by examining Conciliation as a holistic concept and evaluating its relative importance in the Qur'anic discourse. This will necessarily result in a broader interpretation of Conciliation than mere Qur'anic references to *ṣulḥ*, and may bring to light new concepts whose relevance and significance becomes fully apparent only after a detailed investigation. In examining Conciliation in the Qur'an, I consider the notion of Conciliation in its modern usage, where most definitions indicate the following two meanings:

1. the informal restoration of good relations between two parties or perspectives, and
2. the use of certain formal processes to resolve actual or potential legal disputes through an intermediary.

In line with my holistic approach, I will also examine those matters that deal with the avoidance of conflict, which may be considered a form of pre-emptive Conciliation. A holistic study of my subject will also necessitate a study of both Social and Divine-Human Conciliation, given the Qur'an's dual societal and theological narrative, although Divine-Human Conciliation will predominantly be studied as a means to informing the primary study of Social Conciliation. In order to provide an appropriately balanced analysis, I will additionally engage with significant segments of text which deal extensively with conflict, although my study will be limited to how conflict relates to Conciliation rather than providing a complete study on conflict of itself. I will also discuss the use of persuasive argument in the Qur'anic discourse, in order to explain its essential role in the proper contextualisation of the Qur'an's engagement with conflict.

In order to analyse and assess the relative importance of Conciliation within the Qur'anic discourse, I will address the following specific questions:

1. How pervasive is Conciliation in the Meccan and Medinan suras?
2. What range of aspects of Conciliation are manifest?
3. What, if any, literary techniques are used to emphasise Conciliation?
4. How coherent is the Conciliation material?

Question 1 will include a comparison of how pervasive Conciliation is in the Meccan and Medinan suras, to evaluate a suggestion of greater belligerence in Medinan suras (Cragg, 2001, p.90), as explained in the following section of the Introduction. Question 2 is self-explanatory and follows from my holistic approach to the study of the subject. Question 3 acknowledges the important role of literary techniques in fully understanding the meaning of a text and conveying the attitude a text imbues towards a given subject, as explained towards the end of the Introduction in the section 'Research Framework and Methodology'. Finally, Question 4 follows from an increasing contemporary academic interest in perceptions of the Qur'an as a coherent text based on different theories of *naẓm* (arrangement), which are explained and discussed further below in the section of the Introduction entitled 'The Development of Coherence Studies'. Although there may be an element of 'inherent' coherence in Qur'anic exegesis, as explained in the Research Framework and Methodology, it should be possible to go beyond this interpretive level to evaluate overall patterns of structural and thematic coherence in the Conciliation material examined.

Meccan and Medinan Suras

In Western literature, some writers have perceived a distinct contrast between the tone of the Meccan and Medinan revelation. Cragg (2001, pp.90, 95), for example, contrasts the 'innocent preachment' of the Meccan period with the 'transition to belligerence' in the Medinan period, seeing combat as the 'central feature' of the Medinan Qur'an. By contrast, other writers emphasise the freedom of religion and peace treaties established by the Prophet in the Medinan period, referring to a *'pax Islamica'* (Watt, 1961, pp.219–20). Furthermore, the prominent conciliatory teaching emphasising human equality in Q.49:13, quoted at the Prophet's Conquest of Mecca in 8 A.H. (Iqbal, 1965, p.43), has been judged later revelation but 'essential doctrine from the beginning' (Levy, 1969, pp.55, 192), suggesting a consistency between the two periods. Levy also recognises that such 'ethical doctrine in Islam is intimately connected with the law'. The development of Islamic Law is generally attributed to the Medinan period of revelation (Hallaq, 2005, pp.21, 195; Hallaq, 2016).

Whilst the generally shorter length, formulaic structures and common themes of the Meccan suras have made them accessible to academic writers (see, for example, Dayeh, 2010), the Medinan suras have largely escaped a systematic study due to their sheer size and divergence of style and theme. This is clearly illustrated by the extensive work on Qur'anic register and arrangement provided by Robinson (2003) in relation to Meccan suras, whilst dealing with only one Medinan sura. Even the comparative study of Locate-Timol (2009) provides structural, thematic and textual analysis of *selected* Medinan suras. Neuwirth (n.d., "Types of Medinan suras") considers a systematic study of the Medinan suras 'an urgent desideratum' in the field. I will partially address these issues, by examining the concentration of Conciliation passages in the Meccan versus the Medinan Qur'an comparatively to assess whether Conciliation is more or less emphasised in the Medinan Qur'an.

The Development of Coherence Studies

Classical commentators on the Qur'an often focussed on specific verses or concepts in the Qur'an in an isolated manner which may be referred to as an 'atomistic' approach. Perhaps surprisingly, therefore, Faiq (2011, para. 2) argues that there was always a historical desire amongst early scholars to find coherence in the Qur'an although it was expressed through different disciplines and sectarian doctrines. These early scholars, he argues, considered the choice of words, content and eloquent composition of the Qur'anic material to be demonstrative of its *iʿjāz* (miraculous nature), but the most significant advancement and contribution was that of ʿAbd Al-Qāhir Al-Jurjānī (d. 471/1078). According to Faiq (2011, paras. 7–8), Al-Jurjānī's theory sees all language as a system of relations so that the precise and holistic arrangement of words within a single discourse becomes instrumental to the overall meaning. Al-Jurjānī expounded a developed theory of *naẓm*, which remains of great importance in *al-balāgha* (study of the rhetorical style of the Qur'an).

Another perspective on Qur'anic coherence is highlighted by Abdul-Raof (2003, p.73) in the notion of *al-munāsaba* (conceptual and textual chaining) within Qur'anic discourse. Amongst classical exegetes who emphasised this notion, he refers to Fakhr Al-Dīn Al-Rāzī (d. 606/1209), and amongst contemporary exegetes he highlights Sayyid Quṭb's (d. 1966) *tafsīr Fī Ẓilāl Al-Qur'ān.* However, I believe it is important to distinguish between Al-Rāzī's focus on drawing connections of meaning between specific verses, and Quṭb's focus on a *miḥwar* (central thematic axis) in suras which takes the concept of coherence to the level of a much more systematic arrangement of internally and externally coherent blocks of text. Abdul-Raof (2003, pp.74–75) draws a contrast between the classical view of the Qur'an as being highly coherent based on the concept of chaining, and the view of modern Western scholars who often viewed the Qur'anic text as being disconnected and disparate.[1] Abdul-Raof (2003, p.92) also argues that the application of text linguistic strategies demonstrates that lexical items and grammatical structures are not random but rather support a continuity of meaning and sequentiality of concepts which is an essential feature of the Qur'anic discourse. Furthermore, he finds that the juxtaposition of

1 Abdul-Raof investigates the chaining phenomenon at the *micro* level (inter- and intra-verse) and at the *macro* level (inter- and intra-consecutive suras, p.74). His terminology must be distinguished from that of Neuwirth (n.d.) who refers to the sura as the most prominent *micro*-structure of the Qur'an, highlighting the use of similar terminology with different meanings by the two authors.

suras provides a natural progression of related themes and development of concepts, such as Prophethood or the Book.

It is surprising that Faiq's earlier discussion of subsequent modern approaches does not mention the important contributions of the Indian scholar Ḥamīd Al-Dīn Al-Farāhī (d. 1930) and his student and successor Amīn Aḥsan Iṣlāḥī (d. 1997) to the study of coherence, discussed in detail below. Abdul-Raof (2003, p.74) also makes only passing reference to these scholars, although his conclusions appear to be based almost entirely on the Farāhī-Iṣlāḥī theory, despite using the terminology of chaining in his analysis.

The Farāhī-Iṣlāḥī Theory

In his Urdu *tafsīr Tadabbur-e-Qur'ān*, Iṣlāḥī argues the apparent existence of well-defined themes in verse sequences, the pairing of complementary suras and the grouping of suras into seven distinct groups, with each group systematically developing a master theme. His teacher Farāhī's original Qur'anic structural schema is outlined in his own Arabic work *Dalāil Al-Niẓām*. Despite originating from the Indian subcontinent, Farāhī has authored several important works on Qur'anic Studies in classical Arabic, demonstrating his linguistic expertise and command of the language.

The Farāhī-Iṣlāḥī theory has been brought to light in Western academia in particular through the writing of Mir (1983b, 1986, 2013) and, to a lesser extent, of Khan (2002, 2008). Mir (1983a) emphasises that the work of exegetes such as Al-Rāzī merely highlights that the Qur'an is a *connected* text, which is to be contrasted with the modern phenomenon of Muslim scholars presenting the Qur'an as a text with significant thematic and structural *unity*, a point on which he considers there to be an increasing consensus (see also Nadeem, 2015). The modern trend amongst Muslim scholars identified by Mir towards recognising the sura as an important building block in the overall Coherence of the Qur'anic arrangement has also been recognised by Neuwirth (n.d., "Canonization and the problem of the 'sūra' as a unit", para. 6).

The apparent approval of the Farāhī-Iṣlāḥī theory by other writers is further confirmed by the work of Farrin (2014) who bases his book on the same theory, agreeing with many of its principles and additionally finding a concentric symmetry in the Qur'anic arrangement around a central group of suras. El-Awa (2006, p.20), another important writer in the field of Coherence Studies, also recognises the significant contribution of the Farāhī-Iṣlāḥī theory to the field. El-Awa's pioneering work represents a further advance in the methods used to study the Qur'anic text (in this regard, see Arkoun, n.d.). She examines two suras Al-Aḥzāb and Al-Qiyāma in detail and applies two linguistic theories for the study of textual relations: Relevance Theory and Coherence Theory.[2]

The Farāhī-Iṣlāḥī theory uses the terminology of *naẓm* but must be distinguished from the limited principle-based theory of Al-Jurjānī, by its comprehensive theory of Qur'anic textual arrangement. In light of all the above, the Farāhī-Iṣlāḥī theory arguably represents the most systematic, contemporary and accepted theory of Qur'anic arrangement to date. Despite the above merits, however, the Farāhī-Iṣlāḥī model remains a theory and should not be considered proven, as highlighted by Rippin (2013, p.1). In his view, this approach to coherence reflects contemporary ideas based on trends in Biblical studies and general literary theory. I would argue that if this is the case, then it can at least be observed that studies of Qur'anic coherence are developing in line with the wider study of other religious texts and literary theory in general. This in turn should provide greater credibility and accessibility to the findings of those studies.

Research Framework and Methodology

In my own Qur'anic analysis, I will adopt a contextual hermeneutic, interpreting text in light of both the immediate and related context, in line with the classical approach. It is an established maxim of Qur'anic exegesis that: *al-Qur'ānu yufassiru ba'ḍuhū ba'ḍā* (different parts of the Qur'an explain each other). A context-based approach is also emphasised in contemporary works on the subject of Qur'anic interpretation (Abdel Haleem, 2017). Linguistically, I will also examine the wording and rhetorical usage of language to construe the Qur'anic text both literally and purposively, seeking to ascertain the Qur'an's attitude to Conciliation. In support of this approach to analysing and interpreting texts, Bauer et al. (2014, pp.3, 10, 20) highlight both the need to enter into a 'reflexive dialogue' with the text, and the special importance of 'higher orders of text' such as narratives, rhetorical proofs and argumentation, metaphors and the framing of ideological discourse. In light of the above, my proposed dual contextual and linguistic approach is in line with established textual analysis

2 Another work on feminist interpretation (Hidayatullah, 2014), although apparently *naẓm*-based, is used merely to advocate an intra-textual method of Qur'anic interpretation and an interpretation of specific Qur'anic verses in light of their *maqāṣid* (underlying aims) of justice and human equality. Also see Ramsey (2015) for discussion of what I would term 'extra-Qur'anic Coherence' between the Qur'an and other prophetic revelation in the works of Sayyid Ahmad Khan.

practice and also results in what I consider an accurate interpretation. Where I sometimes derive principles of general application based on language, whilst restricting the scope of other verses by context, this is not for the purpose of achieving a desired outcome but follows from my hermeneutic approach.

For my overall Qur'anic analysis, I draw extensively on the two influential commentaries of the renowned exegete Fakhr Al-Dīn Al-Rāzī and the innovative scholar of the Indian subcontinent, Amīn Aḥsan Iṣlāḥī (for biographical information, see Nadeem, 1998), offering a balanced perspective between classical and contemporary exegesis. These commentaries are also highly complementary with the first providing linguistic emphasis and the other providing structural insight, both of which are especially pertinent to my specific research questions. In the Arabic language, Al-Rāzī's highly analytical *tafsīr* (exegesis) *Mafātīḥ Al-Ghayb* has been selected for its authoritative elucidation of key terminologies based on comprehensive and encyclopaedic reference to linguistic resources, legal rulings, historical context, Prophetic narrations and the opinions of earlier commentators (regarding Al-Rāzī's methodology, see Jaffer, 2013). Iṣlāḥī's Urdu *tafsīr Tadabbur-e-Qur'ān*, based on the works of his teacher Ḥamīd Al-Dīn Al-Farāhī (for biographical information, see Esposito, 2007), has been selected for its relatively unique insights and systematic approach to the structure and coherence of the Qur'an (regarding Iṣlāḥī's methodology, see Khan, 2008).

Despite its significance as perhaps the only comprehensive *tafsīr* of the Qur'an based on a coherence approach, the study of Iṣlāḥī's *tafsīr* has previously been limited due to it being written in the Urdu language; I will draw extensively upon this *tafsīr* providing new insight into this voluminous work, although without endorsing the Farāhī-Iṣlāḥī schema. Importantly, my study is not dependent on the validity of the Farāhī-Iṣlāḥī theory, but analyses the theory critically. It is also my intention to use Farāhī and Iṣlāḥī's hierarchical classification to frame my thematic study of Conciliation in the Qur'an, providing an organisational framework for my data analysis, segmenting my data in accordance with its sura groups and referencing its sura and group themes in my own thematic analysis. I believe this innovative approach to a thematic study has not previously been undertaken, with thematic and coherence studies often perceived as distinct research areas in Qur'anic Studies. In light of the above, this work provides an original contribution to research in the field, both through engagement in a holistic thematic study of Conciliation in the Qur'an, and by utilising and presenting a significant portion of Iṣlāḥī's comprehensive *tafsīr*, developing and implementing a methodology which combines thematic and coherence studies of the Qur'an.

In analysing the Qur'anic material, I conducted a manual survey of the entire Qur'an selecting some 250 verses relating to Conciliation. I then conducted a second more structural review in which I studied large segments of text surrounding these Conciliation verses, identifying and tabulating text segments of around 10–100 verses in which Conciliation featured in a sustained fashion. By analysing this structural review data, I identified key Conciliation themes which form the skeleton of my argument. Having also recorded the sura groups, pairing and themes according to the Farāhī-Iṣlāḥī theory (based on Farāhī (1968), the introduction to Iṣlāḥī's *Tadabbur-e-Qur'ān* and Mir (1986)), I critically assessed this classification in light of my review. For each text segment, I then reviewed Iṣlāḥī's sura overview and *tafsīr*, tabulating material pertinent to my research questions, and then reviewed Al-Rāzī's more detailed *tafsīr* of key terminologies within the segment. In total, around 1500 pages of Iṣlāḥī's *tafsīr* in Urdu and several hundred pages of Al-Rāzī's *tafsīr* in Arabic were reviewed. My approach of conducting a preliminary global structural analysis of the text followed by a more in-depth analysis of the constituent segments is broadly in-line with the iterative combination of recursive surface thematic mapping and in-depth interpretive work, argued for by Davidson et al. (2019) in analysing large-scale qualitative data sets. Davidson et al. refer to this as a 'breadth-and-depth' method.

From this *tafsīr* material, I have selected those insights which are most relevant to my research questions, and which facilitate my analysis by providing in-depth linguistic or structural focus. I have adduced such material not only where it supports but also where it challenges my argument, providing critical discussion. Given the volume of research material and the desire for greater depth of analysis, I have generally restricted my research to the work of two principal exegetes, albeit carefully selected to provide a complementary balance and range of insights as highlighted above. Given the long-standing tradition of scholarship around interpretations of the Qur'an, I believe it would be difficult to provide a plausible purely subjective contemporary analysis, detached from reputable and authoritative classical *tafsīr* works. At the same time, I do occasionally utilise what might be considered contemporary terminology such as 'freedom of religion' and 'conflict management systems' in my own analysis in seeking to correlate a historical text with a relevant, contemporary understanding of the notion of Conciliation and its related discourse.

I have tabulated the layout of Conciliation verses and segments across each sura group, providing a 'Conciliation Map' at the end of each chapter. The tabulated presentation of Qur'anic data is a common contemporary format in Qur'anic analysis. These Maps serve both as an interim figurative summary of key verses and an incremental device for the consolidation of data through the chapters, ultimately informing the structural and thematic analysis in the overall Conciliation Map and final conclusions at the end of the book. Subjectivity is inherent in original Qur'anic research (El-Awa, 2006, p.21) and the content of my study is similarly limited by the subjectivity of my analysis. I have counter-balanced this by greater transparency in presenting underlying material. The research is based primarily on historical texts and does not deal with any human subjects. Ethical issues should therefore be limited to proper acknowledgement and referencing of primary source material and secondary literature.

In English translations of the Qur'an, I use Abdel Haleem (2005) as my main translation due to its academic authorship, literary focus on the Qur'anic text and contemporary English language. I also occasionally refer to Yusuf Ali (2001), Nasr (2015) and Asad (2003) for additional insight into some key verses based on their comparative translations, elucidatory alternative meanings and explanatory notes – although I give much greater emphasis to primary sources of *tafsīr*, namely Al-Rāzī and Iṣlāḥī, in accordance with my general methodology. For Qur'anic and Arabic dictionaries, I refer to *Mufradāt Alfāẓ Al-Qur'ān* (Al-Iṣfahānī, 2009), *Al-Muʿjam Al-Mufahras Li-Alfāẓ Al-Qur'an Al-Karīm* (ʿAbd Al-Bāqī, 2001), the *Dictionary of Qur'anic Usage* (Abdel Haleem and Badawi, 2013) and *Lisān Al-ʿArab* (Ibn Manẓūr, 2014). Variant Qur'anic readings, often indicated by Al-Rāzī or otherwise highlighted in this work, are listed in *Muʿjama Al-Qirā'āt Al-Qur'āniyya* (ʿUmar and Mukarram, 1983).

In presenting my Qur'anic analysis in each chapter, I progress sequentially through the respective sura group, discussing in turn the key Conciliation verses or longer text segments identified in my structural review, as explained above. Where necessary, I adduce relevant intertextual references from further on in the sura group or elsewhere in the Qur'an to enrich my analysis of these verses, for example where a Qur'anic concept under discussion features elsewhere. Key Conciliation verses or text segments are identified in the initial overview of each chapter and also included in the summary table at the end of each chapter. Due to the volume of Qur'anic material, references to English translations of Qur'anic text and Al-Rāzī's *tafsīr* are by Qur'anic verse number, whilst references to Iṣlāḥī's *tafsīr*, which is less readily searchable by verse number, are by volume and page number. Due to the number of references, I use 'Prophet', capitalised, to refer to the prophet Mohammed, mentioning other prophets by name (in Islamic convention, the names of prophets are customarily followed by the honorific expression 'peace be upon him'). Although I generally translate each instance of Arabic and Urdu terms, I omit recurrent translations where the meaning should be apparent from frequency of use or a proximate earlier translation. English translations of Qur'anic text without citations are my own. All translations of Urdu and Arabic *tafsīr* are my own.

Having introduced the motivation behind this research as well as its scope and methodology, the following section now provides the historical and contemporary context for this thematic study of Conciliation in the Qur'an.

Conciliation in Context

Definitional Scope of *Ṣulḥ*

The root *ṣ-l-ḥ* features 240 times in 10 derivations in the Qur'an, including only 2 instances of *ṣulḥ* (reconciliation, settlement) but 28 instances of the form IV verb *aṣlaḥa*, 7 instances of its verbal noun *iṣlāḥ* (reconciliation, reform/order, proper conduct) and 5 instances of its active participle *muṣliḥ/muṣliḥūn* (Abdel Haleem and Badawi, 2013, p.531). Further dictionary analysis of key Conciliation terminology is provided in Sections 2.2.1, 3.1 and 5.1.

For background information not discussed below, Rozmus and Skoczek (1997) provide discussion of the root word *ṣ-l-ḥ* in Arabic and Hebrew. Rhetorics surrounding *ṣulḥ* are discussed by Diab (2016). The historical context of *ṣulḥ* and society structures in Meccan society, which provides background to the now ensuing discussion, is discussed by Denny (n.d.) and Al-Humaidhi (2015, pp.93–95).

Islam (2012, p.32) highlights that, according to Ḥadīth, *ṣulḥ* is considered a meritorious form of charity and in order to attain *ṣulḥ* even certain liberties with the truth are allowed. In this research, further examples will be sought where Conciliation may be exempted from other general principles as this could be an indication of its relative importance. When construed as an Alternative Dispute Resolution (ADR) mechanism, there is a wide range of Conciliation processes available within an Islamic system. Islam (2012) distinguishes *ṣulḥ*, including negotiation, mediation/conciliation and compromise of action, from other forms of ADR such as *taḥkīm* (arbitration), *ṣulḥ/taḥkīm* (med-arb), *muḥtasib* (ombudsman), informal justice by the *walī al-maẓālim* (chancellor) and *fatwa* of muftis (expert determination). Further distinction from arbitration in particular is provided by Alsheikh (2011, pp.378, 399). He defines *ṣulḥ* as a binding contract based on agreement between two parties, with concession of rights and after a dispute has occurred, with a 'defendant' denying, accepting or remaining silent as to his liability. Conversely, he considers arbitration binding upon issue of an award, from a third party satisfying certain formal criteria, and based on agreement to be bound by arbitration before, during or after a dispute occurs.

Although Al-Ramahi (2008, p.12) suggests that a *ṣulḥ* agreement is only binding when it occurs before a court, this position has been criticised (Alsheikh, 2011, p.377), justifiably in my view, as private agreements would still be binding in an Islamic system. I believe the practice of registering private *ṣulḥ* agreements in Ottoman courts (Tamdoğan, 2008) is more likely to be a result of

https://doi.org/10.1515/9783110747348-002

the evidential and enforcement benefits. An important reference to *sulh* at Q.4:35 in marriage disputes also refers to the appointment of a *ḥakaman* (arbiter) on behalf of each spouse, giving rise to a significant debate as to whether the intended process is a mutually agreed *ṣulḥ* or a binding arbitration imposed by third parties. Alsheikh (2011, p.382) states that the majority of jurists consider the arbiters' 'ruling' binding on the parties, whilst a minority of jurists including Ibn Ḥazm, Ibn Taymiyya and some Malikis consider it non-binding with the arbiters being merely agents of the parties. In Fazaluddin (2016, p.342), I supported the latter view, arguing that the arbiters have no legal authority to separate or reconcile the parties without their consent. The question of when a *ṣulḥ* is or is not binding will be considered further in this research.

Confusion in terminology arises from the use of *taḥkīm* to describe the above arbiter process. Sayen (2003, p.927) stresses the consensual nature of Islamic *taḥkīm* in contrast to binding Western arbitration, and is then criticised by Alsheikh (2011, p.382) for confusing 'arbitration' between spouses with normal Islamic arbitration. Although Alsheikh's criticism is reasonable since *taḥkīm* generally refers to binding arbitration, Alsheikh's own distinction between the two becomes unclear once *ṣulḥ* under Q.4:35 is considered binding, which he advocates. Q.4:35 itself refers to the root *ṣ-l-ḥ* and I would therefore argue that the above process should be referred to as *ṣulḥ* rather than either *taḥkīm* (per Sayen) or arbitration (per Alsheikh).

The limited application of *ṣulḥ* to criminal law is discussed by Hossain (2013, pp.2, 7–9). A *ṣulḥ* contrary to mandatory injunctions or prohibitions of Islamic Law is not permitted and neither is a *ṣulḥ* pertaining to the rights of God as opposed to the rights of people. One consequence of this is that *ṣulḥ* cannot remit *ḥadd* punishments (mandatory punishments in criminal cases), which are considered as falling within the rights of God or *maṣlaḥa ʿāmma* (public interest). These apply, for example, in the case of offences such as *zinā* (unlawful sexual intercourse) and theft. In accordance with various *ḥadīth*, however, the burden of proof to establish liability for such offences is high and construed in favour of the defendant, and *ṣulḥ* is also allowed if the offence is not brought before the authorities. Furthermore, *ṣulḥ* remains highly relevant in criminal law since, even in the case of homicide, liability for *qiṣāṣ* (retaliation) can be waived or the sentence mitigated under a *ṣulḥ*, based on provisions stipulated in the Qur'an and Ḥadīth. Tamdoğan's work below indicates a roughly equal distribution between *ṣulḥ* in Ottoman courts relating to criminal acts of wrongful death or injury and civil actions of debt or inheritance. All of this indicates that despite certain limitations, *ṣulḥ* has a significant role in criminal as well as civil matters, reinforcing its importance in Islamic Law and society.

Ṣulḥ in History

Conciliation is an essential aspect of Islamic history and development: the final 'genuine reconciliation' with the Meccan chieftains was considered the Prophet's 'greatest achievement' by Watt (1961, p.210). Another famous example of *ṣulḥ* in Islamic history is Ṣulḥ Al-Ḥudaybiya (6 A.H.). Following a Prophetic vision of their pilgrimage to Mecca, the Prophet and his 1400 followers arrived at Ḥudaybiya where, having been refused access to the Kaʿba, they eventually entered into a 10-year peace treaty with their Meccan opponents (see Ḥijāzī, 1986 for a full account). A remarkable feature of the historical context was the Prophet's determination to achieve a settlement, even making apparently unbalanced concessions to the distress of his followers (Ahmad, 2009, pp.190–92). The concessions made by the Prophet at Ḥudaybiya were so significant that, according to the Hanafi jurist Al-Sarakshī, they constituted a legal precedent for the acceptance of humiliating terms for the general good (Lecker, 2010, p.74). This highlights the need for a long-term perspective in dispute resolution, focussing on the future needs, objectives and interests of the parties and going well beyond the circumstances of the current conflict. Ahmad (2009, pp.216–18) argues that a triumphal refrain at Q.48:28 marked the progress of Islam after the landmark Treaty of Ḥudaybiya, with two similar Qur'anic references marking other expansive phases. Such triumphalism in the face of an apparently unfavourable treaty indicates a tremendous confidence in the long-term benefits of Conciliation.

Further examples of Conciliation in the Prophet's own lifetime are provided by Iqbal (1965, pp.3–5, 13–18). A particularly early example is the pre-Islamic tribal dispute in Mecca for the honour of replacing the Black Stone in the walls of the rebuilt Kaʿba, in which the Prophet conciliated by instructing the tribes to carry the stone collectively on a cloth. It is notable here that solutions which offer mutual benefit have been identified in Western literature as a common feature of ADR techniques (Cohen, 2001, pp.27–28, 35). Later, the 'seemingly authentic' (Lowry, 2010, p.84) Constitution of Medina established by the Prophet on his arrival in that city apparently established freedom of religion, equality of rights and mutual security. Lecker (2010, p.75) provides a relevant extract of the Constitution of Medina in English. These examples indicate that the ideology and skills of the Prophet with respect to Conciliation reflected some continuity from his early Meccan days to his early Medinan times. Whether the Meccan and Medinan periods reflected a consistent or disjunct approach to Conciliation is discussed further in this research.

Interestingly, the Prophet appears to have used a range of techniques to achieve Conciliation (Iqbal, 1965, pp.48–49, 52–53). On one occasion, he addressed the Medinan *Anṣār* (Helpers) making them feel valued by special association with the Prophet to overcome their sense of injustice after the Battle of Ḥunayn, when a greater share of spoils was given to the Meccans than the Medinans. The harnessing of positive emotions can play an important role in Conciliation (Shapiro, 2005, pp.74–75). Doubts have been expressed, however, as to whether the Prophet actually came to Medina in the specific role of a peacemaker and the extent to which conflicts amongst the inhabitant tribes of Aws and Khazraj were manifest through physical battles (Lecker, 2010, pp.66–67). There are also mixed narratives regarding the Prophet's relations with the Jews of Medina, some highlighting instances of conflict (Lecker, 2010, pp.72–73) and others highlighting peaceful co-existence outside of specific instances of political conflict (Watt, 1961, p.175). Ultimately it must be recognised, as cogently argued by Tolan (2010, p.245), that the portrayal of the Prophet in history has varied significantly with change of time and authorship, from exaggerated and highly critical caricatures to the 'irenic', often reflecting the issues of the age.

After the Prophet's lifetime, both the individual, spiritual and the societal, administrative aspects of *ṣulḥ* have found an important emphasis in two different historical contexts. These two contrasting paradigms illustrate the richness of *ṣulḥ* as a concept and the range of motivations behind its promotion. Firstly, Derin (2005, pp.1–2, 7–10) discusses *ṣulḥ* around the thirteenth century C.E. in Sufi ideology, perhaps most famously advocated by Ibn Al-ʿArabī and later reflected in the work of the Turkish writer Yunus Emre. These writers emphasised Conciliation from an esoteric spiritual perspective. In this approach, the focus on compassion and preference for verses in the Qurʾan emphasising mercy, provide a natural propensity towards Conciliation based on forgiveness rather than retaliation, even where retaliation is permitted by Islamic Law. Anger management is emphasised to provide a more sustainable conclusion to conflicts than cycles of retaliation. The notion of forgiveness as a means to controlling conflicts is discussed in this book.

Secondly, by contrast, in the eighteenth century a fascinating insight into the systematised use of *ṣulḥ* in legal disputes is obtained from the records of two Ottoman courts in Uskudar and Adana. Out-of-court *ṣulḥ* agreements, even oral ones, were according to Tamdoğan (2008, p.63) integrated into the court system through endorsement by a *qāḍī* (judge). This accords with Othman's argument (Othman, 2007, pp.65, 73–81) that *ṣulḥ* is an integral part of an Islamic justice system and not merely a private settlement process, since a judge can refer the parties for *ṣulḥ* or engage in *ṣulḥ* with them. Othman discusses the historical juristic debates about whether a *ṣulḥ* agreement should also be required to be fair and just, and whether a judge should act as mediator himself. This highlights the significant competitive tensions between *ṣulḥ* and justice. This book discusses the inter-relationship between these two important notions and the question of whether a Conciliation agreement is required to be fair and just.

The interplay of *ṣulḥ* and justice has been the subject of a recent PhD thesis (Amadu, 2015), commented on further in this work.

Ṣulḥ agreements in the Ottoman courts received threefold recognition from customary practice, civil law and religious law, the Hanafi school being prevalent in the Ottoman empire (Tamdoğan, 2008, pp.68, 75, 82). Around 40% of cases in both courts related to wrongful death and bodily injury, with the majority of the remainder relating to debt and inheritance matters, reflecting an equal importance of *ṣulḥ* in criminal and civil matters as mentioned above. A noteworthy variation in customary practice between the two courts is the extensive use of symbolic gifts such as Qur'an copies, horses and swords in *ṣulḥ* agreements in the Adana regional court, compared to exclusively cash payments in the Uskudar district of the capital. The significance of this will be highlighted in the immediately following discussion. Further discussion of *ṣulḥ* in the Ottoman and post-Ottoman period is provided by Sartori (2011) and Mutaf (2004).

Ṣulḥ in Contemporary Peace Negotiations

In the context of Palestine/Israel peace negotiations, the study of local cultural *ṣulḥ* practices (Gellman and Vuinovich, 2008, pp.129–31, 135, 139–40) has shown *ṣulḥ* to be a cross-religious grouping practice, sometimes used in tandem with legal process. Crucially, it focusses on the restoration of human dignity and is forward-looking, 'recalibrating' communities and allowing them to resume good relations, something which is less likely to be achieved by a purely legal process. This recalibration is, in my view, an important concept highlighting two particularly meritorious features of *ṣulḥ*. Firstly, it provides a check on escalation of the dispute and further deterioration of the relationship before the 'point of no return' is reached. Virtuous cycles of cooperation and trust are particularly important in productive ongoing relationships (Allred, 2005, p.95). Secondly, it aims to maintain the relationship even at the cost of individual concessions, rather than achieving justice at the cost of a relationship, which can often be the outcome of litigation.

An interesting point is that external rituals such as eating together are used to achieve this result by masking any residual inner resentment, even if the parties are not entirely reconciled internally. This demonstrates parallels with the exoteric approach of using symbolic gifts in the Adana court examples above, highlighted by Tamdoğan, whilst contrasting with the more spiritually purist esoteric approach of the Sufi ideology discussed by Derin which aims for a more complete inner satisfaction. The proposed use of training (Gellman and

Vuinovich, 2008, pp.140, 143) to facilitate long term Conciliation goals has also been discussed extensively by Abu-Nimer (2003, pp.9–17) and provides a proactive approach to dispute resolution which I argued in my earlier research was consistent with the Qur'anic approach (Fazaluddin, 2016).

Conciliation in divorce proceedings is discussed in Malik and Muda (2015) and Carlisle (2007), and a social study of *ṣulḥ* in a contemporary Muslim diaspora (Keshavjee, 2013), but for brevity has not been discussed in this work given that Conciliation in marriage has not been discussed in detail in this research. It does, however, highlight the relevance of *ṣulḥ* in the family context, as well as the international and commercial contexts discussed above.

Ṣulḥ in Commercial Disputes

In the commercial context, *ṣulḥ* is gaining increasing recognition as a means of resolving disputes both efficiently and appropriately. Hassan (2006, p.189) argues that *ṣulḥ* is particularly suited to resolving employment disputes since the relationship is based on contract and therefore lends itself to resolution by agreement. Furthermore, the remedy sought by an employee will either be reinstatement to his position or damages, both of which fall within the scope of specific benefits, credit or rights, all matters which are permitted in a *ṣulḥ* claim, according to cited sources.

Another area of increasing interest is the use of *ṣulḥ* in Islamic Finance disputes. As discussed by Rasyid (2013, pp.354, 362), *ṣulḥ* was officially adopted by the Malaysian *Sharīʿa* Courts in 2001, with apparently 70% of cases being resolved. The Indonesian Supreme Court also introduced mandatory mediation in 2003, failing which legal rulings are void. In Malaysia, the Financial Mediation Bureau also provides a hybrid Med-Arb procedure which has been popular. Rasyid (2013, pp.1, 367) argues that *ṣulḥ* is the preferred method of dispute resolution in Islam and that alternative ADR processes provide the parties with choices in effectively and efficiently resolving their disputes. By introducing mandatory *ṣulḥ* processes, however, I would argue that the parties have little actual procedural choice, although they are not of course obliged to come to an agreement.

Oseni (2015, pp.381–83, 390–93) discusses the recent Malaysian Islamic Financial Services Act 2013, which appears to have introduced further procedural changes which support *ṣulḥ*, whilst the International Islamic Centre for Reconciliation and Arbitration (IICRA) established in 2005 also appears to have had some successes. The merits of *ṣulḥ* over litigation in Islamic Finance are strongly advocated by Oseni, who argues that litigation of disputes actually goes against one of the five fundamental *maqāṣid* (underlying aims) of Islamic Law, namely *ḥifẓ al-māl* (preservation of wealth); he cites from Al-Ghazālī that anything which safeguards the *maqāṣid* is justifiable as *maṣlaḥa* (public interest). Although Oseni's discussion is in an Islamic context, I believe his arguments concerning financial efficacy, participant-driven solutions and mutual satisfaction are of general application in highlighting the merits of Conciliation over litigation.

Ṣulḥ and the Western Perspective

Investment by the Western business community in countries where Islamic Law is applicable poses legal risk as a result of uncertainty as to how those laws will be implemented and interpreted. Sayen (2003, p.906) highlights this issue and provides a detailed review of the Saudi legal and extra-judicial dispute resolution system, with a view to ascertaining how the Western business community can be confident that commercial disputes will be settled in an Islamic Law-based system promptly, fairly, objectively and predictably. After discussing the potential legal challenges facing arbitration awards, leading to uncertainty, Sayen concludes (2003, pp.944–48) that *ṣulḥ* offers an efficient and relatively robust mechanism for resolving disputes, whilst also providing sought-after familiarity with 'Roman law'. He highlights that *ṣulḥ* was the Prophet's preferred method of dispute resolution. As essentially a new contract between the parties, *ṣulḥ* would not generally be open to legal challenge and would only be open to limited challenge on the facts. This conclusion highlights the merits of *ṣulḥ* over both litigation and arbitration even to a non-Islamic Western entity, pursuant to the commercial imperative of achieving certainty.

Eastern and Western concepts of dispute resolution have been compared and contrasted by various writers. Al-Ramahi presents an interesting observation that the nature of the intermediary and his/her role is different in the two systems. The intermediary will typically have close relations with the participants in the East but would often be a previously unknown third party in the West. In an anthropology paper, Greenhouse (1985, pp.91–92, 98–107) uses the terminology of 'Inclusive' to describe the first model and 'Exclusive' to describe the second. Cultural differences are clearly an important aspect of any conflict situation and relevant to its resolution, a point which also finds support from other authors (Al-Humaidhi, 2015, p.99; Cohen, 2001).

Al-Ramahi (2008, pp.17–20) argues that Eastern systems focus more on tribal collectives, informal models of dispute resolution and religious values, in contrast to the focus on individuals, formal models and secular values in Western systems. Al-Ramahi's tone is somewhat overly critical of Western models, however, suggesting that they leave little room for emotions and values and view conflict as cathartic, which appears to be difficult to substantiate evidentially. Further, Al-Ramahi portrays an emphasis on objectivity and fairness in Western models as an alternative to the emphasis on preservation of relations and restoration of dignity in Eastern systems. Such divergent polarity of emphasis may be considered unhelpful given that all of these factors are relevant and valuable in any given conflict. One illustration of this is that justice in *ṣulḥ* agreements has also been an important point of debate for Islamic jurists, as highlighted above.

The richness of the notion of *ṣulḥ* is illustrated by the range of perspectives offered: some historical such as the discussion of Ṣulḥ Al-Ḥudaybiya, some ideological such as the Sufi perspective on *ṣulḥ* and some contextual such as the current discussion on dispute resolution in Islamic Finance. A key point arising from the above discussion of *ṣulḥ* in history and the contemporary application of *ṣulḥ* is that the systematised use of *ṣulḥ* in historical Islamic contexts has enjoyed a level of continuity in contemporary Islamic contexts such as Islamic Finance and Western dispute resolution contexts. The continued importance of the more esoteric aspects of *ṣulḥ* in Islamic history is less easy to discern, although it does seem to have retained at least some contemporary importance in the realm of peace negotiations.

The above discussion has highlighted a number of issues and debates around the notion of Conciliation, and a number of these will be addressed in this work. The presentation of the research now commences with an original analysis consisting of six chapters, dealing sequentially with the material relating to Conciliation in the entire Qur'an. Each chapter begins with an overview of the suras covered in that chapter, highlighting the themes and key Conciliation verses to be discussed, and then closes with a summary table mapping the key Conciliation verses and a conclusion. Finally, the book concludes with a comprehensive summary table which maps the Conciliation themes identified in the entire Qur'an and addresses the research questions outlined in the Introduction.

1 Conciliation Discourse and Conflict Management Systems

Overview: Group 1 Suras – Q.1–Q.5

Group 1 consists of one short Meccan sura (Q.1 Sūrat Al-Fātiḥa) followed by four lengthy Medinan suras (Q.2 Sūrat Al-Baqara, Q.3 Sūrat Āl ʿImrān, Q.4 Sūrat Al-Nisāʾ and Q.5 Sūrat Al-Māʾida) which deal predominantly with legal rulings, as well as certain doctrinal themes and historical narratives. Sūrat Al-Fātiḥa is often considered an executive summary of the Qurʾanic themes, whilst the Medinan Qurʾanic discourse in this group instructs the Muslims, challenges the hypocrites, debates with the Jews and Christians and addresses the issue of conflict with the disbelievers. In the Farāhī-Iṣlāḥī schema, the theme of this group is The Law, with Q.2–Q.3 forming a pair dealing with Faith and Islam and Q.4–Q.5 forming a (less distinct) pair dealing, respectively, with the Law as a Mercy to Mankind and a Covenant with God.

Based on my own extensive analysis, I argue below that a significant Conciliation theme emerges in Q.2 and continues into Q.3 challenging the sufficiency of adopting the apparent exoteric aspects of religion, and thus focussing attention inwards on an esoteric transformation. An apparent administrative framework for managing conflicts is also provided – Q.2 and Q.4 in particular deal with specific social contexts such as unlawful killing, inheritance of wealth, marriage disputes and commercial dealings. Another Conciliation theme, of unity, emergent in Q.2, is developed in a sustained discourse in Q.3 and continues into Q.4. Conciliation and its relationship with justice and conflict are punctuated through Q.2 to Q.5, with the former dealt with in brief but emphatic instructions and the latter presented in lengthier discourse. The Summary Table at the end of Section 1.3 below details the layout of the key verses in Group 1 suras relating to these Conciliation themes.

The key Conciliation verses analysed in the first section of this chapter are those relating to *birr* (dutiful conduct) at Q.2:177, the inner dimension of worship at Q.2:183–187 and Q.2:189–203, and those relating to *silm* (submission to God) at Q.2:204–208. The second section includes an analysis of the verses relating to homicide at Q.2:178–179, inheritance at Q.2:180–182 and Q.4:7–14 and commerce at Q.2:282. The third section concludes with an analysis of inter-faith and intra-faith commonality at Q.3:64 and Q.3:103, respectively.

https://doi.org/10.1515/9783110747348-003

1.1 Esoteric Focus

Ṣulḥ has been seen to be important in Islamic history, both at the individual, esoteric level in Sufi ideology and at the societal, administrative level in the Ottoman context. However, the limited contemporary literature on *ṣulḥ*, reviewed above, has tended to focus exclusively on the use of *ṣulḥ* as an administrative dispute resolution process. In Surat Al-Baqara, both the esoteric and exoteric aspects of Conciliation feature, but the esoteric aspect of Conciliation features first, through the notion of *birr* (righteousness, dutiful conduct), suggesting that the Qur'anic vision of Conciliation begins with internal change. This also indicates that the Qur'an adopts a more holistic approach to Conciliation than is currently apparent in the contemporary usage of *ṣulḥ*.

1.1.1 *Birr*

A structural analysis of Surat Al-Baqara reveals several important early references to Conciliation and then a sustained treatment of Conciliation in a text segment commencing at Q.2:177. After occasional references to *fasād* (disorder, corruption) by hypocrites at Q.2:11, *fasād* by mankind in general at Q.2:30 and the sowing of discord between married couples at Q.2:102, Surat Al-Baqara turns towards *iṣlāḥ* (reform) at Q.2:160. Further discussion on the important notions of *fasād* and *iṣlāḥ* in relation to Conciliation will follow in Chapter 2. After this at Q.2:177, the sura turns towards *birr* (dutiful conduct), a concept which I consider fundamental to the ensuing discourse on the teachings of the new religion, as I explain below. Further on, Q.2:224 explicitly demonstrates the essential connection between *birr* and Conciliation: *birr* is connected by *al-wāw al-ʿaṭf* (a conjunctive particle) with *taqwā* (God-consciousness) and *iṣlāḥ bayn al-nās* (conciliating between people). Q.2:224 even enjoins breaking otherwise sacrosanct oaths made to God, to allow Conciliation, highlighting its importance.

The initial reference to *birr* at Q.2:177 immediately draws the reader's attention through a dramatic opening negation: *laysa 'l-birra* (*birr* is *not*), immediately shifting focus away from the exoteric aspect of facing East or West in prayer and instead towards the esoteric aspects of faith, generosity, obedience, integrity and patience. This re-calibration prioritises core values over external acts, even essential conditions of worship. There is also what I consider an opening grammatical signal in Q.2:177 which alerts the reader to its foundational role in setting the tone for the ensuing Conciliation material. The particle *laysa* in Arabic grammar would normally take an *ism marfūʿ* (nominative case noun) and provide a *khabar manṣūb* (accusative case predicate). The unexpected *naṣb* (accusative case) on *birra* therefore draws attention to the essential notion of *birr*. Iṣlāḥī makes a similar point in relation to *naṣb* in the word *ṣābirīn* at Q.2:177 (vol.1, p.427); he describes this usage as *ʿalā sabīl al-ikhtiṣāṣ* (by way of distinction). A grammatical justification for the construct is the *taqdīm* (advancement) of *birra*, a *khabar* and therefore *manṣūb*, in order to highlight its strategic importance at this juncture in the narrative (there is, however, also a variant reading *birru* with *rafʿ* (nominative case)).

Al-Rāzī provides lengthy grammatical explanations for the *naṣb*, such as *laysa* acting as a present tense verb with *birra* as its object, although this is somewhat contradicted by the *rafʿ* (nominative case) in Q.2:189 which also follows *laysa*. He also considers whether the term *laysa* is a *fiʿl* (verb) or a *ḥarf* (particle). However, Al-Rāzī's grammatical focus, and the lack of structural analysis in his methodology, distracts him from the essence of this verse. Only at the very end of his analysis of the term *birr* does he, eloquently but incredibly briefly, mention what in my view is the crucial exhortation in the verse: *aʿmāl al-qulūb ashrafu ʿind Allāh min aʿmāl al-jawāriḥ* (actions of the heart are more worthy before God than actions of the limbs). The phrase *ʿalā ḥubbi**hī*** in Q.2:177 also indicates a test of internal state, negating the giving of wealth being regarded as a mere act of the limbs, and is discussed further where the same phrase recurs at Q.76:8 in Section 6.3.

Both Iṣlāḥī and Al-Rāzī's commentaries agree that *birr* encompasses all forms of rewardable behaviour. However, Iṣlāḥī's structural macro-analysis of Q.2:177 produces a radically different level of emphasis on the esoteric aspect of religion, which supports my analysis above. His commentary notably begins an entirely new structural and thematic text segment at Q.2:177 (vol.1, pp.420–30), with the first marginal summary opening his analysis with a heading stating *dīn meḥeḍ chand rusūm o ẓawāhir ka nām nahīn* (religion is not merely a few rituals and external acts). He continues his section summary by emphasising that religion encompasses all *aʿmāl* (acts) and *akhlāq* (character) which are deeply connected to life. His opening comment of the verse itself (p.421) defines *birr* as the **fulfilment of rights**, be they rights of God or His people. This definition highlights the underlying conciliatory theme of this verse, given that non-fulfilment of basic human needs is often a primary cause of disputes (Abu-Nimer, 2003, p.9, based on Burton 1990). Samḥān (2006, p.120) also concludes from his jurisprudential study that the fundamental importance of *ṣulḥ* agreements at the individual level lies in their consensual restoration of rights and the removal of mutual hostility between disputants. Despite Samḥān's conclusion, however, as discussed later in Sections 1.2.1 and 5.3.2, concession of rights can also be an important means of achieving settlement.

Fulfilment of rights includes good relations with kin and others. After faith, the first rewardable act mentioned in Q.2:177 is generosity towards relatives, preceding even generosity to the destitute or mandatory acts of worship. Iṣlāḥī (vol.1, p.425) cites a *ḥadīth* that the best charity is spent on a close relation who holds enmity against the donor, emphasising its conciliatory effect. Q.4:36, further on in Group 1, also enjoins *iḥsān* (gracious conduct) towards parents, relations and then others, such as orphans, the destitute, neighbours, travellers and slaves, insisting that God does not like those who are haughty and arrogant. *Iḥsān*, and particularly with relatives, is an exceptionally important Conciliation concept, as shall be seen in Chapter 3 onwards. *Birr* too is mentioned again in Chapter 3, at Q.19:14 and Q.19:32, highlighting the exemplary character of the prophets John and Jesus in being dutiful to their parents, rather than being *jabbāran* (domineering, Abdel Haleem). *Birr* and *iḥsān* are thus complementary notions which emphasise good relations and humility in dealing with others, particularly with family members, clearly maintaining social cohesion.

Long-term conciliatory behaviour is particularly emphasised in Q.2:177 through a grammatical shift, from the use of verbs to the tense-less use of the grammatical *fāʿil* (actioner) to describe those who fulfil their agreements and are patient. Iṣlāḥī argues convincingly (vol.1, pp.427–29) that this shift indicates the performer's *kirdār* (character), in contrast to his temporary action, the development of such character being the *rūḥ* (essence) of religion. Fulfilment of agreements for Iṣlāḥī constitutes the basis for the fulfilment of all rights and duties towards God and creation. He cites the memorable example of the Prophet's return of Abū Jandal, a Muslim suffering persecution, to the Meccans immediately after the Treaty of Ḥudaybiya (see Al-Liḥyānī, 2007, p.45 and Section 5.2.2).

Following Q.2:177, *birr* features in a sustained fashion through the Group 1 suras, demonstrating the continuing importance of esoteric development. At Q.2:189 *birr* is again used to negate the adequacy of feigned external piety, in this case, the pre-Islamic custom of pilgrims entering their houses from the rear, and to again prioritise the esoteric state: *wa lākinna 'l-birra man ittaqā* (rather, *birr* is that you have *taqwā* (God-consciousness)). Further on, Q.2:224 defines a trinity of key esoteric concepts: *birr*, *taqwā* and *iṣlāḥ bayn al-nās*. Collectively, these three notions provide what I would term a "Conciliation Relationship Triangle". *Birr* regulates the individual's own relationship with others, *taqwā* regulates the individual's relationship with God, and *iṣlāḥ bayn al-nās* regulates the individual's effect on relationships between others. After Q.2:224, *birr* features yet again at Q.3:92 in overcoming the love of wealth, in a different form at Q.3:193 in a prayer which indicates the importance of *birr* and similarly at Q.3:198 in relation to the attainment of Paradise, and even features as late as Q.5:2 where mutual assistance is commanded in attaining *birr*.

The emphasis of internal morality through the concept of *birr* in Q.2:177 provides an effective prelude for the immediately ensuing legal verses on Conciliation in relation to unlawful killing (Q.2:178–Q.2:179) and inheritance (Q.2: 180–182). This collocation, like Q.2:224 above, binds *birr* and Conciliation emphatically, indicating that developing *birr* is essential preparation for exoteric Conciliation. As Hallaq (2009, p.57) notes, religious morality served in Islamic systems as an 'effective and pervasive mechanism of self-rule', conducive to informal mediation and dispute resolution. The juxtaposition of morality and law also highlights the 'morality inherent in law itself' (Berman, 1974, p.37).

The Qur'anic discourse is inter-woven such that the above-mentioned Q.2: 178–182 suspends the theoretical discussion of internal morality to address practical legal systems, before returning to a strong underlying moral emphasis when discussing ritual worship (see the Summary Table at the end of the chapter for more details). To maintain continuity in my argument, therefore, I will now depart somewhat from the sequential order of the text segments, dealing first with the esoteric emphasis in ritual worship at Q.2:183–203 and then the esoteric notion of entering into *silm/salm* at Q.2:208, before coming back to address the legal conflict management systems at Q.2:178–182 in Section 1.2.

1.1.2 The Inner Dimension of Worship

Sūrat Al-Baqara deals with the religious obligations of fasting at Q.2:183–187 and pilgrimage at Q.2:189–Q.2:203. Although these are acts of worship, in my view they also aim to bring about internal change and provide essential Conciliation training, developing mutual cooperation and restraint. In relation to fasting, Iṣlāḥī notes (vol.1, p.445) that the Arabs used the word *ṣāma* to describe the training of horses and would have understood the element of training inherent in the word *ṣiyām* (fasting). Q.2:183 provides the underlying objective of fasting – *laʿallakum tattaqūn* (that you may be mindful of God, Abdel Haleem). The concept of *taqwā*, indicating internal change, provides continuity and coherence to a whole set of relatively sequential verses which relate to Conciliation – Q.2:177: *muttaqūn*, Q.2:179: *tattaqūn*, Q.2:180: *muttaqīn*, Q.2:183: *tattaqūn* and Q.2:197 dealt with immediately below.

The pilgrimage too contains an inherent Conciliation command. Despite the multi-ethnic global gathering and hardships of travel, Q.2:197 enjoins *lā jidāla* (no quarrelling, Abdel Haleem) in *ḥajj*. The emphatic *lā al-nāfiya li 'l-jins* (negation of a genus) followed by the *manṣūb* noun is further reinforced by implied accountability in the Hereafter, from the mention of God's complete knowledge and two explicit references to *taqwā* (God-consciousness). According to Iṣlāḥī (vol.1, p.486), there is arguably also a third implied reference to *taqwā* after *tazawwadū* which is *ḥadhf* (ellipted). Al-Rāzī's *tafsīr* explains a variant reading in which *rafath* and *fusūq* are read with *rafʿ* and *tanwīn* (nunation) and only *jidāl* with *naṣb*, by arguing that *jidāl* encompasses all *qubḥ* (detestable) behaviour and thus Allah distinguished it *bi mazīd al-zajr wa 'l-mubālagha fi 'l-nafy* (with greater prohibition and exaggerated negation). This emphasises the distinct importance given to Conciliation, even as compared to other forms of personal development, during the pilgrimage. Q.3:97 notably describes those entering the pilgrimage sites in Mecca as being *āminan* (at peace) and Abdel Haleem's translation of Q.5:97 notes from Al-Rāzī a reference to the pilgrimage as 'bringing people together in peace'.

It is also pertinent to mention here that the gradual prohibition of alcohol alluded to later in Surat Al-Baqara at Q.2:219 is again related to its social detriment in giving rise to disputes. Iṣlāḥī's *tafsīr* of Q.2:219 (vol.1, pp.514–15) argues that the word *ithm* indicates *akhlāqī mafāsid* (moral corruption) rather than physical harm, which would have been indicated by *ḍarar*. It is also clear that the final prohibition of alcohol at Q.5:90–91, which mentions *ʿadāwata wa 'l-baghḍāʾa* (enmity and hatred, Abdel Haleem), is a form of preventative Conciliation. The prohibition is reinforced by two mentions of Satan, one emphasising Satan's desire to instigate such conflict, and a final command, albeit phrased as a rhetorical question: will you then desist? (see Hāshmī, 2008, p.102 on this rhetorical usage). There is also a further condemnation implied in the evocative term *rijs* (impurity) used to describe alcohol, which eloquently contrasts with the regulations regarding pure food (Q.5:5, Q.5:87–88) and ritual purity for worship (Q.5:6), providing a sense of emphatic antithesis.

It can be seen that these passages of the Qurʾanic discourse promote both God-consciousness in ritual worship and maintaining presence of mind through sobriety as a means of pre-emptively avoiding argument and conflict. Bad speech leading to arguments is also prohibited at Q.4:148, whilst thorough investigation of information is enjoined at Q.4:83 and Q.4:94. These issues, which also relate to the avoidance of conflict, will be discussed in Chapter 5, where they are dealt with more comprehensively in Q.49.

1.1.3 *Silm* vs Hypocrisy

It has been argued above that an esoteric focus is emphasised strongly in Surat Al-Baqara and pervades Group 1, forming a key Conciliation theme. This esoteric focus culminates in a fundamental dichotomy between hypocrites, a key target audience in the early Medinan context, and sincere believers. The description of disputing hypocrites at Q.2:204–206, linked to *fasād* (disorder) in Q.2:205, contrasts with the immediately ensuing injunction at Q.2:208 for believers to enter into *silm* (submission to God/peace, Abdel Haleem) completely. Importantly, in one variant reading *silm* is read *salm*, even more clearly indicating Conciliation. Ibn Manzūr (2014, vol.3, p.348) also states: *wa 'l-ṣulḥ al-silm*, equating *silm* with *ṣulḥ* (reconciliation).

The description of hypocrites in Q.2:204 condemns their anti-Conciliation stance through the phrase *wa huwa aladdu 'l-khiṣām* (yet he is the bitterest of opponents, Abdel Haleem), using the elative form. This indication towards severe disputation is, as Al-Rāzī highlights, particularly poignant after the injunction seven verses earlier at Q.2:197: *wa lā jidāla fī 'l-ḥajj* (no quarrelling in the *ḥajj*). Al-Rāzī also emphasises the *nifāq* (hypocritical duality) between the hypocrites' superficially appealing words and their inner hostility and *fasād* (disorder), which includes sowing discord between others leading to bloodshed and broken relations, as well as physical destruction. A particularly strong condemnation of their conduct is provided by the implied threat and removal from Divine favour indicated by *wallāhu lā yuḥibbu 'l-fasād* (God does not like disorder).

Q.2:208 contrasts with Q.2:204 in a number of respects.[3] Q.2:208 addresses believers, faith being an inner quality, and enjoins them: *udkhulū fī ('l)-ssilmi kāffa* (enter wholeheartedly into submission to God, Abdel Haleem). Both the imperative verb *udkhulū* (enter) and the emphasising state *kāffa* (wholeheartedly) indicate passage into a new depth, which contrasts with the hollow core of the hypocrites mentioned at Q.204. A notable insight from Al-Rāzī at Q.2:208 is that the subsequent instruction to the believers not to follow *khuṭuwāti ('l)-shshayṭān* (Satan's footsteps) is potentially a reference to the sowing of discord and doubts by hypocrites in Q.2:204. This association between the sowing of discord and Satan, the epitome of evil, adds further condemnation and prohibition to the actions of the hypocrites which lead to conflict. The formula regarding Satan here is identical to that used in Q.2:168 in restricting people from eating other than pure food. The prohibition of alcohol at Q.5:90–91 above also uses a similar association with Satan to indicate prohibition of a substance indicated as leading to conflict.

Silm/*salm* in Q.2:208 also contrasts with *khiṣām* at Q.2:204. Al-Rāzī eloquently highlights this important contrast, noting that the word *silm* originates

3 Methodologically, it is interesting to note here that Al-Rāzī refers to *naẓm al-āya* in his *tafsīr* of Q.2:204, an apparent reference to *intra-verse* Qur'anic arrangement or *munāsaba* (chaining; see Abdul-Raof, 2003). Al-Rāzī also cross-refers to Q.2:204 in his commentary of Q.2:208, this time an *inter-verse* example of *munāsaba* and an attempt to illustrate some localised coherence in the text.

from *inqiyād* (submission) and that, in the *ṣulḥ* meaning of *silm/salm*, *yanqādu kullu wāḥidin li ṣāḥibihī wa lā yunāziʿahū fīhi* (each person submits to his companion and does not dispute with him). In another reference, he takes *silm/salm* to refer even more explicitly to ***al-ṣulḥ*** *wa tark al-muḥāraba wa ʻl-munāzaʿa* (**Conciliation** and abstinence from warfare and disputation) going on to paraphrase Q.2:208 as an instruction to avoid all *munāzaʿa maʿa ʻl-nās* (disputation with people in general) incited by Satan. Yet further linguistic emphasis is provided by Al-Rāzī's explanation of *kāffa* as a preventive barrier indicating *tark al-intiqām* (abstaining from reprisal), and enjoining unity and preventing *tafarruq* (division). It is clear from these numerous examples that Al-Rāzī appreciates the entering into *silm* by people of sincere, rather than merely professed and hypocritical, faith as a clear indication of their abstaining from both the initiation and reciprocation of disputation and conflict.

Despite its clear importance in advocating Social Conciliation and condemning conflict, this aspect of Q.2:208 can easily be overlooked because *silm* is often taken in a purely theological sense as referring to Islam (Yusuf Ali) or submission to God (Abdel Haleem, although he footnotes the alternative meaning of *silm* as 'peace'). It can be seen that a forensic iterative analysis and careful reflection have been required to unmask several important esoteric Conciliation concepts in this section. Firstly, *birr* (righteousness, dutiful conduct) is advocated as a catalyst for change. In this sense, *birr* is a precursive value instilled to bring about a positive Conciliation culture. Secondly, *birr* and *taqwā* (God-consciousness) are inter-dependent, as indicated in their semantic coupling in Q.2:177 and Q.2:189, such that for example an individual's greater *taqwā* (God-consciousness), even in ritual worship such as fasting and pilgrimage, would naturally encourage better relations with others, as encapsulated in *birr*. Finally, *silm* (peace) is a state in which those of sincere belief are enjoined to renounce conflict and maintain peaceful relations with those they engage with.

This concludes the discussion of esoteric concepts in Group 1, although the fundamental notion of *birr* will be encountered again in Chapter 6. The discussion will now turn back to the exoteric conflict management systems beginning at Q.2:178, whose examination was deferred above.

1.2 Conflict Management Systems

In this section, there will be a discussion of homicide, inheritance of wealth and commercial dealings. These relate to social contexts in which disputes frequently arise and notably the practical management of each of these is explicitly legislated for in Q.2. Iṣlāḥī (vol.1, p.430) notes that the strength of interpersonal relations depends on the protection of life and wealth, thus identifying a direct Conciliation-based link between the content of Q.2.177 and the immediately following verses which deal with these two topics. The section ends with a discussion of commerce, another area of frequent disputes related to wealth, dealt with at length in Q.2:282.

Before beginning this section, there are two points to be made regarding the Conciliation material in Q.2 and the structure of this book. First, after homicide and inheritance, the narrative of Q.2 turns to fasting and pilgrimage discussed above, and then conflict at Q.2:190–194 and Q.2:216–218. This theme and its relationship with Conciliation continues at Q.4:71–76, Q.4:89–91 and elsewhere in Group 1, with restrictions on fighting and opportunities for peace mentioned at Q.4:75, Q.4:90–91 and Q.4:114. The discussion of this material will be deferred to Chapter 2, due to the substantive continuation of this theme in Group 2, particularly in Q.8 and Q.9.

Secondly, after the discussion of hypocrites versus sincere believers at Q.2: 204–208, dealt with above, *iṣlāḥ* and *fasād* in the context of guardians mixing trust property of orphans with their own are mentioned at Q.2:220, followed by a lengthy discussion of matrimonial issues from Q.2:221 to Q.2:242. Conciliation in marriage is also dealt with extensively at Q.4:19–Q.4:35 and Q.4:127–Q.4:130, with direct references to *ṣulḥ* and a formal reconciliation process at Q.4:35 and Q.4:128. The *tafsīr* and discussion of this material has not been included in this book, as mentioned in the Introduction, due to the extensive discussion of the marriage relationship, reconciliation procedure, reconciliation ethics, and provisions relating to divorce, already provided in my earlier research (Fazaluddin, 2016, pp. 341–44). In summary, however, the encouragement of positive thinking and forgiveness between spouses, the appointment of arbiters from each family to negotiate reconciliation where problems arise, and the maintenance of magnanimity and the mutual negotiation of child-care responsibilities even in a divorce scenario were all highlighted. The use of a metaphor of clothing to symbolise the proximity of marriage relations at Q.2:187, the invoking of suitable emotional appeal at Q.30:21 and the triple repetition of Conciliation through the noun *ṣulḥ* and its related verb and cognate accusative form at Q.4:128 were notable literary features emphasising Conciliation.

We will now turn to the first topic of this section: homicide.

1.2.1 Homicide

Islamic jurists maintain that a *ṣulḥ* settlement is not permitted where the rights of God are violated and a *ḥadd* (mandatory) punishment is prescribed (Hossain

2013, 2, 7–9), for example in theft. Despite this, *ṣulḥ* can be utilised in the sphere of wrongful killing or injury and in Ottoman times appears to have been as prevalent as *ṣulḥ* in civil disputes (Tamdoğan, 2008, p.68). The four legal schools agree that such a settlement is permissible 'in the rights to retribution for the destruction of life and limb' on the basis that 'retribution is a right for human beings' (Al-Zuhayli, 2007, vol.2, pp.215–16). However, this logic could equally be applied to theft, where the victim could exact retribution through return of goods and/or financial compensation. A better explanation in my view, therefore, for the permissibility of *ṣulḥ* in homicide is that it is a Divine exception, based on the specific Qur'anic sanction in Q.2:178. This reflects the Qur'an's emphasis on the sanctity of life and prevention of further loss of life through escalation of violence. This was a real risk in tribal Arab society where exacting vengeance for a kinsman was considered a sacred duty, although even then mediation was one of several control mechanisms (Hoyland, 2001, pp.113–14).

Q.2:178 sets out the principle of *qiṣāṣ* in cases of unlawful killing. Linguistically *qiṣāṣ* means to follow (Iṣlāḥī, vol.1, p.431) or track down (Abdel Haleem), and contextually means 'retribution' (Abdel Haleem). Although *ṣulḥ* is not mentioned in this verse, the word *ʿufiya* (pardoned) signals the inherent concept of Conciliation, despite the apparent prescription of a mandatory punishment indicated by *kutiba* (prescribed). Iṣlāḥī (vol.1, pp.432–33) explains this distinction by suggesting that *kutiba* indicates society's obligation to pursue justice, discussed below, whilst *ʿufiya* allows the aggrieved individual (next of kin) an opportunity to show *iḥsān* (gracious conduct) through forgiveness or acceptance of an alternative financial compensation. *ʿUfiya*, in Al-Rāzī's preferred view, also indicates *isqāṭ al-ḥaqq* (concession of rights). It is striking that in such a grave context, the Qur'an turns so immediately towards concession, rather than justice. Perhaps again the potential for escalation and loss of further life motivates the Qur'anic narrative *fattibāʿun bi 'l-maʿrūfi wa adāʾun ilayhi bi iḥsān* (then grant any reasonable demand, and compensate him with handsome gratitude, Yusuf Ali). The escalation of negative conduct is truncated and diverted towards a positive cycle of mutual agreement and good will. All of this follows from the initial pardon indicated by *ʿufiya* which opens the door to the path of Conciliation (see Bin Salamah, 2002, p.79 for more discussion of *ʿafw* in *qiṣāṣ*).

Justice is a fundamental principle in the Qur'an, mentioned alongside the unity of God at Q.3.18, and as the basis of creation at Q.55:7–9. *Qisṭ* and *ʿadl* (both meaning justice) also feature in a number of Qur'anic verses which emphasise due process in the settlement of disputes (Q.2:188, Q.2:282, Q.4:58 and Q.4:135). Justice is also a transcendental principle, with Q.5:2 and Q.5:8 cautioning against injustice even with former enemies, a reference to past hostilities with the Meccans. Although a full discussion of this topic would be premature at this stage, some of the key verses on this topic arise in Group 1 and are therefore listed in the Summary Table at the end of this chapter. The important theme of justice and its relationship to Conciliation will recur incrementally throughout the book. A detailed study on justice in the Qur'an is also provided by Harvey (2018).

The Qur'an demonstrates high expectations in human conduct, setting aside intuitive negative feelings. The contextually surprising word *akhīhi* (his brother) at Q.2:178 is used to describe the relationship of the victim's next of kin to the killer (a similar technique is used at Q.2:237 to enjoin *faḍl* (graciousness) in the context of a divorce). Al-Rāzī's discussion of the term *akhīhi* centres on the brotherly relation based on *common belief* in Q.49:15. However, the conciliatory effect of the term *akhīhi* is much more significant in light of Q.15:47 which describes the inhabitants of Paradise as *ikhwānan* (brotherly) after the removal of their internal rancour, also mentioned in Q.7:43. At Q.3:103, God's favour in substituting old enmity with heart-felt love makes people *ikhwānan* (like brothers). Thus, the term *akhīhi* in Qur'anic usage is a highly charged persuasive term, evoking a cleansing of rancour and a sense of deep-seated affection. Al-Rāzī also confirms that God *dhakarahu bi lafẓ al-ukhuwwa li yaʿṭif aḥaduhumā ʿalā ṣāḥibihi* (mentioned him with the term of brotherhood to incline each of them towards his companion) but adds *nadaba ila 'l-ʿafw ʿani 'l-qātil* (recommended pardon for the killer).

In fact, the persuasive effect of *akhīhi* is addressed to the *killer* to encourage him to agree to any reasonable settlement: according to Al-Zuhayli (2007, vol.2, p.217), the word *shay'un* implies full discretion in the settlement amount where killing is intentional. Furthermore, *man* signals a *jumla sharṭiyya* (conditional sentence) and *ʿufiya* is passive. This shows remarkable delicacy and avoidance of direct pressure on the aggrieved party to forgive such a serious crime, allowing him a free choice which is more conducive to Conciliation. Thus, whilst the killer is taught positive behaviour by instruction, the next of kin is instead taught to forgive by example with more sensitivity to his aggrieved state. Q.2:178 continues *dhālika takhfīfun min rabbikum wa raḥma* (this is an alleviation from your Lord and an act of mercy, Abdel Haleem). The Divine example of concession and mercy serves as a subtle but persuasive inspiration. Al-Rāzī explains that the Jews were commanded to retaliate and the Christians to forgive, whilst the Qur'an introduces *takhyīr* (choice) between *qiṣāṣ* and *diya* (financial compensation). This choice allows more complete Conciliation: Iṣlāḥī notes (vol.1, p.433) that the discretion offered helps to heal the hurt of the victim's family, whilst the availability of an alternative financial remedy allows social assistance.

Q.2:178 appears to balance the somewhat conflicting appeals of justice and mercy, but overwhelmingly aims to achieve Conciliation and contain the dispute, stating *faman iʿtadā* (whoever exceeds these limits) and threatening eschatological sanctions for anyone who further escalates tensions after resolving the matter through mutual agreement. It is perhaps the avoidance of these further hostilities, as well as the potential forgiveness of the killer's own life, which is indicated in Q.2:179: *wa lakum fi 'l-qiṣāṣi ḥayātun* (there is life for you in *qiṣāṣ*). Later, in Q.4, expiation through freeing a slave, or two successive months' fast, and potentially financial compensation for accidental homicide, including in case of war or treaty with the victim's people, is dealt with at Q.4:92, and deliberate homicide is condemned to Divine punishment at Q.4:93. Kamali (2003, pp.173–75) discusses how in deliberate homicide, the explicit *qiṣāṣ* ruling of Q.2:178 takes precedence over the alluded meaning of non-expiation in Q.4:93, although the alluded meaning of Q.4:93 takes precedence over the inferred meaning of Q.4:92 which requires the freeing of a slave (although the Shāfiʿī school disagrees on the latter point).

The subject of homicide and *qiṣāṣ* is brought to an impactful climax in the narrative of Cain and Abel at Q.5:27–32. These verses provide context for Q.5:45 which recalls the Judaic law of retaliatory *qiṣāṣ* for unlawful killing and lesser forms of personal injury. A notable Conciliation feature in the narrative occurs at Q.5:28 in which the victim declares that he will not retaliate even if he is attacked. The *ism al-fāʿil, bāsiṭin*, rather than a verb in the phrase *mā ana bi bāsiṭin yadiya ilayka li aqtulak* (I shall not raise my hand against you to kill you) indicates, in my view, a long-term resolve (see Q.109:4 for a similar usage). The clear implication is that Conciliation through de-escalation and containment requires one party to be steadfast in non-retaliation, even when faced with aggression from the other. This point will be discussed further in Chapter 5 by reference to Q.41:34–35.

A persuasive implied prohibition against violence is provided through the use of *khāsirīn* (losers) in Q.5:30 and through *al-nudba* (lamentation) in the form of *al-taḥassur* (regret): the terms *yāwaylatā* and *nādimīn* in Q.5:31 highlight the regret of the perpetrator. Against the canvas of this impactful and dramatic narrative of the sons of man's common ancestor Adam, Q.5:32 provides a clear injunction that one unlawful killing is *ka annamā* (as if) he has killed all of mankind, magnifying the value of each and every human life. This formulation emphatically supports my argument above that Conciliation in homicide is a Divine exception reflecting the Qurʾan's emphasis on the sanctity of life.

1.2.2 Inheritance

Immediately after discussing *qiṣāṣ*, Q.2:180 stipulates the making of a will for parents and near relatives *bi 'l-maʿrūf* (reasonable, Yusuf Ali), the subsequent word *ḥaqqan* indicating a binding duty. The term *bi 'l-maʿrūf* recurs in other Conciliation contexts: *qiṣāṣ* Q.2:178, marriage Q.2:234 and Q.4:19 (and *bi maʿrūfin* at Q.2:229, Q.2:231), providing counsel (*aw maʿrūfin* at Q.4:114) and parental rights (*maʿrūfā* at Q.31:1). The phrase *bi 'l-maʿrūf* suggests a reference to social norms or 'Explicit' group values, rather than 'Implicit' values which are personal to the parties, in Greenhouse's classification of values invoked in mediations (1985, pp.91–92, 98–107). Kamali (2003, p.369 onwards) provides further discussion of the term *ʿurf* and the role of 'custom' in Islamic Law.

Q.2:181 warns against unlawful alteration of the will, with accountability implied by mentioning God's qualities of being *Samīʿ* and *ʿAlīm* (All-Hearing, All-Knowing). The subsequent Q.2:182 is distinguished in its explicit sanctioning of a pre-emptive Conciliation (Ṭāhā, 2009, pp.14, 19), as indicated by *man khāfa* (if anyone fears, Yusuf Ali; although Abdel Haleem translates *khāfa* as 'knows'). This conditional phrase anticipates a *future* dispute, and Al-Rāzī considers that it indicates early intervention to facilitate dispute resolution. According to Yusuf Ali's footnote, this could entail advising the testator to change his mind or, after his death, seeking agreement from the beneficiaries to a more just distribution. The ensuing phrase *fa aṣlaḥa baynahum* (conciliates between them) in Q.2:182 is considered by both Al-Rāzī and Iṣlāḥī (vol.1, p.441) as being achieved by the removal of bias and unfair distribution, and the consequent restoration of rights. Bias is indicated by *janafan*, which is unintentional, according to Al-Rāzī, whilst *ithman* indicates intentional unfairness. Impartiality is also emphasised in other Conciliation contexts such as marriage (Q.4:129), and group disputes (Q.49:9) discussed in Chapter 5. The restoration of rights, emphasised in *birr* and again here at Q.2:182, is central to the prevention of disputes and provides cohesion between Q.2:180–182 and Q.2:177.

A specific exception, indicated by the phrase *lā ithma* (no sin), is provided in Q.2:182 for altering wills to achieve Conciliation, this time implicitly encouraged by mentioning God's qualities of being *Ghafūr* (Forgiving) and *Raḥīm* (Merciful). The importance of Conciliation is therefore highlighted both by the objective legal fetter placed on the testator's subjective discretion and the rendering lawful of an otherwise unlawful action based purely on the intent to conciliate. Another example of the latter features in Ḥadīth where the intent to conciliate overrides the usual prohibition on untruthful speech and renders it lawful (Samḥān 2006, p.25).

Turning now from Q.2 to Q.4, I would argue that the inheritance provisions in Q.4:7–8 are a similar form of pre-emptive dispute resolution to that encountered immediately above, achieving certainty and balancing interests in a contentious area: wealth distribution amongst family and friends. These relationships are naturally jeopardised due to the competition for assets and implied affection, and unrealised expectations or needs. My argument finds support from Iṣlāḥī's commentary of Q.4 which mentions ending disputes, oppression and *fasād* (disorder) such as cutting off relationships, by fixing inheritance shares (vol.2, pp.257, 262). Specifically, he cites *ghayra muḍār* (with no harm done to anyone, Abdel Haleem) in Q.4:12 as an indication of avoiding detriment to inheritors. The explicit Conciliation mechanism in Q.2:182 in the context of *waṣiyya* (a will) also supports the inference of a dispute avoidance mechanism in the prescribed shares in Q.4:7–8, particularly since these very provisions supersede the earlier will provisions, rendering them *mansūkh* (repealed).

As with the *diya* (financial compensation) for unlawful killing, social welfare and social justice feature in the range of Qur'anic inheritors, compared to the more limited inheritors possible in feudal or discretionary systems. Hallaq (2009, pp.134–37) provides a related discussion of modern implementation of inheritance laws in Islamic countries. Q.4:8 also stipulates that relatives, orphans and the needy present at a distribution be provided for, even if they are not otherwise legally entitled (up to one third of an estate may be distributed on a discretionary basis). This is clearly a Conciliation mechanism since it is also stipulated that they should be spoken to with *qawlan maʿrūfā* (a kindly word). The collocation of the inheritance procedures in Q.2:180–182 after the subject of Conciliation pursuant to unlawful killing, and in Q.4:7–14 (with an addendum at Q.4:176) immediately before the subject of matrimonial dispute resolution, indicates their common Conciliation theme. Indeed the innovative allotment of a substantial, though not equal, inheritance share to women, 'unprecedented in Arabia' coupled with the new 'financial independence of wives' (Hallaq, 2005, p.23), can readily be argued as constituting a specific prevention of disputes arising from previous curtailment of women's rights.

Having discussed the Conciliation of disputes arising from unlawful killing and inheritance of wealth, the discussion now turns to the third social context of disputes introduced at the start of Section 1.2: commercial dealings.

1.2.3 Commerce

Uncertainty of contractual terms is a significant legal issue, giving rise to commercial disputes and potentially invalidating contractual terms. In the Qur'an, commercial disputes are restricted through encouraging leniency towards debtors at Q.2:280 and through improving certainty of contractual terms and evidential process at Q.2:282. This verse, its importance apparent from its distinction as the longest verse in the Qur'an, provides a detailed formal framework for written financial contracts, including legal processes such as appointing scribes and witnesses.[4] There is *takrār* (repetition) no less than six times of the notion of writing, three times in the imperative, providing further *tawkīd* (emphasis). The conclusion of the verse makes clear that a new system is being taught: *wa yuʿallimukumu ʻllāh, wa ʻllāhu bi kulli shay'in ʿalīm* (and [God] will teach you: He has full knowledge of everything, Abdel Haleem).

Q.2:282 also provides a trinity of *ʿilla* (underlying purpose) for its rulings, perhaps acknowledging the onerous nature of introducing an obligation to write in a predominantly oral culture. The first is *aqsaṭu ʿinda ʻllāhi* (more equitable in God's eyes, Abdel Haleem) which reinforces two earlier references to *ʿadl* (justice) and two references to *taqwā* (God-consciousness). The second is *aqwamu li (ʻl)-shshahāda* (more reliable as testimony, Abdel Haleem) and the third is *adnā an lā tartābū* (more likely to prevent doubts arising between you, Abdel Haleem). It is clear the second and third *ʿilla* are directed at preventing disputes. The trinity sits well with the Conciliation Relationship Triangle identified in Section 1.1.1: addressing respectively justice before God, evidentiary benefit before others in society and personal certainty to the individual and his contract party.

Al-Rāzī provides further confirmation that the third *ʿilla* is a form of pre-emptive Conciliation in his explanation *yaʿnī aqrab ilā zawāl al-shakk wa ʻl-irtiyāb ʿan qulūb al-mutadāyinīn* (i.e. more conducive to erasing doubt and mistrust from the hearts of the parties to the loan agreement). This, he continues, indicates prevention of harm to the self through providing certainty of contractual terms and to the other through avoidance of back-biting and slander. Al-Rāzī also provides some structural thematic *naẓm* analysis in his commentary, commenting that after enjoining charity and prohibiting interest in the earlier verses, the Qur'an encourages the preservation of wealth in this verse to facilitate and complement the earlier commands. Notably, preservation of wealth or life is a common feature of all three conflict management systems discussed in Section 1.2.

4 The extraordinary length of the verse supports Goitein's argument that the Qur'an contains more legal content than is apparent from the mere number of legal verses (Hallaq, 2005, pp. 20–21). The systematic framework, however, contradicts Hallaq's assertion that only with the revelation of verses in Q.5 around the end of 5 A.H. did the Qur'an provide substantive legislation beyond matters of ritual, such as prayer and pilgrimage. Indeed, the inclusion of the famous Q.5:3 *alyawma akmaltu lakum dīnakum* (today, I have perfected your religion for you, Abdel Haleem) signifies that Q.5 provides the finishing touches to the legislation already enacted in suras such as Q.2 and Q.4. This is also indicated by the subject matter of Q.5 which deals with purity of food, for example, rather than the fundamental social constructs dealt with in Q.2 and Q.4 and tends to update topics such as ritual purity or pilgrimage, rather than initiate commandments.

This concludes the discussion of conflict management systems, which followed after the earlier examination of esoteric concepts. As mentioned in the Overview, my analysis of Group 1 demonstrates a third level of Conciliation, based on the notion of unity, which is now discussed.

1.3 Conciliation Through Unity

After assessment of the hypocrites, Jews, Christians and Meccans in the early Medinan period towards the commencement of Q.2, the Qur'anic discourse shifts towards what I consider an appeal to inter-faith, and also intra-faith, unity which becomes fully apparent in Q.3. Historical narratives (Ramadan, 1961, pp.114–17) of peace treaties formed in the early Medinan period by the Prophet with the Jews and Christians, in particular, provide support for such an inclusive interpretation.

As early as Q.2:62, the emphatic *inna* begins a declaration that Muslims, Jews, Christians or Sabians shall enjoy eschatological rewards, provided they believe and *ʿamila ṣāliḥan* (do good deeds). Q.2:160 further on extends an olive branch to those who the Qur'an accuses of distorting their own faiths, if they *aṣlaḥū* (reform), adding encouragingly that God is *Tawwāb* (Relenting) and *Raḥīm* (Merciful). Q.2:213 then provides an inspirational utopian vision of unity: *kāna (ʿl)-nnāsu ummatan wāḥidatan* (mankind was one nation), going on to clarify that the purpose, indicated by the *lām* of *taʿlīl*, of sending prophets and scriptures was *li yaḥkuma bayna (ʿl)-nnāsi fīma ʿkhtalafū fīhi* (to judge between people in their disagreements, Abdel Haleem), providing resolution of theological disputes. This point is reinforced by several verses in later sura groups, including Q.10:19, Q.21:92 and Q.23:51–3.

Emphasised by its position immediately after the famous Throne Verse, Q.2:256 goes on to declare: *lā ikrāha fī (ʿl)-ddīn* (there is no compulsion in religion), providing complete negation of any religious compulsion, a potential source of conflict, through the *lā al-nāfiya li ʿl-jins* with a *manṣūb* noun. Further discussion of non-compulsion and its greater significance will follow in Chapters 4 and 6. Having cited the narratives of past prophets including Adam, Abraham, Jacob, Moses, David and Jesus, and with Q.2:253 having mentioned the elevated status of the various prophets, Q.2:285 concludes the discourse on a remarkably conciliatory and unified note: *lā nufarriqu bayna aḥadin min rrusulih* (we make no distinction between any of His messengers, Abdel Haleem). This verse provides a strategic concluding highlight to the sura which enhances its unifying Conciliation message and provides an introductory frame to the following sura.

In Q.3, after an introductory theological discourse and the narrative of Jesus's birth leading up to the verse of *mubāhala* (prayer for Divine adjudication) at Q.3:61, there is a sustained dialogue with the earlier faiths using the term of address *yā ahl al-kitāb* (O People of the Book; see Gwynne (2007) on patterns of address in the Qur'an). This term features no less than six times at Q.3:64, 65, 70, 71, 98 and 99, the first and last two being prefixed with an address to the Prophet *qul* (say). The term of address appears significant given that in Q.2 the same people were addressed *yā Banī Isrā'īl* (O Children of Jacob) at Q.2:40, 47, 122, perhaps in preparation for the narrative and argument presented at Q.2:133 about Jacob's religious bequest to his children. That precedent indicates that here again the term of address is used to reinforce the ensuing arguments of common ancestry and scripture presented at Q.3:65–68.

In my earlier research (Fazaluddin, 2016, p.351), I argued using intertextual Qur'anic examples, such as Aaron's conciliatory appeal to calm Moses by referring to their common mother at Q.7:150 and Q.20:94, that the term *yā ahl al-kitāb* was itself a conciliatory appeal (*al-ighrā'*; see Hāshmī (2008, p.116) on this rhetorical usage) invoking a shared identity. Based on the conciliatory narrative preceding and succeeding Q.3:64 as discussed above and below, the surrounding *siyāq al-naṣ* (textual context) also indicates a genuine appeal. Furthermore, the immediate textual context indicates the same: the word *ta'ālaw* (come) is undoubtedly a word of appeal and invitation and the reference to *kalimatin sawā'in* (common word) together with the *ḥarf nidā' (yā)* and the *ṣīghat al-amr* (imperative form): *qul* (say) all indicate a willingness to engage in dialogue.

Al-Rāzī supports this positive analysis, considering the invitation *kalām mabnī 'ala 'l-inṣāf wa tark al-jidāl* (discourse based on justice and abandonment of conflict), which confirms its conciliatory effect. He also considers the term of address itself *min aḥsan al-asmā' wa akmal al-alqāb* (amongst the best of names and most perfect of titles) *yadullu 'alā anna qā'ilahu arāda 'l-mubālagha fī ta'ẓīm al-mukhāṭab wa fī taṭyībi qalbihi* (evidencing that the speaker intends magnification in honouring the addressee and in placating his heart). All of this provides the strongest argument in considering the term of address and the invitation at Q.3:64 to be a prime example of inter-faith Conciliation. Furthermore, I believe Q.2:122, which talks of God's favour on and preference of *Banī Isrā'īl*, strongly supports an honorific interpretation of Q.3:64. Shapiro (2005, pp.74–75) emphasises the importance of harnessing positive emotions in Conciliation. It is clear from historical examples highlighted by Iqbal (1965, pp.48–49, 52–53), as outlined in the early discussion on *Ṣulḥ* in History, that the Prophet, who becomes the medium here through the instructive *qul* (say), was sensitive to such conciliatory effects.

There is however a palpable contrast between the inviting tone of Q.3:64 and the five repetitions of *lima* (why), in Q.3:65, 70, 71, 98 and 99 which indicate a sustained reproach. Iṣlāḥī (vol.2, pp.116–17) refers to the *malāmat* (reproach) and *afsaws* (regret) he considers to be indicated through the term *yā ahl al-kitāb* in Q.3:70. He considers this to be directed at the religious scholars who are charged with knowingly concealing their scripture, which accords with Al-Rāzī's commentary of Q.3:70, and the reference to a *farīq* (faction) at Q.3:23 charged with turning away from scripture in their disputes. Remarkably, however, Iṣlāḥī (vol.2, p.109) virtually ignores the positive use of *yā ahl al-kitāb* in Q.3:64 that I have argued above, which in my view provides an unbalanced assessment of this important term.

I have traced above a conciliatory inclusive and unified approach towards other faiths in Q.2 and the narrative continues in the same vein in Q.3. Q.3:34 reinforces the common ancestries of the prophets of previous faiths. Q.3:75 emphasises the trustworthiness of some People of the Book, whilst Q.3:113–114 and Q.3:199 highlight the piety of others, referring to them as *ṣāliḥīn* (righteous) at Q.3:114. Q.3:81 again highlights the commonality of faiths through a common prophetic covenant.[5] Q.3:84, like Q.2:285 above, stresses common belief in the prophets of past religions. Q.3:89, like Q.2:160 above, again offers an olive branch to those who *aṣlaḥū* (reform), again confirming invitingly that God is *Ghafūr* (Forgiving) and *Raḥīm* (Merciful).

After Q.3, Q.4:150–152 again stress that faith, as advocated by the Qur'an, includes a belief in all prophets without differentiation. Q.4:162 praises those People of the Book who are *rāsikhūna fī 'l-ʿilmi* (well-grounded in knowledge, Abdel Haleem). Q.5:5 permits certain inter-marriage with the People of the Book and makes their food lawful. Given the intimate connection and emotional effect of mingling in food consumption and matrimonial relations, this ruling in itself is a powerful Conciliation verse, promoting mutual good relations. Q.5:13 encourages a tolerant attitude towards the People of the Book who have deviated from scripture, saying *faʿfu ʿanhum waṣfaḥ, inna 'llāha yuḥibbu 'l-muḥsinīn* (overlook this and pardon them: God loves those who do good, Abdel Haleem). Q.5:57 restricts a non-friendship injunction to those who mock the new faith and Q.5:69 closes by return the pluralistic sentiments of Q.2:62, declaring again that Muslims, Jews, Sabians and Christians who believe and *ʿamila ṣāliḥan* (do good deeds) shall enjoy salvation (Hamidullah, 1945, pp. 39–43 provides a concurring discussion).

Turning now from inter-faith unity to intra-faith unity, the ultimate goal of the new religion being to set aside past differences and form a unified group based on common beliefs is confirmed at Q.3:103 in the impactful *istiʿāra* (metaphor) of a rope, which gains strength through the multiplicity of intertwined

5 There is debate over whether this is a covenant *by* all the prophets or *about* all the prophets (the grammatical question is whether *nabiyyīn* is a *fāʿil* (subject) or *mafʿūl* (object)).

threads (variations in the use of *istiʿāra* (metaphor) are presented by Abu-Deeb (2000, p.343)). The believers are enjoined *waʿtaṣimū bi ḥabli ʻllāhi jamīʿan wa lā tafarraqū* (hold fast to God's rope all together; do not split into factions, Abdel Haleem). Past enmity is encapsulated in a further metaphor as being on the edge of a pit of fire, and the aforementioned unity is contrasted with the fragmentation of past communities who *tafarraqū wakhtalafū* (split into factions and (fell) into disputes, Abdel Haleem). There is powerful *ṭibāq* (antithesis; see Gwynne (2004, pp.140, 149–50) for a discussion of antithesis in the Qurʾan) between the ascension offered by the salvific 'rope' of Conciliation and the descent into the destructive abyss of conflict. The Conciliation of past disputes is indicated by *idh kuntum aʿdāʾan fa allafa bayna qulūbikum* (you were enemies and then He brought your hearts together, Abdel Haleem) and the gradual transformation to brotherly relations through the teachings of the new religion is indicated by *fa aṣbaḥtum bi niʿmatihī ikhwānā* (you became brothers by His grace, Abdel Haleem). Brotherhood, as discussed in the homicide context above, is a key Conciliation concept denoting mutually harmonious relations.

Reviewing the structure of Group 1 as a whole, in the Farāhī-Iṣlāḥī schema, Q.2 centres around the theme of faith and Q.3 around the theme of Islam, suggesting a distinct progression from an internal to an external dimension of religion. In Qurʾanic Conciliation discourse, however, we saw an esoteric focus in Q.2 inter-woven concurrently with an exoteric framework of conflict management systems, which also features in Q.4. In Q.3, the central concept, according to my structural review, is inter-faith and intra-faith unity, seeking Conciliation rather than confrontation despite the emergence of a new ideology.

Summary Table: Group 1 Conciliation Themes Map by Sura and Verse

	Conciliation through internal transformation	**Conciliation through conflict management processes**	**Conciliation through unity**	**Conciliation and justice**
Q.2	177 *birr* 183–187 fasting, *taqwā* 189–203 *ḥajj*, *taqwā* 208 internalisation 224 *birr*, *taqwā*, *iṣlāḥ*	178–179 homicide 180–182 inheritance 219 alcohol 221–242 marriage 280–282 commerce	62 religious pluralism 213 one nation 285 common belief	182 inheritance 188 corruption 282 commerce

(continued)

	Conciliation through internal transformation	Conciliation through conflict management processes	Conciliation through unity	Conciliation and justice
Q.3	92 *birr* 134 *iḥsān* (see Chapter 3) 159 prophetic exemplar (see Chapter 2)		23, 75, 113–4, 199 differentiation 81 common belief 64 interfaith dialogue 103 unity, brotherhood	
Q.4	36 *iḥsān*	7–14 inheritance 19–35 marriage 83 defamation 85 mediation 92–93 homicide 127–130 marriage 148 defamation	1 universal kinship (see Chapter 3) 152, 163 common belief 162 differentiation	58–65 judgements (see Chapter 2) 135 justice
Q.5	2 *birr*	27–32 homicide 90–91 alcohol	5 common food and inter-marriage 13 tolerance 69 religious pluralism	1 contracts 8 justice 41–50 judgements (see Chapter 2)

Conclusion

Hierarchically, it can be seen that Conciliation is pervasive in the content of the Group 1 suras at three levels, commencing with an esoteric focus which is introduced at Q.2:177 and then developed subsequently in the same sura before re-surfacing periodically. The second level from Q.2:178 to the end of Q.2 is an administrative framework of conflict management systems which is resumed in Q.4. Q.3 appears to provide the focal point for the third level, a strategic vision of unity which pervades the suras before and after it. Q.5 concludes with updating or highlighting references to concepts largely dealt with in the previous suras. Exceptions to normal ethical principles (such as integrity of wills and keeping Divine oaths (Q.2:182, Q.2:224)) are made to prioritise Conciliation, highlighting its over-riding importance and indicating a similar exception in the case of homicide.

Despite the absence of structurally distinct demarcation of thematic content in the Qur'an, therefore, thorough analysis identifies clear Conciliation themes which are interwoven cohesively, with each theme receiving primary focus in its place before assuming a supportive function for the subsequently emerging primary theme. Q.2 introduces all three concepts and acts as a base for the thorough development of administrative provisions in Q.4 and of the vision of unity in Q.3. Furthermore, the sequential order of the themes indicates a micro-level-to macro-level-directed Qur'anic Conciliation paradigm, arguing for change from within at the individual level, then radiating outwards to support societal systems and finally being bound together by a strategic-level global human unity – in three words: Values, Processes, Vision. This demonstrates both a high level of thematic coherence in the Conciliation material and a broad range in the aspects of Conciliation in Group 1 suras.

At the first level, the notion of *birr*, accompanied by references to *taqwā*, provides the internal catalyst for change, demanding good relations with others through altruism, integrity and restraint. A focus on fulfilling the rights of others leads to the proactive avoidance of disputes and the instilment of a Conciliation-based value system. Disputes are also emphatically denounced by negatively associating them with Satan, a notable literary technique. Ritual worship, which might superficially be considered the essence of religion, is given a powerful correctional esoteric re-focus through the emphatic negation in the phrase *laysa 'l-birra* at Q.2:177. Q.2:224 inextricably joins the trinity of esoteric concepts: *birr*, *taqwā* and *iṣlāḥ bayn al-nās* which support a Conciliation Relationship Triangle.

At the administrative level, Conciliation processes provide a supportive skeletal framework for the management of disputes. Underlying causes of disputes, such as the desire for retribution for loss of life, perceived unfairness in wealth distribution, mutual expectations of rights and duties in family relationships and the need for certainty in commercial dealings are all addressed. Indeed upon reflection, Conciliation of disputes in relation to each of the five subjects of the *Maqāṣid Al-Sharīʿa* (underlying aims of Islamic Law) is addressed: faith through an appeal to scriptural commonality and religious pluralism; life through *qiṣāṣ*, *diya* and forgiveness; lineage through Conciliation psychology and arbiter processes in marriage; intellect through alcohol prohibition; and wealth through inheritance laws and the writing of financial contracts. Crucially, in each context, the specific underlying cause of disputes is addressed both psychologically and procedurally.

The strategic vision of unity is particularly rich with special literary features such as grammatical signals, unifying terms of address, impactful metaphors and the notion of brotherhood. Such literary features, in my view, are hallmarks of primary Conciliation verses, where Conciliation is presented with a special prominence of expression. I would include verses such as Q.2:177, Q.2:208, Q.3:64 and Q.3:103 in this category. In future chapters, I will also highlight similar verses, for example where they appear to be seminal in relation to a Conciliation theme or of paramount importance in a sura.

The Farāhī-Iṣlāḥī schema works well at the group level with Law constituting an important aspect of the Conciliation content, although this is supported from below and above by values and vision, respectively. At the sura level, Q.2 and Q.4 form a cohesive pair in providing legal content supplemented by Q.5, rather than the pairing suggested by the Farāhī-Iṣlāḥī schema, with Q.3 focussing more on vision. The Farāhī-Iṣlāḥī method shows strength in addressing the structural significance of verses such as Q.2:177 as compared to Al-Rāzī's generally more localised analysis. However, Al-Rāzī shows his strength in providing unmatched linguistic depth of insight into key Conciliation concepts.

The analysis of Group 1 provides avenues for further exploration. Firstly, the inter-relation between justice and Conciliation is an area of rich debate, given the apparently symbiotic relationship suggested in the commercial context, but the inherent tensions between the two concepts highlighted in the context of homicide and the early discussion of *Ṣulḥ* in History. Secondly, the entire content of Group 1 with the exception of the introductory Q.1 is Medinan and yet contains extensive and substantive Conciliation content. Conciliation is therefore an important theme in the Medinan suras reviewed. However, a balanced assessment in this regard requires a thorough examination of the conflict theme which now follows in Chapter 2.

2 Conciliation and Conflict in the Meccan and Medinan Qur'an

Overview: Group 2 Suras – Q.6–Q.9

Group 2 consists of two lengthy Meccan suras (Q.6 Sūrat Al-Anʿām and Q.7 Sūrat Al-Aʿraf) followed by two lengthy Medinan suras (Q.8 Sūrat Al-Anfāl and Q.9 Sūrat Al-Tawba). The first two being addressed to a Meccan audience focus on fundamental theology, in particular the unity and power of God the Creator and the reckoning of the Day of Judgement, with reference to the fate of past nations and visions of the Hereafter. After this, Q.8 and Q.9 deal with the historical events of the Medinan period involving the Muslims, the Meccans, other faiths in Medina and the hypocrites, including repeated specification of when and where the Muslims should or should not engage in military conflict.

In the Farāhī-Iṣlāḥī schema, the theme of this group is Abrahamic Religion, with one pair of suras dealing with the unity of God in Q.6 and warning of the prevalence of the Truth in Q.7, and a connection between Q.8 dealing with obligations concerning fighting and Q.9 dealing again with the prevalence of Truth. Iṣlāḥī suggests that the primary addressees in Group 2 are the Meccans, in contrast to Group 1 where the primary addressees were the People of the Book (vol.3, p.10).

In my analysis, the notion of Conciliation was examined and implemented through detailed provisions in a range of social contexts in Group 1. In Group 2, the Qur'an elaborates more conceptually the role of Conciliation in three historically important contexts: (i) ideological conflict arising from propagation of the monotheistic Islamic faith, (ii) conflict arising in Divine–human relations and social relations and (iii) military conflict arising from political differences based on religious identity. The Summary Table at the end of Section 2.3 details the layout of key verses in Group 2 in relation to these three sustained Conciliation themes; some content from Group 1 suras has been included due to its thematic relevance.

The key Meccan Conciliation verses analysed in this chapter deal with non-confrontational faith propagation at Q.6.106–108 and Q.7:199–200. In Divine–human and social relations, a discussion of Divine mercy analyses Q.6:54, and social responsibilities are expounded at Q.6:151–153 and Q.7:56. In the Medinan period, community cohesion is discussed at Q.8:1 and Q.8:63, whilst conflict restriction and peace treaties are addressed by reference to Q.8:39, 61 and 72 and Q.9:1–16, 29 and 73.

https://doi.org/10.1515/9783110747348-004

2.1 Conciliation in Faith Propagation and the Prophetic Exemplar

This chapter analyses two lengthy Meccan suras (Q.6 and Q.7) followed by two lengthy Medinan suras (Q.8 and Q.9). The first two being addressed to a Meccan audience focus on fundamental theology, in particular the unity and power of God the Creator and the reckoning of the Day of Judgement, with reference to the fate of past nations and visions of the Hereafter. After this, Q.8 and Q.9 deal with the historical events of the Medinan period involving the Muslims, the Meccans, other faiths in Medina and the hypocrites, including repeated specification of when and where the Muslims should or should not engage in military conflict.

At first read, the content of Q.6 has little to do with a conventional understanding of Conciliation. A thorough analysis of the same material however reveals two important aspects of Conciliation. The first of these is a non-confrontational etiquette in the propagation of faith which pervades Q.6 and is also referred to in Q.7. The second aspect of Conciliation in Q.6 is an injunction to abide by both Divine rights and human rights, thus maintaining good relations in these relationships. This second theme is introduced later in Section 2.2, which analyses Q.7 in more detail.

Q.6 presents a number of passages such as Q.6:1–3, Q.6:59–65 and Q.6:95–105 in which the Qur'an espouses God's unity and omnipotence. Within the general rhetorical eloquence of these passages, the relevant literary feature is the use of sustained cosmological and teleological arguments, introduced here and discussed in greater detail in Chapter 4. The repetition of introductory refrains such as *wa huwa 'lladhī* (it is He who; three times at Q.6:97–99) and *qul* (say; three times at Q.6:63–65) indicates a sustained argument. All-encompassing phraseology such as heavens and earth, darkness and light (Q.6:1), hidden and apparent (Q.6:3), land and sea, wet and dry (Q.6:59), unseen and seen (Q.6:73) and living and dead (Q.6:95) create a sense of Omnipotence, whilst titular references such as *fāliqu 'l-iṣbāḥ* (Cleaver of the daybreak, Q.6:96) and *badīʿu ('l)-ssamāwāti wa 'l-arḍ* (Originator of the heavens and the earth, Q.6:101) indicate qualities which are unique.

Indeed, Q.6 itself makes numerous references to the use of *ḥujja* (evidential proof) and *āyāt* (signs; Q.6:4, Q.6:46, Q.6:65, three times in Q.6:97–99, Q.6:105) as well as *baṣā'ir* (visible proof – juxtaposed for impact with the *invisibility* of God, Q.6:103–104) and *bayyina* (clear proof, Q.6:57). Q.6:149 declares that God's argument is *al-ḥujjatu 'l-bāligha* (the conclusive argument, Abdel Haleem), whilst accusing the opposing polytheists in the previous verse of pursuing mere *ẓann* (conjecture). At Q.6:74–83, the narrative of Abraham and his people presents a further sustained argument, this time using dramatic dialogue, contrasting the everlasting God with the daily extinguishing of various heavenly bodies. Again, this is referred to as a Divine *ḥujja* (Q.6:83).

The above points all serve to illustrate that the Qur'an goes to great lengths to persuade its audience of its fundamental theological assertions through literary arguments, supporting the foundational conciliatory tenet encapsulated in the Medinan verse Q.2:256: *lā ikrāha fī ('l)-ddīn* (there is no compulsion in religion). Iṣlāḥī (vol.3, p.134) also points out that at Q.6:106–107, the Qur'an uses *iltifāt* (turning; a style of dynamic shifts in address, see Abdel Haleem, 2001, pp.184–210) to address the Prophet directly, a point of impact, advocating disengagement and also presenting non-compulsion in the propagation of faith as a Divine example for the Prophet's own conduct: *wa aʿriḍ ʿani 'l-mushrikīn, wa law shāʾa 'llāhu mā ashrakū, wa mā jaʿalnāka ʿalayhim ḥafīẓā* (Turn away from those who join other gods with Him. If it had not been God's will, they would not have done so, but We have not made you their guardian, Abdel Haleem). In his abridged study *Muhammad: Prophet and Statesman*, Watt (1961, pp.219–20) cites historical examples of Jewish and Christian minority communities with whom the Prophet entered into treaties granting protection in return for a payment, a so-called '*pax Islamica*', but crucially highlights that they 'were not asked to become Muslims'. This is especially pertinent to the discussion in this chapter given that the historical context of these treaties was the Prophet's expedition to Tabūk in 9 A.H./630 C.E., which coincides with the circumstances of the revelation of verses dealing with military conflict in Q.9, discussed in the final section of this chapter.

Whilst advocating its own theological position, as discussed above, Q.6 also expressly enjoins the avoidance of confrontation in theological matters. The Prophet is educated, using the example of past prophets as role models, in bearing persecution and rejection with patience (Q.6:34). The Prophet in turn is an exemplar for his followers, elevated to a pre-eminent status in the Qur'an (see Q.33:21 and Q.33:6, 40, 45–46, 56 and Q.68:4; also see Ernst, 2010, p.132). More generally, Q.6:68 again instructs *iʿrāḍ* (disengagement) from those who ridicule the Qur'an rather than retaliation, although even this disengagement is temporary for the duration of such conduct. The same instruction is repeated at Q.6:106 with a further injunction at Q.6:108 that the gods worshipped by the polytheists are not to be abused, so as to prevent their retaliatory abuse directed at Allah, resulting in an escalation of conflict. Iṣlāḥī (vol.3, pp.134–35) notes that the restriction on disputation with the (Meccan) polytheists here mirrors the similar restriction on disputation with the (Medinan) hypocrites at Q.4:148, indicating a consistent approach across the two historical periods.

In exploring the *ʿilla* (underlying objective) of the legislative prohibition on abuse of the polytheists' deities at Q.6:108, Al-Rāzī highlights that such conduct would cause *tanfīrihim ʿan qubūl al-dīn* (their being repulsed from accepting faith) as well as causing *idkhāl al-ghayẓ wa ʻl-ghaḍab fī qulūbihim* (the entering of rage and fury into their hearts). The form II verbal noun *tanfīr* and the form IV verbal noun *idkhāl* both indicate, through their forms, a causative effect. It can be seen that these two consequences would, respectively, undermine the conciliatory faith propagation advocated and practised by Q.6 and result in inflammatory conflict. The prohibition on abuse thus supports Conciliation by avoiding both of these undesirable outcomes. There is a linguistically rich effect in Al-Rāzī's choice of words, in that the *qulūb* (hearts) of the polytheists are prevented from *qubūl* (acceptance), the alternation of the medial and terminal consonants mirroring the alternation in the underlying meaning of the respective words.

The Prophet's character is also the subject of Q.3:159, in Group 1, where the Qurʾan commends his lenient attitude, apparently towards those who fled the battlefield at Uḥud. The Prophet is told that by God's mercy he is *linta lahum* (gentle in [his] dealings with them, Abdel Haleem). Had he been *faẓẓan ghalīẓa ʻl-qalbi* (harsh, hard-hearted), *la ʻnfaḍḍū* (they would certainly have dispersed) from around him. He is instructed: *faʿfu ʿanhum wa ʻstaghfir lahum wa shāwirhum fī ʻl-amr* (forgive them, seek forgiveness for them and consult with them in matters). As in Q.6:108 above, behaviour is to be controlled in light of its effect on the attitude of others towards religion. There is delicate wordplay in the juxtaposition of the two similar sounding stressed syllables in the words ***fa**ẓẓan* and *(i)n**faḍ**ḍū*. This accentuates the causative nexus between the two behaviours, with harsh conduct causing others to disperse. A gentle approach therefore appears to be integral to the prophetic role of attracting people towards religion (also see Q.20:44, discussed in Chapter 3).

The principle of disengagement at Q.6:68 and Q.6:106 is again reinforced strategically at the end of Q.7, the ensuing sura, which appears to complete the teachings of Q.6. Q.7:199 enjoins: *khudhi ʻl-ʿafwa wa ʾmur bi ʻl-ʿurfi wa aʿriḍ ʿani ʻl-jāhilīn* (be tolerant and command what is right: pay no attention to foolish people, Abdel Haleem). As well as a further reference to *iʿrāḍ* (disengagement), the Prophet is instructed here to adhere to the quality of *ʿafw* (complete forgiveness), whilst being steadfast in his propagation. The ensuing verse Q.7:200 suggests that the converse of Q.7:199, a retaliatory approach, is a prompting of Satan from which God's refuge should be sought, concluding with an emphatic reminder that God is All-Hearing and All-Knowing. Al-Rāzī cites a prophetic narration in which the Angel Gabriel is credited with explaining Q.7:199 to mean 'maintaining relations with those who have cut relations with you, giving to those who have withheld from you, and forgiving those who have wronged you'. The central importance of these conciliatory behaviours in personal character development, as espoused by the Qurʾan, is also highlighted by Al-Rāzī's quotation from the celebrated Jaʿfar Al-Ṣādiq – *wa laysa fī 'l-Qur'ān āya ajma' li makārim al-akhlāq min hādhihi 'l-āya* (there is no verse in the Qur'an more comprehensive than this one regarding noble character traits).

The specific instruction to *consult* at Q.3:159, mentioned above, also goes beyond non-recrimination, showing a willingness to move forward and work together constructively and respectfully in a unified manner, overlooking past differences. A similar conciliatory emphasis on consultation between a couple after their divorce, for the benefit of their children, is found at Q.2:233 and Q.65:6. Both Q.7:199 and Q.3:159 encourage the Prophet to rise above the apparent injury suffered and to focus instead on his intended objective. In this sense, forgiveness of wrongs shows strength of character and offers a platform for progress. Gopin (2001, pp.93–97), who examines the importance of forgiveness in conflict resolution, highlights that forgiveness thus becomes an 'empowering act', which goes beyond ritual forgiveness and achieves true Conciliation. He also argues that forgiveness goes beyond justice, enabling progress even where justice cannot be achieved. This discussion is developed further on in this book and particularly in Section 5.1.3 below.

It can be seen above that in Q.6 and the conclusion of Q.7 the Qur'an not only engages with its audience to present its theological arguments persuasively but also provides education in the parameters within which such engagement should be restricted, to maintain a conciliatory approach and avoid conflict. This correlates with the influential work of Abu-Nimer (2003, pp.9–17) on reconciliation, which advocates the use of persuasion and training to promote long-term change and avoid physical conflict.

The second important Conciliation theme mentioned above, of fulfilling God's rights and human rights to preserve good relations at both levels, is now introduced by reference to Q.6, and further developed by reference to Q.7.

2.2 Conciliation in Divine–Human and Social Relations

2.2.1 God's Mercy in Divine–Human Conciliation and the Notion of *Iṣlāḥ*

Concurrent with the theological narrative of Q.6 is an engaging message of Divine invitation whose central feature is the boundless mercy of God, an important Conciliation concept in Divine–human relations. Conflict arises in Divine–human relations through human conduct which opposes the Divine will, inviting retribution. Such retribution is, however, avoided through human repentance which invokes Divine forgiveness, achieving what Neuwirth (2000, p.13) describes as 'divine–human conciliation'. It should be understood that, whilst the term 'Conciliation' has been used in this context, the *basis* of such Conciliation is inherently less bilateral and consensual than might be expected in Social Conciliation. A key verse in this regard is Q.6:54, in which the Prophet is instructed to welcome believers with the greeting of *salām* (peace) and the message: *kataba rabbukum ʿalā nafsihi (ʾl)-rraḥma* (your Lord has ordained that He will be merciful), continuing that if someone does wrong out of ignorance, then *tāba* (repents) and *aṣlaḥa* (reforms), then God is *Ghafūr* (Most Forgiving) and *Raḥīm* (Most Merciful).

Al-Rāzī considers whether Q.6:54 refers specifically to the poor but sincere believers reviled by the Meccan chieftains just mentioned at Q.6:52–53, but inclines towards a general meaning which refers to all believers who repent from knowingly committed sins due to personal desires. However, I would argue that a wider contextual analysis suggests that the verse is in fact a general invitation towards Divine–Human Conciliation based on acceptance of the Qurʾanic message, targeted at the Meccan audience in general. This is significant because the verse becomes both integral to the over-arching propagation discourse of Q.6 and manifests a greater magnitude of forgiveness and conciliatory reach across the population. From my perspective, it makes little sense for such an expansive and highly motivational verse to be targeted at the relatively small number of early believers to the exclusion of the disbelieving majority of the Meccan audience. In addition, Al-Rāzī himself explicitly prefers a relatively broad interpretation of the verse, as mentioned above. Furthermore, Al-Rāzī states that commentators agreed that Q.6 was revealed *dafʿatan wāḥidatan* (in a single instalment). As such, the primary audience of this sura, as confirmed by Iṣlāḥī (vol.3, p.10) in his structural analysis, are the Meccan polytheists.

The reference in Q.6:54 to *salām* and the selective and emphatic mention of God's names associated with forgiveness and mercy are clear signals towards Divine–Human Conciliation. As Al-Rāzī quotes from earlier sources, *salām* constitutes a prayer for safety. *Salām* is also a symbolic assurance of security, diffusing tension, indicating non-retaliation and avoiding or confirming the resolution of a dispute. Both Abu-Nimer (2003, p.7) and Cohen (2001, p.42) discuss the conciliatory impact of rituals such as greetings. In the instant case, *salām* offers an assurance of non-retribution from God for past sins for those who accept the new faith. As in the context of Prophetic conduct above, forgiveness goes beyond justice to repair relationships.

At Q.6:54, after belief and *tawba*, it is *iṣlāḥ* (reform) which finally unlocks Divine mercy and ultimately achieves Conciliation. *Iṣlāḥ* is both an expansive and fundamental concept. ʿAbd Al-Quddūs (1999, pp.34, 242) cites the classical scholar Al-Rāghib Al-Iṣfahānī (d. circa fifth/eleventh century) as distinguishing *ṣulḥ* from *iṣlāḥ* on the basis that *ṣulḥ* is more specific and refers to the removal of disputes, whilst *iṣlāḥ* is a broader notion referring to the removal of *fasād*, which includes disputation and other matters (see Al-Iṣfahānī, 2009, pp.489–90). ʿAbd Al-Quddūs adds that *iṣlāḥ* can be used in the sense of *ṣulḥ* with the addition of the restrictive phrase *bayna ('l)-nnās* (between people, as in Q.4:114). In Q.6 to Q.9, although *ṣulḥ* does not feature, *aṣlaḥa* occurs at Q.6:48, Q.6:54 and Q.7:35, *aṣliḥ* occurs at Q.7:142, *aṣliḥū* occurs at Q.8:1, *iṣlāḥ* occurs at Q.7:56 and Q.7:85 and *muṣliḥīn* occurs at Q.7:170 ('Abd Al-Bāqī, 2001, p.410). These verses will be discussed below. Ten further references to righteous people or righteous deeds from the root *ṣ-l-ḥ* are not discussed,[6] except one reference to *ṣāliḥīn* (the righteous) at Q.7:196.

Tawba and *iṣlāḥ* are also the means to Divine–Human Conciliation at Q.3:89 (addressing People of the Book) and Q.4:146 (directed at the hypocrites). At Q.6:48, a general conditional statement provides an assurance of Divine non-retribution for whoever believes and *aṣlaḥa* (reforms). This message is reinforced again at Q.7:35, with the same assurance for those who believe, show *taqwā* (God-consciousness) and *aṣlaḥa* (reform). The active form IV verb *aṣlaḥa* indicates the Qur'anic call to action leading to Divine–Human Conciliation, a notion mentioned repeatedly in the Qur'an: see Q.2:160 (concealing revelation), Q.4:16 (adultery), Q.5:39 (theft), Q.16:119 (lawful foods) and Q.24:5 (slander). Notably Q.7:35 addresses mankind in general: 'O Children of Adam', like Q.3:89 and Q.4:146 going beyond addressing only sincere believers. These three verses support my broad interpretation of Q.6:54 as not restricting its central message of *tawba* and *iṣlāḥ* to the small community of early believers in Mecca.

In addition to *iṣlāḥ*, the notion of *tawba* incorporates a sense of penitence and submission, leading to Divine mercy, which contrasts sharply with arrogance and rebellion, leading to Divine retribution. Two archetypal models, the prophetic example of Adam's penitence (Q.7:23; also see human penitence and submission at Q.7:149–155, 206) and the Satanic example of arrogance (Q.7:12), are presented to the Meccan audience as a stark choice for emulation (human arrogance is also mentioned at Q.7:36, 40, 76, 88 and 146). Persuasive impact is provided in this passage by the above term of address 'O Children of Adam', a title used at Q.7:26–27 and 31 in addition to Q.7:35 above, reinforcing the precedent of Adam's penitence as an exemplar for his descendants. Iṣlāḥī (vol.3, pp.237, 246) highlights that this use of the term of address 'O Children of Adam' to appeal to Adam's descendants to follow his path is as an example of the Qur'an's customary eloquence and brevity.

Further persuasive impact is provided by the intransigent tone of Q.7:40, which famously declares that the arrogant shall not enter Paradise 'until the

6 The references to righteous people or righteous deeds from the root *ṣ-l-ḥ* are: Q.6:85, Q.7:168, Q.7:189, Q.7:190, Q.7:196, Q.9:75, Q.9:102 and Q.9:120; two references to the Prophet *Ṣāliḥ* occur at Q.7:73 and Q.7:77.

camel' (Yusuf Ali) or 'even if a thick rope . . .' (Abdel Haleem; although 'camel' may have greater rhetorical effect, see Q.77:33) can pass through the eye of a needle, highlighting the loss of Divine favour consequent in following the example of Satan. Q.7:16 warns of Satan's promise to lead people away from the 'straight path' as revenge for his expulsion from Paradise. As discussed further below, the 'straight path' is used to refer to a body of conciliatory behaviours, indicating a polarity between the Divine encouragement towards Conciliation (Q.6:151–153) and Satan's encouragement towards conflict (see Q.7:200 above). The choice of the primary narrative of Adam and Satan at this juncture in the Qur'anic discourse demonstrates both the fundamental importance and the universality of the message of Divine–Human Conciliation. The insightful analysis by Neuwirth (2000, p.7) of the recurrent Adam–Satan narrative in various suras of the Qur'an considers Q.7 the 'most comprehensive' account of the narrative.

The above argument of a general message of Divine–Human Conciliation in Q.6 is further supported by Q.6:147, where the Prophet is instructed to say first *even to those who reject his message* that: *rabbukum dhū raḥmatin wāsiʿatin* ('Your Lord has all-encompassing mercy', Abdel Haleem), suggesting that the door of Divine mercy is never closed. *Rabbukum* (your Lord) here adds an inviting sense of proximity, although the message of mercy is then tempered with a message of retribution for those who persist in wrongdoing. Q.6:155 indicates that Divine mercy will be the reward of those who follow the Qur'anic teachings. Q.6:160 adds a quantitative demonstration of God's mercy by indicating that He will reward each good deed with tenfold reward whilst punishing a wrongful action as a single deed.

Finally, Q.6:165 concludes the sura with an impactful reversal of Q.6:147, this time with God's retribution mentioned first so that God's qualities of forgiveness and mercy, reinforced by the affirming particle *inna* and the *lām* of *tawkīd* (emphasis), are thrown into focus as the final thought in the audience's mind at the conclusion of Q.6 and the commencement of Q.7: *inna rabbaka sarīʿu 'l-ʿiqābi wa innahū la ghafūru ('l)-rraḥīm* (your Lord is swift in punishment, yet He is most forgiving and merciful, Abdel Haleem). In short, the narrative of Divine mercy is taken to its furthest limit, in persuasive correlation with the exhaustive arguments of God's unity also presented in Q.6.

2.2.2 Social Conciliation in the Meccan Period

In Q.6, the focus on theology and Divine mercy suggests that Social Conciliation is not emphasised in this narrative. However, a close study shows that this is not the case. After a lengthy discussion regarding prohibited and permitted *foods*, Q.6:151–153 uses this context for impact by providing an extensive list of prohibited and prescribed *conduct*. This list includes a prohibition on infanticide due to poverty (also see Q.6:137 prohibiting infanticide due to idolatry), immodesty, homicide and unlawful use of an orphan's property, as well as enjoining *iḥsān* on parents, weighing with *qisṭ* (justice) and speaking with *ʿadl* (justly) without bias (in the following sura, Q.7:8 also refers to the eschatological scales of Divine justice whilst Q.7:29 enjoins justice as a temporal Divine command). It can be seen that many of the notions in Q.6:151–153 are essential in dispute avoidance since they are the cause of disputes in individual, familial, tribal, commercial and societal level relationships. We will now consider the significance of this collective social message.

First, the phrase *qul taʿālaw* (say, come) is reminiscent of the fundamental injunction towards inter-faith dialogue with the People of the Book at Q.3:64,[7] and indicates an inviting style and quest for common ground (here, common Divine injunctions) to engage with other faiths, particularly the Jewish faith mentioned before and after in Q.6:146 and Q.6:154. Secondly, the above list of Social Conciliation concepts at Q.6:151–152 is securely encapsulated at both ends within Divine–Human Conciliation by commencing the list at Q.6:151 with a prohibition on polytheism and terminating the list at Q.6:152 with abiding by God's covenant. All of these commandments are linked with the *wāw* of conjunction indicating that they are a single set of teachings, referred to in Q.6:153 with a singular demonstrative particle *hādhā*. Thirdly, this set of teachings – all relating to Social or Divine–Human Conciliation – is fundamental to the Qur'an's message, as now discussed below.

Q.6:153 describes the above conciliatory teachings as *ṣirāṭī mustaqīman* (my (i.e. the Prophet's) way, the straight path). As the Prophet is the medium of the Qur'anic message and a role model for its implementation, a reference to his way is an indication of the Qur'an's central message. Furthermore at Q.6:161, the Prophet is instructed to say that he has been guided by his Lord to *ṣirāṭin mustaqīmin*, the true, monotheistic religion of Abraham indicating a reference to the essential message of previous faiths. Another commandment regarding permitted and prohibited foods and the message of God's unity is followed by a reference to *ṣirāṭu rabbika mustaqīman* (the straight path of your Lord, Q.6:126), linking the Prophet's way to God's way. In addition to these references, the juxtaposition of the two words *ṣirāṭ* and *mustaqīm* directly correlates to the phraseology of Q.1:6. Since Q.1

7 This seminal verse on inter-faith dialogue has given rise to much literary discussion by both Islamic and Western writers; see El-Ansary and Linnan (ed.) (2010), *Muslim and Christian Understanding: Theory and Application of a "Common Word"*.

is considered a distillation of the Qur'anic message, notions contained within it are of fundamental importance. Conciliatory conduct is thus the Prophet's way, the message of past religions, God's way and the essence of the Qurʾanic discourse.

The above Social Conciliation themes are developed further in Q.7, where a central feature is the Divine establishment of *iṣlāḥ* and prohibition of *fasād*, explicitly highlighted at Q.7:56: *wa lā tufsidū fī 'l-arḍi baʿda iṣlāḥihā* (do not spread corruption in the earth after it has been set in order). In this verse, the Qurʾan speaks in its own direct and commanding voice using the prohibitive *lā*. The sense of Divine authority is reinforced by the surrounding verses Q.7:54 and Q.7:57, which drive home the notion of Divine power. Q.7:54 in particular states: *alā lahu 'l-khalqu wa 'l-amr* (all creation and command belong to Him, Abdel Haleem). Both at Q.7:56 and elsewhere in the Qurʾan (for example Q.2:11, Q.11: 116–117, Q.26:152, Q.27:48), *fasād* is frequently contrasted with *iṣlāḥ*, providing semantic opposition between the two concepts. Even linguistically, scholars such as ʿAbd Al-Raḥmān Ibn Al-Jawzī (d. 597/1200) and Al-Rāzī consider *fasād* to be the opposite of *ṣalāḥ* (Muṣṭafā, 2007), which is grammatically and semantically directly linked to *iṣlāḥ*. Ibn Manẓūr (2014, vol. 3, p.348) states: *al-ṣalāḥ ḍidd al-fasād* (*ṣalāḥ* is the opposite of *fasād*). *Ṣalāḥ* is a form I verbal noun meaning a 'thriving state of affairs' and shares a grammatical root with the form IV verbal noun *iṣlāḥ* meaning 'reform/order'. The significance of opposition between *iṣlāḥ* and *fasād* in the Qurʾan will become apparent in the ensuing discussion.

Al-Rāzī provides two helpful elucidations of the above quotation from Q.7:56. Firstly, he considers the prohibition on *fasād* to be a prohibition *ab initio* on any corruption in relation to the five *maqāṣid* (objectives) of Islamic law: the corruption of life, for example, through unlawful killing; wealth, for example, through stealing (see Q.7:85 below); religion, for example, through disbelief; lineage, for example, through fornication; and intellect, for example, through alcohol consumption. Secondly, Al-Rāzī suggests that *iṣlāḥ* of the earth, the opposite of *fasād*, refers to the sending of prophets and scriptures with regulations, a view which Iṣlāḥī (vol.3, pp.280–83) also appears to support. Al-Rāzī's elucidations of Q.7:56 collectively provide valuable insight into the full significance of Q.6: 151–153, discussed above. The first elucidation highlights that, since Q.6:151–153 prohibit conduct causing detriment to life, wealth, religion and lineage – which are all objectives of Islamic law, they constitute a prohibition on *fasād*. The second elucidation indicates that these same teachings constitute *iṣlāḥ*, because they signify 'the Prophet's way' and are enshrined in scripture.

Further on at Q.7:85, the people of Madyan are told not to weigh goods inequitably and cause *fasād* (corruption) in the land after its *iṣlāḥ* (order). Al-Rāzī provides further legal insight here, including in Q.7:85 a general prohibition on theft, taking bribes, highway robbery and unlawful acquisition of wealth by force, arguing that any form of taking another's property without consent necessarily leads to *al-munāzaʿa wa ʾl-khuṣūma* (conflict and disputation) which in turn leads to *fasād*. Just as conciliatory conduct correlates to *iṣlāḥ* and is enjoined, therefore, conflict correlates to *fasād* and is prohibited. Al-Rāzī also provides further insight into the fundamental notions of *fasād* and *iṣlāḥ*, commenting that Q.7:85 distils down to two essentials: accepting the unity of God and prophethood, and *shafaqa ʿalā khalqi ʾllāh* (compassion for God's creation). The consistent juxtaposition of these two notions in the above discourse illustrates both the importance of Social Conciliation in being situated alongside fundamental theological doctrines, and the essential nexus between Divine–Human Conciliation and Social Conciliation.

The above general prohibition on *fasād* is complemented by an impactful series of specific historical narratives, citing Divine retribution against nations accused of rejecting their prophets and spreading *fasād*. At Q.7:74, the nation of Thamūd is instructed by their prophet Ṣāliḥ: *wa lā taʿthaw fī ʾl-arḍi mufsidīn* (and do not spread corruption in the land, Abdel Haleem), before narrating their mutilation of a she-camel. Elsewhere, nine individuals amongst the same community who *yufsidūna fī ʾl-arḍi wa lā yuṣliḥūn* (spread corruption in the land and did not reform; Q.27:48–49) are chastised for their plot to assassinate their prophet, bearing notable similarities with the conduct of the Meccans referenced at Q.8:30. After Thamūd, at Q.7:85 onwards the narrative of Madyan and their prophet Shuʿayb is presented in which Madyan, accused of dishonesty in trading, are warned of the past fate of the *mufsidīn* (those who used to spread corruption, Abdel Haleem, Q.7:86). The latter epithet is also specifically applied to Pharaoh at Q.7:103 in relation to his oppressive conduct. Welch, who provides valuable insights into the formulaic features of punishment stories in the Qur'an, considers the examples in Q.7 'one of the most important and rhetorically powerful versions'. In spite of this, he considers that they have 'little connection' with the sura's other themes which he considers fragmented (Welch, 2000, p.85). This is in keeping with his broader view, since Welch (2000, p.112, n.18) also rejects the notion of central themes providing coherence within individual suras. In contrast, my analysis of Q.6 and Q.7 above and below suggests that the stories in Q.7 are an integral part of a sustained thematic engagement with *iṣlāḥ* and *fasād*.

Iṣlāḥ and *fasād* also feature prominently in the fundamental Adam–Satan narrative. The notion of *iṣlāḥ* in the Adam–Satan narrative of Q.7 has already been discussed in relation to Divine–Human Conciliation in Section 2.2.1. Another instance of this narrative occurs at Q.2:30, in which God announces His intention to appoint a *khalīfa* (vicegerent) on earth. In this early creation account, the Qur'an explicitly envisages the spreading of *fasād* in the earth by humans, leading to bloodshed, a pre-emptive charge levelled against mankind by angels: *qalu ataj alu fīhā man yyufsidu fīhā wa yasfiku (ʻl)-ddimāʼ* (they said, ‘How can You put someone there who will cause damage and bloodshed, Abdel Haleem, Q.2:30). Two immediately ensuing references to God’s supreme knowledge (*innī aʿlamu*: I know) at the end of Q.2:30 and to His teaching the prophet Adam (*wa ʿallama*: He taught) at the start of Q.2:31 indicate that Divine education of humans through prophets is the means by which *fasād* will be held in check and the Divine order maintained on earth.

I would argue that the Divine education through prophets envisaged in Q.2:30, at man’s very inception, as a force to oppose *fasād* and bloodshed, is itself the notion of *iṣlāḥ* – a notion which is therefore integral to the limitation of conflict. In the above discussion of Q.7:56 and Q.7:85, both Al-Rāzī and Iṣlāḥī consider that *iṣlāḥ* of the earth features the sending of prophets and scriptures to oppose *fasād*, which supports my argument in relation to Q.2:30. Neuwirth (2000, pp.13, 15) also appears to support my position: she argues that the Adam–Satan narrative surrounding Q.2:30 presents the ‘primordial exemplum’ for the co-existence of Divine guidance and the adversarial practitioners of *fasād*. Although she differs from my position somewhat by juxtaposing *fasād* with *īmān*, I have already argued above that the Qurʾan contrasts *fasād* with *iṣlāḥ*, a semantic opposition which is also supported linguistically by scholars such as Ibn Al-Jawzī and Al-Rāzī. Although the notions of *īmān* (faith) and *ṣāliḥāt* (righteous deeds) are linked (see Q.2:25, a recurrent refrain in the Qurʾan: ʿAbd al-Bāqī (2001, p. 411) lists 62 instances of *ṣāliḥāt*, many of which are coupled with references to *īmān*), the challenge against *fasād* at Q.2:30 and in Q.7 demands action in the form of *iṣlāḥ* rather than faith alone. Furthermore, the Adam–Satan narrative at Q.7 is embedded within a sustained engagement with *fasād* and *iṣlāḥ*, as I have demonstrated above, which indicates a similar thematic emphasis in the narrative at Q.2:30. The implication of my argument is significant: the notion of *iṣlāḥ* at Q.2:30 creates a fundamental connection between Conciliation and the origin of creation.

A number of Qurʾanic examples also support the above argument. Firstly, I have argued above that Q.6:151–153 constitute *iṣlāḥ* and a prohibition on *fasād*, whilst also signifying both God’s way and the Prophet’s way. Secondly, at Q.7:85 above, Shuʿayb chastises his people: *wa lā tufsidū fī ʻl-arḍi baʿda iṣlāḥihā* (do not spread corruption in the earth after it has been set in order), vocalising the essential message of *iṣlāḥ* presented in Q.7:56 in identical wording, dramatically bringing revelation to life and reflecting Divine education in prophetic instruction. Thirdly, Moses’ parting advice to Aaron, his delegated representative enjoins, at Q.7:142: *(u)khlufnī fī qawmī wa aṣliḥ wa lā tattabiʿ sabīla ʻl-mufsidīn* (‘Take my place among my people: act rightly and do not follow the way of those who spread corruption’, Abdel Haleem). This indicates the role of a prophet is to *aṣliḥ* (uphold right) within his nation and not give way to the *mufsidīn* (those who spread corruption). Each of these examples confirms that the central role of prophets is to receive through Divine revelation and transmit to their people through prophetic instruction the essential message of prohibiting *fasād* and effecting *iṣlāḥ*.

The imperative verb *(u)khlufnī* (take my place) at Q.7:142 also correlates well with the notion of man as a *khalīfa* (vicegerent) at Q.2:30, providing a cohesive link between the two verses. Similar terminology, *khalaftumūnī* (you stood in my place), is also used in Moses' later chastisement of his people and his brother Aaron, at Q.7:150, for apparently failing in this role. In my view, Q.2:30 and Q.7:142 collectively indicate that the prohibition of *fasād* and effecting *iṣlāḥ*, entrusted to the prophets, is man's primary role as God's vicegerent. Although Amadu (2015, p.185) argues that man's role as God's vicegerent is to uphold *justice*, his position lacks clarity due to the significant variations in the types and definitions of *ʿadl* (justice) presented (pp.117–19, 178–79) and the supplementing of notions such as equality, love for humans and *iḥsān* which he also occasionally includes within the responsibilities of the vicegerent (pp.165, 202). In my view, justice is also an example of *iṣlāḥ*: at Q.6:151–152 above, just conduct is one example of a list of ordained conciliatory behaviours constituting *iṣlāḥ*. Conversely at Q.7:85, injustice in the form of inequity in weights and measurement is one example of *fasād* and a violation of the earth's *iṣlāḥ*. The above discussion culminates in a profound and fundamental connection between Conciliation through the notion of *iṣlāḥ* on the one hand and man's inception and the essential purpose of religion on the other. *Iṣlāḥ* is not merely a broader notion than *ṣulḥ*, as indicated by ʿAbd Al-Quddūs above, it is a remarkably expansive and fundamental concept in Qurʾanic discourse, providing education in conciliatory conduct and thus maintaining order in accordance with the Divine will.[8]

Iṣlāḥ and the removal of *fasād* feature recurrently both in Divine–Human Conciliation, and again in Social Conciliation, providing thematic continuity between these two closely related types of Conciliation. The offer of Divine mercy to encourage *iṣlāḥ* in social dealings is seen in Q.7:56, which goes on to say that God's mercy is near the *muḥsinīn*; an important quality of such people is being gracious towards others (see the discussion of Q.3:134 in Section 3.1 and further on in Chapter 3). Section 2.2.1 discussed how God's mercy awaits those who *aṣlaḥa* (reform). Simultaneously, by way of contrast, the historical narratives described above at Q.7:74 and Q.7:85 highlight that Divine retribution awaits those

8 For a related discussion of classical theological debates regarding God's knowledge versus His will and His creation of 'order' and 'harm', see Griffel (2009, pp.225–34).

who oppress others and cause *fasād*. In this way, the Qur'an creates a direct motivational link between Social Conciliation and Divine–Human Conciliation.

In the above sections, we encountered a significant emphasis on fundamental doctrines and the positive development of personal character and social relations, primarily by reference to Q.6 and Q.7. It was also noted that these were Meccan suras. In contrast, however, as the Qur'anic discourse moves further on, a sustained engagement with the theme of military conflict emerges in Q.8 and Q.9, which appears to coincide with the shift towards the Medinan period of revelation. Conciliation between believers, however, is still emphasised – with unity providing a source of strength.

2.2.3 Social Conciliation in the Early Medinan Period

Q.8 is considered by commentators to have been revealed in the context of the early Medinan battle at Badr between the believers, now established at Medina, and the Meccan disbelievers. From the outset, Q.8:1 establishes a central theme of Conciliation and unity, albeit in the specific post-conflict context of a distribution of war booty: *aṣliḥū dhāta baynikum* (make things right between you, Abdel Haleem). An imperative form is used to instruct mutual conciliatory relations through the active form IV verb *aṣliḥū*. This central command is reinforced by a preceding warning *fattaqu 'llāh* (fear God) and a subsequent enjoinder *wa aṭī'u 'llāha wa rasūlahū* (obey God and His Messenger), articulated as a condition of faith for further emphasis: *in kuntum mu'minīn* (if you are true believers, Abdel Haleem).

Al-Rāzī considers Q.8:1 a definitive pronouncement on the authority of God and His Messenger, as a means of prohibiting *al-munāza'a wa 'l-mukhāṣama* (conflict and disputation). I would supplement this by adding that the specification of allocated shares in war booty at Q.8:41 provides a final resolution of the issue, similar to the allocation of inheritance shares at Q.4:11–12 and Q.4:176. The purpose in both cases is, I would argue, to prevent disputes by addressing the root cause, namely uncertainty over the allocated shares in a large capital sum, which naturally incites personal greed and mutual confrontation (also see Q.4:128 which highlights the dangers of personal greed in obstructing Conciliation in marriage). The pairing of *aṣliḥū* with the reference to *taqwā* in Q.8:1 also suggests a focus on internal transformation. Iṣlāḥī (vol.3, p.430) elaborates that the believers are expected to wholeheartedly accept the Divine distribution of war booty, and to avoid jealousy or rancour regarding the shares allocated to their brethren. *Dhāta baynikum* clarifies that this is a command towards improving social relations yet, as illustrated by the surrounding commands and argued in the preceding section, integrally linked to maintaining good relations with God.

The formulaic refrain *wa aṭīʿu 'llāha wa rasūlahū* (obey God and His Messenger) in Q.8:1 not only emphasises the preceding command to conciliate, but acts as a unifying motif, binding individual believers together into a single, aligned collaborative. The same refrain recurs further on at Q.8:20 and Q.8:46, and with slight variations of expression at Q.8:24 and Q.8:27. It is also recurrent elsewhere in the Qur'an, notably at Q.4:59 mentioned below, where it is also associated with the settlement of disputes. At Q.8:46, the refrain, which commands general obedience, is accompanied by a specific injunction *wa lā tanāzaʿū* (do not dispute with one another), the mutual form VI verb emphasising non-confrontational mutual relationships. The verse goes on to specify a consequential *ʿilla* (underlying reason) for the injunction, stating *fatafshalū wa tadhhaba rīḥukum* (you may lose heart and your spirit may desert you, Abdel Haleem), thus conjoining three related notions of unified obedience, non-disputation and strength (a similar collocation of disputation and lost spirit features at Q.3:152).

Further on at Q.8:63, the emergent unity of the believers – *wa allafa bayna qulūbihim* (and He unified their hearts; similar terminology is used in the seminal verse on unity at Q.3:103) – is highlighted as a Divine miracle. The verb *allafa* is mentioned three times, emphasising unity. The repeated reference to hearts also highlights the internal transformation, and the indication of a matter beyond human capability stresses the magnitude of the transformation. Amongst the community of believers, a fundamental difference of classification was that of 'emigrants', who had arrived from Mecca, and 'helpers' who were native to Medina. Their ancestry, history, culture and perspectives were naturally divergent. Q.8:72 and Q.8:74 towards the conclusion of Q.8 declare these two groups to be mutual *awliyā'* (allies) who will be rewarded by (Divine) forgiveness.

Addressing another classification within the Medinan Arab community, who were divided into the tribes of Al-Aws and Al-Khazraj, Lecker (2010, p.66) asserts that the Prophet 'did not come to Medina as an arbiter and peacemaker . . . as the two tribes had already started a process of reconciliation before his arrival and were no longer in a state of war'. Both Lecker and Watt (1961, pp. 87–89) refer to the Battle of Buʿāth, which appears to have embroiled the Medinan Arabs and Jews a few years before the Prophet's migration. In contrast to Lecker, however, Watt considers the Battle to have left Medina in a 'state of tension', with the Prophet invited to Medina as an ideal, neutral arbiter of the perpetual disputes, whose arrival might herald 'a new era of peace'.

In the Qur'an, the Prophet does appear to be presented as an authoritative adjudicator of disputes, as evidenced by Q.4:59, Q.4:65 and Q.5:42, in Group 1.

At Q.4:59, believers are instructed to obey God, the Prophet and those in authority, referring any form of dispute to God and the Prophet. At Q.4:65, total acceptance of the Prophet's adjudication in disputes, without rancour, becomes a condition of faith. This point is reinforced by an oath, which Iṣlāḥī (vol.2, p.329) notes is stronger because oaths are unusual in this part of the Qur'an and because the oath is an oath by God himself rather than his qualities or natural phenomena. At Q.5:42, the prophet is at liberty to adjudicate in disputes brought to him, but is enjoined to adjudicate with *qisṭ* (justice). The Qur'anic portrayal is also supported by historical reference to the 'seemingly authentic' (Lowry, 2010, p.84) Constitution of Medina which stipulates that all disputes between Muslims, and even certain significant disputes between the Jews of Medina, will be referred to the Prophet (Lecker, 2010, p.75).

Al-Rāzī's commentary also supports Watt's position regarding the tension in Medina preceding his arrival. Al-Rāzī presents Q.8:63 as evidence that prior to the advent of Islam, the community of believers – specifically the Medinan Arab tribes of Al-Aws and Al-Khazraj – was *fī 'l-khuṣūma al-dā'ima wa 'l-muḥāraba al-shadīda* (in perpetual dispute and severe combat), whilst after the advent of Islam *zālat al-khuṣūmāt wa irtafa'at al-khushūnāt wa ḥaṣalat al-mawadda al-tāmma wa 'l-maḥabba al-shadīda* (the disputes dissipated, the harshness was lifted, and complete friendship and strong affection were attained). Al-Rāzī also states that before the Prophet's arrival, the Arabs readily fell into a state of war, being prevented from harmonious relations by their desire for wealth, prestige and vain-glory. In this sense, the stipulated allocation at Q.8:41 achieves Conciliation on a specific issue, as argued above, by directly addressing the Arabs' particular propensities.

Q.8 therefore closes by return, beginning at Q.8:1 and ending at Q.8:63 with a central Conciliation theme of unity and cohesion amongst the community of believers. In contrast, however, the tone of some verses addressed to the disbelievers, in Q.8 in the early Medinan period, and then in Q.9 in the later Medinan period, is *prima facie* remarkably confrontational. In his important study *Muhammad in the Qur'an*, Cragg (2001, pp.90, 95) contrasts what he terms the 'innocent preachment' of the Meccan Qur'an with a 'transition to belligerence' in the Medinan period, even asserting that combat is the 'central feature' of the Medinan Qur'an. Such a far-reaching assertion merits a close and thorough investigation since it has clear implications for the relative importance of Conciliation in the Qur'an as a whole. Conflict in the Qur'an, firstly in the early Medinan period and then in the later Medinan period, is now examined in Section 2.3. Although Q.8 and Q.9 represent only a sample of the material in the Medinan Qur'an, they include the most sustained treatment of conflict as a theme and also the verses which have the greatest reputation for 'belligerence'.

2.3 Conciliation and Conflict

2.3.1 Conflict in the Early Medinan Period – '*Fitna*' and Peace Treaties

Some verses in Q.8 appear to indicate physical confrontation with certain disbelievers. These verses will be analysed in turn below, with supporting cross-reference to Q.2:190–193, which provide relevant elucidation on the subject of conflict. To begin with, Q.8:12 twice mentions *faḍribū. . . waḍribū* (strike). This command, however, is addressed to angels and follows four near-successive uses of the word *idh* ((recall) when) at Q.8:7, 9, 11, 12 mentioning a premonition of a battle, the believers' plea for Divine help, the Divine supportive grant of slumber and rain and God's address to the angels to assist the believers (another sequence of five uses of the term *idh* occurs at Q.8:42–44, 48–49). The recurrent use of *idh* indicates a specific historical episode of conflict tied to a particular set of circumstances, rather than a general ratification of conflict. Q.8:13 justifies the preceding verse on the basis that the disbelievers *shāqqu 'llāha wa rasūlahu* (opposed God and His Messenger). This reference should, in my view, be considered as referring to an initiation of hostilities by the Meccans justifying a defensive response, as I will argue below.

Q.8:39 instructs, this time addressed to the believers, *wa qātilūhum hattā lā takūna* ***fitnatun*** (fight them until there is no more **persecution**, Abdel Haleem). *Fitna* is translated by Nasr as 'strife' and by Yusuf Ali as 'tumult or oppression'. Cragg (2001, p.91) himself appears to take the meaning of 'persecution'. Iṣlāḥī too explains *fitna* as 'persecution' (vol.3, p.475; and vol.3, p.518 where he provides the same meaning of 'persecution' for another reference to *fitna* at Q.8:73). Al-Rāzī explains *fitna* in Q.8:39 as firstly the persecution of the early Muslims in Mecca which led to some being instructed to migrate to Ethiopia, and secondly a further escalation of persecution which manifested in the period before the migration to Medina. The translations and commentaries presented thus appear unanimous in presenting Q.8:39 as a restrictive justification, allowing fighting only to end persecution. Contextually, this view is strongly supported by the prelude to Q.8:39 which offers justifications at Q.8:30, namely the disbelievers' plot to capture, assassinate or expel the Prophet from Mecca, which led to his migration. Q.8:34 also cites the disbelievers' preventing the Muslims from access to the Sacred Mosque at Mecca for worship. Strong support for this view is also provided by another verse, Q.4:75, which urges believers to respond to the call of the weak inhabitants of Mecca for liberation from oppression. Annotating his translation of Q.4:75, Yusuf Ali (2001, p.208, n.593) refers to the persecution of believers in Mecca citing various examples. Elsewhere at Q.85:10 also, the related verb *fatana* clearly refers to the use of fire by the 'people of the trench' to persecute (pre-

Islamic) believers. In construing the meaning of *fitna*, however, some alternative meanings demonstrate the importance of context. At Q.8:25 *fitna* refers to 'discord' (Abdel Haleem, Yusuf Ali) and at Q.8:28 a 'test' (Abdel Haleem). At Q.7:27, the related verb *yaftinannakum* means 'seduce you'.

The term *fitna* also occurs at Q.2:191 mentioning the term immediately after an apparent reference to the believers being forced out of Mecca: *wa akhrijūhum min ḥaythu akhrajūkum wa 'l-**fitnatu** ashaddu mina 'l-qatl* (and drive them out from where they drove you out, for **persecution** is more serious than killing, Abdel Haleem). Al-Rāzī's encyclopaedic approach demonstrates inconsistency here, compared to his own commentary at Q.8:39, presenting several disparate possible meanings of *fitna* and leading with a narration at Q.2:191 from Ibn ʿAbbās that *fitna* refers to disbelief in God, and then going on to comment personally on the 'sinfulness' of disbelief in general. Although Abdel Haleem (2010, p.165, n.15) highlights authenticity issues associated with narrations attributed to Ibn ʿAbbās, such narrations nonetheless remain influential. In my view, Al-Rāzī's speculative and inconsistent potential extension to the meaning of *fitna* is unwarranted by the Qurʾanic text. Instead, the narration by Ibn ʿAbbās should be seen as a reference to oppressive conduct by the Meccan disbelievers, such as forced eviction cited at Q.2:191 and its related Q.2:217, a point supported by Al-Qurṭubī's version of the narration discussed below. This is also consistent with Al-Rāzī's explanation of 'if they desist' in Q.2:192 which includes a restrictive narration from Ibn ʿAbbās specifying *ʿani 'l-qitāl* (from fighting). This indicates Ibn ʿAbbās's emphasis on the aggression of the Meccans, rather than their disbelief.

Al-Qurṭubī (2006, vol.3, pp.246–47 (Q.2:193)) relies on Ibn ʿAbbās and others to take the meaning of *fitna* as a reference to 'disbelief' and a broad justification of conflict. This position demonstrates inconsistency since Al-Qurṭubī continues that the reference to 'desist' in the same verse means desisting from disbelief either by accepting Islam or paying the *jizya* (a tax; see the discussion at Q.9:29 in the following section below) despite the latter not affecting disbelief. On close inspection, it becomes clear that the correct emphasis in the narration of Ibn ʿAbbās is on persecution and not on disbelief, since Al-Qurṭubī's version of the quotation states: *al-fitna hunāk al-shirk **wa mā tābaʿahu min adha 'l-muʾminīn*** (*fitna* here means polytheism **and the harming of believers which followed from it,** my emphasis). The conjunctive *wa* clarifies that polytheism which is disjunct from persecution is not intended.

Q.8:39 continues: *wa yakūna ('l)-ddīnu kulluhū lillāh* (and all worship (at the Sacred House) is devoted to God alone, Abdel Haleem). Like Abdel Haleem, Al-Rāzī and Iṣlāḥī (vol.3, p.475) also consider the verse as referring to the establishment of God's religion in the Sacred Precinct at Mecca. Iṣlāḥī (vol.3, p. 556) explains that after the Conquest of Mecca in 8 A.H., the polytheists remained free to trade and worship according to pagan traditions in the Sacred Precinct of the *Kaʿba* for one year, after which they were given notice at the *ḥajj* gathering of 9 A.H. (see Q.9:28) that they would not be permitted access for trade and pagan worship the following year in 10 A.H., which coincided with the Prophet's own *ḥajj* pilgrimage. Yusuf Ali translates the above Qur'anic phrase in Q.8:39 more broadly as: 'and there prevails justice and faith in Allah altogether and everywhere'. Such a broad interpretation sits uneasily alongside the Qur'an's own principle of non-compulsion at Q.2:256. In addition, such an interpretation fails to contextualise the restrictive and consistent collocation, and indeed inalienable conjunction of this phrase (indicated by the *wāw*), with the eradication of persecution in Q.8:39 (and also Q.2:193). Another important Qur'anic reference at Q.22:39–40, in Group 3, collocates a permission to fight being granted to the oppressed who were driven from their homes, with preventing the destruction of various places of worship, again linking persecution and freedom of religion. In my view, therefore, *wa yakūna ('l)-ddīnu kulluhū lillāh* in Q.8:39 is best explained, in context, as a reference to the establishment of freedom of worship apparently denied to the believers at Mecca through the examples of persecution listed above. The two principles I have argued for in Q.8:39, freedom from persecution (implied through mutual security) and freedom of religion, both featured in the Constitution of Medina at a time and place of relative Muslim hegemony, highlighting their importance to the believing emigrants of Mecca.

It is also contextually clear that Q.8:39 provides a highly restricted mandate directly linked to a series of grievances, listed at Q.8:30 and Q.8:34, collectively amounting to *fitna* (persecution). The preceding Q.8:38 offers an apparent olive branch: *in yantahū yughfar lahum mā qad salaf* (if they desist their past will be forgiven, Abdel Haleem), with the end of Q.8:39 repeating the concession: *fa in intahaw. . .* (so if they desist). Similarly, Q.2:192 offers Divine forgiveness if the disbelievers 'desist', alongside references to *fitna* in both Q.2:191 and Q.2:193. This recurrent collocation of 'desist' with references to *fitna* (persecution) strongly indicates that the conduct referred to is a specific charge, only temporarily justifying conflict. Q.8:73 couples another reference to *fitna* in the earth with a reference to *fasādun kabīr* (widespread disorder): *illā tafʿalūhu takun fitnatun fi 'l-arḍi wa fasādun kabīr* (if you do not [support one another] there will be persecution in the land and widespread disorder). It becomes clear that Q.8:39 ultimately provides a limited mandate to prevent *fasād*, consistent with the emphasis on *iṣlāḥ* and prohibiting *fasād* discussed in Section 2.2. The repeated reference to forgiveness at Q.8:38 and Q.8:39 indicates a desire to achieve complete Conciliation as soon as the catalyst for hostility is removed.

Another reference to hostility with an alternative justification is provided further on in Q.8. Q.8:56 mentions those who flagrantly and repeatedly breach the treaties they have made, going on to say at Q.8:57 that if they are encountered in battle, *fasharrid bihim man khalfahum* (frighten through them, those who follow them; the form II imperative verb *sharrid* means 'frighten away' (Abdel Haleem and Badawi, 2013, p.480)), thus rescinding the treaty as a form of admonition to others. Iṣlāḥī (vol.3, pp.498–99) suggests Q.8:56 refers to the Jewish and other tribes the Prophet made treaties with after migrating to Medina. Watt (1961, pp. 130–31, 148–51, 170–75) discusses the periodic tensions between the Prophet and the three major Jewish clans of Medina, concluding that this was largely due to their *political alignment* with the Prophet's internal and external opponents. Lecker (2010, pp.72–73) offers an alternative insight into competition between the *economic interests* of the Jewish clans and the Prophet's 'economic strategy'. Notably, neither author suggests the tensions were based on religious compulsion.

Q.8:65 goes on to address the Prophet directly, saying *ḥarriḍi 'l-mu'minīna 'ala 'l-qitāl* (urge the believers to fight, Abdel Haleem). The verse immediately leads onto two lengthy verses which suggest that the believers were apparently hopelessly outnumbered. The same verses refer to the believers' *ḍa'fan* (weakness). There are indications in the plea for Divine assistance (at Q.8:9) and the discussion of relative numbers here that the believers were very much on the back foot in terms of military strength. All of this suggests a defensive rather than aggressive engagement in the conflict, consistent with a natural reluctance to fight those who have previously been dominant. Q.2:190, in Group 1, another verse supporting this view, explicitly restricts conflict to fighting 'those who fight against you' and warning against transgression, with Q.2:191–193 adding one use of *hattā* (until) and no less than three uses of the conditional particle *in* to regulate conflict. A natural reading of Q.2:190–193 prohibits both conflict initiation and conflict continuation beyond a direct response.

At Q.2:191, Al-Rāzī comments that whilst Q.2:190 sanctions only a response to an attack, Q.2:191 goes further, limiting this restriction to conflict in the Sacred Precinct and thus sanctioning conflict initiation in other circumstances. Although Al-Rāzī rejects the opinion of Muqātil that Q.2:191 abrogates Q.2:190 and prefers the notion of *takhṣīṣ* (specification) at Q.2:191, he arrives at much the same result. In my view, Q.2:190–193 should be read as a collective progressive discourse, with Q.2:190 first stating a general principle sanctioning fighting only in self-defence, and even reinforcing a caution against transgression through Divine disapproval. Crucially, this principle *remains effective* in spite of the subsequent specific confirmation of its application in the Sacred Precinct at Q.2:191. Q.2:192–193 then terminates conflict upon cessation of hostilities by the opponents consistent with the non-transgression principle of Q.2:190. Over-riding the general application of the emphatically formulated principle of Q.2:190 without justification appears to me entirely unwarranted.

In summary, each of the above verses apparently enjoining conflict are phrased reactively rather than proactively, suggesting a defensive response rather than an initiation of conflict, aimed at ending practices such as persecution, prohibition on free worship and breach of peace treaties. Limiting constructs, such as clauses beginning *hattā* (until) and conditional clauses beginning *in* (if), define parameters which contain and provide a marker for the conclusion of conflict. In this sense, they provide a form of conflictregulation. At both Q.8:42 and 44, the particle *idh* (when) is used alongside a statement that the battle was a matter decreed by God. This collocation appears to confirm the conflict referred to as a specific historical event. Out of 75 verses in Q.8, the above verses indicating physical confrontation represent a relatively small handful of verses, despite the sura primarily dealing with the theme of conflict between believers and disbelievers. In each case, the verses are surrounded by fact-specific reasons. This suggests the Qur'an sees conflict as an anomalous situation requiring justification, rather than a default state of affairs.

Having examined verses pertaining to conflict in Q.8, we will now focus on verses explicitly advocating Conciliation. Q.8:61 provides an important Conciliation principle: *in janaḥū li ('l)-ssalmi fa 'jnaḥ lahā* (if (the disbelievers) incline towards peace, you (Prophet) should also incline towards it). In the word *salm* we encounter another important term, previously mentioned in Chapter 1, denoting Conciliation and specifically indicating a state of peaceful relations. The notably symmetrical linguistic construct in this verse is commensurate with its purport and is, in my view, a recurrent feature in Conciliation verses (Fazaluddin, 2016, pp.341, 351, 353, 356). This verse stresses the importance of reciprocating peace initiatives and correlates with the preceding condemnation at Q.8: 56–58 of those who violate peace treaties. Al-Rāzī's commentary of Q.8:61 confirms *fa 'l-ḥukm qubūl al-ṣulḥ* (the legal ruling is to accept a peace agreement), once the opponent inclines towards peace terms.

In light of Q.8:61, an interpretation by Al-Rāzī of the reference to 'desist' in Q.8:39 as inferring that the Meccans should abandon their disbelief, repent from their sins and accept faith, appears to be an overly subjective perspective which is unjustified and contradicts his own interpretation of *fitna* as persecution in the same verse, mentioned above. I would argue that Q.8:61 strongly refutes any interpretation of Q.8:39 as suggesting that conflict should continue until the universal acceptance of Islam has prevailed, a point discussed further in the next section. Rather, it suggests that the Meccans should desist their hostilities and negotiate terms such that the believers are allowed to co-exist peacefully.

Iṣlāḥī (vol.3, p.505) argues by reference to Q.8:61 that Islam emphasises truth and justice at a personal, social and international level and advocates a receptive approach to positive initiatives, even accepting the risk of betrayal, indicated by the injunction *wa tawakkal ʿala ʾllāh* (and rely upon God). Given the multiple references to betrayal in Q.8:58, 62 and 71, Q.8:61 demonstrates that the command to conciliate overrides the command to engage in conflict despite a significant and real risk of betrayal. Al-Rāzī considers the reference in Q.8:61 to God as All-Hearing and All-Knowing to be *tanbīhan bi dhālik ʿala ʾl-zajr ʿan naqḍ al-ṣulḥ* (by way of a warning of the prohibition on violation of a peace agreement). An almost identical emphatic formulation regarding Divine omniscience was encountered in the important Conciliation verses at Q.7:199–200 above.

Q.8:72 further emphasises the maintenance of peace agreements. As discussed above, Q.8 repeatedly stresses the unifying bonds between believers. In this verse, however, the believers are instructed not to interfere to protect their non-migrating co-religionists until they have migrated, thus preserving the territorial integrity of the Meccan authorities. An exception is where they seek help in matters of *dīn* (persecution, Abdel Haleem). The related verse Q.4:75 expressly refers to fighting in the way of God and for the deliverance of the weak men, women and children who pray for salvation from the oppressors of their town. Even in such cases, however, Q.8:72 expressly prohibits the provision of assistance against those with whom there is a *mīthāq* (peace treaty). The prohibition in Q.8:72 is, like Q.7: 199–200 and Q.8:61 above, reinforced by a reference to God as *Baṣīr* (Watchful), another caution of Divine sanction for any violation of peace treaties. This demonstrates clearly the relative priority given to Conciliation and the prevention of military conflict, particularly conflict initiation, even in the Medinan period.

It can also be seen that the Qur'an places great emphasis on the binding nature of *ṣulḥ* agreements, a point debated in the early section on Definitional Scope of *Ṣulḥ*. Both at Q.8:72, and later at Q.9:4 and Q.9:7, the Qurʾan emphasises the upholding of *ṣulḥ* agreements, even in situations where there has already been an outbreak of war. As well as containing conflict, this strongly supports the view that *ṣulḥ* agreements are binding, irrespective of a judicial or non-judicial context. This also accords with the nature of *ṣulḥ* agreements, which are contractual, and derive effect from the intention of the parties to be bound by their obligations. The binding nature of a Conciliation agreement is an important feature of its effectiveness in *concluding* a dispute (Bin Salamah, 2002, p.159). Fulfilment of obligations is a fundamental principle in the Qurʾan, with Q.5:1 stipulating *awfū bi ʾl-ʿuqūd* (fulfil your obligations). As noted by Hamidullah (1945, p.269), the famous Treaty of Ḥudaybiya was considered binding by the Prophet upon agreement, even prior to its formal execution, with an escaping Muslim refugee, Abū Jandal, extradited back to the Meccans (see Section 5.2.2).

The above discussion on the importance of peace treaties indicates a desire to secure a sustainable peace at the social level, despite the former grievances of persecution and obstruction to freedom of religion. Q.8 also addresses the issue of Divine–human relations, where opportunities for Conciliation are also apparent. The Prophet is presented as the medium of Divine–Human Conciliation. At Q.8:33, his former presence in Mecca served to shield the disbelievers against Divine wrath and the disbelievers are given the on-going opportunity to repent. At Q.8:38 he is instructed to communicate a conditional offer of Divine forgiveness for past wrongs, and at Q.8:70 he is instructed to communicate the hope of Divine forgiveness to those captives in his control. Iṣlāḥī (vol.3, p.515) argues that Q.8:70 provides Divine ratification of the Prophet's policy of releasing war captives, criticising un-named commentators for suggesting the Prophet was chastised by God (see Q.8:67) for this relatively conciliatory approach. Cragg (2001) provides some related discussion of Q.8:67 at pp. 94–95.

In spite of the above opportunities for Divine–Human Conciliation, the losses inflicted by the believers and the Prophet's symbolic throwing of a handful of dust before the battle are described as God's acts at Q.8:17, implying a level of temporal Divine retribution. The threat of Divine retribution is also implied at Q.8:52 and 54, where the Meccans are charged with conduct akin to that of Pharaoh and transgressing nations past who incurred Divine wrath. The proportion of discourse emphasising Divine forgiveness also appears to have gradually declined from Q.6 to Q.8. Yet the continued presence of several important verses offering opportunities for redemption and emphasising peace treaties *even at the point of conflict* is highly significant, as it indicates that conflict should be curtailed wherever possible and Conciliation rather than conflict remains the ultimate desideratum. Cragg (2001, p.105) himself acknowledges, by reference to Q.47:4 which states: *hattā taḍaʿa 'l-ḥarbu awzārahā* (until war lays down its burdens, Nasr), that conflict in the Qur'an is ultimately presented as onerous rather than appealing. He states: '"burdens" (*awzār*), not glamour, was the word for what belligerence involved.'

However, Al-Rāzī's commentary of Q.8:61 cites the opinion of Qatāda that Q.8:61's emphasis on peace treaties is abrogated by Q.9:5 and Q.9:29, although he clarifies that other commentators have not taken such an absolute interpretation. Earlier at Q.7:199, Al-Rāzī also mentions that one view considered the majority of the conciliatory teachings in Q.7:199 abrogated by Q.9:5, the so-called 'Sword Verse', although expressing frustration with such commentators for being *mashghūfūn bi-* (infatuated with) over application of abrogation without justification. In light of these apparently anomalous but far-reaching assertions regarding the scope of Q.9:5, we will now turn to a discussion of Q.9, the final sura to be analysed in this chapter.

2.3.2 Conflict in the Late Medinan Period – Contextualising Q.9:5, the 'Sword Verse'

Q.9 is considered to have been revealed primarily in the context of the Battle of Tabūk in 9 A.H., when the Muslims marched to confront the Byzantines, although no conflict actually ensued (Yusuf Ali, 2001, p.435). Q.9:1–42 deals primarily with the polytheists, including a section Q.9:29–35 which deals with People of the Book. Q.9:43–110 deals primarily with the hypocrites, including several specific references to the desert Arabs from Q.9:90 onwards. Q.9:111–128 primarily addresses the believers. The sura's two names Sūrat At-Tawba and Sūrat Barā'a offer an apparently contrasting emphasis, one on Divine forgiveness (based on Q.9:104) and the other on Divine severance of relations (based on Q.9:1). The absence of the usual *Basmalla* which opens every sura of the Qur'an except Q.9 in the name of God, citing His Divine qualities of kindness and mercy, may be perceived as an indication of Divine intransigence (see the narration from the Companion ʿAlī cited in Nasr (2015, p.503)) but is equally explained rather benignly by the possibility that Q.8 and Q.9 structurally form a single sura, an opinion preferred by Iṣlāḥī (vol.3, p.523) and noted by Abdel-Haleem.

Explicit commands to fight are apparently found at Q.9:5 which enjoins *faqtulū* (slay) and Q.9:12, 14, 29, 36, and 123 which all enjoin *qātilū* (fight), with Q.9:73 adding *jāhidū* (strive) and both Q.9:73 and Q.9:123 referring to the notion of *ghilẓa* (sternness). These verses primarily target the polytheists, with only Q.9:29 referring to People of the Book and Q.9:73 referring additionally to the hypocrites. The justification provided for hostilities against the polytheists centres on their breach of peace treaties. This is emphasised through repetition in two pairs of verses at Q.9:8 and Q.9:10 which both refer to a failure to respect ties of *illan wa lā dhimma* (kinship or treaty), and Q.9:12 and Q.9:13 which both refer to *nakathū aymānahum* (they have broken their oaths). Q.9:8 and Q.9:12 both use the conditional particle *in* (if) which indicates that as a principle the hostility urged is contingent upon breach of treaties, whilst Q.9:10 and Q.9:13 are both absolute, confirming that the contingency has been fulfilled and justifies hostility in the present circumstances.

Given the context above, I would argue that the above commands to fight are permissive rather than immediately instructive (see, for example, the use of a command to permit rather than command hunting at Q.5:2), in the sense that they indicate a Divine authorisation of release from peace treaties which have already been violated. This public declaration of release is indicated in Q.9:1 and Q.9:3, with a notice period of four months recognising the sanctity of the sacred months, according to Q.9:2 and Q.9:5 (and later Q.9:36). Sanctity of place was recognised earlier in the Qur'an at Q.2:191 and sanctity of time at

Q.2:194, with both verses permitting conflict only in response to an attack. The apparent general release in Q.9:1 and Q.9:3 is in fact qualified in another pair of verses, Q.9:4 and Q.9:7, which explicitly restrict the believers from fighting those polytheists with whom there is a treaty which they have not violated. Both verses instruct the believers to uphold such treaties in full, consistent with the import of Q.8:61 and Q.8:72 in the previous sura. Both Q.9:4 and Q.9:7 encourage such maintenance of peace agreements through the repeated refrain *inna 'llāha yuḥibbu 'l-muttaqīn* (surely, God loves those who are conscious of Him). Q.9:7 incorporates an eloquent symmetrical construct, reminiscent of Q.8:61, discussed above, stating *fama 'staqāmū lakum fa 'staqīmū lahum* (so long as they are true to you, be true to them). At Q.9:4 and Q.9:7, *inna 'llāha yuḥibbu 'l-muttaqīn* encourages the maintenance of peace treaties whilst at Q.2:190, a converse declaration on the same pattern *inna 'llāha lā yuḥibbu 'l-mu'tadīn* (God does not love those who transgress) reproves those who initiate conflict.

The above illustrates clearly that, even at this late stage in the Medinan period of revelation, there was no general declaration of conflict against the polytheists. Indeed, the language used even in Q.9:5 is far from the boldness and breadth to be expected from the recurrent assertions of its universal abrogating status. Q.9:5 is subject to a four-month suspension period, applies only to the specific treaty-breaching Meccans as discussed above and below, devotes around half its content to repentance, and ends by specifying God's qualities of forgiveness and mercy.

Iṣlāḥī (vol.3, p.540) and Abdel Haleem (2005, p.116, n.(c)) both concur with the application of Q.9:5 only to the treaty-breaching polytheists, which is also apparent from the surrounding verses. The phrase *ḥaythu wajadtumūhum* (wherever you find them) merely disapplies the usual prohibition on fighting (such Meccans) in the Sacred Precinct. Iṣlāḥī (vol.3, p.540) and Abdel Haleem (2005, p.116, n.(b)) specify that the wording sanctions conflict (with the treaty-breaching polytheists) both outside and inside the Sacred Precinct. The similar ***ḥaythu*** *thaqiftumūhum* (wherever you encounter them, Abdel Haleem) at Q.2:191 is explained by Al-Rāzī's comment ***ḥaythu*** *kānū fi 'l-ḥilli wa 'l-ḥaram* (whether they are outside or inside the Sacred Precinct). A similar comment is provided by Al-Rāzī at Q.4:89. Muhammad Asad (2003, p.289, n.7, and p.289, n.9) comments that Q.9:5 relates to conflict 'already in progress' with aggressors who have violated peace treaties, and sanctions conflict 'only in self-defence'. Nasr (2015, p.506) similarly comments that, in light of the surrounding verses regarding upholding treaties with idolaters who have not repudiated such treaties, 'a more plausible reading of this passage would not see the very fact that certain persons were idolaters as a reason to fight them'.

Even the declaration in Q.9:1 refers exclusively to those who *'āhadtum* (made an agreement with you), indicating this to be the primary consideration, only then going on to specify for clarification *min al-mushrikīn* (amongst the polytheists). The particle *min* emphasises that only *some* polytheists are intended; at Q.14:40, Al-Rāzī argues the same point in respect of Abraham's offspring, referring to the notion of *tabʿīḍ* (partition). Even from the specific sub-set of polytheists who have entered into treaties, Q.9:4 and Q.9:7 guarantee security to those who maintain such treaties, despite the fact that they remain *mushrikīn*. This supports my interpretation above of Q.8:39 as permitting fighting to prevent persecution and preserve freedom of religion, rather than to enforce Islam.

Finally on the subject of conflict with the disbelievers, in Q.9, the *ʿilla* (underlying reason) for permitting fighting is so that those who have breached their peace agreements and reviled the believers' faith may desist (Q.9:12); Q.9:13 provides further detail of such conduct in the form of driving the Prophet out (of Mecca) and initiating conflict. Opportunities for avoidance of Divine retribution in the Hereafter are also provided, through repentance, at Q.9:3, 5, 11 and 15. Q.9:3 addresses this point to the polytheists directly for impact. Q.9:6 also expressly provides that any polytheist seeking sanctuary should be given an opportunity to hear the word of God and then conveyed to a place of safety. The verse does not suggest that conversion to Islam is a condition of such safety. Structurally, only the first 16 verses of Q.9 deal in a sustained manner with the theme of fighting the polytheists, and it can be seen that even a number of these verses are either justificatory, exemptive or conciliatory.

Further into Q.9, Q.9:29 apparently enjoins fighting against the People of the Book. Yet the same verse in fact talks of fighting people who do not believe in God and the Last Day and who do not follow the teachings of the People of the Book. The ensuing verse Q.9:30 discusses polytheistic beliefs amongst the People of the Book, yet it would be inconsistent to enjoin fighting on this basis, whilst endorsing peace treaties with the polytheists above. Similarly, Q.9:34 accuses priests and monks of unjustly enriching themselves at the expense of the masses. However, Q.9:35 threatens eschatological sanction of this conduct, rather than temporal retribution.

In my view, therefore, Q.9:29 must be understood *in context* as having permitted fighting against People of the Book who sided with the covenant-breaking polytheists, discussed in Q.9:1–16 above and more generally in Q.9:17–19, 28. Contextually, Q.9:32–33, a recurrent portent regarding the prevalence of Islam (see the discussion of Q.48:28 in Section 5.2.1 below), would then refer to the desire of such people to eliminate the nascent Islamic faith in conflict with God's will to establish it. The restriction in Q.9:29 on fighting such people only until they pay the much-debated *jizya* tax,[9]

---

9 A tax charged to so-called *dhimmis* (non-Muslim citizens). The notion has attracted mixed comments from writers. Watt (1961, pp.219–20) describes it as a 'system of protected minorities'.

thus refers to their agreement to cease hostilities, at which point it was no longer permitted to fight them. Abdel Haleem (2010, pp.154–55), however, places greater emphasis on the reference to *jizya*, considering the purpose of Q.9:29 is to 'enforce tax regulations' consistent with Abū Bakr's later enforcement of the *zakāt* tax against Muslims. This does not appear to acknowledge the context of the surrounding verses, relating to the polytheists, or align with the relevant historical circumstances.[10] Had the two situations proved so readily analogous, it is unlikely that Abū Bakr's decision would have met with initial resistance by his advisers, as recorded by Al-Suyūṭī, or that he would have failed to adduce Q.9:29 in response.[11] I find strong support for my view regarding the scope of Q.9:29 from Iṣlāḥī (vol.3, p.561), who clarifies that it relates only to those *dhimmis* (non-Muslim citizens) who *Islāmī ḥukūmat se jang kī* (made war against the Islamic authority) – he goes on to clarify that those who are on peaceful terms with the Government would be governed according to the terms of their agreements.

Iṣlāḥī (vol.3, pp.1–15, 419) holds a relatively consistent position that Q.6 to Q.9 substitute the believers in place of the Meccan disbelievers as custodians of the Kaʿba. As such, Iṣlāḥī (vol.3, pp.524, 560) argues that Q.9:29 establishes a more tolerant position towards the People of the Book than it does towards the

---

Levy (1969, pp.66–67) reproduces an extract from a document described as the Testament of the second Caliph ʿUmar which also refers to 'protection' conditional on payment. Levy considers the document 'fairly accurately represented' the division of society but is sceptical of the ascription to ʿUmar. However, he goes on to describe such people, including Jews, Christians, Sabians and Zoroastrians, as having 'no rights in the State at all' and 'at times . . . subject to numerous restrictions'. Yusuf Ali (2001, p.445) suggests that the payment was 'merely symbolical' and partly a 'commutation for military service' charged only to able-bodied men. Abdel Haleem (2012) provides a detailed linguistic analysis which challenges many interpretations of Q.9:29 provided by classical Islamic commentators as being unfounded in the text of the verse itself, and also challenges some modern Western perceptions of the *jizya* as a 'poll tax', highlighting (on p.76) that those who are liable to *jizya* are exempt from the *zakāt* tax payable by Muslims.

10 Abdel Haleem draws a parallel between the enforcement of the *jizya* tax against the People of the Book pursuant to Q.9:29 and the enforcement of the *zakāt* (alms) tax against Muslim tribes by the Prophet's successor Abū Bakr. In my opinion, although the *conclusion* of conflict upon payment of *jizya* in Q.9:29, signifying cessation of hostility, and upon enforcement of the *zakāt* (alms) by Abū Bakr shares some ostensible similarity, the context of *initiating* conflict differs. This is because the primary context of initiating conflict in Q.9:29 is that of siding with the hostile polytheists, whilst in Abū Bakr's case the primary context was the instability resulting from the precedent of selective observance of fundamental obligations.

11 See the relevant dialogue in Al-Suyūṭī's *Tārīkh al-Khulafāʾ* (2013, p.159). Furthermore, had the Muslims been accustomed to warfare against mere tax evaders, they would have been unsurprised by Abū Bakr's decision, whereas even the usually combative ʿUmar (Iqbal, 1965, p.52) was apparently incredulous.

Meccan polytheists, against whom Iṣlāḥī considers that Q.9 espouses continuous conflict until they repent and accept Islam. I have already argued above that this is not the position taken by the earlier verses dealing with the polytheists, and Iṣlāḥī's argument that the polytheists were more accountable due to the Prophet being sent directly to them, is unconvincing. It could just as easily be argued that the People of the Book should have been more accountable due to their prior knowledge of Scripture. Furthermore, Iṣlāḥī (vol.3, p.538) suggests that at least the initial verses of Q.9 dealing with the polytheists were revealed between the Treaty of Ḥudaybiya in 6 A.H./628 C.E. and the Conquest of Mecca in 8 A.H./630 C.E., in which case the generally non-retributional nature of that Conquest belies Iṣlāḥī's position. Cragg himself, despite his position on belligerence in the Medinan context, refers to the Prophet's conduct at the Conquest of Mecca as 'magnanimous' and showing 'no instinct to be vindictive' (2001, p.109).

In my view, Q.9 takes a consistent position across the two groups of people, polytheists and People of the Book, having permitted conflict only in response to hostility and only until peace was established by agreement. The verses presented above contradict the assertion that fighting should continue until either the polytheists or the People of the Book convert to Islam, which would openly conflict with the Qur'an's own (Medinan) principle of non-compulsion in faith (Q.2:256). Q.22:40, in Group 3, refers to permitting fighting not only to preserve mosques but also monasteries, churches and synagogues, indicating an alignment of interests with other monotheistic faiths. The promotion of dialogue and commonality of faith with the People of the Book, centred around Q.3:64 (also Medinan) as discussed in Chapter 1, is also an essential context in construing Q.9:29 narrowly as relating to a single specific context. I discuss this approach in more detail in my earlier research, identifying a conciliatory Qur'anic principle of 'Differentiation' which restricts criticised behaviour from impacting an entire relationship or a relationship with an entire group, thus containing conflict (Fazaluddin, 2016, pp.345, 351, 354). Despite the criticisms in Q.9:30–35, other People of the Book are commended at Q.3:113–115, Q.4:162, Q.7:159 and also in Q.7:170 where they are even described as *muṣliḥīn* (righteous). Sections 1.3 and 4.1.1 provide further examples where People of the Book are commended. Similarly, polytheists who abide by peace treaties (see Q.9:4 and Q.9:7) have been clearly distinguished above from those who do not, a further application of the Differentiation principle.

It remains now to deal with the verses relating to the hypocrites. They are accused of reluctance to join the believers in military conflict (Q.9:42–47), sowing discord and scheming (Q.9:48), insulting the Prophet (Q.9:61), mocking (Q.9:64), enjoining wrong and forbidding good and being miserly (Q.9:67), infidelity (Q.9:74), and mocking the charitableness of others (Q.9:79). One specific reproach against the hypocrites at Q.9:107 is their construction of a mosque *tafrīqan* (to sow discord). The Prophet is distanced from discord, being instructed at Q.9:108 never to stand in their mosque. That mosque is contrasted with a mosque founded on *taqwā*, providing an implied correlation between *taqwā* and unity. At Q.9:109, the mosque founded for discord is described as being founded on the edge of a 'crumbling precipice' (Abdel Haleem) about to fall into the fire of Hell, an analogy reminiscent of Q.3:103 which also emphasises unity and condemns discord.

Although Q.9:73 enjoins 'striving' (*jāhidū*) and sternness against the hypocrites, there is no command of conflict. The Qur'an itself rarely uses the term *jihād* in connection with the subject of military conflict, as seen in the verses above. I provide examples at Sections 3.3.2 and 4.2 which illustrate that the term *jihād* is often used to denote internal struggle or rational argument. Abdel Haleem (2010, pp.147–48), who provides a detailed examination of the term *jihād* in the Qur'an, considers that Q.9:73 has 'nothing to do with fighting', criticising translations which have suggested otherwise. Iqbal (1965, pp.49–53), in his detailed study of diplomacy in Islam, discusses the Prophet's creative avoidance of confrontation in dealing with the leader of the hypocrites, apparently to avoid detrimental public perception. The Prophet's 'successful diplomacy' is also remarked upon by Lecker (2010, p.73). Al-Rāzī confirms that it would have been impermissible to fight the hypocrites given they ostensibly sided with the Muslims, and therefore he says that Q.9:73 advocates striving against them through disclosure of their reality, severance of amicable relations and reprimand.

One specific example is a severance of faith-based relations relating to the Hereafter, with Q.9:80 rejecting any Divine acceptance of a prayer for their forgiveness and Q.9:84 similarly prohibiting any prayer for their forgiveness after death. However, in the context of the desert Arabs, Q.9:101 condemns to Divine retribution only those who are *persistent* in their hypocrisy, another example of Differentiation. Instead, Q.9:102–106 opens the door of repentance to those who acknowledge their sins, instructing the Prophet to purify them through his acceptance of their charity and his prayer for them, providing them with *sakanun* (solace). Q.9:102 and Q.9:104, respectively, refer to God as Forgiving and Merciful, and Accepting of Repentance and Merciful.

Fighting is, however, enjoined against the hypocrites at Q.4:89 and Q.4:91. Yusuf Ali (2001, p.212, n.606) suggests this is in the context of those deserters who left the believers' army at the Battle of Uḥud, and then deserted again after being given a second chance. Even these verses provide a specific exemption at Q.4: 90–91, in favour of those who seek refuge with people who have a *mīthāq* (treaty) with the believers, or those who are non-combatants and offer *salam* (peace terms). A nearby reference at Q.4:114 condemns secret counsels, except those which enjoin charity, good conduct or *iṣlāḥin bayna ('l)-nnās* (conciliation between people). Both contexts demonstrate the importance given to Conciliation as a universal principle, overriding other contexts and considerations. Al-Rāzī mentions that some commentators considered the exemption in Q.4:90 abrogated by Q.9:5, but indicates that the majority view opposes this. I have also argued above that Q.9:5 itself is subject to the preservation of peace treaties, rendering it fully aligned with Q.4:90.

After praising and advising the believers at Q.9:111–122, Q.9 concludes at Q.9:123–Q.9:129 briefly reiterating the permission to fight, but reminding the believers to show *taqwā*, by respecting treaties and sacred months according to Iṣlāḥī (vol.3, p.664), and then chastising the hypocrites at greater length for their continued non-repentance. The sura concludes on a perhaps surprisingly soft note, emphasising the Prophet's qualities of compassion and mercy towards the believers, finally instructing the Prophet that if people turn away from him, he is to place his trust in God.

Summary Table: Group 2 Conciliation Themes Map by Sura and Verse

	Conciliation in faith propagation	Conciliation in Divine–human relations	Conciliation in societal relations	Conciliation in military conflict
Q.2		30–31 Divine education and *fasād*		190–194 justification and limitation 216–218 justification and limitation
Q.4				75 justification 89–91 peace treaties
Q.6	68–70 disengagement and engagement 106–107 non-compulsion 108 prohibition on abuse	54 *tawba* and *iṣlāḥ* 147 Divine mercy 165 Divine mercy	151–153 social order	
Q.7	199–200 forgiveness and disengagement; also see Q.3:159	23 Adam's penitence 35 *taqwā* and *iṣlāḥ*	56 *fasād*, *iṣlāḥ*, *iḥṣān* 85–86 *fasād* and *iṣlāḥ* 142 *fasād* and *iṣlāḥ*	

(continued)

	Conciliation in faith propagation	Conciliation in Divine–human relations	Conciliation in societal relations	Conciliation in military conflict
Q.8			1 *iṣlāḥ* and unity 46 unity 63 uniting hearts	39 justification and limitation 56 peace treaties 61 peace treaties 72 peace treaties
Q.9		102–106 Divine mercy		1–16 justification and limitation, peace treaties 29 limitation

Conclusion

Although not always readily apparent, Conciliation is pervasive throughout Q.6 to Q.9. It is emphasised in the Meccan component, in Q.6 and Q.7, in the form of prophetic restraint and Divine mercy, and the central notion of *iṣlāḥ*. In the Medinan component, Conciliation is also apparent in the form of maintaining unity in Q.8, and crucially and emphatically through the persistent instruction to establish and maintain peace treaties in Q.8 and Q.9. The Medinan component of the above suras reflects injunctions to fight which are absent in the Meccan component. The offer of Divine mercy is less emphasised but has not been entirely withdrawn, as indicated by the common reference to Q.9 as Sūrat Al-Tawba, despite its reputation for intransigence. The Medinan injunctions to reciprocate efforts to make peace with the polytheists and to cease hostilities with the People of the Book, subject to the *jizya*, support the principle of non-compulsion in faith, which notably is also Medinan (Q.2:256).

Quantitatively, the number of verses enjoining fighting is around 10 out of around 200 verses in Q.8 and Q.9. This represents a relatively low proportion of around 5%. A significant portion of Q.8 deals with unity rather than conflict and around two thirds of Q.9 is directed at the hypocrites' undermining of unity, with no express command to fight them. Q.8 and Q.9 preserve the establishment and upholding of peace treaties as a sacrosanct principle, demonstrating that Conciliation overrides conflict, with the cessation of hostilities apparently remaining the ultimate desideratum. There is certainly a shift of tone and emphasis between the Meccan and Medinan components of the analysed suras, but Conciliation is still of paramount importance, even in circumstances of conflict, in this significant sample of the Medinan Qurʾan.

A broad range of Conciliation concepts are manifest in Q.6 to Q.9. The Prophet is given extensive education in exercising restraint, disengagement, non-disputation and forgiveness – a conciliatory approach which is integral to his propagation function. Divine mercy and non-retribution are also crucial features in Divine–Human Conciliation. The fundamental Conciliation notion of *iṣlāḥ* is recurrent. *Iṣlāḥ* is considered a broader notion than *ṣulḥ* in Islamic scholarship, being defined as the removal of all *fasād*, including but not limited to social disputes. Restrictive justification is frequently presented for conflict, suggesting that conflict is anomalous: the key justification of *fitna* refers to 'persecution' of the early believers by the Meccan polytheists, whilst another justification is the rescinding of treaties which have already been breached. The unification of hearts in the diverse Medinan community, centred around the Prophet's key function of resolving disputes, presents a further manifestation of Conciliation, whilst a Divine allocation of financial shares directly addresses a significant cause of conflict. The emphasis on negotiating, agreeing and upholding peace treaties, and the condemnation and warnings against breaching such treaties, provides clear evidence of the contractually binding nature of Conciliation agreements.

From a literary perspective, extensive cosmological and teleological arguments are used in Q.6 to persuade the audience. The vocalisation of key Qurʾanic messages relating to *iṣlāḥ* by various prophets brings theoretical instruction dramatically to life, for example in Q.7. The use of persuasion and education is integral to preserving the insistence on non-compulsion. In Q.8, the triple repetition of *allafa* is used to emphasise the 'miraculous' unification of hearts, whilst the recurrent motif 'Obey God and His Messenger' enhances the message of unification. Symmetrical textual constructs in Q.8 and Q.9 are used to reflect the mutually supportive nature of the peace treaties they aim to inspire. Emphatic reminders of Divine omniscience provide additional gravitas to the maintenance of treaties at Q.8:61 and Q.8:72, and to the conciliatory teachings at Q.7:199–200. Restrictive and conditional particles such as *hattā* and *in* are used to delineate limiting parameters to conflict. Strategic location of key concepts such as Divine mercy at the end of Q.6, and the Prophet's compassion and mercy at the end of Q.9, provides impactful focus.

The thematic development of Q.6 to Q.9 displays a high level of coherence. The recurrent notions of *iṣlāḥ* and *fasād* provide a sustained thematic continuity. There is close correlation between the Prophet's forgiveness and Divine forgiveness, with both emphasised in the Meccan period and still featuring in the Medinan period. Forgiveness enables relationships to progress where justice is unachievable or even undesirable. Divine–Human Conciliation is directly inter-connected with Social Conciliation, serving as a motivation for the latter. The Prophet is also a binding figure in both Divine–Human and Social Conciliation, invoking Divine mercy, and settling disputes and maintaining unity in Medinan society. The undermining of this unity by the hypocrites is extensively criticised towards the end of the group of suras analysed, as is the hostility initiated through breach of peace treaties by the Meccans. The above Conciliation concepts demonstrate a progression through three hierarchical levels, from personal qualities such as forgiveness and mercy, to the intra-societal level featuring *iṣlāḥ* and the settlement of disputes, and then the resolution of inter-societal disputes through peace treaties. It should be noted that, although *iṣlāḥ* indicating reform of corrupt practices has a practical intra-societal manifestation in the prevention and resolution of disputes, it is also very much a universal principle indicating maintenance of the Divine world order.

Given the extensive body of fundamental conciliatory teachings emphasised throughout Q.6 to Q.9, any abrogation would be expected to be obvious and explicit. It is implausible that Q.9:5, a single verse lacking any clear abrogation language, could conceivably abrogate the import of some or all of these verses. There is profound irony in the attempt by some commentators to abrogate conciliatory verses such as Q.7:199 and Q.8:61, whose gravity is reinforced by explicit reference to Divine omniscience and implied sanction, whilst elevating the conflict-related Q.9:5 to abrogating status despite it being surrounded by caveats and exemptions, and softened by a reference to Divine forgiveness and mercy. Despite his apparent disapproval, Al-Rāzī appears compelled by his own encyclopaedic approach to relay such anomalous minority views, which unfortunately can have significant societal implications for the perceived message of the Qurʾan. A further issue arises from Al-Rāzī's apparently inconsistent intra-verse and inter-verse explanations of the significant term *fitna*. Failing to consistently distinguish *persecution by* the Meccan polytheists from polytheism itself contradicts the Qurʾan's own principle of Differentiation. Although I have also disagreed above with Iṣlāḥī's conclusions on the scope and purpose of conflict, his coherence-based approach demonstrates greater consistency and clarity. The depth of his analysis, however, is rarely as rich as Al-Rāzī's.

3 The Notion of *Iḥsān* in Conflict Resolution

Overview: Group 3 Suras – Q.10–Q.24

Group 3 consists of 15 primarily Meccan suras of moderate length spanning some 8 of the 30 parts of the Qur'an and thus forming the largest of the 7 groups in the Farāhī-Iṣlāḥī schema. The suras are: Q.10 Sūrat Yūnus, Q.11 Sūrat Hūd, Q.12 Sūrat Yūsuf, Q.13 Sūrat Al-Ra'd, Q.14 Sūrat Ibrahīm, Q.15 Sūrat Al-Ḥijr, Q.16 Sūrat Al-Nahl, Q.17 Sūrat Al-Isrā', Q.18 Sūrat Al-Kahf, Q.19 Sūrat Maryam, Q.20 Sūrat Ṭāhā, Q.21 Sūrat Al-Anbiyā', Q.22 Sūrat Al-Ḥajj, Q.23 Sūrat Al-Mu'minūn and Q.24 Sūrat Al-Nūr. According to Iṣlāḥī only the last sura is Medinan, although Abdel-Haleem for example also considers Q.13 and Q.22 Medinan, in likelihood reflecting a mixed content. Alongside the persuasive recurrent enumeration of God's favours and signs in creation, this sura group presents numerous historical narratives of past nations and their prophets, the various punishments of the former serving as a warning to the Meccan polytheists and the strength of character displayed by the latter serving as an exemplar to the Prophet and his followers.

In the Farāhī-Iṣlāḥī schema, the theme of this group is The Struggle Between Truth and Falsehood and Related Divine Law. The suras are paired Q. 10–11, Q.12–13, (Q.14–15 informally paired), Q.16–17, Q.18–19, Q.20–21, Q.22–23 with Q.24 forming an appendix to Q.23. According to Iṣlāḥī (vol.4, p.9), the Meccan suras towards the end of Group 3 were revealed near to the Prophet's migration from Mecca to Medina. *Sīra* accounts (Lings, 2005, pp.88, 96, 101) of this period describe the historical contextual background of a two-year social boycott by the Meccan disbelievers against the Prophet's clan, the Banū Hāshim, closely followed by the grievous personal loss of the Prophet's longstanding wife Khadīja and his patron and uncle Abū Ṭālib. The sura themes are thus centred around delivering final warnings to the Meccan polytheists and delivering good tidings of future success to the Prophet and the early Meccan believers, exhorting them to patience and anticipating relief from persecution through their imminent migration. In the Medinan content, Q.22 briefly mentions physical conflict and Q.24 deals in detail with social relationships.

After examining the systematic legal content of Group 1 and the conceptual ideological content of Group 2, the below analysis of Conciliation themes in Group 3 now illustrates a sustained focus on *khuluq* (character or moral constitution), previously touched upon in the esoteric focus discussion in Chapter 1 and the discussion of the Prophetic exemplar in Chapter 2. According to my analysis, three primary themes feature across Group 3, in some instances individually and in other cases collectively. These Conciliation themes are: (i) the notion of *iḥsān*

https://doi.org/10.1515/9783110747348-005

(which I will translate as 'gracious conduct' based on my analysis), (ii) preserving ties of kinship and (iii) the etiquette of good speech. I will argue that these positive character traits are promoted, particularly in this section of the Qur'an, both as a means of conflict resolution and of conflict avoidance. The Summary Table at the end of Section 3.4 details the layout of key verses in Group 3 in relation to these three sustained Conciliation themes; some content from Group 1 suras has again been included due to its thematic relevance.

The key Conciliation verses analysed in the first section of this chapter are those promoting *iḥsān* at Q.3:134, Q.10:26, Q.11:115 and Q.12:22, 36, 56, 78 and 90. Kinship and its obligations are analysed in the second section by reference to Q.4:1, Q.11:50, Q.13:20–25, Q.15:47, Q.16:90 and Q.17:23–24. In the third section, the importance of good speech is examined through a discussion of Q.14:24, 35–41 and the related Q.19:41–50, Q.16:125–127, Q.17:53 and Q.24:1–35. The significance of these three sections becomes apparent through the concluding analysis of Q.21:107 regarding the Prophet's designation as a 'mercy', and the historical events relating to Joseph's assurance of non-retribution at Q.12:92.

3.1 The Notion of *Iḥsān* in Conflict Resolution and Joseph as the Epitome of *Iḥsān*

The notion of *iḥsān* is, in my view, central to the narrative in Group 3 of the Qur'an. In the previous chapter, we discussed Q.7:56 which connected the central Conciliation notions of *iṣlāḥ* and *fasad* with Divine mercy and human *iḥsān*. In this chapter, it will be demonstrated that this notion of *iḥsān*, now examined in Section 3.1, also pervades the two further key Conciliation themes which are discussed in Sections 3.2 and 3.3. The full significance of this sustained engagement with the notion of *iḥsān* as an instrument of Conciliation will come to light at the end of the chapter in Section 3.4. Linguistically, however, *iḥsān* does not share a grammatical root with words such as *ṣulḥ* and *iṣlāḥ*, encountered in Chapters 1 and 2 and more naturally associated with Conciliation, and its importance is therefore easy to under-estimate. Despite a thorough analysis of the terms *ṣulḥ* and *iṣlāḥ*, the detailed study by ʿAbd Al-Quddūs (1999, p.195), for example, does not include *iḥsān* in her selection of 10 words which are closely related to *ṣulḥ* and *iṣlāḥ* in meaning. Given this context, a thorough analysis of the notion of *iḥsān* is essential to reveal its true importance and relevance to Conciliation.

According to Abdel Haleem and Badawi (2013, p.209), the root *ḥ-s-n* features 195 times in the Qur'an in 14 derivations, including 12 references to the form IV *maṣdar* (verbal noun) *iḥsān* (doing good/piety), 39 references to those who do *iḥsān*, 21 references to the form IV verb *aḥsana* (to perfect/to beautify/do good/treat well) and 28 references to the noun *ḥasanatun* (good deed/benefit/good reward). The meanings show significant variation from beautification to piety to human or Divine benefaction. According to the citations in ʿAbd Al-Bāqī (2001, p.202) the root *ḥ-s-n* features 56 times in Group 3 suras, which is in reasonable proportion to the length of Group 3 in the Qurʾan. There are notable concentrations of the root in several suras such as Q.12, Q.16 and Q.17. Closer inspection and analysis of each entry is essential, however, to appreciate concentrations of *iḥsān* meaning good conduct towards others in particular suras or sections of the Qurʾan, as opposed to other meanings concerned with beauty or perfection which are less relevant to Conciliation.

In Group 1, in the Medinan period, we find references to *iḥsān* in spending at Q.2:195, in showing forgiveness at Q.5:13 and in avoiding prohibited consumption at Q.5:93. We have also encountered an important reference to *iḥsān* in avoiding *fasād* in the Meccan period at Q.7:56. At Q.3:134, however, we find a more elucidatory reference, providing a Qurʾanic 'definition' of *iḥsān*: *alladhīna yunfiqūna fī ('l)-ssarrāʾi wa ('l)-ḍḍarrāʾi wa 'l-kāẓimīn al-ghayẓa wa 'l-ʿāfīna ʿani ('l)-nnās, wa 'llāhu yuḥibbu 'l-muḥsinīn* (those who spend in prosperity and adversity, who restrain their anger and forgive people, God loves those who are gracious towards others, my translation). The use of the *ism al-fāʿil* (active participle) in *kāẓimīn* and *ʿāfīna* indicates a constancy which amounts to a permanent character trait rather than a temporary behaviour. A particular emphasis on such compassion, restraint and mercy has been symbolic of the esoteric, spiritual approach to Conciliation in Sufi ideology (Derin, 2005, pp.1–2, 7, 9, 10), although the above definition also has wider implications for the theory and practice of Conciliation as we shall see in the rest of this chapter and beyond.

Contextually, Q.3:134 is preceded at Q.3:130 by a prohibition on devouring interest, reinforced by three references to *taqwā* at Q.3:130, 131 and 133, which suggests a motivation towards gracious conduct towards debtors, also enjoined in Q.2:280 in the form of literally offering a 'grace' period. Surrounding references to Divine mercy at Q.3:133 and 135 offer an enticing incentive for those who reflect such Divine mercy through their own gracious conduct, as does the promise of Divine Love in Q.3:134 itself. The *ism al-mawṣūl* (relative pronoun), *alladhīna*, not only generalises the principle of the verse but also creates a direct link between the *muttaqīn*, the final word of Q.3:133 and the *muḥsinīn*, closely connecting the quality of *taqwā* in Divine–human relations with the quality of *iḥsān* between people. In Chapter 1, I argued that Divine–human relations served as a motivation and exemplar for better social relations, identifying the existence of a Conciliation Relationship Triangle by reference to a similar link between *taqwā* and *birr* at Q.2:189 and Q.2:224.

This Conciliation Relationship Triangle is manifest at Q.10:26 at the start of Group 3, whose suras we shall now start to analyse thematically. Q.10:26 highlights the importance of *iḥsān* through the magnitude of Divine reward proffered motivationally to inspire *iḥsān*, declaring: *li 'lladhīna* ***aḥsanu 'l-ḥusnā*** *wa ziyāda* (those who did well will have the best reward and more besides, Abdel Haleem). According to the views expressed in Al-Rāzī's commentary, the reward for *iḥsān* ranges from eschatological reward, multiplied 10 to 700 times, to Paradise supplemented by no less than the vision of God. The proximate verses Q.10:4 and Q.10:9 also refer to eschatological reward for those who believe and perform *ṣāliḥāt* (righteous deeds, from the root *ṣ-l-ḥ*). Although the human provider of *iḥsān* is ostensibly disadvantaged through the non-reciprocated harm of another or the provision of gratuitous benefit, it can be seen that in fact balance is restored in the Conciliation Relationship Triangle by the bestowal of Divine *iḥsān* upon the provider of human *iḥsān*. This Divine *iḥsān* therefore serves not only as a motivation and exemplar for such human *iḥsān* but also a compensatory reward.

The final verse of Q.10, Q.10:109, enjoins *ṣabr* (patience, restraint; see Section 5.1 for further explanation) on the Prophet. The strategic concluding location of this verse emphasises the essential importance of this injunction. The same command enjoining *ṣabr* is given in Q.11:115 (see also Q.11:49), again strategically placed towards the conclusion of the following sura, with similar concluding references further on in Group 3 at Q.16:127 and Q.20:130. After explicitly enjoining *ṣabr*, Q.11:115 directly affirms that God does not leave the *muḥsinīn* (those who do *iḥsān*) unrewarded, both indicating that gracious conduct in social relations is rewarded by Divine grace and directly linking *ṣabr* and *iḥsān*. Although Al-Rāzī suggests that Q.10:109 and Q.11:115 refer to perseverance in *worship*, I would argue that the purpose of such worship is to distract and console the Prophet and thus encourage forbearance and restraint. This is because Q.16:127–128 again directly connect *iḥsān* with *ṣabr* in dealing with the disbelievers' hurtful dealings, whilst Q.20:130 explicitly conjoins constant engagement in prayer and an injunction towards *ṣabr* with the disbelievers' speech. From the definition in Q.3:134 it can also be seen that *ṣabr*, meaning restraint, fits within the second limb of the definition of *iḥsān*.

The notion of *iḥsān*, incorporating *ṣabr*, is developed to maturity in Q.12, which details the story of Joseph, particularly his separation from his father and his homeland, a notable parallel with the Prophet's pending migration and his eventual attainment of high status (see Abdel Haleem, 1990 for a comparison with the Biblical account). Adopting a dramatic style, the sustained narrative of Q.12 vocalises its key messages through the dialogue of the various characters and the accompanying supportive narrative. Jacob, separated first by space and then also by time from his most beloved son, declares a memorable motif twice at Q.12:18 and 83. *faṣabrun jamīl* (patience is best). The expression is rendered more succinct and impactful by the apparent *ḥadhf* (ellipsis) of the *mubtada*ʾ or *khabr*, as indicated by both Al-Rāzī and Iṣlāḥī (vol.4, p.199). The intermediate 65 verses unfold a narrative spanning many years of grief-stricken separation which nonetheless yield an apparent constant patience from Jacob, accentuated by the identical wording in the 2 verses. This provides an illustrative exemplar for the Divine enjoinder at the conclusion of Q.10 and Q.11 towards continued patience by the Prophet and by extension his followers.

Joseph too serves as an exemplar of prophetic patience and an aspirational embodiment of *iḥsān*. The recurrence of the notion of *iḥsān* in Q.12 cannot fail to impress the attentive reader of the Arabic text of the Qurʾan, inviting a closer examination of these references. At Q.12:90, Joseph looks back on the above events, reflecting: *innahū man yyattaqi wa yaṣbir* (surely whoever is conscious of God and patient), God does not leave the *muḥsinīn* unrewarded, again including patience within *iḥsān* and emphasising its Divine reward as in Q.10 and Q.11 above. Joseph's statement is mirrored earlier in the Divine narrative voice at Q.12:56, which crucially Al-Rāzī describes as testimony from God that Joseph is amongst the *muḥsinīn*. Similar wording is used again at Q.12:22. The depersonification in the formulation of the above three affirmatory statements serves to establish a universal principle, although contextually they clearly refer to Joseph. Two other dramatic scenes include personalised affirming dialogue from the supporting actors, first by his fellow prisoners at Q.12:36 and then by his brothers at Q.12:78, that Joseph is visibly amongst the *muḥsinīn*. Ibn Manẓūr (2014, vol.16, p.271) indicates, with reference to this specific description of Joseph, qualities such as assisting the weak, the oppressed and the sick. The word *narāka* (we see you) is evidentially emphatic, highlighting the observed experience of collective orators in each instance. The significance of Joseph being bestowed with the title of *muḥsin* from all sides is, in my view, crucial to a proper appreciation of his exemplary status.

The above five recurrences of the word *muḥsinīn* referring directly or indirectly to Joseph in the same sura are a remarkable literary feature, whose impact is rather lost in translation. Abdel Haleem translates them as 'those who do good' (Q.12:22), 'knowledgeable' (Q.12:36), 'those who do good (Q.12:56), 'a very good man' (Q.12:78) and 'those who do good (Q.12:90). Unfortunately, such attempts to appreciate *wujūh al-Qur*ʾ*an* (alternative meanings of Qurʾanic words), rather dilute the impact of the Arabic term which is translated into different words in different instances, masking the actual frequency of its recurrence. The variation in translation between Q.12:36 and Q.12:78, for example, retracts from the affirmative evidential impact of the identical Arabic wording.

A further problem is that the word 'good' in English is so generic as to lack the richness of the Arabic term *muḥsinīn*. Reinhart (2016, "Virtuous acts", para. 5) says, 'it is difficult to translate *ḥ-s-n* and its derivatives more precisely than with the word "good"'. Translations of the Qurʾan thus neutralise the importance of *iḥsān* through generic translations of the word as meaning 'good' in an effort to find a sufficiently encompassing one-to-one correspondence with the term. In my view, the most appropriate translation in this context would be 'gracious'. Yusuf Ali helpfully supplements his translation by adding the word 'benevolent' in explaining Q.12:36 and 'gracious' in explaining Q.12:78. Al-Rāzī offers four possible meanings of *muḥsinīn* at Q.12:36 – *makārim al-akhlāq* (nobility of character), compassionate, pious and knowledgeable, leading with the first, which I prefer due to its consistency with the central theme of the sura, and expressing the others only with the less affirmative *qīla* (it is said).

For Iṣlāḥī, Q.12:90 above, which emphasises Divine reward for *iḥsān* based on *taqwā* and *ṣabr*, constitutes the *rūḥ* (spirit or essence) of the narrative and the *ʿamūd* (central theme) of the sura. However, Iṣlāḥī's elaboration (vol.4, p.250) reveals his diversion of emphasis towards Divine–human relations rather than social relations. He explains Q.12:90 as commending *taqwā* and *ṣabr* based on the *bunyādī sharṭ* (foundational condition) of *iḥsān*, which he considers a state in which the individual behaves as if he is beholding the Divine or is in the Divine gaze, a reference to a famous Prophetic narration in which the Prophet and the Archangel Gabriel converse regarding this meaning of *iḥsān*, but crucially *in the context of worship* rather than social interaction. Furthermore, Al-Iṣfahānī (2009, p.236) clearly distinguishes two different usages of the term *iḥsān*: *iḥsānun fī fiʿlihi* (excellence in one's performance of an action), which is the obvious meaning indicated in the Prophetic narration, and *al-inʿām ʿala 'l-ghayr* (providing benefit to another), which is the more contextually appropriate meaning in Q.12:90.

I would argue that the true magnitude of Joseph's *iḥsān* and the actual emphasis on *iḥsān* in social relations at Q.12:90 cannot be fully understood without additional reference to Q.12:92. After revealing his identity and hearing the expression of remorse from his brothers at Q.12:90–91, Joseph immediately reassures them at Q.12:92: *lā tathrība ʿalaykumu 'l-yawm*, going on apparently unsolicited and without hesitation to pray for their forgiveness, invoking God's mercy with the title *Arḥam al-Rāḥimīn* (the most Merciful of the merciful; see for contrast Q.12:98 where Jacob's prayer for forgiveness is both solicited and delayed as indicated by *sawfa* (presently)). The *manṣūb* case of *tathrība* grammatically indicates complete negation of the genus and is highly emphatic, whilst the titular reference to God's ultimate mercy provides a Divine exemplar for human mercy and *iḥsān*.

Joseph's lack of inner rancour and resentment is demonstrated by his apparently instantaneous forgiveness, despite the years of separation from his father and the hardships of abandonment, servitude and imprisonment. The same quality is demonstrated as Joseph signals his willingness to excuse the brothers of fault, referring to them at Q.12:89 as *jāhilūn* (ignorant), and later readily externalises the cause of their dispute. At Q.12:100, rather than calling the brothers to account for their jealousy and deception, Joseph attributes their failures to Satan's conduct of *nazagha* (sowing discord, Abdel Haleem), following the example set by his father in Joseph's childhood at Q.12:5. Joseph's *iḥsān* achieves the reconciliation of his family and his story ends appropriately on the word *ṣāliḥīn* from the root *ṣ-l-ḥ*, whose connection to Conciliation was discussed in Chapter 2. Joseph prays to be joined with the *ṣāliḥīn*, perhaps not coincidentally a word also used to describe his great-grandfather Abraham emphatically at Q.16:122, another Qur'anic model of forbearance (see Q.9:114, Q.11:75 and Q.19:47).

Upon evaluating Joseph's conduct against the 'definition' of *iḥsān* in Q.3:134 above, it can be seen that Joseph has gratuitously supplied his brothers in prosperity and educated his fellow prisoners in adversity, has restrained his anger – particularly at Q.12:77 when the brothers unknowingly slander him as a thief in his own presence – and has forgiven them with alacrity. In respect of the first quality of spending, Al-Rāzī clarifies that *infāq* (spending) includes educating and guiding others, as Joseph does to his co-prisoners from Q.12:37–41. In return, at Q.12:100, Joseph affirms that he has been temporally rewarded with Divine grace, also referred to as *iḥsān*, through the reunion of his family. At Q.12:101, he also acknowledges the temporal Divine gifts of dominion and knowledge and then prays for eschatological reward: (to die with faith and) be joined with the *ṣāliḥīn* (righteous).

With respect to the second quality of restraint in Q.3:134, Al-Rāzī cites a Prophetic narration stating that the strong man is not one who throws another to the ground, but rather the one who controls himself when angry, emphasising restraint and strength of character over physique. Restraining oneself from reciprocating harm, Al-Rāzī also clarifies, protects the other from harm in this world, whilst the third quality of forgiveness protects them from accountability in the Hereafter. Crucially, Al-Rāzī's additional quotation, this time from the prophet Jesus, affirms that *iḥsān* is not merely to reciprocate good conduct: *innama 'l-iḥsān an tuḥsin ilā man asā' ilayk* (rather, *iḥsān* is doing *iḥsān* towards one who has harmed you, my translation). Ibn Manẓūr (2014, vol.16, p.272) states: *wa 'l- iḥsān ḍidd al-isā'a* (*iḥsān* is the opposite of oppression/harm). It can be seen from these statements that *iḥsān* is crucial in breaking a vicious cycle of negative conduct and thus avoiding the perpetual escalation of a dispute.

We now see that *iḥsān* serves as a counter-intuitive but empowering self-help remedy which enables one who has been harmed to contain a dispute and set a conciliatory example for his or her counterpart, re-defining the relationship from a relationship of conflict to a relationship of Conciliation. A conciliatory approach can effectively be maintained by the party suffering harm irrespective of the confrontational approach of the other. Without retaliation, the fire of disputation is deprived of inflammatory oxygen and ultimately extinguished. Allred (2005, p.95), a professional mediator himself, has argued that productive ongoing relationships benefit from virtuous cycles of cooperation and trust and that neutral mediators can often facilitate Conciliation by overcoming bias which leads to a vicious cycle of suspicion and contention.

The above discussion introduces the theory and practice of *iḥsān* in social relations as a means to resolving conflicts, and its motivation through the offer of Divine reward. This initial examination will be developed as *iḥsān* continues to feature as a pervasive concept throughout this chapter in the sections below, and again in Chapter 5. The notion of *iḥsān* in Q.12 is presented in the specific context of fraternal relations of kin. This aspect of Q.12 will be examined further in Section 3.2.1 and it will be seen that this specific illustration is succeeded structurally in Q.13 by a more general enjoinder towards preserving relations of kin. This is the second important Conciliation theme of this chapter and is now introduced below.

3.2 Conciliation and Relations of Kin

3.2.1 The Importance of Kinship in Social Relations and Faith Propagation

The seminal verse highlighting the importance of kinship is found in the Medinan Qur'an at Q.4:1, an appropriate introduction to a sura which deals generally with the regulation of several aspects of family life, such as inheritance and marriage, and the legal and supra-legal rights of women and children in particular. Q.4:1 unifies all mankind as a single body of humanity within creation through the opening address *yā ayyuha ('l)-nnās* (O Mankind), and then by declaring God's Lordship as the Creator of mankind from *nafsin wāḥidatin* (one soul). Women are then given special mention both through their partnership in marriage indicated by the phrase *zawjahā* (its spouse) and their constitution as half of society through the word *nisā'ā* (women). Q.25:54 elsewhere mentions that kinship is by both *nasaban* (blood ties) and *ṣihran* (marriage ties). Conciliation through marriage ties has been discussed briefly in Chapter 1 and in this chapter Conciliation through blood ties will be discussed in detail.

Al-Rāzī considers the possibilities that the address in Q.4:1 is to all mankind or the Arabs in particular, but inclines towards mankind in general based on the notion of *al-istighrāq* (encompassing) indicated by the *alif* and *lām* before *nās*. He reconciles the contrary opinion of Ibn ʿAbbās, however, by suggesting that the later reference to fearing God and relationships of the womb could be specific to those things which were particularly sacrosanct amongst the Arabs and were therefore culturally invoked by them for the purpose of *munāshada* (entreaty), as alluded to in Q.4:1.

Al-Rāzī also enumerates the implications of mentioning mankind's creation from one soul, including *li ziyādat shafaqat al-khalq baʿḍihim ʿala ʾl-baʿḍ* (to increase the compassion of all people towards each other) and so that they *tarakū al-mufākhara wa ʾl-takabbur wa aẓharū al-tawāḍuʿ wa ḥusn al-khuluq* (they desist from boasting and arrogance and show humility and excellence of character). The conciliatory appeal of Q.4:1 is, I believe, strongly supported by another striking Qurʾanic example where the prophet Aaron, whose brotherhood with Moses is previously highlighted at Q.20:30 and Q.20:42, is distanced through being addressed by name by his younger brother Moses at Q.20:92. Moses' anger, demonstrated by his grasp of Aaron's hair and beard, is apparently silenced when Aaron appeals to him at Q.20:94 not only as a brother but more explicitly and evocatively *ya'bna umma* (O son of my mother). It is manifest from the above that the impressive opening address of Q.4:1 is not only a powerful argument for human equality and social justice but also a compelling argument for mutual cooperation and Conciliation. The effective use of terms of address as a form of *al-ighrāʾ* (appeal; see Hāshmī, 2008, p.116) is apparent in both Q.4:1 and Q.20:94 and, as shall be seen below, in numerous other instances, making them an important literary device in Conciliation.

The mandatory importance of the above subject-matter in the Qurʾanic text is indicated in Q.4:1 by the twice-repeated mention of *ittaqū* (fear (God)) and a further emphatic closing reference to God as *raqībā* (ever-watchful). This is reinforced by the *ʿatf* (conjoining) of God's name with the word *arḥām* (relations of the womb), the imperative voice demanding from mankind continued honouring of both the Divine–human relationship and social relationships of kin. Al-Rāzī cites numerous classical authorities to highlight the use of the *manṣūb* (accusative) case to conjoin the word *arḥām* with God's name, and also by way of *al-ighrāʾ* (appeal) to invoke the obligation of maintaining ties of kin. The word *arḥām*, he states, affirms *taʿẓīm ḥaqq al-raḥm wa ta'kīd al-nahī ʿan qaṭʿihā* (honouring the rights of relationships of kin and emphasising the prohibition on breaking them). He goes on to cite various Prophetic narrations, including the following in which God links Divine mercy with human mercy, declaring: 'I am Al-Raḥmān (the Merciful), and it is *al-raḥm* (the womb or kinship, from the grammatical root meaning to be merciful) – I have derived its name from my name, so whoever joins it, I will join with him, and whoever cuts it off, I will cut off from him.'

It can be seen from the above discussion that the relationship of humans by kin is a fundamental principle of creation in the Qurʾan, and that the importance of honouring ties of kinship is heightened by its conjunction with honouring the rights of God. This general principle appears to acquire a special significance in the context of faith propagation, as will now be discussed, primarily by reference to Q.11. At Q.11:50, 61 and 84, three out of five prophetic narratives in the sura introduce the prophets Hūd (the eponymous prophet of the sura), Ṣāliḥ and Shuʿayb, sent to their various communities, as *akhāhum* (their brother). This kinship appears to act as a limited preventative impediment to greater conflict, with Shuʿayb's people exercising restraint from certain physical abuse out of regard for his *rahṭ* (kinsfolk, Q.11:91). Shuʿayb in turn is careful to point out his earnest desire to achieve *iṣlāḥ* (reform), in place of the *fasād* (corruption) of inequitable measurement in commerce, for the mutual benefit of himself and his people rather than desiring their opposition (Q.11:85, 88). The limiting phrase *ma 'staṭaʿt* (as far as I can, Abdel Haleem) at Q.11:88 accentuates his conciliatory approach of non-compulsion.

In his commentary of Q.11:50, Al-Rāzī recounts that the Prophet's people, that is the Meccans, would distance the Prophet from themselves in spite of his being of their tribe. The purpose of stressing the brotherhood of the above prophets with their nations was thus *li izālat hādha 'l-istibʿād* (to remove this distancing) and thus *istimālat* (conciliating) the Prophet's people. It can be seen that the kinship of a prophet to his people is, from the Qurʾan's perspective, an important aspect of his conciliatory appeal and the success of his propagation. Elsewhere, in the Medinan Qurʾan at Q.9:128, reference to the Prophet being *min anfusikum* (from amongst yourselves) again creates proximate relations between the Prophet and his people collocated with a statement of his sincere compassion and goodwill, in the appealing style of Shuʿayb's statement at Q.11:88 above.

The Prophet is also instructed at Q.20:132 to enjoin prayer upon his family, and later at Q.26:214: *wa andhir ʿashīrataka 'l-aqrabīn* (warn your nearest kinsfolk, Abdel Haleem). Al-Rāzī's account of the surrounding circumstances suggests that the Prophet gathered his relatives publicly on Mount Ṣafā and addressed them with titles of tribal and even individual kinship. The Qurʾan thus makes faith propagation in respect of kin specifically incumbent upon the Prophet, invoking duties of kinship – sacred to the Arabs – bilaterally between the Prophet and his people to promote mutual proximate relations. As mentioned earlier in Chapter 1, Greenhouse (1985, pp.91–92, 98–107) discusses how such common values, in this case Explicit values common to the Arabs as a group, can be invoked to facilitate Conciliation.

Finally in this section, returning to the narrative of Q.12 examined in Section 3.1 in light of the above discussion, it can be seen that the story of Joseph is not only a story of *iḥsān* but is more specifically a story of *iḥsān* towards relatives and maintaining relations of kin. Although reiterated expressly in other suras in this group, this notion is enacted dramatically and embodied practically in Q.12. The context of familial relations is everywhere apparent. Fraternal relations are highlighted at Q.12:5, 7, 8, 59, 65, 69, 70, 76, 77, 89, 90 and 100. Filial relations are expressly highlighted at Q.12:**5, 67,** 81 and **87,** whilst paternal relations are similarly highlighted at Q.12:**4,** 9, **11,** 16, **17**, 59, **63, 65**, 68, 78, 80, **81**, 93, 94, **97**, 99 and **100**. The preceding bold references indicate emphasis of the relationship of kin through terms of address.

Subtle insight into the state of relations is provided through these references. Jacob's fatherly concern is manifest through his consistent reference to all his sons by their relationship to him. The sons, vying for paternal affection, consistently refer to their father by relationship. However, Joseph's brothers distance Joseph from themselves referring to him only by name. Although they refer to Benjamin as their brother to reassure their father at Q.12:65, they are quick to distance both Joseph and Benjamin, respectively – as Benjamin's brother rather than their own at Q.12:77, and as their father's son rather than their brother at Q.12:81. Joseph, by contrast, draws to himself first Benjamin at Q.12:89 and 90 and then the remaining brothers at Q.12:100, referring to all as his brothers. It is also Joseph's instruction which finally unites the family as he states at Q.12:93: *wa ʾtūnī bi ahlikum ajmaʿīn* (then bring your whole family back to me, Abdel Haleem).

Having established the significance of kinship in both social relations and faith propagation primarily by reference to Q.4 and Q.11, respectively, and briefly re-examined Q.12 to highlight the context of familial relations, we will now turn to a discussion of earthly and heavenly relationships of kin by reference to Q.13.

3.2.2 Temporal and Eschatological Ties of Kinship

The importance of maintaining family ties, practically demonstrated by Joseph, is explicitly brought to the fore in the narrative of Q.13, which in this respect appears to be justifiably paired with Q.12 in the Farāhī-Iṣlāḥī schema. Although there is a shift from the narrative style of Q.12 to the enumeration of the signs of God's power and grace in Q.13, thematically there is a cohesive continuity in the focus on maintaining relations of kin. Q.13:20–24 offer an honorific, lengthy character description followed by the promise of an angelic salutation of *salām* (peace) in gardens everlasting to those who, amongst other qualities, *yaṣilūna mā amara 'llāhu bihī an yyūṣala* (join together what God commands to be joined, Abdel Haleem) and *yadra'ūna bi 'l-ḥasanati ('l)-ssayyi'a* (who repel evil with good, Abdel Haleem). In stark contrast, Q.13:25 offers a rather dismissively brief but ominous account of the eschatological fate of those who *yaqta'ūna* (sever) such relations and *yufsidūna fi 'l-arḍi* (spread corruption on earth, Abdel Haleem).

Although Q.13:21 does not explicitly mention relations of kin, reference to other Qur'anic verses is in my view conclusive as to the intended meaning. Firstly, Q.2:83 refers to a *mīthāq* taken from Banī Isrā'īl regarding worshipping God alone, immediately following with the notion of *iḥsān* towards relatives (a similar collocation is presented at Q.4:36 and Q.17:23, 26). Secondly, Q.4:1 mentions God's Lordship and immediately follows with the notion of mankind's creation from one soul and *arḥām* (ties of kinship). Thirdly, Q.47:22 includes the phrase *tufsidū fi 'l-arḍi wa tuqaṭṭi'ū arḥāmakum* ((could it be that) you will go on to spread corruption all over the land and break your ties of kinship, Abdel Haleem), explicitly juxtaposing *fasād* on the earth with the cutting of ties of kinship – the same terminology is used in Q.13:25 (Q.9:8 and 10 also condemn the polytheists' failure to respect either ties of kinship or agreements).

The importance of the reference to maintaining ties of kinship in Q.13:21 is emphasised by its proximate juxtaposition and link through the connective *alladhīna* (those who) to the fundamental notion of abiding by *'ahdi-'llāhi* (God's covenant) and *mīthāq* (pledge) in Q.13:20. The legislative style, which adds impact to the mandatory nature of the obligations specified, is further enhanced by the above-mentioned reference to God's command and the retributive sanctions implied by references to fearing God and accountability in Q.13:21. In my view, 'God's covenant' refers to the testimony of Divine Lordship taken from all Children of Adam at Q.7:172. This interpretation provides a cohesive link through the notion of Divine unity and authority to the ensuing reference to God's command. It also forms a coherent and comprehensive statement of Conciliation in first Divine–human and then social relations across Q.13:20 and Q.13:21, with further detail of both notions in Q.13:22.

Support for the above position is provided by Iṣlāḥī's structure-based commentary (vol.4, pp.285, 287) which also takes *mīthāq* as a reference to Q.7:172, and Q.13:21 as a reference to joining ties of kinship, and then conjoins the two notions coherently by declaring them to be the twin foundational pillars – one the unity of God and the other the unity of mankind – which support a *ṣāliḥ* (righteous) society. In his commentary of Q.15:44, whose related verse Q.15:47 is discussed below, Iṣlāḥī also stipulates that in his analysis the seven fundamental behaviours which the Qur'an identifies as leading to destruction are: polytheism, severance of ties of kinship, homicide, fornication, false testimony, oppression of the weak and transgression. Within this already essential schema, severance of ties of kinship is given special importance by its collocation with polytheism, which also reflects the Qurʾanic approach in Q.13:20–21.

Although Abdel-Haleem translates Q.13:20 as 'those who fulfil the agreements they make in God's name and do not break their pledges', I find this interpretation less preferable than the position taken in my analysis above for several reasons. Firstly, the notions of covenant and pledge in Q.13:20 are both individually singular rather than plural, and together refer to a single concept, a point made clear at Q.13:25. Furthermore, the contextual relevance of mentioning the upholding of inter-personal contractual agreements after the enumeration of God's power and grace is significantly less than the contextual relevance of acknowledging God's authority and joining ties of kinship, rather than spreading corruption on the earth. It is also not entirely clear in Abdel-Haleem's translation what the 'join(ing) together what God commands to be joined' refers to, whether the agreements mentioned or something else unmentioned. In the former contingency, I would argue that the word *yaṣilūna* sits well with joining ties of kinship and is the terminology used in Prophetic narrations in this context, whilst *yūfūna* (fulfil) would be more appropriate for contractual agreements: see Q.13:20 and Q.5:1.

Although Al-Rāzī does consider the possibility that Q.13:20, and even Q.13:21, may refer to the fulfilment of agreements, he opens his discussion of Q.13:20 with the opinion of Ibn ʿAbbās that it refers to the Divine covenant in Q.7:172. He also concludes his discussion of Q.13:20 and Q.13:21 by summarising that Q.13:20 alludes to *al-taʿẓīm li amri 'llāh* (honouring God's command) whilst Q.13:21 alludes to *al-shafaqa ʿalā khalqi 'llāh* (compassion towards God's creation), a notion within which he includes *ṣilat al-raḥm* (joining ties of kinship). It will be seen later in Section 3.2.3 that Al-Rāzī is referring here to the recurrent notion of *iḥsān* and its two branches, one linked to Divine–human relations and the other to social relations.

Concurrent with the legislative style used to emphasise the importance of maintaining relations of kin is a motivational portrayal of the inhabitants of Paradise at Q.13:23. Their conciliatory character is highlighted through their description as *ṣalaḥa*, often translated as 'righteous' but offering in my view a direct link to the joining of ties of kinship mentioned above and a clear contrast to the reference to the severing of relations and *fasād* in Q.13:25. I would argue that there is an unmistakable alignment between the surrounding familial relationships of ancestors, spouses and descendants presented in Paradise at Q.13:23 and the temporal maintenance of relations of kin enjoined above (see also Q.43:67 regarding the maintenance of positive earthly relationships by righteous people in the Hereafter). In the context of this representation of eschatological familial harmony, it is in my view clear that the textual focus in the fundamental command in Q.13:21 is on maintaining relations of kin, which also accords with the central theme of the previous sura, Q.12.

Moving forward two suras, Q.15:47 presents a further insight into the conciliatory internal state of the *muttaqīn* (righteous) inhabitants of Paradise: *wa nazaʿnā mā fī ṣudūrihim min ghillin ikhwānan ʿalā sururin mutaqābilīn* (and We shall remove any bitterness from their hearts: [they will be like] brothers, sitting on couches, face to face, Abdel Haleem). A similar statement regarding the removal of malice at Q.7:42–43 mentions the *ṣāliḥāt* (good deeds, from the root *ṣ-l-ḥ*) of such people, whilst Q.44:53 also highlights their facing position with the term *mutaqābilīn*. The opposition of Divine will and Satanic influence is accentuated, at Q.15:47, by the verb *nazaʿa*, which is reminiscent of the verb *nazagha* (sowing discord) used at Q.12:100 to describe Satanic influence leading to conflict (see further examples at Q.7:200 and Q.17:53). In my view, the removal of the dot on the letter *ghayn* symbolises the removal of the blot of rancour from discordant hearts, whilst the collective personal pronoun in *nazaʿnā* indicates Divine power ultimately overcoming Satan's influence.

References to *ṣudūr* (hearts) and *ghill* (bitternesss) highlight that outward behaviour is a manifestation of the inner state of the heart and Conciliation ultimately requires a cleansing of the emotions inside the heart, in this case bitterness or rancour. In dealing with cross-cultural negotiations, Cohen (2001, pp.27–28, 35) emphasises the need for inner transformation in Conciliation, a point which we shall see reiterated several times by reference to the Qur'anic material later in the chapter. Al-Rāzī mentions the cleansing of all spiritual malaise, including *al-ḥiqd* (malice), *al-ḥasad* (envy), *al-ghill* (rancour) and *al-ghaḍab* (anger). Q.19:96 similarly states that Al-Raḥmān (God, the Lord of Mercy, Abdel Haleem) will create *wuddā* (love) in the hearts of those who believe and do *ṣāliḥāt* (good deeds), the context of the previous verse and the futuristic prefix *sa* both indicating a reference to the Day of Judgement. The form VI verb *mutaqābilīn* (facing each other) in Q.15:47 also demonstrates visually the mutually open and good relations of the inhabitants of Paradise, whilst the same active participle represents the perpetually harmonious state of those who never turn their backs on each other and are never estranged.

The entire conciliatory scene (see the notion of *taṣwīr* in Boullata (2000, p.356) regarding the Qur'anic style which dramatically brings scenes to life) is encapsulated with immense concision in the single word *ikhwānan* (brotherly) in the *manṣūb* case which adverbially describes relations in Paradise as akin to those who have shared a common mother's womb and common paternal lineage.

The notion has bilateral effect, serving both as an aspirational model for earthly brotherly relations such as those of Joseph and his brothers, and as a means of highlighting the proximate relations of the inhabitants of Paradise (also see Q.59:10 which refers to spiritual brothers in a prayer for removal of malice). Whilst the analogy of fraternal relations has universal human appeal, it is especially effective in the context of the fiercely loyal tribal relations of the Arab audience.

A keen sense of antithesis is evident from the scenes portrayed in Hell, of mutual recrimination and blame. Gwynne (2004, pp.148–51) provides a full discussion of the use of antithesis in the Qur'an, highlighting its use particularly in passages relating to Paradise and Hell. At Q.7:38–39 we are told of communities driven to Hell cursing their predecessors and accusing them of being responsible for misguiding them, whilst the earlier communities will hold the latter equally responsible and punishable. At Q.40:47, the mutual quarrelling of those in Hell is mentioned, with the weak followers appealing to their proud leaders for respite, but in vain. Q.43:67 declares that, on the Day of Judgement, friends shall turn into enemies except for the righteous. Q.23:101 also signifies the breaking of ties by the people destined for Hell, in contrast to the maintenance of relations in Paradise at Q.13:23. The manifest conflict of Hell provides a stark contrast with the conciliation of Paradise, each accentuating the effect of the other. This creates a negative distasteful association between Hell and conflict and a positive motivational association between Paradise and Conciliation.

The above section examined the motivational eschatological scenes of Paradise, with its harmonious relations, promised to those who maintain ties of kinship on earth. In the following section, the gracious conduct required to maintain such ties of kinship is expounded, also providing additional clarity regarding the notion of *iḥsān* itself, previously introduced in Section 3.1.

3.2.3 The Obligation of *Iḥsān* Towards Relatives

The notion of *iḥsān* re-surfaces conspicuously at Q.16 and Q.17, featuring with its derivative forms recurrently at Q.16:30, 41, 90, 96, 97, 122, 125 and 128 and Q.17:7, 23, 34 and 53. A number of these verses such as Q.16:30, 41, 96, 97 promise both temporal reward and the eschatological reward discussed above, motivating the Meccan believers to remain steadfast, showing *ṣabr* (patience, Q.16:96), some migrating in the face of persecution (Q.16:41), and to continue *ʿamila ṣāliḥan* (do (ing) righteous deeds, Q.16:97). Others such as Q.17:7 and 34 address Banī Isrāʾīl and deal with orphans' wealth, respectively. In this section, we will consider *iḥsān* from the perspective of those obligations which the Qur'an stipulates in respect of relatives, examining particularly the general principle of good treatment of relatives at Q.16:90, and the specific injunctions in respect of parents and others at Q.17:23 onwards. Q.16:125 and Q.17:53 deal with good speech and will be dealt with subsequently in Section 3.3.1.

Although Iṣlāḥī's *ʿamūd* (central theme) for Q.16 is the message of Q.16:30 (vol.4, pp.383, 438), both he and Al-Rāzī agree on the fundamental importance of Q.16:90 as a summative statement of principle in respect of Qurʾanic injunctions and prohibitions. As such, it is a distillation of the fundamental behaviours which are incumbent upon believers, rendering each item of the utmost importance. The verse is introduced with the emphatic particle *inna* reinforced with the legislative verb *yaʾmuru* (commands). The advancement of the subject in the word order, creating a nominal sentence, casts special prominence on the name Allah, referring to God Himself rather than His individual attributes. These grammatical constructs and the vocabulary selection together yield a sense of Divine majesty and power which adds much emphasis to what follows.

Q.16:90 is composed of no more than three commands and three prohibitions. The three commands are: *ʿadl, iḥsān* and *ītāʾi dhi ʾl-qurbā* (justice, gracious conduct and generosity towards relatives). The specific mention of relatives in a verse of such concision, in which other beneficiaries remain concealed, is highly significant and shows the relative importance attached to their treatment. Furthermore, *ʿadl* refers to justice and naturally includes the legal rights of relatives such as the rights of inheritance expressly legislated in tremendous detail in Q.4. *Iḥsān* denotes supra-legal kindness and grace and is repeatedly enjoined expressly in respect of relatives, for example at Q.2:83, Q.4:36 and Q.17:23. Al-Iṣfahānī (2009, p.236) states, with specific reference to Q.16:90, that *iḥsān* goes beyond justice, since justice involves giving what is due and taking one's entitlement, whilst *iḥsān* is to give more than is due and to take less than one's entitlement. The good treatment of relatives thus acquires remarkable significance as it pervades all three injunctions in Q.16:90, which are themselves considered summative of all Qurʾanic injunctions. The three injunctions also have a progressive effect indicating that in the case of relatives, they should be given their legal rights, treated with additional grace and forbearance and yet further have gifts bestowed upon them with unwavering generosity.

In distinguishing between *ʿadl* and *iḥsān*, Iṣlāḥī (vol.4, p.439) considers *iḥsān* as conduct which goes beyond the fulfilment of legal rights and is *karīmāna* (gracious) and *fayḍāna* (beneficent). Iṣlāḥī also considers *ītāʾi dhi ʾl-qurbā* an essential 'branch' of *iḥsān* to which relatives are also entitled. If *ītāʾi dhi ʾl-qurbā* is an aspect of *iḥsān*, then looking back at the 'definition' of *iḥsān* in Q.3:134 which itself incorporates the notion of *infāq* (spending), the reference to *ītāʾi dhi ʾl-qurbā* could serve an emphatic function in respect of their entitlement, or indicate a demand of extraordinary generosity in the case of relatives. Iṣlāḥī appears to incline towards the latter, mentioning that relatives are *mazīd infāq ke mustaḥaq* (literally: additional – spending – entitled to). Unfortunately, the Urdu wording includes an element of ambiguity as it could mean 'entitled to (additional expenditure)' or 'additionally (entitled to expenditure)'.

Al-Rāzī's commentary of Q.16:90 concludes his discussion of various narrations and opinions on the subject of *ʿadl* and *iḥsān*, by defining the former as *qadr al-wājib min al-khayrāt* (the mandatory extent of good deeds) and the latter as *al-ziyāda fī tilka 'l-ṭāʿāt bi ḥasb al-kammiyya wa bi ḥasb al-kayfiyya* (exceeding such obedience in magnitude and manner). He then elaborates that ***iḥsān*** includes ***al-taʿẓīm li amri 'llāhi taʿālā wa 'l-shafaqa ʿalā khalqi 'llāh*** (honouring the command of God the Exalted and compassion towards God's creation; Al-Rāzī uses the same phrase in his commentary of Q.13:20 and 21 above and, apparently quoting a Prophetic narration, at Q.17:23 below). Crucially, Al-Rāzī states that whilst compassion towards creation obviously takes many forms, *ashrafihā wa ajallihā ṣilat al-raḥm* (the most noble and exalted of them is joining ties of kinship).

The legislative command of mandatory generosity towards relatives is also reinforced elsewhere in the Qur'an, with Q.17:26 and Q.30:38 both stating that the near of kin (and the needy and traveller) should be given *haqqahū* (his due). Q.17:27 contrasts such dutiful conduct with the squanderers of money who are termed the 'brothers of Satan', whilst Q.17:28 stipulates that where a potential donor is unable to realise the demand of a relative he should at least satisfy them with *qawlan maysūrā* (some word of comfort, Abdel Haleem). Q.4:36 follows a detailed passage regarding Conciliation between spouses with a general stipulation towards monotheism followed by an injunction of *iḥsān* on parents, relatives, orphans, the needy, neighbours related and unrelated, companions and slaves – extending the conciliatory reach of the injunction of *iḥsān* throughout the social circle and with a focus on those who are most proximate and in need.

The summative commands and prohibitions of Q.16:90 are, according to Iṣlāḥī's structural commentary (vol.4, pp.469, 471, 491), elaborated into a series of more detailed regulations from Q.17:23 to Q.17:37, a body of teachings collectively unitised at Q.17:38 and 39 in the demonstrative *dhālik* (these/this). These regulations Iṣlāḥī considers a reflection of the Biblical Ten Commandments and the essential tenets of all Abrahamic faiths. Once again, a body of conciliatory teachings is encapsulated at both ends (at Q.17:23 and Q.17:39) by the central theological doctrine of God's unity, elevating their position amongst the Qur'anic discourse to a fundamental status. *Iḥsān* upon parents, generosity to relatives, the poor and travellers and by association moderation in expenditure, *iḥsān* in the use of an orphan's wealth, fulfilment of promises and fair measurement are all enjoined whilst infanticide, fornication and homicide, and reliance on unverified information and arrogance are all prohibited – any breach of these regulations is denounced as evil and hateful in the sight of God (Q.17:38).

The status of parents is particularly sanctified by a two-fold association between duties owed to parents and duties owed to God. Firstly, the phrase *wa bi ʻl-wālidayni iḥsānā* (and *iḥsān* on parents) is conjoined with a prohibition on the worship of anyone other than God at Q.17:23. Both Al-Rāzī and Iṣlāḥī (vol.4, p.496) consider the indefinite *iḥsānā* indicative of a *ḥadhf* (ellipsis) of the verb *aḥsinū* (be gracious) reflecting an emphatic *mafʿūl muṭlaq* (cognate accusative) construct, signifying *iḥsān* of the highest order. Secondly, the parental care of children is linked to Divine care through the use of the verb *rabba* (bring up) to describe the parental role and the noun *rabb* (Lord), alluding to the same quality in a Divine sense, to refer to God at Q.17:23 and 24. This conveys a sense of continuity between the required dutiful conduct towards nurturing parents, and the required dutiful worship of a providing Lord. The entire stipulation of obligations towards parents is mandated through the recurrent use of the prohibitive and imperative voice and further given a legislative status, which Al-Rāzī also describes as conclusive and irrevocable, by the imposing introductory declaration: *wa qaḍā rabbuka* (your Lord has decreed).

As the child attains maturity and the parents attain *kibara* (old age), parental care becomes less evident and indeed it is often the child who adopts the role of carer leaving the parents feeling redundant and burdensome. This can result in tension and conflict which interferes with the previously proximate and affectionate parent–child relationship. In such circumstances, verses Q.17:23–24 elevate the parents' status, ennobling them and restoring their dignity through an injunction on the child to avoid external derogatory behaviour such as impatient or discourteous speech and instead *qul lahumā qawlan karīmā* (speak to them graciously). Simultaneously, the child is instructed: *wakhfiḍ lahumā janāḥa (ʻl)-dhdhulli mina (ʻl)-rraḥma* (lower to them the wing of humility out of mercy; see also Q.15:88 where the Prophet is instructed to 'lower his wing' to the believers), lowering themselves before the parent with a gentleness indicated by the image of the wing, thus recalibrating the parent–child relationship and restoring its balance. Two motivational prophetic examples are provided two suras on at Q.19:14 and Q.19:32 of the prophets John and Jesus being *barran* (dutiful) rather than insolent towards their parents.

The Qurʾan also evokes an internal emotional response in the parent–child relationship by promoting a cycle of merciful conduct. After being humble and showing mercy on the parents, the child is also instructed to invoke God's Divine mercy upon the parents through a specific prayer whose wording reminds the child of the parents' own merciful conduct towards the child, indicated through the comparative *kamā* (just as) which once again strikingly connects Divine mercy with the provision of parental care. The strategically located final word of Q.17:24 *ṣaghīrā* (little) transports the child temporally to its most vulnerable state when it was most dependant on parental care, maximising the emotional impact of the instructions and evoking the desired reciprocal response of *iḥsān*. The searching reference to Divine knowledge of what is in the hearts at Q.17:25 highlights the desired internalisation of this conciliatory conduct, the latter indicated through the description of earnest reformers of filial conduct as *ṣāliḥīn* (righteous, from the root *ṣ-l-ḥ*).

The conciliatory approach of demonstrating *iḥsān* towards parents, enjoined at Q.17:23, is based on human kinship and is not therefore restricted to believing parents, as presumed by Levy (1969, p.195, n.3). Levy cites Q.9:23 in support of his position, a late Medinan revelation which seems however, in context, a prohibition on maintaining personal alliances in opposition with communal loyalties during a conflict situation (see the discussion of Q.58:22 and Q.60:1–9 in Chapter 6 which supports this view). The general principle is actually presented at Q.31:15, like Q.17:23 a Meccan verse, in which the child is directly addressed, presenting a Divine resolution to a conflict of loyalties arising from the twin principles of monotheism enjoined at Q.31:13 and *iḥsān* on parents at Q.31:14. Even in a situation where the parents incite the child towards *shirk* (association with God), violating a fundamental Qur'anic prohibition and referred to in Q.31:13 as *ẓulmun aẓīm* (a terrible wrong, Abdel Haleem), the child is not entitled to cut off relations with the parents. On the contrary, the child is instructed to differentiate between the theological and the material worlds, obeying God in the former but crucially maintaining company with the parents in the latter: *wa ṣāḥibhumā fī ('l)-ddunya ma'rūfā* (yet keep their company in this life according to what is right, Abdel Haleem). To my mind, *ṣāḥib* here signifies quantity and *ma'rūfā* signifies quality in respect of their accompaniment, indicating a constancy of companionship which remains untainted by estrangement or conflict.

At Q.17:23 above, good speech was encountered in the context of the parental relationship of kin, also concurrent with the theme of *iḥsān*. Around this focal verse, the wider textual landscape of the central sura pair Q.16 and Q.17 demonstrates a concurrency of all three conciliation themes, as can be seen clearly by reference to the Conciliation Map at the end of Section 3.4. Affirming the remarkable 'compositional coherency' of the Qur'an, Saleh (2010, p.34) justifiably refers to its 'self-referencing nature, its constant cross-referencing of motifs and themes'. Dual concurrency of Conciliation themes was also featured in Q.12 above and in verses such as Q.16:90 discussed above. This dual concurrency feature will continue to manifest as we now turn to focus on good speech in more detail, firstly in relation to good speech in faith propagation at Q.14, Q.16, Q.17 and Q.19, and then in relation to a prohibition on defamatory speech at Q.24. The dual theme of *iḥsān* features again in the first topic and the dual theme of kinship is again pertinent to the teachings in Q.19 and Q.24.

3.3 Conflict Avoidance and the Etiquette of Good Speech

Conciliation themes in the Qur'an often demonstrate both a specific relevance in faith propagation and a general advancement of desirable conduct in social relations. This was apparent in the discussion of kinship in Section 3.2.1 and is again apparent in the now ensuing discussion of good speech. These two facets of good speech are addressed in Sections 3.3.1 and 3.3.2, respectively.

3.3.1 Good Speech in Faith Propagation

Immediately after Q.14:23 mentions that those who believe and *ʿamilu (ʻl)-ṣṣāliḥāt* (work righteousness, Yusuf Ali) will be entered into Paradise and greeted with *salām* (peace), Q.14:24 compares *kalimatan ṭayyibatan* (a good word) to *shajaratin ṭayyibatin* (a good tree). The phraseology of Q.14:24 is doubly supported by the use of the particle *ka* of *tashbīḥ* (simile) before *shajaratin ṭayyibatin*, and the word *mathalan* (example), which is grammatically *badl* (substitution) with *kalimatan ṭayyibatan* rather than the *iḍāfa* (possessive) construct used at Q.14:26 for a bad word. The strong comparison facilitates the mental transition of the audience from an apparently ephemeral and intangible concept, like speech, to a concrete image symbolic of longevity and growth. The symbolic value of the image is enhanced by specific mention of its firm roots, expansive branches and perpetual fruit. All of this serves to heighten the importance of good speech, with its sound basis and perpetual and far-reaching consequences, to its maximum effect.

In commenting on the image of the tree, Al-Rāzī considers its branches extending in both the Divine realm and the material world and explains each in turn, once again by reference to the two limbs of the fundamental notion from Prophetic tradition of *al-taʿẓīm li amri ʻllāhi taʿālā wa ʻl-shafaqa ʿalā khalqi ʻllāh*. According to Al-Rāzī, the love of God and what it entails is included in the former limb whilst human mercy, forgiveness, assistance and returning harm with *iḥsān* (gracious conduct) is included in the latter. The image of the tree is so fundamental to the sura that it also features in Iṣlāḥī's *ʿamūd* (central theme) in which he focusses on the establishment of the 'tree' of Islam in Mecca by the Prophet and the uprooting of polytheism. In this connection he also cites Abraham's initial migration to Mecca and his prayers for its establishment as a centre of monotheistic worship, both of which feature later in the sura at Q.14.35–41 in an apparent appeal to the Meccan disbelievers who traced their ancestry to Abraham.

As discussed in Section 3.2.1, prophetic duties to propagate faith hold a special significance in respect of kin. Abraham makes specific prayers, including seven appeals through the recurrent *rabb* (Lord), for the faith and worship of his offspring and then the forgiveness of his parents (Q.14:35, 40, 41). Abraham's efforts to divert his father from polytheism to monotheism are recounted further on in Group 3 at Q.19.41–50. Iṣlāḥī (vol.4, p.658) disagrees with the suggestion by some commentators that the individual addressed was Abraham's paternal uncle. Abraham's conciliatory dialogue is evident from his four-fold repetition of the address *yā abati* (O my father, Q.19:42–45), drawing attention to their proximate relationship by way of appeal – Iṣlāḥī (vol.4, p.658) refers to Abraham's *istimālat* (appeal). In contrast, his father distances him addressing him by name at Q.19:46 (for contrasting examples of filial endearment, see Q.12:5 and Q.31:13), threatening to stone him and banishing him from his sight. Al-Rāzī highlights that the contrast between Abraham's tone of endearment and gentleness, and the harshness of his father's rebuff, is presented to empathise with the Prophet's own experience with the polytheists of Mecca. He raises a similar point in his commentary of Q.11:50, as mentioned in Section 3.2.1.

Abraham's response (Q.19:47, 48) is one of *salām* (peace) and withdrawal (an apparent allusion to the Prophet's pending migration, as in the narrative of Joseph above), both manifest avoidances of conflict. I disagree with Iṣlāḥī's suggestion (vol.4, p.660) that Abraham's *salām* is a mere salutation indicating departure. I would argue that this is a significant formulaic indication of a non-confrontational response in the face of hostile speech: Q.25:63, which will be discussed in Chapter 4, proffers the ideal of a peaceful response of *salām* in the face of an 'aggressive' address (see Yusuf Ali's note to Q.25:63), in turn rewarded with a greeting of *salām* in Paradise (Q.25:75). In addition, verses Q.14: 23–24 above, whose arrangement is mirrored at Q.22:23–24, suggest that righteous deeds (from the root *ṣ-l-ḥ*) include good speech and are rewarded by *salām* in Paradise. Abraham's conciliatory approach in faith propagation and steadfast adherence to his belief serve as an illustrative exemplar for the Prophet and his followers, whose instruction is now discussed.

In Group 2, the Prophet and his followers were instructed at Q.6:108 to avoid abusing other deities worshipped by the polytheists to avoid retaliation, and at Q.7:199 to show forgiveness towards and disengage from their adversaries, rather than to retaliate. In Group 3, these teachings are developed into the notion of *iḥsān* through the use of appealing speech to propagate faith. After presenting the example of Abraham as constituting a role model at Q.16:120 and as being from the *ṣāliḥīn* at Q.16:122, Q.16:125 instructs the Prophet: *udʿu ilā sabīli rabbika bi ʾl-ḥikmati wa ʾl-mawʿiẓati ʾl-ḥasanati wa jādilhum billatī hiya aḥsan* ([Prophet], call [people] to the way of your Lord with wisdom and good teaching. Argue with them in the most courteous way, Abdel Haleem). Q.17:53 instructs the Prophet to enjoin his followers to behave in a similar way, persuasively enticing the believers to compliance by addressing them with the appealing term of endearment *ʿibādı* (my servants). After recounting the various contentions of the Meccan disbelievers, Q.17:53 regulates the believers' response, saying: *wa qul li ʿibādī yaqūlu ʾllatī hiya aḥsan* (tell My servants to say what is best, Abdel Haleem).

Al-Rāzī's discussion suggests that Q.16:125 refers to the use of *ḥikma*, which he interprets as definitive demonstrative proofs, in dealing with the intellectual elite, the use of *mawʿiẓati ʾl-ḥasana*, which he interprets as persuasive inductive rationale, in dealing with the masses, and *al-jadl al-aḥsan*, which he interprets as overwhelming argument distinguished from invitation, to deal with *al-mushāghibīn* (troublemakers). Al-Rāzī, therefore, in this verse but not in Q.17:53 below as we shall see, overlooks the important notion of the *manner* of debate focussing instead on content. Iṣlāḥī (vol.4, p.463), on the other hand, considers *ḥikma* as referring to the use of proofs and evidence and *mawʿiẓati ʾl-ḥasana* as referring to the use of a *mushfiqāna andāz* (gracious manner), the latter stressed to avoid any detrimental impact on the effectiveness of faith propagation. This interpretation encompasses both manner and content but appears to misplace these notions in the verse. In my view, *ḥikma* refers to a judicious approach customised to the addressee, *mawʿiẓati ʾl-ḥasana* refers to rationally appealing exhortation and *al-jadl al-aḥsan* refers to maintaining a courteous manner in the exchange of arguments. This is also consistent with the tone of Abdel Haleem's translation above.

Notably, it is the *manner* of the exchange rather than its content for which the elative form *aḥsan* (best) is reserved. Furthermore, it is I believe the same factor which is individually referenced and emphasised in the following sura by way of summary reminder at Q.17:53 using exactly the same formulation *allatī hiya aḥsan* (that which is best; see also Q.29:46 which provides the same exhortation in respect of the People of the Book and Q.3:64 discussed in Chapter 1). This view is supported by the immediately ensuing reference at Q.17:53 *inna (ʾl)-shshayṭāna yanzaghu baynahum* (Satan sows discord among them). The emphatic *inna*, the advancement of the subject in the sentence, and the continuing reference to Satan as man's open enemy casts all blame and malevolent sentiment arising from contentious debate onto Satan and disengages the participants from any enduring negative emotions in respect of each other. The same technique has been illustrated above by Joseph in Q.12. In Fazaluddin (2016, p.346), I identified such Externalisation as an important Conciliation ethic in the Qurʾan.

I would argue that the elative is reserved for the manner of debate for the essential reason that the manner of debate goes to the crux of the desired objective. As indicated by *udʿu* (invite) at Q.16:125, and *taʿālaw* (come) at Q.3:64, the Qurʾan endorses a conciliatory approach of unifying people of different faiths through rational discourse and courteous dialogue. For this reason, in addition to the quality of the arguments presented, it is imperative that the quality of the character displayed by the propagator of faith should be exemplary. In each of Q.3:64, above at Q.17:23 and here at Q.16:125, good speech performs an ennobling function in respect of the addressee which enhances the conciliatory appeal of the spoken words. A striking example is presented at Q.20:44 where Moses and Aaron are initially instructed to speak with *qawlan layyinan* (gentle speech) to address the transgression of Pharaoh and encourage him to take heed. Only after thus stressing the *manner* of speech and its desired effect in isolation is the content of the speech presented three verses later at Q.20:47.

At Q.17:53 Al-Rāzī, somewhat belatedly, focusses on the manner of debate – *al-ṭarīq al-aḥsan* (the best way), stressing *wa huwa an lā yakūna dhikr al-ḥujja makhlūṭan bi 'l-shatm wa 'l-sabb* (the presentation of the proof should not be tainted by (literally, co-mingled with) insult and abuse). Such insult, contrary to Q.6:108, he points out would result in *yazdād al-ghaḍab wa tatakāmal al-nafra wa yamtaniʿ ḥuṣūl al-maqṣūd* (anger is increased, aversion is completed and the attainment of the objective is obstructed). The converse, presentation of the argument *bi 'l-ṭarīq al-aḥsan* without insult or abuse, he elaborates further, would *athara fī 'l-qalb taʾthīran shadīdan* (influence the heart with great (persuasive) effect) – the formulation is highly emphatic including both the cognate accusative construct to emphasise the verb *athara* and the highly expressive adjective *shadīdan*. Iṣlāḥī (vol.4, p.463) also highlights the apparent Qurʾanic concern at impeding effective faith propagation through confrontational speech. It is clear that a conciliatory approach in religious dialogue, denoted by the term *aḥsan*, is absolutely integral to the Qurʾan's core objective and is intended to appeal to the listener's heart. As highlighted above, such internal change is an essential part of Conciliation.

Immediately subsequent to Q.16:125 discussed above, verses Q.16:126–127 caution against excessive retribution, limiting any such conduct to the extent of injury and immediately continuing *wa laʾin ṣabartum lahuwa khayrun lil-ṣṣābirīn – wa 'ṣbir . . .* (but if you are patient, that is indeed best for those who are patient – be patient . . .). A progressively higher standard is enjoined here, beginning with the minimum standard of just retribution, then moving to the level of preferring and recommending *iḥsān* through *ṣabr* (patience) as an alternative in principle, and finally *commanding* the Prophet himself to be patient and cleanse his heart of distress regarding the Meccan disbelievers' conduct, by implication avoiding retribution and response to provocation entirely. Although Abdel Haleem translates Q.16:126 in terms of 'respond(ing) to an attack', in my view, the context of Q.16:125 indicates that Q.16:126 relates to showing patience rather than retaliating against verbal abuse (see Q.20:130 for a similar example). The principle of just retribution is reiterated further on at Q.22:60, however, where Abdel Haleem's above interpretation seems more appropriate.

The entire enjoinder of effective and courteous speech and patience ends with a strategically located final reference at Q.16:128, fittingly concluding Q.16, a sura with numerous references to patience and *iḥsān*, on the word *muḥsinūn* (righteous people) who are assured of God's proximity to them. Extraordinarily in my view for a commentary which is ostensibly based on a coherent development of Qur'anic themes, Iṣlāḥī (vol.4, p.465), as he does at Q.12:90 in Section 3.1, again interprets this reference to *muḥsinūn* as a reference to those who worship God as if they behold him, alluding once more to the Prophetic narration mentioned above defining *iḥsān* in the context of worship. I would argue that this one-dimensional approach entirely misdirects the point of the narrative, which is to motivate the Prophet and the Meccan believers towards patience and *iḥsān* in their social conduct and particularly good speech in dealing with the contentions of the disbelievers, as enjoined at Q.16:125–127. The reference to *taqwā* in Q.16:128 is in accordance with the similar reference preceding Q.3:134 which also promotes *iḥsān* towards people, in that case by promising God's love. As mentioned above, Al-Rāzī's explanation of *iḥsān* has two limbs, one relating to honouring God's command and the second relating to compassion towards creation. At Q.16:128, Al-Rāzī's commentary expressly states that the reference to *taqwā* refers to the former, whilst the reference to *muḥsinūn* refers to the latter. This accords with my view which is both based on a contextual reading and produces a coherent result.

Section 3.3.1 above deals with the notion of effective speech in faith propagation and the avoidance of conflict in religious debate. In the following section, we will deal with another aspect of the regulation of speech in the Qur'an, namely a prohibition on the spreading of defamatory rumours, this time in a general social context, to avoid conflict arising from perceived insult to reputation and retaliatory response, specifically a severance of ties of kin and consequent financial assistance. This is dealt with in Q.24, a Medinan sura in contrast to the majority of Group 3 suras which are Meccan.

3.3.2 Prohibition on Defamatory Speech

The segment Q.24:1–34 deals with issues relating to chastity, defamatory speech and social etiquette, whilst verses Q.24:35–40 provide supportive inspirational colour. Q.24:11 refers expressly to an incident regarding an accusation against ʿĀʾisha, the wife of the Prophet and the daughter of his close companion Abū Bakr, which is referred to as *ifk* (slander) and is considered the instigating event resulting in the surrounding revelation. It is quite apparent that the spreading of rumours, particularly relating to chastity and involving close familial relations, would prove a highly contentious issue. What is remarkable, however, is the intervention of the Qurʾan, characterised as sublime revelation, to provide conciliatory instruction even in such ostensibly mundane domestic issues, and with such intensity and expansiveness as will now be explained.

From the outset, Q.24:1 emphasises that the entire sura's purpose is to stipulate mandatory obligations through the term *faraḍnāhā* (we have mandated it). After this, the *ḥadd* (mandatory penal sanction) for adultery is closely followed by an almost equivalently severe penalty (at Q.24:4) for those who falsely accuse chaste women without producing *four* witnesses. An additional penalty is imposed by rendering their future testimony perpetually inadmissible, branding them *fāsiqūn* (wicked transgressors, Yusuf Ali; lawbreakers, Abdel Haleem) and encouraging them to *aṣlaḥū* (reform, Q.24:5). The conduct of false accusation is reviled both through the implicitly distasteful notion of 'pelting' in the word *yarmūna* (accuse, Q.24:4, 23) and through the explicit references to *ifk* (lie) at Q.24:11 and 12, *kādhibūn* (liars) at Q.24:13 and *buhtān* (slander) at Q.24:16. The passage contains five verses, Q.24:11, 14, 15, 16, 23 with terminal instances of the word *ʿaẓīm* (great), which emphasise the perceived magnitude of the conduct in question. Three of these are in successive verses and three of them, Q.24:11, 14, 23 are paired with the word *ʿadhāb* (punishment) threatening retributive sanction (Q.24:19 also threatens severe punishment and Q.24:23 refers to being 'cursed').

Reliance upon and circulation of unverified information is castigated throughout the passage which refers to *ẓann* (supposition, Q.24:12) falling short of *ʿilm* (knowledge, Q.24:15). After providing a specific procedure to resolve situations involving accusations of matrimonial infidelity between spouses at Q.24:6–9, at Q.24:12 a pointed reference to male and female believers rails upon the accused participants in the circulation of the slander to effectively demonstrate their faith and unity by thinking well of their own people. The recurrent formulation *law lā* (why . . . not?) is used at Q.24:12, 13 and 16 to insist on the presumption of innocence, in the absence of evidence meeting the stipulated standard of proof, and the denouncement of unverified slanderous rumour. The entire admonition climaxes with progressive intensity at Q.24:17: *yaʿiẓukumu ʾllāhu an taʿūdū limithlihī abadan in kuntum muʾminīn* (God warns you never to do anything like this again, if you are true believers, Abdel Haleem).

In spite of the emotionally charged human context coupled with the literary intensity of the scriptural text, a strong conciliatory framework and outcome emerges. The accusers and the participants in circulation have been variously put to proof and chastised above to prevent recurrence. The aggrieved party is also instructed at Q.24:22 not to swear against offering financial assistance to relatives and those in need (an apparent reference to Abū Bakr's orphan nephew Misṭaḥ who Abū Bakr had sworn to cease supporting financially) in retaliation for their participation in circulating the slander, rather: *wa l-yaʿfū wa l-yaṣfaḥū* (let them pardon and forgive, Abdel Haleem). The exhortation to forgive is motivationally rendered irresistible to the earnest believer by the immediately subsequent *alā tuḥibbūna an yyaghfira 'llāhu lakum* (do you not wish that God should forgive you? Abdel Haleem), reinforced by the terminal exemplary reference in the verse to God being Most Forgiving and Merciful. The cycle of contention is broken by Divine censure of the offensive conduct, a restriction on retaliation and a motivational offer of Divine *iḥsān* to appease the aggrieved party.

The Qurʾanic annulment of Abū Bakr's oath indicates the overriding importance of Conciliation (see also Q.2:224), given the usual importance given to the fulfilment of promises (see for example Q.5:1). Al-Rāzī's commentary provides a number of elucidatory Prophetic narrations which to me collectively demonstrate an injunction towards *iḥsān* and a restoration of mandatory rights of kinship. The first narration emphasises the value placed on providing benefit to others, declaring *khayrun nās man yanfaʿun nās* (the best of people is he who benefits the people). Spending on others is also the first limb of the 'definition' of *iḥsān* at Q.3:134 and a matter emphasised in the rights of relatives in particular.

The second is a Prophetic narration declaring upon return from battle *rajaʿnā min al-jihād al-aṣghar ila 'l-jihād al-akbar* (we have returned from the lesser struggle towards the greater struggle). This is adduced by Al-Rāzī to highlight the severity of the *internal struggle* faced by Abū Bakr in being told to revert to his former benevolence after being hurt by the betrayal of his own relative. Controlling anger is the second limb of the 'definition' of *iḥsān* at Q.3:134 and severance of ties of kin is also prohibited as argued in Section 3.2. The third narration highlights the value of forgiveness stating *afḍalu akhlāqi 'l-muslimīn al-ʿafw* (the greatest of character traits in Muslims is forgiveness). This is the third limb of the 'definition' of *iḥsān* at Q.3:134 and completes the erasure of lingering resentment and the restoration of good relations. The above teachings also align with the notions of justice, *iḥsān* and generosity towards relatives enjoined in the fundamental teachings at Q.16:90.

The above narrative is punctuated throughout by the recurrent refrain *wa law lā faḍlu 'llāhi ʿalaykum wa raḥmatuhū* (if it were not for God's bounty and mercy towards you, Abdel Haleem, see Q.24:10, 14, 20, 21) on occasion coupled with other Divine qualities indicating mercy. As well as indicating respite from punishment, these references serve to emphasise the educational benefit provided through the above teachings. Divine qualities of knowledge and wisdom are highlighted at Q.24:10, 18, 19 and 21 indicating the imparting of knowledge, also indicated by the references to Divine clarification at Q.24:1, 18 and 25. Pitted against this Divine illuminating knowledge is the calling of Satan, the phrase *khuṭuwāti ('l)-shshayṭān* (Satan's footsteps) alluding to the path of deviation from the 'straight path' of Qur'anic guidance, in this case the instigation and promotion of slander leading to conflict, severance of ties and resentment. References to indecency and evil at Q.24:21 (see also Q.24:19) enjoined by Satan are reminiscent of the matters prohibited by God at Q.16:90 and focus attention on the opposing forces apparently at work (see the discussion of Q.15:47 above in Section 3.2.2.). The entire scriptural passage of educational elucidation is elevated to sublime status, emphasising its illuminating Divine guidance, by its collocation with the immediately subsequent *Āyat Al-Nūr* (the Light Verse) – Q.24:35.

This ends the individual examination of the three Conciliation themes of this chapter, which have demonstrated significant overlap and inter-relationship, and a pervasive recurrence of *iḥsān*. As indicated at the opening of the chapter, the full significance of this sustained engagement with the notion of *iḥsān* as a means to Conciliation, also coupled with an insistence on the upholding of ties of kinship, will come to light in the next section which considers the Qur'anic material in its historical context.

3.4 *Iḥsān*, Kinship and Prophetic Reconciliation at the Conquest of Mecca

It has been demonstrated above that *iḥsān*, in both conduct and speech, and kinship are key Conciliation themes in Group 3. They feature both in the contexts of faith propagation and in the general social context and are often interlinked. To understand the full significance of these themes, it is necessary to reflect on the historical circumstances of the Prophet's experiences during this period of revelation. As Cragg (2001, p.2) remarks, the Prophet's persona is paramount in the Qur'an: 'he is everywhere the immediate agency whereby the text supervenes on the situation in which everywhere he is crucial to its incidence.' We have already seen in this chapter that the Prophet is frequently directly addressed in the Qur'an, often at the end of suras, providing a personal instructive epilogue by reference to the ostensibly universal preceding material. More specifically, as mentioned in the initial Overview section of this chapter, the Prophet was subjected to a two-year social boycott of his clan resulting in significant hardship. This was a remarkable departure from the usual tribal loyalty of the Arabs and the Qur'an goes to some lengths to highlight that the mutual kinship of the Prophet, the Meccan believers and the Meccan disbelievers should have been a basis for unity rather than division.

In the face of protracted persecution, the Prophet is repeatedly taught to respond with *iḥsān*. Even Draz (2000, p.130) who argues, apparently addressing the issue of authorship of the Qur'an, that the Qur'an mostly bypasses the Prophet and treats him as a 'total abstraction', acknowledges that 'as soon as his life is concerned with a matter of moral conduct, we see him in the grip of its legislative authority'. At Q.20:114, the Prophet is commanded to pray for an increase in his knowledge, demonstrating the emphasis on his ongoing education. Q.12:102 highlights the Divine revelation to the Prophet of events previously unknown to him and beyond his experience (see also Q.4:113 which refers to the Prophet being taught what he did not know, by God's grace). The *iḥsān* of Joseph here and the good speech and forbearance of Abraham elsewhere are both presented to him as prophetic exemplars.

In addition to the recurrent exhortation to patience often found at the end of suras highlighted earlier, at Q.23:96 – towards the end of Group 3 – the Prophet is specifically instructed: *idfaʿ bi 'llatī hiya aḥsanu ('l)-ssayyiʾa* (repel evil with good, Abdel Haleem) with a consoling reference to God's full knowledge of the conduct of the Meccan disbelievers. Shortly after mentioning that the earth will be inherited by the *ṣāliḥūn* (righteous, Q.21:105), the Prophet is also reminded at Q.21:107 of the conciliatory capacity in which he was sent: *wa mā arsalnāka illā raḥmatan lil-ʿālamīn* (We sent you only as a mercy to all people, Abdel Haleem). The grammatical construct *wa mā . . . illā* here provides a total restriction on all conflict and retribution, which is contrary to mercy. The direct address to the Prophet here indicates that this emphasis on his merciful character is highlighted for his own reflection and development, and not merely to highlight this mercy as a Divine favour for the appreciation of others (cf. Q.3:164).

The development of a conciliatory disposition by the Prophet appears to be at the forefront of his Qur'anic instruction. Iṣlāḥī (vol.4, p.9) stresses the importance of good character in faith as a central theme of Q.23 and Q.24, later highlighting at Q.23:97–98 (vol.5, p.346) that after the injunction towards *iḥsān* at Q.23:96, the Prophet is instructed to pray for Divine sanctuary from the prompting of 'devils' and their *beheth, jidāl, sharr and fasād* (disputation, confrontation, evil and corruption). At Q.21:107, Al-Rāzī refers to Q.68:4 which emphasises the Prophet's 'exalted standard of character' (Yusuf Ali) and quotes a narration from the Prophet saying he was sent as a mercy not as a punishment, drawing attention to his avoidance of personal or invoked retribution. Moral excellence appears to have been a defining characteristic of the Prophet to the early Muslims to such an extent that being foremost in its emulation was considered an indication of seniority in the receipt of state stipends and in inheriting his leadership (Asfaruddin, 2010, pp.182–85, 196–97).

At first consideration, such enjoinders to mercy seem somewhat theoretical. The Prophet and his few followers were in any case relatively ill-equipped to provide an equal retaliatory response in the face of persecution by the influential Meccan chieftains. Close analysis, however, reveals that this training provided to the Prophet by the Qur'an was intended to prepare him for a long-term engagement. Abu-Nimer (2003, pp.9, 14, 17) has long been an advocate for a training approach to Conciliation in resolving long-running, deep-seated communal conflicts. He considers this approach more effective in proactively preventing conflict and achieving long-term conciliatory attitudes. The exemplary story of Joseph details to the Prophet not only Joseph's patience during his initial trials and tribulations but also his demonstration of *iḥsān* towards his offending kin at the pinnacle of his own power. Some 10 years after the period leading up to the Prophet's migration to Medina, during the Conquest of Mecca in 8 A.H., the Prophet would find the tables turned in a similar fashion to Joseph's experience, elevating him to a position of power and strength over the Meccans as his overwhelming and largely unopposed army entered the city.

Al-Rāzī's commentary of Q.12:92 includes a narration that the Prophet grasped the two jambs of the door of the Kaʿba on the day of the Conquest and addressed his tribe, the Quraysh, asking how they expected him to deal with them. He continues that they responded *naẓunnu khayran akhun karīmun wa 'bnu akhin karīmin* (we suppose beneficence, generous brother and son of a generous brother; Al-Mawrid lists both beneficence and *iḥsān* for the meaning of doing *khayr*, the term *karīm* is also referenced by Iṣlāḥī to explain *iḥsān* at Q.16:90 above). The Prophet is said to have replied, "I say what my brother Joseph said: 'there is no reproach upon you this day.'"

The response of Quraysh signals a clear appeal to mutual kinship and the reciprocation of harm with goodness. The repetition of the term 'brother' is evocative of direct kinship and is repeated across two generations to indicate additional proximity. There is profound irony in such an appeal for the Prophet to uphold kinship from those apparently responsible for the social boycott of his clan in opposition to the universal principle of maintaining kinship, also specifically sacred to the Arabs. The term *karīm* signifies their expectation of a magnanimity that could look beyond this irony and the injustice of the protracted Meccan era of persecution.

According to Tolan (2010, pp.245, 249), accounts of the Prophet in European history have included a significant period which portrayed him as conciliatory or 'irenic', but have also often been polarised between either considering him an 'embodiment of error or a symbol of religious freedom and tolerance', reflecting the polemical agendas of the writers and the historical circumstances of their times. Yet the persistent Qurʾanic instruction towards the upholding of ties of kin and *iḥsān* does appear ultimately to have culminated in a 'genuine reconciliation' with the leading Meccans, described by Watt as one of the Prophet's 'greatest achievements' (1961, p.210).

Summary Table: Group 3 Conciliation Themes Map by Sura and Verse

	Conflict resolution and *Iḥsān*	Conciliation and relations of kin	Good speech and conflict avoidance
Q.3	134 *iḥsān:* spending, restraint and forgiveness		
Q.4	(36 includes reference to *iḥsān*)	1 universal kinship 36 *iḥsān* on parents and relatives	
Q.10	26 Divine reciprocation of *iḥsān*		
Q.11		50, 61, 84 prophets brothers of their nations	
Q.12	22, 36, 56, 78, 90 Joseph is amongst the *muḥsinīn*	5, 100 jealousy of brothers attributed to Satan 92 Joseph: no vengeance against brothers	
Q.13		21 Divine command to join ties of kinship	
Q.14			24 good speech compared to a good tree
Q.15		47 brotherly relations in Paradise	
Q.16	(125 includes reference to *iḥsān*)	90 Divine command to help relatives	125 religious discourse to be rational and courteous
Q.17	(23, 53 include reference to *iḥsān*)	23 rights of parents 26 rights of relatives	53 good speech cf. Satan's incitement

(continued)

	Conflict resolution and *Iḥsān*	Conciliation and relations of kin	Good speech and conflict avoidance
Q.18			
Q.19		14, 32 prophets show *birr* in respect of parents	47 Abraham's *salām* in response to father's hostility
Q.20		94 Moses and Aaron's fraternal relationship	44 gentle words to Pharaoh
Q.21	107 Prophetic exemplar: mercy for the worlds		
Q.22			
Q.23	96 respond with *iḥsān*		
Q.24		22 provision for relatives to be maintained, forgive, link to Divine forgiveness	17 prohibition on defamation 35 Divine guidance and light

Conclusion

Conciliation pervades Group 3, which is predominantly Meccan, primarily through the central notion of *iḥsān* as a means of conflict resolution. *Iḥsān* also features in the contexts of good relations with kin and good speech, which also demonstrate important Conciliation themes in their own right. Through the relatively robust wider Qurʾanic narrative of the punishment of heedless past nations runs a conciliatory core message of conflict resolution based on the above three Conciliation themes, whose consistent and unyielding focus is to train the Prophet, and by emulation his followers, to reflect a merciful and non-retributional character. This sustained focus on good character, centred on the Prophetic persona, reflects a proactive long-term approach which, according to Islamic and some Western sources, ultimately culminated in an otherwise unforeseeable epic reconciliation with significant repercussions, at the Conquest of Mecca. The Qurʾanic portrayal of the Prophet as an embodiment of merciful character is uniquely essential to the plausibility of this historical narrative.

The range of aspects of Conciliation is again extended in this chapter. The secondary engagement with personal character in Chapters 1 and 2, which dealt respectively with a social legislative framework and the regulation of engagement and conflict, burgeons in this chapter into a sustained engagement with the development of a conciliatory character demanding internal personal development. This emphasis is manifest both in the context of faith propagation and leadership and in wider social relations, and indicates a gradual transition from reform at the societal macro-level in Groups 1 and 2 to reform at the individual micro-level in Group 3. In this chapter, we see a clear distinction between Conciliation and justice, with Conciliation going beyond justice and retribution to the more elevated notion of *iḥsān*, or gracious conduct. Conceptually, such *iḥsān* aims to interrupt a vicious cycle of negative response and conflict escalation, containing disputes and facilitating Conciliation through a virtuous cycle of gratuitous benefit, anger-management, forgiveness and non-retribution. Linguistically, references to *iḥsān*, and some other forms of conciliatory behaviour, are often collocated with *ṣāliḥīn* (the righteous) or the performance of *ṣāliḥāt* (righteous deeds), also providing linguistic cohesion between the notion of *iḥsān*, Conciliation and the root *ṣ-l-ḥ*.

This chapter contains a number of literary techniques used to emphasise and promote Conciliation. The narratives of Joseph and Abraham, brought to life through the dramatic use of dialogue, provide exemplary role models of conciliatory conduct for the Prophet and his nation, who are often directly addressed strategically at the end of suras. The recurrent integrated presentation of Divine–human duties and social duties, coupled with legislative language, and in one case the overriding of an oath against assisting kin, add gravitas and impact to the fundamental message of non-severance of ties of human kinship. This serves to admonish the Meccan disbelievers who had severed ties of kinship with the Prophet and his followers against their own sacred values, and also to proactively remind the Prophet and his followers not to respond in kind. Terms of address in the Qurʾanic voice and prophetic dialogue are used to make conciliatory appeals to proximate relations of human kinship. Satan is targeted as the recurrent instigator of conflict, channelling enmity towards his persona and externalising it from the participants in social relations. Finally, the image of the good word as a good tree in Q.14 and verses such as the Light Verse at Q.24:35 provide sublime elevation and impact to the exhortation towards Conciliation and good speech.

Coherence in this chapter is structurally less obvious than the sequential progression of themes in Chapter 2, but the tapestry of interwoven Conciliation themes in this chapter is cohesively linked by the recurrent notion of *iḥsān*. The frequency of this *takrār* (emphatic repetition) is remarkable and provides a sense of unrelenting insistence on the display of such behaviour by the Prophet under Divine command, and his followers by emulation of the Prophetic example.

The parallel concurrence of Conciliation themes also portrays a coherent interrelationship whose significance is finally revealed on the canvas of the history of the Conquest of Mecca. A notable confluence of the three Conciliation themes of the chapter features in the central sura of the Group, Q.17, highlighting a significant parallel between dutiful filial conduct towards nurturing parents, and dutiful human conduct towards a beneficent Lord.

The two commentaries of Al-Rāzī and Iṣlāḥī provide elucidating analysis of the notion of *iḥsān* and concur in particular on the fundamental importance given in the Qurʾan to maintaining relations of kin. Al-Rāzī's definition of *iḥsān*, *al-taʿẓīm li amri 'llāhi taʿālā wa 'l-shafaqa ʿalā khalqi 'llāh* (honouring the command of God the Exalted and compassion towards God's creation), crucially identifies *two* branches of *iḥsān*, one dealing with Divine–human relations and the other with social relations. Iṣlāḥī designates a number of key Conciliation verses in several suras as an *ʿamūd* (central sura theme), demonstrating the central importance of the notion of Conciliation in the sura group. This is also supported by the Qurʾan's dedication of the entirety or large sections of suras, such as Q.12 and Q.24, to the fulsome elaboration of Conciliation themes. Iṣlāḥī's sura pairing also demonstrates some strong coherent links, such as Q.12–13 and Q.16–17 in particular. Surprisingly, it is Iṣlāḥī's purportedly coherence-based commentary which I consider displays a fatal flaw, fallaciously misdirecting two important references enjoining *iḥsān* in social relations, towards the display of *iḥsān* in worship. Further analysis on the significant and recurrent notion of *iḥsān* will follow in the next chapter, and beyond.

4 Conciliation Models and Conciliatory Appeal

Overview: Group 4 Suras – Q.25–Q.33

In Group 4, a cluster of Meccan suras (Q.25 Sūrat Al-Furqān, Q.26 Sūrat Al-Shuʿarāʾ, Q.27 Sūrat Al-Naml, Q.28 Sūrat Al-Qaṣaṣ, Q.29 Sūrat Al-ʿAnkabūt, Q.30 Al-Rūm, Q.31 Sūrat Luqmān, Q.32 Sūrat Al-Sajda) is followed by a single Medinan sura (Q.33 Sūrat Al-Aḥzāb). The Meccan suras predominantly present arguments advocating the Unity of God, admonish the Meccan disbelievers by denouncing past disbelieving nations and motivate the Meccan believers to remain steadfast in the face of the disbelievers' opposition. Sūrat Al-Aḥzāb also reflects the latter situation in a Medinan context as the Muslim community is besieged by their allied opponents' armies. The same sura also focusses on the persona and status of the Prophet. The Prophet is positioned as a pre-eminent, binding figure in the diverse new Medinan community, providing him with a platform for exemplifying and effecting Conciliation. This aspect was discussed in Chapter 2 where it was relevant to the discussion of the Prophetic exemplar and will therefore not be discussed in this chapter.

In the Farāhī-Iṣlāḥī schema, the theme of Group 4 is proof of the veracity of Prophethood. The suras are paired Q.25–Q.26, Q.27–Q.28, Q.29–Q.30, Q.31–Q.32 – all centred around the theme of promised help and victory to the believers, with Q.33 serving as a concluding appendix to the group and centred on the importance of the believers' loyalty to the Prophet. Group 4 is a relatively shorter group of suras within Iṣlāḥī's seven-group schema, spanning just over 3 of the 30 parts of the Qur'an.

Conciliation is an important but relatively understated notion in Group 4, as compared to its preceding Group 3 in particular. Explicit references to Conciliation are less numerous and this is only partly explained by Group 4's significantly shorter length, being less than half the length of Group 3. Furthermore, the conciliatory response of *iḥsān* (gracious conduct) in the face of persecution and confrontation, foregrounded and elucidated at length in Group 3, is now relegated to a secondary theme. Nonetheless, the sustained recurrence of the notion of *iḥsān* across Groups 3 and 4, as a means of containing conflict, is significant. With close study, the three sections of the chapter do demonstrate a sustained focus on Conciliation.

In Section 4.1, the notion of *iḥsān* is augmented by several inspirational pericopes which portray various models of conciliatory conduct advocated by the Qur'an: the *ʿIbād Al-Raḥmān* (the Servants of the Lord of Mercy), certain People of the Book, the sage Luqmān and the story of Moses' conciliatory

https://doi.org/10.1515/9783110747348-006

attitude against Pharaoh's oppressive and socially divisive governance, which constitutes *fasād* (disorder). In Section 4.2, another Conciliation theme, whose significance was introduced previously in Chapter 2, assumes a primary status: the sustained use of rational argument by the Qur'an to persuade its audience. This theme is contextually important in explaining the wider Conciliation narrative of the Qur'anic discourse, evidencing the Qur'an's insistence on persuasion and Conciliation rather than compulsion and conflict. Finally, Section 4.3 examines the richness of the modes of appeal utilised, from the personal to the universal and the temporal to the eschatological. The important notion of man's *fiṭra* (natural disposition) is discussed, together with man's ability to make 'free' choices which result in eschatological punishment and reward based on binding obligations.

Key Conciliation verses examined in the first section of this chapter include the exemplary models of God's special servants at Q.25:63–76 and certain People of the Book at Q.28:52–55, Luqmān's wisdom at Q.31:12–17, the significance of the story of Moses at Q.28:4–6, 14 and 44 and the enjoinder towards migration at Q.29:56. In the second section, an exposition of Divine arguments from natural phenomena and historical narratives references Q.25:1–61, Q.26:10–189, Q.27:7–66 and Q.30:11–27. The final section analyses the sense of individual and communal appeal invoked by Q.30:30 and Q.31:12, respectively, and the notion of man's culpability at Q.32:12–22 and Q.33:7.

A discussion of the above-mentioned Conciliation Models now begins with the *'Ibād Al-Raḥmān.*

4.1 Conciliation Models

4.1.1 *'Ibād Al-Raḥmān* (The Servants of the Lord of Mercy)

At the opening of the Group 4 suras, the segment Q.25:1–62 presents a sustained engagement with the Meccan disbelievers' arguments for denigrating the Prophet and his message. The Prophet is accused by his opponents of fabricating revelation (Q.25:4) and being bewitched (Q.25:8), and apparently subjected to ridicule (Q.25:41). In these circumstances, Q.25:20 challenges the Prophet and his followers to remain patient and steadfast: *ataṣbirūn* (will you stand fast?, Abdel Haleem). An aspirational model of conciliatory conduct is presented to the believers in an arresting pericope, highlighted by its strategic situation at the conclusion of the sura, defining at some length the characteristics of the *'Ibād Al-Raḥmān* (the Servants of the Lord of Mercy, Abdel Haleem, Q.25:63). These characteristics are both fundamental and integral to the sura according to Johns (2000, p.218) who states that they 'summate the ethical principles of Islam' and 'realize and give specificity to [the sura's] moral and ethical implication by a variety of devices'.

The coining of a specific and unique title, *'Ibād Al-Raḥmān*, at this juncture both memorably identifies and elevates this passage and the individuals described within it. The use of the Divine name *Al-Raḥmān* (the Lord of Mercy) positively re-asserts the Divine name incredulously repudiated by the disbelievers at Q.25:60 immediately above: *wa ma ('l)-Raḥmān* (what is the Lord of Mercy?, Abdel Haleem). The *iḍāfa* (possessive) construct of the title *'Ibād Al-Raḥmān* also creates a binding proximity between God and His servants, adding a sense of Divine endorsement of their conduct. Q.25:63 to Q.25:76 enumerate the characteristics of the *'Ibād Al-Raḥmān* as: walking humbly on earth and responding to the ignorant by saying *salām* (peace); worshipping at night; praying for the aversion of Hell's torment; spending moderately; abstaining from polytheism, unlawful killing and adultery; not bearing false witness and passing by frivolous talk with dignity; not being heedless of their Lord's signs; and praying for their families to set a good example for others.

This extensive descriptive list dedicates 14 continuous verses, including no less than 8 emphatic recurrences of the *ism al-mawṣūl* (relative pronoun), to the elaboration of a single notion, the *'Ibād Al-Raḥmān*. For comparison, the introductory definition of the fundamental notion of the *muttaqīn* (pious) at Q.2:2–5 spans only four verses and includes merely two instances of the relative pronoun. Even the more extensive definition of the eponymous 'believers' in Q.23 spans only 11 verses and includes 7 recurrences of the relative pronoun. The remarkable weight given to the description at Q.25:63 to Q.25:76 serves both to ennoble those described as *'Ibād Al-Raḥmān* and to hold them out as role models for others, as alluded to by their own concluding prayer in which they ask to be at the forefront of the *muttaqīn*.

At Q.25:63, the leading characteristic of the above definitional list is given: *alladhīna yamshūna 'ala 'l-arḍi hawnan* (those who walk humbly on the earth, Abdel Haleem). The inclusion of this already leading quality in the only verse which explicitly mentions the *'Ibād Al-Raḥmān* gives it further prominence and merits special focus. Al-Rāzī defines the noun *al-hawn*, from which the adverb or *ḥāl* (state) *hawnan* is derived, as meaning *al-rifq wa 'l-līn* (gentleness and leniency). This conciliatory characteristic can be seen to be semantically linked to *iḥsān* (gracious conduct), discussed in Chapter 3, and is also reminiscent of the terminology of Q.3:159, discussed in Chapter 2, which commends the Prophet as lenient, enjoining him to show forgiveness. One narration cited by Al-Rāzī also elucidates the meaning of *hawnan* as not desiring *fasād* (disorder) on the earth, another conflict management concept discussed in Chapter 2.

Q.25:63 continues *wa idhā khāṭabahumu 'l jāhilūna qālū salāmā* (and when the ignorant address them, they reply 'peace'). As discussed in Chapter 3, such references to *salām* signal non-requital and non-escalation of hostility initiated by another (for example at Q.43:89, the Prophet is instructed to forgive those who contend with him and say *salām*). The external vocalisation of the conciliatory prayer of *salām*, indicated by *qālū* (they say), evidences an absence of internal rancour and malice, as well as an active response to de-escalate tension. Al-Rāzī suggests that the earlier reference to walking on the earth *hawnan* means *tark al-iydhā'* (refraining from harming (others)) whilst the ensuing reference to responding to the ignorant with *salām* indicates *taḥammul al-ta'adhdhā* (tolerance of harm suffered). This interpretation suggests a bilateral regulation of conflict, both initiation and response, to both prevent and control conflict situations. The ideal Qur'anic model of such conduct is presented by Abraham at Q.19:46–49, discussed in Chapter 3, where Abraham responds to his father's banishment of Abraham and his father's threat to stone him by responding with *salām* and a declaration of his departure: *wa a'tazilukum* (I will leave you, Q.19:48). Abraham's declaration of departure also signals disengagement, another important conciliatory response.

The ensuing verse, Q.25:64, highlights another aspect of the *'Ibād Al-Raḥmān*'s conciliatory conduct, namely their spending of the night in prayer: *wa 'lladhīna yabītūna li rabbihim sujjadan wa qiyāmā* (those who spend the night bowed down or standing, worshipping their Lord, Abdel Haleem). This indicates a balanced focus on harmonious social relations, usually effected by day, and on harmonious Divine–human relations by night, a point highlighted in Al-Rāzī's commentary. The reference to God as creator of the night and day shortly before at Q.25:62 adds a sense of dutifulness to the *'Ibād Al-Raḥmān*'s obedience to the Divine will during both periods of time. The complementary reference to the activities of the day and night also indicates perpetual conciliatory conduct, whilst the complementary focus on both social (see Q.25:63, 67–68, 72) and Divine–human relations (see Q.25:64–65, 68, 73–74) indicates the *'Ibād Al-Raḥmān*'s holistic conciliatory attitude.

A further reference at Q.25:72 provides elaboration of the harmonious social conduct indicated above: *wa idhā marrū bi 'l-laghwi marrū kirāmā* (when they see some frivolity, pass by with dignity, Abdel Haleem). The repetition of *marrū* (pass by) adds emphasis to the *'Ibād Al-Raḥmān*'s withdrawal and non-engagement in confrontation even when subjected to provocation: Al-Rāzī suggests that *marrū kirāmā* refers to disengagement from and non-participation in polytheism, frivolity regarding the Qur'an or abuse of the Prophet. Both the opening and near to closing qualities of the *'Ibād Al-Raḥmān*'s portrayal at Q.25:63 and Q.25:72 thus laud their exercising of restraint in the face of opposition and their avoidance of disputation and conflict.

The twin themes of Social Conciliation and Divine–Human Conciliation alternating throughout the description of the *ʿIbād Al-Raḥmān* are terminally conjoined near the end of Q.25 at Q.25:75, as those whose leading quality is responding to the contentions of the 'ignorant' with ***salām*** are themselves welcomed into Paradise *taḥiyyatan wa* ***salāmā*** (with greetings and peace, Abdel Haleem). A remarkable and subtle antithesis also highlights the eschatological elevation of those who have been steadfast in their temporal humility walking on the earth ***hawnan*** (**humbly**): *ulāʾika yujzawna* ***'l-ghurfata*** *bimā ṣabarū* (these servants will be rewarded with the ***highest place*** in Paradise for their steadfastness, Abdel Haleem). In light of the preceding context at Q.25:1–62, it can be seen that the concluding pericope defining the *ʿIbād Al-Raḥmān* from Q.25:63–77 is intended to serve simultaneously as a concluding reproach, implicitly highlighting the Meccan disbelievers' own contrasting social and theological failures and contentions, and as an inspirational motivation for the Prophet and his followers to remain firm in their faith whilst emulating the conciliatory conduct modelled by the *ʿIbād Al-Raḥmān.*

The description of the *ʿIbād Al-Raḥmān* is both integral and complementary to its preceding discourse regarding the contentions of the Prophet's opponents and the impending state of potential conflict. In response, the description of the *ʿIbād Al-Raḥmān* presents a conciliatory paradigm whose importance is apparent from their honorific title and notably expansive description. The leading term of this description, *hawnan*, indicates conflict avoidance, whilst the ensuing reference to responding with *salām* promotes amicable disengagement and de-escalation of conflict. The harmonious maintenance of social relations by day is holistically complemented by the *ʿIbād Al-Raḥmān's* dutiful remembrance of God by night, resulting in eschatological reward. Social Conciliation is thus situated alongside Divine–Human Conciliation in a powerful and balanced model of perpetual conflict avoidance, which is seamlessly conjoined with the natural alternation of night and day.

Three suras later, the above portrayal of the *ʿIbād Al-Raḥmān* is reinforced by a similar characterisation of certain People of the Book. Q.28:52–53 specifically refer to people who were given scripture prior to the Qurʾan saying *yuʾminūn* (they believe) and then quoting them as being *muslimīn* (those who have submitted to God), highlighting their commonality of faith with the Muslims. Q.28:54–55 highlight a number of characteristics of such people. After the defining quality of faith testified to by these People of the Book, a reference to the doubling of their eschatological reward is foregrounded for apparent emphasis at Q.28:54, although stylistically contrasting with the deferred mention of eschatological reward for the *ʿIbād Al-Raḥmān* above. The promise of such reward in both cases provides Divine endorsement and commendation of the conciliatory conduct modelled. The exposition of the conciliatory conduct of the People of the Book cited at Q.28:54–55 then becomes the entire focus of their remaining description.

Q.28:54 declares that the above People of the Book will be doubly rewarded ***bimā ṣabarū*** *wa yadra'ūna bi 'l-**ḥasanati** ('l)-ssayyi'a* (because they are **steadfast**, repel evil with **good**, Abdel Haleem). Both Q.28:54 here and Q.25:75 above, regarding the *'Ibād Al-Raḥmān*, promise reward for being patient and steadfast using the same phrase: *bimā ṣabarū*. Q.28:54 follows with an additional explicit reference to the important conciliatory notion of *iḥsān* (gracious conduct) highlighted in Chapter 3, an elaboration only implied in the notion of *hawnan* (humbly) regarding the *'Ibād Al-Raḥmān*. This description is followed by a reference to the financial generosity of the People of the Book, correlating with a similar generosity which, according to Iṣlāḥī (vol.5, pp.487–88), is implied by moderation in the expenditure of the *'Ibād Al-Raḥmān* at Q.25:67. This quality is frequently cited in the Qur'an in connection with the provision of social assistance to the needy.

After this, Q.28:55 provides a more direct correlation with the conciliatory conduct of the *'Ibād Al-Raḥmān*. Q.28:55 declares: *wa idhā sami'u 'l-laghwa a'raḍū 'anhu* (and turn away whenever they hear frivolous talk, Abdel Haleem). The instant reference to *laghwa* (frivolity) mirrors the reference in Q.25:72 above, the former using the terminology of disengagement indicated by *i'rāḍ* (turning away) and the latter referring to *marrū kirāmā* (pass by with dignity). In Q.28:55 the point is further expounded by a specific quotation indicating a 'live and let live' attitude: *wa qālū lanā a'mālunā wa lakum a'mālukum* (saying 'We have our deeds and you have yours', Abdel Haleem). As well as indicating non-confrontation with others through tolerance of their conduct, this quotation demonstrates a notable symmetry of expression which I have argued earlier is a feature of conciliatory verses in the Qur'an. This feature provides a visible and palpable textual balance indicative of the harmony resulting from the conflict containment and non-escalation demonstrated by these People of the Book.

The quotation in Q.28:55 continues: *salāmun 'alaykum, lā nabtaghi 'l-jāhilīn* ('Peace be with you! We do not seek the company of ignorant people.' Abdel Haleem). This quotation again mirrors the conduct of responding to the ignorant with *salām*, praised above at Q.25:63. The choice of *jāhilīn* (ignorant) to describe the proponents of provocative contentions in both Q.28:55 and Q.25:63 provides semantic encouragement towards temporal excuse of their conduct, although the immediately preceding symmetrical reference to the respective deeds of the parties implies ultimate eschatological reward and sanction. Avoidance of the company of the ignorant indicated by the quotation again declares an expression of disengagement and a desire not to clash with or confront such people.

The notable similarities in the above description of the People of the Book in Q.28 and the *'Ibād Al-Raḥmān* in Q.25 are unmistakable. References to *ṣabr* (patience), disengagement, altruism, *iḥsān* and *salām* all demonstrate a close connection between these two conciliatory paradigms. In Section 4.1.3, which examines Q.28 in more detail focussing on the story of Moses, we shall see that in fact the conciliatory conduct of Moses and the People of the Book also serves as a historical aspirational model for the Prophet and his followers. After the above models of the *'Ibād Al-Raḥmān* and People of the Book, a further conciliatory exemplum in the Group 4 suras appears in an eight-verse sustained admonishment from Q.31:12–19: the sage Luqmān's advice to his son.

4.1.2 Luqmān's Ideal

Q.31 cites the sage Luqmān's memorable advice, drawing attention to its special significance by a specific reference to God's bestowal of *al-ḥikma* (wisdom, Q.31:12) upon Luqmān. The sura also endorses and appropriates Luqmān's advice by self-referencing its own verses, which contain that advice, as originating from *al-kitāb al-ḥakīm* (the wise Scripture, Abdel Haleem, Q.31:2). The rich use of monologue by the eponymous central character of the sura adds impact by the direct quotation of his words, apparent from the triple recurrence of the address *yā bunayya* (my dear son, Q.31:13, 16, 17) giving dramatic voice to the Qur'anic message. The endearing diminutive form of address highlights the benevolence inherent in the paternal advice, stylistically enhancing the sense of appeal within the passage. The presentation of Luqmān's advice to appeal to the Meccan audience is further enhanced by Luqmān's apparent status, noted by Iṣlāḥī (vol.6, p.116) and discussed further in Section 4.3.2, as a celebrated sage featuring in pre-Islamic Arab literature. Iṣlāḥī (vol.6, p.125) also suggests that Luqmān was a leader of his people and provided this advice to his son upon handing over the responsibilities of office, providing a sense of occasion and solemnity which lends additional weight to the advice proffered.

The narrative is introduced by a Divine injunction to be thankful to God at Q.31:12, and a Divine two-verse interjection regarding the rights of parents at Q.31:14–15 consequent on their favours, particularly child-bearing and suckling by the mother. Both Q.31:12 and Q.31:14 enjoin gratitude upon man: *ani 'shkur lī* (be thankful to Me (i.e. God)), with Q.31:14 adding *wa li wālidayk* (and to your parents). Inextricably interlaced with these contributions in the Divine voice, Luqmān's own advice across five verses at Q.31:13 and 16–19 admonishes his son to abstain from *shirk* (polytheism), be aware of accountability before God, establish prayer, enjoin what is right and forbid what is wrong, bear afflictions with patience, avoid arrogance with people and walking on the earth arrogantly, walk at a moderate pace and lower the voice.

As with the description of the *ʿIbād Al-Raḥmān*, the subject matter of these injunctions is relatively balanced between dutiful conduct towards God and conciliatory dealing with people, relating the notion of *shukr* to both Divine–Human and Social Conciliation. In the Divine–human context, it is difficult to overlook the apparent semantic dichotomy between *shukr* (thankfulness, Q.31:12, 14) and *shirk* (polytheism, Q.31:13, 15), enhanced by the commonality of root letters in the two words but with the letters *kāf* and *rā* reversed. *Shukr* is enjoined by God and thus apparently results in Divine–Human Conciliation whilst *shirk* is prohibited by Him and is therefore a cause of Divine–human conflict. Iṣlāḥī (vol.6, p.127) argues that *shukr* (thankfulness), the introductory injunction of the above conciliatory paradigm, is so fundamental that it is the basis for recognising all Divine and human rights. Certainly, the stark reminder of the biological reality of maternal favour in these verses is a compelling basis for the imposition of duties on the child in favour of the parents.

It has already been argued in the previous chapter by reference to Q.17:23–24 that dutifulness to parents is a fundamental conciliatory trait emphasised in the Qurʾan alongside dutifulness to God. In the instant passage, it is now made clear that this principle transcends even differences of faith, since Q.31:15 enjoins that should parents attempt to compel their children to engage in polytheism, the children should disobey them in this respect, a point also made at Q.29:8, but *ṣāḥibhumā fī (ʿl)-ddunya maʿrūfā* (yet keep their company in this life according to what is right, Abdel Haleem). The Qurʾan therefore does not entertain severance of ties of kinship with parents even where they openly show hostility towards the Qurʾan's own fundamental message of belief in One God. In Conciliation Ethics in the Qurʾan (Fazaluddin, 2016, p.345), I argued that this was an important example of Differentiation, a conciliatory principle which the Qurʾan advocates as a means of resolving two conflicting duties and maintaining both relationships. Iṣlāḥī (vol.6, p.125) highlights the ironic contrast between Luqmān's admonishment of his son and the teachings advocated by the Qurʾan, and the torture and persecution of their own offspring by the disbelieving Meccans to prevent their children accepting these same teachings, despite the Meccans' cultural and historical acknowledgement of Luqmān's wisdom.

A further, more general, injunction by Luqmān at Q.31:17: *wa ʾmur bi ʿl-maʿrūf* (command what is right, Abdel Haleem) is considered by Iṣlāḥī (vol.6, pp.131–32) as a comprehensive and summary reference to all things pertaining to the fulfilment of (human) rights, such as spending in God's way, providing assistance to orphans, the destitute, neighbours and other deserving recipients of aid. This injunction continues the theme of altruism and social justice already espoused in the Conciliation models discussed above. Social justice is an important Conciliation concept, since non-fulfilment of basic human needs has been found to be a cause of conflicts (Abu-Nimer, 2003, p.9). Iṣlāḥī also highlights that an immediately preceding command to establish prayer connects the servant to God, whilst the injunction *wa ʾmur bi ʿl-maʿrūf* connects the servant to God's creation. Iṣlāḥī links the two notions even more integrally by deducing from Q.31:17, and its preceding verses which refer to *shukr*, that *social responsibilities* are incumbent on those who are *thankful to God*. The consistent juxtaposition of relations with God and with creation again provides a holistic model of both Divine–Human and Social Conciliation, similar to the holistic conciliatory conduct of the *ʿIbād Al-Raḥmān*.

Luqmān's admonition is framed by references at both ends to the important notion of *iḥsān*. Q.31:3 includes in the prelude to Luqmān's admonition a definition of *muḥsinīn* (those who do good, Abdel Haleem) as being those who establish prayer, give alms and believe in the Hereafter. This can readily be construed as an abbreviated reference to those who fulfil God's right, fulfil the rights of people and are conscious of accountability in respect of both. In Chapter 3, it was concluded that the notion of *iḥsān* manifests in both the Divine–human and social contexts, a point which is borne out again here. Shortly after Luqmān's admonition, Q.31:22 again refers to those who submit to God *wa huwa muḥsinun* (and does good work, Abdel Haleem). The terminology of *iḥsān* thus encapsulates the conciliatory teaching of Luqmān's admonition.

Q.31:17 goes on to present another emphatic injunction to show *ṣabr* (patience) in the face of afflictions, reminiscent of the patience of the People of the Book commended at Q.28:54 above and the *ʿIbād Al-Raḥmān* at Q.25:75. In each context, an apparent emphasis on social responsibility and gracious conduct towards others is coupled with a tolerance of the harm caused by others providing a bilateral model of conciliatory conduct. Q.31:18 then emphasises the quality of humility, also commended in the *ʿIbād Al-Raḥmān* as a quality indicating peaceful relations with others, saying: *wa lā tuṣaʿʿir khaddaka li (ʿl)-nnāsi wa lā tamshi fi ʿl-arḍi maraḥā* (do not turn your nose up at people, nor walk about the place arrogantly, Abdel Haleem; also see Q.17:37 for a similar injunction). Here again, humility is a conciliatory quality, indicating an integrated participation in a society of equals and, as indicated in Q.31:17 two paragraphs above, fulfilment of the needs of its most vulnerable members.

It can be seen from the recurrent commendation of qualities such as *ṣabr* (patience), indicating containment of conflict; humility; reciprocation of contention with disengagement and *salām*, indicating conflict avoidance; and reciprocation of harm with good, that these are essential teachings within a fundamental Qurʾanic platform of conciliatory conduct which is frequently rendered into the terminology of *iḥsān*. The maintenance of Divine–human relations is also consistently situated alongside an emphasis on social relations, combining these two branches of Conciliation into an integrated body of teachings and even resolving conflicts between the two when required. Social equality and social justice are both advocated and closely coupled in the above Conciliation models, a message which is further reinforced in the following section by the condemnation of social inequality and social injustice. We will also see that, stylistically, the above generic models are illustrated with specific Qur'anic narratives which serve to accentuate their import and provide dramatic impact, as well as complementing theoretical instruction with practical context. The most comprehensive narrative in the Group 4 suras is that of Moses, in which the very antithesis of the above Conciliation models is epitomised by the arrogance of Pharaoh and his multifarious perpetration of *fasād* (disorder).

4.1.3 The Story of Moses

The Story of Moses in the Qur'an is so recurrent and fulsome that its significance in the Qur'anic discourse is unmistakable. Yet it is this very recurrence that, to the inattentive reader, can result in the obscuring of its specific impact at different instances in the Qur'an. To my mind, the Story of Moses reaches its zenith in Group 4, burgeoning into a dominant and sustained dramatic narrative throughout the Group, and foregrounding its juxtaposition of Conciliation and corruption, embodied respectively by Moses and Pharaoh. The narrative is introduced briefly at Q.25:35–36 and mentioned in conclusion with concision at Q.29:39 and Q.32:23–24. In between, the narrative features prominently and extensively in no less than three consecutive suras, firstly as the leading story in a series of narratives at both Q.26:10–68 and Q.27:7–14. The Story of Moses then dominates the 88-verse contents of Q.28 with a distinct single narrative giving its name (Al-Qaṣaṣ (the Story, Q.28:25)) to the sura, and a sustained account commencing at the outset of the sura at Q.28:3 and continuing until Q.28:82 near the end of the sura, interrupted and supplemented only by supporting Divine commentary. In this respect, Q.28 bears notable similarity with the exemplary Qur'anic narrative of Joseph which spans the entirety of Q.12.

Furthermore, a remarkable coherence between the stories of Joseph and Moses is invoked by the almost exact mirroring of the phraseology of Q.12:22, referring to Joseph, at Q.28:14 in respect of Moses: *wa lammā balagha ashuddahū* ([Q.28:14 adds:] *wa 'stawā) ātaynāhu ḥukman wa 'ilmā, wa kadhālika najzi 'l- muḥsinīn* (When he reached maturity, We gave him judgement and knowledge: this is how we reward those who do good (Q.12:22); When Moses reached full maturity and manhood, We gave him wisdom and knowledge: this is how we reward those who do good (Q.28:14), Abdel Haleem). Both verses refer to the grant of wisdom and knowledge upon maturity to the prophets Joseph and Moses, respectively, as a reward for those who embody *iḥsān*. Crucially, both the narratives of Moses and Joseph present lead characters who serve as conciliatory exemplars for the Prophet and his followers: like Joseph, Moses is given the notable epithet of being amongst *al-muḥsinīn*. This serves to make both prophets role models for the Prophet and his followers who are persistently enjoined to show *iḥsān*, behaving graciously towards those who confront them.

At Q.28:44, the Qur'anic voice uses *iltifāt* (turning from one addressee to another for literary effect), turning from a third-party narration of Moses' story towards addressing the Prophet directly, as it does at Q.12:108 in the story of Joseph, in each case directing these narratives to the context of the Prophet's own experiences. There are direct parallels between the ridicule of the Prophet by his opponents at Q.25:8 and 41 above and Pharaoh's ridicule of Moses at Q.26:27 – Pharaoh's allegation of madness directly mirrors a similar allegation apparently targeted at the Prophet by his opponents (see Q.68:2). The Qur'an too is unified with past Scripture at Q.12:111, where it is described as an affirmation of past Scriptures and a guidance and mercy, at Q.28:43 where the Torah is similarly described as a guidance and mercy, and at Q.28:49 where the Qur'an is closely coupled with the Torah using the dual form *minhumā* (than these two). Q.26:197 goes so far as to declare the correlation of the Qur'an with past scripture, as apparently recognised by the scholars of Banī Isrā'īl, as an *āya* (sign) for the Meccan disbelievers.

Having discussed Joseph's epitomising of *iḥsān* in Chapter 3, we now find subtle but pervasive examples of Moses' conciliatory approach in Q.28. His responsibility to orally *persuade* rather than engage in hostilities with Pharaoh is indicated by his request for support from his brother Aaron who is *afṣaḥu minnī* (more *eloquent* than me, Q.28:33). Upon being insultingly labelled a madman by Pharaoh (Q.26:27), a notable parallel with the Prophet, Moses unhesitatingly continues his identification of God, apparently unruffled. Upon being threatened with imprisonment (Q.26:29), Moses responds only with miraculous 'proof' of his claim (Q.26:30). In doing so, Moses appears to fulfil his conciliatory brief of appealing to Pharaoh with *qawlan layyinan* (gentle words, Q.20:44). Smith (2018, p.92) describes the presentation of Moses in the Qur'an as 'giving signs, calling to repentance, but only actively entering into conflict or challenge when forced to or as initiated by others. Such a model would have stood as important instruction on how to deal with enemies and challenges in the distinct tension-filled circumstances of Mecca.'

Moses also demonstrates a conciliatory tendency to champion social equality and justice, reproaching Pharaoh for his enslavement of Banī Isrā'īl (Q.26:22), assisting his elderly future patron's disadvantaged daughters to water their flocks (Q.28:24), and also responding to his ostensibly oppressed fellow-tribesman's call for assistance in a fight with an Egyptian (Q.28:15). Ironically, Moses' attempt at being a Good Samaritan results in the Egyptian's wrongful death, a point of conflict rather than Conciliation which Moses describes as *min ʿamali (ʾl)-shshayṭān* (Satan's work). Moses is repentant, seeking Divine forgiveness and saying he has wronged himself (Q.28:16), mirroring the penitent language of Adam's similar appeal at Q.7:23. In doing so, he positions himself within the explicit exemption at Q.25:70–71 for those who repent and do good deeds, thus avoiding Divine punishment for wrongful killing, otherwise threatened at Q.25:68.

Earlier at Q.28:4–6, the central paradigm of the Moses/Pharaoh narrative is set out explicitly with Pharaoh positioned as the archetypal nemesis of Qurʾanic Conciliation (see Lawson, 2008 for further discussion of Duality and Opposition in the Qurʾan). Pharaoh is declared to have *ʿalā fī ʾl-arḍi* (made himself high and mighty in the land, Abdel Haleem, Q.28:4), a direct contrast to the humility commended in the conciliation models in Sections 4.1.1 and 4.1.2. Specific charges are then levelled against Pharaoh at Q.28:4 to explain this declaration, namely: dividing society into groups, in contrast to Moses's efforts for social equality, subjugating one such group and killing their sons whilst sparing their women. Such conduct is collectively condemned, as Pharaoh is damningly described as being amongst the *mufsidīn* (those who spread corruption, Abdel Haleem, Q.28:4; see a similar reference at Q.27:14). Q.28:5–6 then proclaims the Divine will to favour the subjugated group, elevating them to leadership, making them inheritors and establishing them in the land, just as Pharaoh and his aides feared.

Yet another archetypal figure representing *fasād* (disorder), like Pharaoh singled out for special mention, is Qārūn (Q.28:76–82) – a wealthy individual from Banī Isrāʾīl itself. In another direct contrast with the humility and altruistic conduct commended in the conciliatory models in Sections 4.1.1 and 4.1.2, Qārūn is condemned for oppressing his own people, and for his amassing and ostentation of personal wealth. Iṣlāḥī (vol.5, pp.713–14) considers the mention of Qārūn a specific parallel to the conduct of the Prophet's wealthy uncle and notable adversary Abū Lahab. Certainly, the emphatic leading mention of Qārūn as being from the people of Moses at the start of his narrative at Q.28:76 has a strong sense of reproach for treachery and disloyalty, equally applicable to Abū Lahab's hostility towards his nephew in opposition to the social norms of their tribal society.

The condemnation of Qārūn is rendered all the more effective by its specific contrast with the *iḥsān* (gracious conduct) and altruistic expenditure of others in his own community, mentioned at Q.28:54 above, and the Qurʾanic criticism of Qārūn in the words of his own people at Q.28:76–77. Qārūn is admonished by his people: *aḥsin kamā aḥsana ʾllāhu ilayka wa lā tabghi ʾl-fasāda fī ʾl-arḍi, inna ʾllāha lā yuḥibbu 'l-mufsidīn* (Do good to others as God has done good to you. Do not seek to spread corruption in the land, for God does not love those who do this, Abdel Haleem, Q.28:77). As we have seen in Chapter 2 and above in Q.26:152 and Q.27:48, the Qur'anic opposite of *fasād* is *iṣlāḥ* (order, reform). At Q.28:77, however, Qārūn is enjoined to demonstrate a higher standard than *iṣlāḥ*, namely that of *iḥsān* or gracious conduct towards others, a reflection of the exceptional Divine grace bestowed upon him. The specific mention of this Divine grace renders Qārūn's descent to the ranks of the *mufsidīn* all the more deplorable.

The clear sense emerging from the narrative of Pharaoh, and the ancillary narrative of Qārūn, is of one societal group dominating and oppressing the other, creating inequality and injustice. The Divine will professes at Q.28:5–6 to restore balance in society and preserve social equality and justice by emancipating and empowering the non-culpable party and restoring their right to peaceful occupation. Such a message would have undoubtedly been intended to admonish the disbelieving Meccan chieftains, who are explicitly compared to Pharaoh's people at Q.8:52, 54 and elsewhere in the Qur'an, and to hearten the persecuted early believers in Mecca. In a concluding address to the Prophet and by extension his followers, the central paradigm of the specific Moses/Pharaoh narrative is broadened to a generic motivational principle at Q.28:83, declaring that the abode of the Hereafter is granted *lilladhīna lā yurīdūna 'uluwwan fī 'l-arḍi wa lā fasādā* (to those who do not seek superiority on earth or spread corruption, Abdel Haleem). The concluding principle once again links arrogance and *fasād*, by implication conversely promising lasting reward to those who demonstrate humility, avoiding and tolerating harm and providing benefit to others as discussed in Section 4.1.1. Such conduct embodies *iḥsān* in accordance with its 'definition' at Q.3:134 and promotes Conciliation.

Conciliation through disengagement is also exemplified in the Moses narrative and other related prophetic stories. A key aspect of the story of Moses is his flight from Egypt, narrated at Q.26:52–68. We are told at Q.26:52 that Moses receives Divine inspiration to depart at night with his people and informed that he will be pursued. In the closely connected story of Joseph – Q.40:34 explicitly mentions Joseph as the predecessor of Moses in Egypt – we find another example of a prophet emigrating, this time *towards* Egypt, but once again separated from his homeland. A further example of a prophet emigrating is given in the story of Abraham, Joseph's great grandfather. At Q.19:46–49 we are told of his banishment by his father and Abraham's withdrawal from his people. At Q.29:26 we are told of a specific migration: *innī muhājirun ilā rabbī* (I shall migrate to my Lord). It is not entirely clear if these words are spoken by Abraham's nephew Lot, who according to Yusuf Ali joins him in his migration, or by Abraham himself. Although Abdel Haleem and Yusuf Ali indicate these to be the words of Lot, my own inclination is to consider them the words of Abraham on the basis that Abraham is the speaker in the previous verse (Q.29:25), the person indicated by the pronoun *hū* (he) immediately prior to the quotation in Q.29:26, and also the person referred to throughout the following verse, Q.29:27.

The three important narratives of Abraham, Joseph and Moses – prophets directly inter-connected by kinship and succession – provide important precedents for the Prophet and his followers. The lesson is one of remaining steadfast and patient but disengaging from their opponents even to the point of migration, necessitating detachment from their homeland, families and possessions. In his explanation of Q.25:63, Al-Rāzī cites the commentator Al-Aṣam as specifying that the *salām* of the *ʿIbād Al-Raḥmān* when addressed by the ignorant is a parting salutation rather than one of greeting. As such, like the *salām* of Abraham at Q.19:47, it is an indication of disengagement and departure. I would also add the two references to *marrū* (pass by) at Q.25:72 also indicate onward movement and departure. At Q.26:216, the Prophet's conditional declaration of detachment: *fa qul innī barīʾun mimmā taʿmalūn* (say, 'I bear no responsibility for your actions', Abdel Haleem), according to Iṣlāḥī (vol.5, p.563) heralds the Prophet's imminent migration.

At Q.29:56, in a sura commencing by declaring at Q.29:2–3 the inevitability of severe tests from God to distinguish true believers from liars, the believers are told pointedly *inna arḍī wāsiʿatun* (surely my earth is vast) – a clear indication towards the potential for migration. Shortly afterwards at Q.29:58–9, the same believers – facing imminent separation from their temporal home – are assured of permanent eschatological lodgings in Paradise for those who *ṣabarū* (remain steadfast) and rely on their Lord. The sura ends at Q.29:69 with an emphatic motivational declaration that God will guide to His ways those who strive for him, ending: *wa inna 'llāha la maʿa 'l-muḥsinīn* (God is with those who do good, Abdel Haleem) – a strategic final reference to the conciliatory notion of *iḥsān*, which contextually appears to refer to remaining patient and steadfast despite opposition. Ultimately, the notion of non-confrontation and disengagement from conflict is promoted to the extent of advocating emigration, leaving behind family, wealth and homeland.

Stylistically, the Moses narrative provides an effective complement to the abstract Conciliation models of the preceding sections, providing context and impact. Thematically, the embodiment of *iḥsān* by Moses and of *fasād* by Pharaoh presents an effective and concrete dichotomy between Conciliation and conflict. Recurrent duality accentuates the Qurʾanic exhortation as the humility commended in the Conciliation models is now expressly contrasted with the arrogance of Pharaoh, and Moses' championing of social equality and justice is pitted against Pharaoh's oppression and enforcement of social division. At the same time, these two central characters, respectively, serve as an exemplar for the Prophet and his largely disadvantaged followers and a condemnation of the entrenched Meccan hierarchy who opposed them. Meanwhile, the temporal continuum of conciliatory conduct exemplified by successive prophets and the apparent unity of their scriptures indicates a timeless conciliatory appeal.

4.2 Conciliation Through Rational Argument: *Itmām Al-Ḥujja*

In Section 4.1, a key notion was the endorsement of disengagement from conflict situations, ultimately culminating in the Qur'an's advocation of migration itself. However, the Qur'an certainly does not promote alienation between disputing parties and in fact adopts and promotes a sustained engagement based on rational argument to persuade its audience. This conciliatory emphasis on persuasion rather than compulsion reflects the Qur'anic principle of non-compulsion in faith (Q.2:256), previously discussed in Chapter 2. In this section, we will see that the Qur'an uses terminology such as 'signs' and 'proofs' indicating a desire to persuade through evidential arguments, demonstrates engagement with its contenders through a dialogical style which recounts and responds to their contentions and supports its theological assertions by extended enumeration of examples of Divine power and grace (see Zebiri, 2017 for a thorough discussion of the Qur'an's use of argumentation).

The Qur'an's use of exhaustive arguments to persuade its audience is sometimes referred to by commentators as *itmām al-ḥujja* (completion of proof). The Urdu equivalent of this term, *itmām-e-ḥujjat*, is explicitly referred to three times by Iṣlāḥī at Q.25:35–60 (vol.5, p.440) in explaining the Prophet's role of presenting Qur'anic arguments to provide both warnings and good tidings. Key to the Qur'an's approach of *itmām al-ḥujja* is the enumeration of *āyāt* (signs), often referencing natural phenomena and historical narratives, which not coincidentally is also the term used by the Qur'an to refer to its own constituent sentences. The Qur'an also frequently highlights its elaboration of emphatic arguments by describing itself as *mubīn* (clear). Although Iṣlāḥī's commentary cited above indicates a rather pessimistic appraisal of the term *itmām al-ḥujja* as ominously sealing the fate of those who were never destined to believe, in my view, the use of *itmām al-ḥujja* indicates a desire to engage in sustained dialogue and rational argument exhausting all efforts at reconciling theological differences, as discussed below.

The disbelievers' contentions against the Qur'an and the Prophet, interlaced with contrasting verses extolling God's transcendent beneficence and majesty, are signalled by recurrent dialogical indicators: ***qāla*** *'lladhīna kafarū* (those who disbelieve **say**, Q.25:4, 32), ***qālū*** (they **say**, Q.25:5, 7), and *wa* ***qāla*** *'lladhīna lā yarjūna liqā'anā* (and those who do not anticipate meeting Us **say**, Q.25:21), with the instructive ***qul*** (**say**, Q.25:6, 57) providing responses vicariously through the medium of the Prophet. The contentions include: allegations of fabrication (Q.25:4), allegations of reproducing fables (Q.25:5); demands for an angelic rather than merely human messenger (Q.25:7, 21); demands for a messenger possessing exceptional wealth, and allegations of being bewitched (Q.25:8); and questioning the gradual revelation of the Qur'an (Q.25:32). Despite its ostensible sublime status as a conclusive Divine scripture, the Qur'an devotes both time and textual space to responding to these apparently mundane and trivial human contentions either directly or indirectly, presenting the rewards of the Hereafter as preferential to temporal rewards (Q.25:10), portraying the realities of the Day of Judgement (Q.25:11–19, 22–31) and the eschatological sighting of angels (Q.25:22), declaring the humanity of previous messengers (Q.25:20) and stressing the reinforcing and interactive nature of the Qur'an's gradual revelation (Q.25:32–33). All of this demonstrates the Qur'an's propensity to engage in rational dialogue and to respond persuasively to each of its opponents' contentions and thus overcome differences.

Verses Q.25:35–44 then present a brief summary citation of various narratives concerning past prophets and a denunciation of the disbelievers' refusal to take heed, with the famous drowning of Noah's people in particular described as an *āya* (sign) for people. After this, an extensive list of natural phenomena is elucidated as evidence of God's creation using the rhetorical indicators *wa huwa 'lladhī* (and He it is who.., Q.25:47, 48, 53, 54, 62) and *alladhī* (who, Q.25:59, 61). These phenomena include: the expansion and contraction of shadows (Q.25:45–46); the provision of night and day for rest and work (Q.25:47, 62); the sending of wind and rain, bringing life to dead land and sustenance to people and animals (Q.25:48–50); the separation of saltwater and freshwater (Q.25:53); the creation from semen and establishment of relationships of blood and marriage (Q.25:43); the creation of the heavens and earth and everything in between in 'six days' (Q.25:59); and the heavenly placement of stellar constellations and the illuminating sun and moon (Q.25:61). Immediately following this list of phenomena is the description of the *'Ibād Al-Raḥmān* whose notable exemplary qualities include not being heedless when reminded of the *āyāt* (signs) of their Lord. This implies that the natural phenomena are also presented as 'signs', a point confirmed explicitly in Q.30, discussed further on in this section.

It can readily be seen that almost the entirety of Q.25 is occupied with responding to the disbelievers' contentions and then expounding arguments from prophetic narratives and natural phenomena, both explicitly or implicitly referenced as signs from God. Notably, this sustained interactive and rational debate in a Meccan sura (prior to the military conflicts of the Medinan period) is referred to by the Qur'an as *jihād*, suspending a list of natural phenomena to instruct the Prophet at Q.25:52: *wa jāhidhum bihī jihādan kabīrā* (strive hard against them with this Qur'an, Abdel Haleem). Further on in Group 4, Q.29:6

declares, immediately following references to withstanding persecution in God's way: *wa man* ***jāhada*** *fa innamā yujāhidu linafsih* (Those who **exert themselves** do so for their own benefit, Abdel Haleem), with Q.29:69 stating at its conclusion *wa 'lladhīna* ***jāhadū*** *fīnā la nahdiyannahum subulanā* (But we shall be sure to guide to Our ways those who **strive hard** for Our cause, Abdel Haleem). These examples of the term *jihād* are remarkably illuminating and perhaps also highly ironic, given contemporary linguistic usage of the Qur'anic term *jihād* to refer to fighting in God's way. Rather, *jihād* in the examples above is a process of persuasive dialogue and engagement, a state of tolerance and self-development, and a source of spiritual guidance towards God's way – those who endure the hardships of this path are assured of God's proximity and described as *muḥsinīn* (those who demonstrate *iḥsān*, Q.29:69).

After examining Q.25:1–44 and Q.25:52 above, the ensuing sura Q.26 can be seen to form a strong complement to Q.25, providing a converse emphasis. In Q.26, natural phenomena indicating God's power of creation are summarised in a single verse (Q.26:7), whilst the narratives of past prophets and the outcome of their nations' actions are related at length: Moses (Q.26:10–66), Abraham (Q.26:69–102), Noah (105–120), Hūd (Q.26:123–138), Ṣāliḥ (Q.26:141–158), Lot (Q.26:160–173) and Shuʿayb (Q.26:176–189). The remarkable feature of this sura is the repetition, no less than *eight times* of a couplet which declares in its first line, regarding the natural phenomena and each individual narrative: *inna fī dhālika la āya, wa mā kāna aktharuhum mu'minīn* (There truly is a sign in this, though most of them do not believe, Abdel Haleem); Q.26:8, 67, 103, 121, 139, 158, 174, 190). The same couplet adds emphatically in its second line: *wa inna rabbaka lahuwa 'l-ʿazīzu ('l)-rraḥīm* (your Lord alone is the Almighty, the Merciful, Abdel Haleem; Q.26:9, 68, 104, 122, 140, 159, 175, 191), apparently a reference to God's ultimate power and grace – at the same time a compelling warning for the intransigent and an inviting indication of clemency towards the repentant. This recurrent motif again demonstrates a highly sustained and apparently persuasive exhortation and appeal.

In Q.27, the Meccan audience are again provided with instruction in the form of both prophetic narratives relating to Moses (Q.27:7–14), David and Solomon (Q.26:15–44), Ṣāliḥ (Q.27:45–53) and Lot (Q.27:54–58), and also natural phenomena at Q.27:60–66. The latter are once again listed emphatically with a five times repeated rhetorical indicator *amman* (who?) asking searchingly ***amman*** *khalaqa* (**who** created..?), ***amman*** *jaʿala* (**who** made..?), ***amman*** *yujību* (**who** responds..?), ***amman*** *yahdīkum* (**who** guides..?), ***amman*** *yabda'u* (**who** initiates..?). The use of *jumla inshā'iyya* (initiating phrase) rather than *jumla khabariyya* (informational phrase) in this instance adds an additional interactive and probing quality to the Qur'anic argument, further accentuating its persuasive effect.

Notably, Q.27 opens with an account of Moses' story which condemns Pharaoh's open rejection of certain miraculous *ayātunā mubṣiratan* (enlightening signs, Abdel Haleem, Q.27:13) and closes with Q.27:93 which declares *sayurīkum ayātihī* (He will show you His signs, Abdel Haleem). The multiple references in Q.26 above to 'signs' of the Qur'an's veracity are also reinforced by the same sura's introductory and near-concluding references to the Qur'an as *mubīn* (clear, Q.26:2, 195). The two succeeding suras also contain references to the Qur'an as *mubīn* (clear) at Q.27:1, 79 and Q.28:2. The Qur'anic text itself thus indicates expressly that it aims to provide *clear and visible proofs* to persuade its audience and delivers an exposition of its arguments at length to achieve this.

Tellingly, both the assertions of God's creation in Q.27 and Q.28 end with a temporal or eschatological challenge for the Prophet's opponents to present their own proof for adhering to their associate gods: *hātū burhānakum* (produce your evidence). Q.29:20 instructs the Prophet to challenge the Meccan audience to see for themselves God's creation in nature: *fanẓurū* (see), contrasting the visibility of the natural phenomena cited by the Qur'an as evidence of God's creation with the fragility of the basis for the polytheists' adherence to their associate gods, which is given the similitude of a cobweb at Q.29:41. Q.27:51 also challenges its audience to *witness* the outcome of Ṣāliḥ's opponents, most likely due to the apparent proximity of their ruined houses to the Meccans' own land, saying: *fanẓur* (see), again indicating a high standard of proof, this time with respect to a prophetic narrative.

Despite the Qur'an's self-assurance of its efforts to persuade its audience, however, it recognises that there remains an apparent difference in expectations between the Qur'an and its contenders, who demand to know why the Prophet does not produce *āyāt* (miracles, Abdel Haleem, Q.29:50) – the same term used by the Qur'an in adducing evidence to support its assertions. In response, Q.29:51 presents the revelation of the Qur'an itself as sufficient as a mercy and admonition for those who wish to believe: it provides assertions supported by 'evidence' from history and nature, leaving its audience to make a final leap of faith. This must be a voluntary exercise and the Prophet is expressly instructed to rely upon God (Q.25:58, Q.26:217, Q.27:79) in the face of opposition to his delivery of the Qur'an's message and absolved of liability for the outcome of his preaching (Q.26:216). Ultimately, persuasion by its nature does not determine the outcome, and the Prophet is therefore instructed to accept that his efforts will only meet with partial success. Q.28:56 declares: *innaka lā tahdī man aḥbabta* (You [Prophet] cannot guide everyone you love to the truth, Abdel Haleem).

Following on from the theme of the above suras, Q.30 provides another thought-provoking and stylistically remarkable catalogue of natural phenomena. A pair of probing, questioning verses at Q.30:8 and 9 ask, respectively: *awa lam yatafakkarū* (have they not reflected?), asserting God's creation for a defined purpose and time, and *awa lam yasīrū fī 'l-arḍi fayanẓurū* (have they not travelled in the land and seen, Abdel Haleem), referring to the ultimate decline of past nations. These two verses highlight the Qur'anic appeal to man's rational intellect and senses, respectively. Further on at Q.30:20–25, six consecutive verses commencing with the recurrent refrain *wa min āyātihī* (one of His signs), highlight natural phenomena as evidential signs of God's creation, listing, respectively: man's creation from dust and dispersal in the earth, the creation of spouses for peaceful co-existence with mutual love and mercy, the creation of the heavens and the earth and the racial diversity of human languages and skin colours, the nightly repose and the daily harvesting of bounties, the vision of lightning and the sending of rain reviving dead earth, and the continued establishment of the heavens and the earth. One additional verse at Q.30:46 commencing with the same refrain references the provision of winds and the sailing of ships. These signs are classified as *dalā'il al-anfus* (signs within humans) and *dalā'il al-āfāq* (environmental signs) by Al-Rāzī at Q.30:22, an apparent reference to these terms in Q.41:53: *sa nurīhim āyātinā fī 'l-āfāqi wa fī anfusihim* (We shall show them Our signs in every region of the earth and in themselves, Abdel Haleem). Natural phenomena are thus sub-classified into internal and external signs of God's creation.

The remarkable sense of appeal to the human intellect and senses in these verses, discussed further in the following section, is accentuated by the conclusion of the four central verses Q.30:21–24, each of which concludes with the repeated emphatic declaration *inna fī dhālika la āyātin* (there truly are signs in this) going on to list the following as beneficiaries of these signs: *li qawmin yatafakkarūn* (for people who reflect, Q.30:21), *lil 'ālimīn* (for those who have knowledge, Q.30:22), *li qawmin yasma'ūn* (for people who listen, Q.30:23) and *li qawmin ya'qilūn* (for people who reason, Q.30:24). Preceding and succeeding the distinguished textual segment at Q.30:20–25 is the assertion of God's power of creation and resurrection at Q.30:11–19 and Q.30:27, respectively. The complete textual segment from Q.30: 11–27 provides a linguistically emphatic, coherently structured and incrementally constructed teleological argument of God's ultimate power and ordered creation, summarised in its terminal phrase: *wa huwa 'l-'Azīz, Al-Ḥakīm* (He is the Almighty, the All Wise, Abdel Haleem, Q.30:27).

At Q.30:42, the Qur'an again enjoins its audience to see the signs it presents: *fanẓurū* (see), with reference to the outcome of past nations' actions, and *fanẓur* (see, Q.30:50), this time with reference to natural phenomena – namely the sending of rain which revives the dead earth. As in Q.26 above, however, the Qur'an absolves the Prophet of responsibility for persuading those who it terms deaf and blind (Q.30:52 and 53) to the signs presented. Regarding this persistent failure to respond to the Qur'an's invitation, Q.30:59 declares: *kadhālika yaṭba'ullāhu 'alā qulūbi 'lladhīna lā ya'lamūn* (In this way God seals the hearts of those who do not know, Abdel Haleem), concluding by instructing the Prophet: *faṣbir…* (be patient…). The entire matter appears to be postponed to be dealt with not by temporal conflict but by eschatological consequence, discussed in Section 4.3.3 which also deals with God's justice and man's free will.

In the following section, the theme of Qur'anic persuasion and appeal will be examined further, going beyond the use of evidence-based rational argument to explore enhanced Qur'anic modes of intrinsic appeal.

4.3 Enhanced Modes of Intrinsic Appeal

In the previous section, the Qur'an's use of rational argument was highlighted by reference to Q.25–Q.30. As well as appealing to man's intellect and senses which are connected to the head, however, the Qur'an also makes a deeper appeal to the listener's heart. This section discusses in turn these enhanced modes of intrinsic appeal, illustrated especially in suras Q.30–33, which include a primordial appeal to man's innate *fiṭra* (natural disposition), a social appeal to Arab cultural wisdom and an emotional appeal to fear eschatological punishment and hope for everlasting reward. Collectively, this multidimensional and incremental appeal to man's thoughts, intuitions, values and beliefs represents an impressive effort by the Qur'an to persuade its audience and reconcile differences. It is also crucial to another fundamental notion in the Qur'anic discourse as will be discussed in this section: man's ultimate destiny to consider the merits of theological arguments through the use of rational intellect and other modes of appeal, to strive for the truth regarding Divinity and creation through personal endeavour, and to make choices in belief and action which ultimately render him accountable and liable to positive and negative eschatological outcomes.

4.3.1 Individual Appeal Through the Notion of *Fiṭra*

In Q.30:20–25 at the end of the previous section, a number of Divine 'signs' were presented, including man's origins from dust and the revival of dead earth by rain, the existence of harmonious spousal relations and racial diversity, and man's daily harvest and nightly repose. These signs not only evoke the cycle of life and death intended by the argument for a defined Day of Judgement but also evoke a picture of cooperative and conciliatory human existence and endeavour. This unified order of creation is presented as emanating from the unity of God and His religion. Shortly after Q.30:20–25, a highly significant verse Q.30:30 enjoins the Prophet: *fa aqim wajhaka li ('l)-ddīni ḥanīfā,* ***fiṭrata*** *'llāhi 'llatī* ***faṭara*** *('l)-nnāsa ʿalayhā* (So [Prophet] as a man of pure faith, stand firm and true in your devotion to the religion. This is the **natural** disposition God **instilled** in mankind, Abdel Haleem). The identification of a religion based on natural disposition suggests a Qurʾanic appeal to an innate recognition within the constitution of man of God's creative power and unity.

For Al-Rāzī, *fiṭrata 'llāh* indicates the general doctrine of *al-tawḥīd* (unity of God) to which mankind testified through the covenant of Divine Lordship referred to at Q.7:172. Although at Q.30:38 Al-Rāzī does connect God's bounty towards people with the command to spend on others and demonstrate *iḥsān*, he does not indicate a social dimension at Q.30:41 in explaining *fiṭrata 'llāh*. For Iṣlāḥī, however, there is another important dimension to what he terms this *dīn-e-fiṭrat* (religion of natural disposition): Iṣlāḥī (vol.6, pp.85–86) draws special attention to the unity of mankind highlighted in the Qurʾanic passage above despite its diversity of gender and race. The two foundations of the religion of natural disposition are, he argues, *tawḥīd* and *hamdardī-e-khalq* (unity of God and compassion for creation, vol.6, pp.98, 100) which the Meccan disbelievers are accused of violating, respectively reflected in the twin obligations of prayer and spending on social welfare – the latter encapsulated in the command to give relatives, the poor and travellers their rights, at Q.30:38. Iṣlāḥī (vol.6, pp.86–87) argues that introducing division in the Divine world order on the basis of colour, race or language is termed in the Qurʾan: *shirk aur fasād fi 'l-arḍ* (polytheism and disorder in the land). Iṣlāḥī's position is supported by the surrounding verses: Q.30:31 distances believers from those who associate partners with God, fragmenting their religion into divergent factions termed *shiyaʿan* (sects). Q.30:41 meanwhile laments: *ẓahara 'l-fasādu fi 'l-barri wa 'l-baḥri bimā kasabat aydi ('l)-nnās* (Corruption has flourished on land and sea as a result of people's actions, Abdel Haleem).

In Chapter 3, numerous instances were highlighted where Al-Rāzī explains *iḥsān* as respect for God's command and compassion for God's creation (a phrase he also mentions at Q.30:38) with a similar emphasis on prayer involving devotion to God, and on spending on others or other examples of maintaining social relations. Although Iṣlāḥī was criticised in Chapter 3 for failing to adequately recognise the second aspect of *iḥsān* in social relations, here he not only recognises both theological and social aspects of the Qurʾanic teachings but also recognises their essential pairing and foundational importance within the Qurʾanic discourse. Taking Al-Rāzī and Iṣlāḥī's positions together, the Qurʾan invokes the unity of God and creation to call upon man to recognise the extensive efforts he should make to conciliate both with God and with his fellow creatures. As highlighted above, the exemplary models of the *ʿIbād Al-Raḥmān* and Luqmān's ideal incorporated an emphasis on making efforts to achieve both Divine–Human and Social Conciliation. The invocation of the human *fiṭra* is a call to recognise and fulfil the rights of both God and creation and thereby maintain harmonious relations with both.

4.3.2 The Wisdom of Luqmān in Arab Literary Culture

After appealing to man's innate disposition through reference to a *dīn-e-fiṭrat*, Q.31 adds yet another incremental level to the Qur'anic appeal through the narrative of the sage Luqmān, drawing on the wisdom of a figure known to and respected by the Arabs in their own literature. Iṣlāḥī (vol.6, p.125) specifically mentions the pre-Islamic Arab poets Ṭarafa bin ʿAbd and Sulmā bin Rabīʿa as referring to the sage Luqmān in their works. Juynboll (1974, p.243) also cites the classical exegete Ṭabarī in relaying an account of an encounter between the Prophet and a prominent poet Suwayd Bin Al-Ṣāmit, in which Suwayd refers to his possession of Luqmān's book of wisdom, asking the Prophet if he has anything comparable. The Prophet commends the book, before praising the Qur'an as surpassing it. Luqmān's wisdom was thus recognised and appreciated both in pre-Islamic and early Islamic times, and the Arab audience would therefore have been socially conditioned to be receptive to its teachings. In Greenhouse's model (1985, pp.91–2, 98–107), this correlates well with the use of so-called Explicit values, acceptable to the disputing parties' social groups, as a basis for facilitating mediated agreements.

On this basis, Q.31's use of material recognised and venerated by the Arabs constitutes yet another calculated conciliatory appeal. It also indicates a willingness to present a relatively objective reference point correlating the Qur'an's wisdom, indicated by the word *ḥakīm* at Q.31:2, and God's wisdom at Q.31:9, indicated by *Al-Ḥakīm*, to the wisdom bestowed upon Luqmān, indicated at Q.31:12 by *al-ḥikma*. The implication is that the Qur'an's arguments are inherently beneficial and correlate to what the Arabs have already recognised as wisdom. Iṣlāḥī (vol.6, p.115) terms this an appeal to the *ʿaql-e-salīm*, which he translates as 'common sense', going on to highlight the related Western branch of philosophy 'Common Sense Ethics' which is based on the moral judgements of ordinary people (see Brown, 1998 for further explanation of this concept). Iṣlāḥī (vol.6, p.116) adds that where man deviates from his natural disposition and common sense, due to his environment and 'abuse' of his *ikhtiyār* (free will; discussed further in Section 4.3.3), the role of prophets and scripture is to make apparent and thus reinstate that innate disposition.

Although Iṣlāḥī presents a rather neat alignment between revelation, social morality and the Qur'anic notion of an innate human *fiṭra*, Griffel (2012, pp.29–32) argues that Al-Ghazālī's seminal classical analysis of the term *fiṭra* distinguishes *fiṭra* from social conventions of morality and from revelation. Instead, *fiṭra* is 'knowledge that any human can arrive at' (Griffel, 2012, p.32), a function of human sense perception and judgements of *wahm* (faculty of estimation) which are verified by the human intellect. Islam then provides 'true moral judgements' (p.30) derived from Qur'anic revelation. A notable practical illustration of the effect of the human *fiṭra* in the Qur'an is indicated at Q.6:75–79: after perceiving and reflecting on the rising and setting of the heavenly bodies, Abraham chooses monotheism over polytheism. The manifestation of the human *fiṭra* in this passage is made apparent in the close mirroring of phraseology in the *fiṭra* verse Q.30:30 which instructs the Prophet to 'set his face' towards the religion *ḥanīfan* (as a man of pure faith, Abdel Haleem), and Q.6:79 which also presents Abraham's conclusive declaration that he has turned his face towards the Creator of the heavens and the earth *ḥanīfan*.

The notion of *fiṭra* and the wisdom of Luqmān present two complementary appeals: one intuitive and individual, the other based on social morality and communal. Beyond this, in the following section the Qur'an also makes an emotional appeal of fear and hope to mankind as a people, thus using a diverse array of modes of appeal and moving gradually from the micro- to the macro-level within the audience population.

4.3.3 Eschatology: Undertakings, Sanctions and Rewards in the Hereafter

After Q.31, discussed in the preceding section, Q.32 is a relatively short sura of some 30 verses which demonstrates a further motivational appeal based on fear and hope in respect of the Hereafter: Q.32:12–22, around one third of the sura, are devoted to an exposition of eschatological outcomes. The apparent culpability of those who fail to heed Qur'anic admonition through presentation of Divine signs is highlighted through their description at the outset and closure of the passage as *mujrimūn* (wrongdoers/guilty, Abdel Haleem, Q.32:12, 22). Despite claiming, at Q.32:12, to be convinced of the accountability of the Hereafter after finally seeing and hearing its reality, they are threatened with perpetual punishment at Q.32:14 and Q.32:20–22, being charged with turning away from their Lord's *āyāt* (verses or signs, Q.32:22) when (temporally) admonished. The customary Qur'anic antithesis is utilised to exacerbate the motivational effect of Paradise and Hell by presenting the two alongside each other for heightened contrast, with those who believe in God's *āyāt*, are 'not arrogant' and spend from God's bounty, promised unimaginable rewards in Paradise (Q.32:15–19). The juxtaposition of heeding God's signs alongside humility and altruistic social tendency provides a cohesive motivational connection with the conduct espoused in the aspirational Conciliation models of Section 4.1. The motivational utilisation of Paradise and Hell is punctuated throughout Group 4, with notable examples at: Q.25:10–19, 22–34 and 75–76, Q.26:90–102, Q.27: 87–90, Q.28:61–67, 83–84 and Q.30:12–16.

The notion of man's culpability and liability to sanction in Q.32 is explained by two fundamental undertakings mentioned in Q.33, the last sura of Group 4 – the first, towards the sura's inception at Q.33:7, obliging prophets to deliver the Divine message notifying mankind of their obligations and the second at Q.33:72, towards the conclusion of the sura, charging mankind with the duty to fulfil those obligations. The first undertaking at Q.33:7 takes the form of a Divine covenant[12] taken from the prophets: *wa idh akhadhnā mina ('l)-nnabiyyīna mīthāqahum.. wa akhadhnā minhum* ***mīthāqan ghalīẓā*** (We took a solemn pledge from the prophets.. we took a **solemn pledge** from all of them, Abdel Haleem). Iṣlāḥī (vol.6, p.192) highlights that *mīthāq* itself refers to a binding covenant, namely to perform *tablīgh* (propagation of faith), whilst *ghalīẓā* adds yet further gravitas.

The second undertaking in Q.33, at Q.33:72, refers to *al-amāna* (the Trust [of reason and moral responsibility], Abdel Haleem) apparently undertaken by mankind, despite the heavens, the earth and the mountains all professing their incapacity to bear its burden. Regarding this Trust, Iṣlāḥī (vol.6, p.279) states that man's undertaking to obey God is *ikhtiyār o irāda kī āzādī par mabnī* (founded on his capacity to make choices and his free will), and is itself the basis for man's appointment as vicegerent on earth (see Q.2:30 and the related discussion in Section 2.2.2). Al-Rāzī explains *al-amāna* as *al-taklīf wa huwa 'l-amr bi khilāf mā fī 'l-tabīʿa* (obligation, which is a command [to do what is] contrary to one's natural tendency). In this respect, he contrasts the obligation placed on man with the earth, mountains, heavens and angels who act perpetually in accordance with their own predisposition. The same obligation and internal tension faced by man is highlighted in Q.33:72's description of man as *ẓalūman jahūlā*. Iṣlāḥī (vol.6, p.281) provides the most coherent explanation of these terms as indicating man's struggle to choose between *ʿadl* (justice) and its opposite *ẓulm* (injustice) and to choose between *ʿilm* (knowledge) and its opposite *jahl* (ignorance). Nonetheless, the description of man by his apparently 'negative' qualities suggests an innate

---

12 Lumbard (2015, pp.6, 15) refers to this covenant as the second of a trio of covenant phases recognised in classical Islamic scholarship. The first of these three covenants is the primordial Divine covenant made with all humans, mentioned in Q.7:172: *alastu bi rabbikum, qālū balā shahidnā* ('Am I not your Lord?' and they replied, 'Yes we bear witness', Abdel Haleem) and referenced at Q.30:30 in the notion of *fiṭra*. The third is an earthly covenant brought by prophets and taken from time to time by humans in affirmation of the first.

propensity which he must challenge – man's *fiṭra* may bring him to recognise God it seems, but man's natural tendency is not necessarily to obey God.

Man's ability to succeed in this onerous endeavour despite his human frailty of disposition is facilitated by the variable tempering of religious obligations. Al-Ṣabāḥī (2016, p.232) highlights the integral existence of *al-tanawwuʿ fī ʾl-takālīf al-sharʿiyya zamānan wa shakhṣan* (variation in religious legal obligations from time to time and according to the individual concerned) in recognition of man's innate weakness of disposition in performing obligations. Obedience to God's decree, and to the Messenger who enunciates the Divine command, is nonetheless required by Scripture: Q.33:36 declares that once God and His Messenger have pronounced their decree in relation to a matter, it is not befitting for any believing man or woman to exercise their *khiyara* (freedom of choice). Q.33:66 and 71 clarify that failure or dutifulness in *iṭāʿa* (obedience) to God and His Messenger will, respectively, correlate to regret or success in the Hereafter. Although man is 'free' to *exercise* choice, therefore, *how* he exercises that choice is in practice heavily regulated.[13]

The solemn tone and legally binding terminology in the two undertakings of Q.33:7 and 72, a specific prophetic duty to convey and a universal human duty to obey, as well as their strategic positioning towards the two ends of the sura all serve to highlight the importance of their contents. The verses succeeding these two verses clarify that the essential purpose of these legally binding commitments is to justify man's eschatological accountability in the Hereafter for his temporal choices and actions, a fundamental tenet of the Qurʾanic discourse. Q.33:8 refers to the questioning of the truthful and the punishment of the disbelievers, whilst Q.33:73 refers to the punishment of the hypocrites and polytheists

13 In discussing man's ability to make 'free' choices, it should be mentioned that man's status as a 'free' agent or a creature of destiny has given rise to much theological debate in classical literature. The principle theoretical positions are set out by Salem (2014), who discusses the influential Epistle to ʿAbd al-Malik, traditionally ascribed to the famous Ḥasan al-Baṣrī, although this authorship has been challenged by Wansborough, Cook and Mourad. The Epistle has often been considered a document championing man's free will, thus preserving the paramount importance of God's justice in holding man accountable for his actions, a theological position advocated by the non-orthodox Muʿtazila theological school of thought. The Epistle has become controversial in its apparent 'rejection' of the important notion of *qadar* (God's unfettered determination of events). Such a rejection of *qadar* is associated with the doctrine of those branded 'Qadarites'. By reconciling *qadar* with man's free will through the fundamental notion of *kasb*, man's acquisition of punishment and reward through the relative merits of his actions, the Ashʿarī school became representative of mainstream Sunni theology. Salem (2014, p.217) argues that a close reading of the historically significant Epistle positions its arguments much closer to this mainstream Sunni theological doctrine, than to the positions of the Muʿtazila or the Qadarites.

and the forgiveness of the believers. Both verses Q.33:8 and Q.33:73 commence with the prepositional *lām* of *taʿlīl* (justification), indicating that the accountability, reward and sanction that they refer to ensue from the binding obligations and responsibilities undertaken in their preceding verses. It can readily be seen that reason and responsibility are closely coupled, as is apparent from Abdel Haleem's above annotation to his translation of Q.33:72. The exhaustive rational appeal to mankind through religious propagation by prophets, and man's ability to make 'free' choices in response, is integral to the imposition of responsibility upon him and to his ultimate accountability.

Moving through the later suras of Group 4, a hierarchy of Qur'anic appeals has emerged from the personal appeal to *fiṭra* in Q.30, to the communal appeal to the Arabs in Q.31 and then the universal appeal to mankind in Q.33. A temporal progression of appeals can also be seen from the association in Q.30 with the primordial past covenant of Divine Lordship to the Qur'anic 'present' of Arab culture in Q.31 and finally the eschatological future in Q.32 and Q.33. The modes of appeal have varied from the intuitive to the social and then, in this section, an emotional appeal of fear and hope coupled with a heightened sense of gravitas and urgency through the use of binding legal contractual language and supportive sanctions. The cross-layering of these appeals, as a supplement to the already exhaustive rational arguments discussed in Section 4.2, demonstrates the extensive Qur'anic effort to persuade its audience. Conversely, propagation of faith based on compulsion rather than this manifest conciliatory appeal would be self-defeating in the Qur'anic schema and would simply not achieve the Qur'an's own purpose of imposing eschatological sanction and reward consequent on a human choice.

Summary Table: Group 4 Conciliation Themes Map by Sura and Verse

	Conciliation models	Conciliation through rational argument	Modes of Appeal
Q.25	63–76 *ʿIbād Al-Raḥmān* – conflict avoidance, *salām* and disengagement	1–34 disbelievers' contentions 35–44 signs – prophetic narratives 45–62 signs – natural phenomena	

(continued)

	Conciliation models	Conciliation through rational argument	Modes of Appeal
Q.26		10–189 prophetic narratives	
Q.27			
Q.28	4 Pharaoh arrogant and amongst *mufsidīn* 15, 24 Moses and social justice 52 Moses' emigration 52–55 People of the Book – *iḥsān* and *salām* 77 Qārūn admonished for *fasād* and failure to show *iḥsān*		
Q.29	46 *iḥsān* in religious debate 56 indication of pending migration 69 God is with those who show *iḥsān*		
Q.30		21–24 sensory and rational argument	30 appeal to *fiṭra* (natural disposition)
Q.31	12–19 Luqmān's advice – social relations, patience, humility 3, 22 Luqmān's advice framed by references to *iḥsān*		12 Arab cultural wisdom in Luqmān's advice
Q.32			12–22 eschatological outcomes
Q.33			72 man encumbered with an *amāna* (trust)

Conclusion

The core Conciliation theme of Qur'anic persuasion is pervasive throughout the suras of Group 4, with the Qur'an apparently striving for Divine–Human Conciliation but ultimately leaving the outcome to human 'free' choice – the latter concept giving rise to much debate. Q.25 and Q.26 in particular specifically address the contentions of the Prophet's Meccan opponents, whilst Q.30 provides a notably strong rendition of the Qur'anic argument in response. Q.30–Q.33 reinforce this argument by presenting an escalating sequence of complementary modes of appeal. Against this sustained thematic canvas, a number of prominent Conciliation models are emphatically punctuated at regular intervals, in particular the *ʿIbād Al-Raḥmān* in Q.25, the People of the Book and Moses in Q.28, and Luqmān's ideal in Q.31. These notably holistic Conciliation models portray exemplary characters which live in harmony with both God and creation, exerting themselves towards the attainment of both Divine–Human and Social Conciliation. The Qurʾan thus exemplifies Conciliation through its own sustained persuasive style and at the same time motivates the Prophet and his followers in particular, and to some extent the Meccan audience at large, to emulate the conciliatory conduct of the aspirational models presented.

As well as the Qurʾan's own persuasive style, the Group 4 suras demonstrate a diverse but inter-related range of Conciliation concepts, both familiar and novel. The recurring notion of *iḥsān* features in the *ʿIbād Al-Raḥmān's* earthly tread described as *hawnan*, reflecting a propensity towards conflict avoidance and containment as well as an innate aversion to *fasād*. The notion of *iḥsān* again frames the exposition of Luqmān's ideal and is an essential feature of the conciliatory conduct of the People of the Book. Also emphasising Social Conciliation in the Group 4 suras, the fundamental dual notions of social equality and social justice, less apparent in previous chapters, become the cornerstones of three important Conciliation models. The recurrent lauding of humble and harmonious co-existence and altruism provide a perfect antithesis to the denunciation of social division and personal greed, personified by the arrogant Pharaoh and Qārūn, respectively. Notably Pharaoh is condemned in the Divine voice as an instrument of *fasād* whilst Qārūn is fittingly reproached by his own people for failing to reflect Divine *iḥsān* in his own social conduct. The migration of Moses, like Joseph before him, serves as an example of ultimate disengagement from conflict, preparing the Prophet for his own pending migration, whilst the valedictory *salām* of the *ʿIbād Al-Raḥmān* and the People of the Book brings to mind the gracious disengagement of Abraham, another example for the Prophet and his followers.

From a literary perspective, the use of narratives such as that of Moses, and defined pericopes to characterise specifically titled individuals such as the *ʿIbād Al-Raḥmān*, personifies and enlivens the illustrative Conciliation models, with the textual weight given to each of the three models also enhancing their exemplary value. A similar dynamic style is reflected in the rhetorical eloquence of the Qurʾanic argument and use of persuasion. Dialogical markers presenting contentions and responses produce a dramatic script with rhetorical markers and recurrent refrains in the Qurʾanic response adding emphasis and impact. The punctuation of this narrative with interactive questions adds a further penetrative quality to an already dynamic narrative.

In terms of structural and thematic coherence, the Group 4 suras demonstrate a coherent sequential progression from dealing with the contentions of the Meccans to presenting *āyāt* in response and then concluding by encumbering mankind with an *amāna* (trust) reinforced by eschatological consequence. The fundamental appeal to man's innate *fiṭra*, a hallmark of his inception, represents a profound and timeless call to Divine–Human Conciliation, also manifest in the binding *iḍāfa* construct in the term *fiṭrata 'llāh* upon which man's *fiṭra* is modelled. I have argued the existence of what I would term a 'Matrix of Appeals', offering a chronological temporal progression from the primordial to the eschatological, a complementary set of appeals based on intellect, intuition, culture and emotion, and a hierarchy of audience reach from the individual to the collective and then universal.

5 Conciliation in Theory and Practice

Overview: Group 5 Suras – Q.34–Q.49

The suras in Group 5 consist of a cluster of Meccan suras from Q.34 to Q.46 (Q.34 Sūrat Ṣabā, Q.35 Sūrat Fāṭir, Q.36 Sūrat Yāsīn, Q.37 Sūrat Al-Ṣāffāt, Q.38 Sūrat Ṣād, Q.39 Sūrat Al-Zumar, Q.40 Sūrat Al-Muʾmin/Sūrat Ghāfir, Q.41 Sūrat Ḥāmīm Al-Sajda/Sūrat Fuṣṣilat, Q.42 Sūrat Al-Shūrā, Q.43 Sūrat Al-Zukhruf, Q.44 Sūrat Al-Dukhān, Q.45 Sūrat Al-Jāthiya and Q.46 Sūrat Al-Aḥqāf) followed by three Medinan suras (Q.47 Sūrat Muḥammad, Q.48 Sūrat Al-Fatḥ and Q.49 Sūrat Al-Ḥujurāt). The Meccan suras continue their admonition of the dominant Meccan audience with reminders of the fate of past nations and graphic scenes of the promised Day of Judgment, whilst the fortitude of past prophets is held out as an exemplar for the Prophet and his long-suffering followers. The historical setting of the Medinan suras provides a contrasting context of a more emboldened Muslim community militarily challenging and then negotiating peace terms with the Meccan leadership.

In the Farāhī-Iṣlāḥī schema, the theme of this group is *tawḥīd* (The Unity of God). The suras are paired 34–35, 36–37, 38–39, (40–41), 42–43, 44–45. Suras 46, 47 and 48 are indicated to be thematically related but are unaccounted for in formal pairing, with 49 an addendum to 48, as discussed by Mir (1986, p.81). This appears to be a notable area of relative weakness in the detailed theoretical framework presented by Iṣlāḥī in particular, an issue which is addressed by the investigations in this chapter. The specified sura themes in the Meccan suras centre around *tawḥīd*, the Day of Judgment, the need for Prophethood and the promise of God's assistance, whilst the Medinan suras deal with war and victory.

Conciliation has featured in earlier chapters in the form of quasi-legal process, contractual agreements, ethical values and a conciliatory style of engagement. I will argue that in this chapter the Conciliation narrative reaches its apex, becoming central to the Qurʾanic discourse, fundamentally shaping the history of the nascent Islamic faith and the Prophet's legacy, and prescribing a comprehensive, detailed and profound Conciliation paradigm. Three principal Conciliation themes emerge: (i) the virtue of patience, which highlights the need for long-term engagement in Conciliation; (ii) a practical example of Conciliation in the landmark historical Treaty of Ḥudaybiya and (iii) a theoretical prospective framework for both Divine–Human and Social Conciliation in Sūrat Al-Ḥujurāt (Q.49). Each of these three central themes is outlined in the Summary Table at the end of Section 5.3 and is now discussed in turn in the following

https://doi.org/10.1515/9783110747348-007

sections of this chapter. It should be noted that due to the distribution of the thematic content across the Group, the numerous Meccan suras are dealt with in a single section, whilst two sections of the chapter are devoted to the relatively few Medinan suras. This reflects the higher proportion of Conciliation material in the Medinan content, as well as the extensive engagement with Meccan themes in previous chapters.

Key Conciliation verses analysed in the first section of this chapter include Q.38:17, 20 and 21–26 regarding the story of David, Q.39:10 regarding migration, Q.41:33–36 regarding perseverance and Q.42:39–43 on the subject of retribution and forgiveness. In the second section, the argument discussing the notion of 'victory' focusses around Q.48:1–4, Q.48:18 and Q.48:26–28. The final section moves systematically through Q.49, addressing first the subject of inner transformation by reference to Q.49:1–8, then the duty of reconciliation at Q.49:9–10 and finally the prohibition of insulting speech at Q.49:11–12, concluding with a verse emphasising unity at Q.49:13.

5.1 The Virtue of Patience

After close investigation of the Conciliation verses in the Group 5 suras of the Meccan period, and a protracted reflection on their core message, it became apparent that the central Conciliation theme in these suras is the enjoinder of patience and perseverance on the Prophet and, by extension, his followers. The Qur'anic notion of *ṣabr* (patience) also featured in the earlier Group 3 suras, notably towards the conclusion of four suras in an enjoinder towards patience directed at the Prophet, at Q.10:109, Q.11:115 (also at Q.11:49), Q.16:127 and Q.20:130. A memorable motif advocating patience was also recurrent in the Story of Joseph at Q.12:18 and 83. As explained in Chapter 3, the instances in Q.11, Q.12 and Q.16 in particular connect *ṣabr* with the notion of *iḥsān* (gracious conduct), a connection which recurs in the ensuing discussion below. It can be appreciated that the notion of *ṣabr* would, as a general concept, be a relevant enjoinder given the 13-year Meccan history of apparent persecution and limited success in religious propagation, as well as the anticipation of a decade of challenges and strife in the forthcoming Medinan period. Through close examination of the Qur'anic text and supporting references, however, further insight can be obtained into the technical meaning of the notion of *ṣabr* and its relevance to Conciliation.

According to Abdel Haleem and Badawi (2013, p.508), the root *ṣ-b-r* features as much as 103 times in the Qur'an across 10 forms and includes in its meanings the notions of 'patience', 'perseverance' and 'restraint'. ʿAbd Al-Bāqī

(2001, p.399) provides further elucidation of the Qur'anic usage, listing no less than 19 instances of the imperative *iṣbir* (be patient), 18 of which are directed specifically at the Prophet. These 19 instances consist of the 5 mentioned above in Group 3 suras (and 1 additional reference in the same group at Q.18:28), 2 references in Group 4, 7 references in Groups 6 & 7 and the following 4 references in Group 5: **Q.38:17**, Q.40:55, Q.40:77 and **Q.46:35**. Numerous additional references to the root *ṣ-b-r* are manifest in Group 5 suras at **Q.42:43**, Q.46:35 (*ṣabara*); **Q.41:35**, Q.49:5 (*ṣabarū*); Q.41:24 (*yaṣbirū*); Q.38:6 (*iṣbirū*); Q.38:44 (*ṣābiran*); **Q.39:10** (*al-ṣābirūn*); Q.37:102, Q.47:31 (*al-ṣābirīn*); Q.34:19, Q.42:33 (*ṣabbārin*). The five verses cited in bold are particularly relevant to Conciliation and will be analysed in context in the discussion below.

5.1.1 The Story of David

In the first sequential instance of the above verses at Q.38:17, the Prophet is enjoined with the command *iṣbir* (be patient) to show patience in the face of the Meccans' ridicule and rejection of the promised Day of Judgement, reinforced with a reminder of the prophet David who is presented as a paragon of fortitude and repentance. At Q.38:20, we are also told of David's power, wisdom and discerning speech. This is followed at Q.38:21–26 by an account of 2 disputants who unexpectedly intrude upon David's privacy seeking his judgement in a matter concerning their respective ownership of sheep, 1 disputant apparently owning 99 whilst demanding his brother's remaining sheep. The story demonstrates some irony in that the plaintiff accuses the defendant at Q.38:23 of overpowering him in speech, despite lucidly presenting his case before David whilst the defendant apparently remains silent and judgement is pronounced against him. Q.38:24 also refers to David having been tested and seeking God's forgiveness for being at fault, giving rise to speculative discussions in the commentaries as to the nature of his test. Despite the opacities mentioned, I would argue that the story itself provides a clear principle advocating the resolution of disputes with justice in no less than three separate dramatic voices, providing successive emphasis and impact; the full significance of this emphasis and some clarification of the opacities mentioned will come to light further in Section 5.3.2.

Firstly, the plaintiff introduces the dispute at Q.38:22 saying: *khaṣmāni baghā baʿḍunā ʿalā baʿḍin fa 'ḥkum baynanā bi 'l-ḥaqqi wa lā tushṭiṭ wa 'hdinā ilā sawāʾi ('l)-ṣṣirāṭ* (we are two litigants, one of whom has wronged the other: judge between us fairly – do not be unjust – and guide us to the right path, Abdel Haleem). To my mind, the plaintiff's concise and emphatic entreaty is given a special resonance by the silence of the defendant. The second dramatic voice is that of David at Q.38:24 who declares that the defendant has *ẓalamaka* (wronged you) and *wa inna kathīran mina 'l-khulaṭā'i layabghī baʿḍuhum ʿalā baʿḍin illa 'lladhīna āmanū wa ʿamilu ('l)-ṣṣāliḥāti* (Many partners treat each other unfairly. Those who sincerely believe and do good deeds do not do this, but these are very few, Abdel Haleem). In addition to his temporal and spiritual authority as king and prophet, David's words are also given special credence by his introduction at Q.38:20 as enjoying the Divine gift of *al-ḥikmata wa faṣla 'l-khiṭāb* (wisdom and a decisive way of speaking, Abdel Haleem). Yusuf Ali (Ali, p.1166, n.4176-A), however, draws attention to the suggestion by some commentators that 'David's fault here was his hastiness in judging before hearing the case of the other party.' In his obvious zeal to do justice, therefore, David may have fallen short of the high standard of fairness expected of him and repented. This point is discussed further in Section 5.3.2.

Finally, the Divine voice itself pronounces ultimate 'judgement' over David, the human authority, using the plural of majesty and drawing special attention by turning dramatically from the third-person reference to David at Q.38:24–25 to a direct address towards him at Q.38:26: *yā dāwūdu innā jaʿalnāka* ***khalīfatan*** *fi 'l-arḍi fa 'ḥkum bayna ('l)-nnāsi bi 'l-ḥaqqi wa lā tattabiʿi 'l-hawā fa yuḍillaka ʿan sabīli 'llāh* (David, We have given you mastery over the land. Judge fairly between people. Do not follow your desires, lest they divert you from God's path, Abdel Haleem). The verse goes on to declare that deviation from God's path ultimately leads to eschatological punishment for those who are heedless of the Day of Judgement.

The above term *khalīfatan* also raises another point discussed in Chapter 2. Abdel Haleem's translation of *khalīfatan* here as 'mastery' retracts, in my view, from appreciating the full import of this statement. Nasr's alternative 'vicegerent' is not only true to the linguistic terminology but also preserves the link to Q.2:30 where the prophet Adam's appointment as vicegerent is first declared by God to the celestial audience at man's inception. As one who combines the spiritual and temporal offices of prophet and king, David is especially entitled to inherit the title of *khalīfa* and to be encumbered with the full responsibility of meting out just decisions to his charges with due process and impartiality. As a holder of such high office and Divinely gifted character, he is also a role model for his nation and future prophets and their followers. In short, David is required to maintain *iṣlāḥ* (order) on the earth which, as I have argued in Chapter 2, is the role of each prophet as God's vicegerent on earth.

My argument is supported by the immediately ensuing verses which declare that God has not created the heavens and the earth *bāṭilan* (without purpose, Abdel Haleem, Q.38:27) but rather to distinguish the eschatological treatment of two types of people. The first are those who *āmanū wa ʿamilu ('l)-ṣṣāliḥāti* (believe and do good deeds, Abdel Haleem). At Q.38:24 above, David uses this same phrase to describe those who do not transgress against others and *ṣāliḥāt* is from the same root as *iṣlāḥ*. The second category, whose treatment is to be distinguished, is the *mufsidīn fi 'l-arḍi* (those who spread corruption on earth, Abdel Haleem). As discussed in Chapter 2, *fasād* (disorder) is the Qur'anic opposite of *iṣlāḥ*. Transgression and injustice then is an example of corruption, and prophets and scripture are sent to rectify precisely such disorder on earth.

Before concluding the discussion of David's story, it is necessary to return to the opening verse Q.38:17 and examine the question of why the Prophet is instructed to be patient and at the same time to remember the prophet David. Iṣlāḥī (vol.6, pp.518, 521, 524) suggests that the Prophet is to console himself by recalling David's forbearance with the disputants' unorthodox manner of approaching him and his patience in hearing their case, as well as to admonish the Meccans by reminding them of David's gratitude to God despite being powerful. A single instance of mild forbearance and patience of this type seems to me an inadequate explanation of the exemplar of patience held forth to the Prophet who apparently faced years of mockery and rejection as described in the prelude to the sura. Further on the sura also holds out the prophet Job, finally cured after years of illness and deprivation, as *ṣābiran* (patient in adversity, Abdel Haleem, Q.38:44) and also cites the example of Jacob (and his forefathers), known for his patience over years of separation from Joseph, describing him as amongst *uli 'l-aydī* (men of strength, Abdel Haleem, Q.38:45). Notably, David is also described as *dha 'l-aydi* (a man of strength, Abdel Haleem) at Q.38:17, the primary characteristic mentioned immediately after his name collocated with the command of patience enjoined on the Prophet.

In light of the above analysis of the story of David, I would argue that the Prophet is instructed to remain steadfast in the face of protracted opposition, like David showing fortitude of character and continued exactitude in compliance with God's command as he progresses to a position of power, and to look forward in preparation for his own future inheritance of the mantle of office. Like David, he will in turn inherit the title of God's vicegerent and combine the offices of prophethood and government in Medina, where he too will be responsible for adjudicating disputes with discernment and upholding justice, thus maintaining *iṣlāḥ* (order). In one particularly relevant *ḥadīth*, the Prophet is quoted as acknowledging his own human frailty in potentially adjudicating unfairly in favour of a litigant, having been swayed by his relative eloquence over the other, and having cautioned against the acceptance of such unjust enrichment (Muslim, Book 4, Ḥadīth 1713). The role of the Prophet in Medina as a conciliator and an adjudicator of disputes has already been discussed in Chapter 2.

Al-Rāzī provides support for my interpretation of *dha 'l-aydi* as fortitude of character and exactitude in compliance with God's command, in contrast to Abdel Haleem and Nasr who translate it as 'strength' and 'might', respectively, indicating physical strength or power. Al-Rāzī states at Q.38:17: *'dha 'l-aydi' ay dha 'l-quwwa ʿalā adāʾ al-ṭāʿa wa 'l-iḥtirāz ʿani 'l-maʿāṣī* (*dha 'l-aydi* meaning one who possesses strength in the accomplishment of obedience and guarding against sin). Commenting on the juxtaposition of the enjoinder towards patience and the mention of David, Al-Rāzī highlights David's exemplary character: *fa amara Muḥammadan ṣalla 'llāhu ʿalayhi wa sallam ʿalā jalālat qadrihi bi an yaqtadī fi 'l-ṣabr ʿalā ṭāʿat Allāh bi Dāwūd wa dhālika tashrīfun ʿaẓīmun wa ikrāmun li Dāwūd* (God commanded Muhammad peace be upon him despite the majesty of his status that he emulate David in steadfastness in obedience to Allah, and that is a great honouring and ennoblement of David).

In summary, the Prophet, who is enduring alienation and ridicule as he strives to propagate the new faith, is presented with an ideal role model in David: a prophet who has gradually risen to earthly power and yet consistently and unwaveringly maintained his sense of exactitude in seeking to implement justice in precise obedience to God's command. Like Joseph's virtues as he ascends to power, the story of David's fortitude of character and just kingdom provides another exemplar for the Prophet who will one day also assume a position of temporal power. The three-fold condemnation of transgression and injustice also accords with a theme which recurs in Sections 5.1.3 and 5.3 further on. After discussing the presentation of David as a practical role model of patience and justice, we will now turn to a more theoretical analysis of how patience is particularly relevant to Conciliation moving sequentially through the relevant Qurʾanic discourse.

5.1.2 Patience as a Means to Conciliation

In the Farāhī-Iṣlāḥī schema, Q.38 is paired with its successor Q.39 and my own analysis demonstrates some notable correlation. Firstly, Q.39:67–75 concludes Q.39 with a particularly detailed and graphic illustration of the Day of Judgement, apparently ridiculed by the Meccans at the commencement of Q.38. Secondly, at Q.38:26, in the above account of David's story, David is commanded to adjudicate *bi 'l-ḥaqqi* (with justice) and is also reminded of *yawma 'l-ḥisāb* (the Day of Reckoning). In adjudicating at Q.38:24, David also finds one disputant has *ẓalama* (wronged) the other. Meanwhile in Q.39, Q.39:69 informs us of God's Divine justice in the Hereafter with the same terminology highlighting the crucial role of man as God's *khalīfa*, mirroring in this world God's Divine justice in the Hereafter: *wa quḍiya baynahum bi 'l ḥaqqi* (judgement will be decided between them with justice) *wa hum lā yuẓlamūn* (and they will not be wronged). The first part of this statement is repeated again at Q.39:75 providing further emphasis.

Thirdly, also adhering to the subject of eschatological outcome whilst returning to the theme of patience discussed at Q.38:17 above, Q.39:10 declares: *li 'lladhīna* ***aḥsanū*** *fī hādhihi ('l)-ddunya ḥasanatun, wa arḍu 'llāhi wāsiʿatun, innamā yuwaffa ('l)-****ṣṣābirūna*** *ajrahum bi ghayri ḥisāb* (Those who do good in this world will have a good reward – God's earth is wide – and those who persevere patiently will be given a full and unstinting reward, Abdel Haleem). The notion of *iḥsān* (gracious conduct) has already been discussed extensively in Chapter 3 and has remained recurrent through Chapter 4. As will become apparent, this recurrence continues through this chapter, highlighting that this term has a uniquely pervasive and integral importance to the theme of Conciliation in the Qur'an. Although the verse does not expressly define *iḥsān* here, its collocation with an apparent allusion towards migration and the promise of eschatological reward for patience indicates remaining steadfast in faith whilst withstanding persecution, and withdrawing from a situation of continuing conflict despite the hardships and loss entailed by emigrating from Mecca. The use of the *ism ul-fāʿil* (active participle) in *ṣābirūn* above denotes an inherent characteristic of lasting patience.

The phrase 'God's earth is vast' at Q.39:10 above (and elsewhere at Q.29:56) alludes to a motivation towards emigration by the Prophet and his followers, a connection which is explicitly apparent from the Medinan verse Q.4:97 which follows a near-identical phrase with *fa tuhājirū* (for you to migrate, Abdel Haleem). In Q.39:10, Al-Rāzī prefers this view to a suggestion by the commentator Abū Muslim that the phrase alludes to the vastness of Paradise, on the basis that the first interpretation is more compatible with the subsequent reference to those who are patient. He explains: *wa 'l-murād hāhunā bi* ***'l-ṣābirīn*** *alladhīna ṣabarū ʿalā mufāraqat awṭānihim wa ʿashāʾirihim wa ʿalā tajarraʿ al-ghuṣaṣ wa iḥtimāl al-balāyā fī ṭāʿat Allāh* (what is intended here by *al-ṣābirīn* are those who endure separation from their homelands and their tribes, and (endure) the swallowing of distress, and the suffering of tribulations in the obedience of God). This temporal loss and suffering is compensated by eschatological reward, Al-Rāzī this time favouring the view that the Divine promise of *ḥasanatun* is the reward of Paradise rather than earthly reward, with the *tankīr* (indefinite) indicating its glory and unimaginable perfection.

The above reference to patience highlights the *magnitude* of forbearance and sacrifice required to remain true to one's beliefs whilst avoiding conflict with those who are hostile to those same beliefs. Two suras later at Q.41:33–36, another passage connecting *iḥsān* and *ṣabr* highlights another aspect of patience, namely the protracted *frequency* with which *iḥsān*, meaning gracious conduct towards others, must be displayed to go beyond conflict avoidance and achieve lasting and complete Conciliation. This passage is remarkable for its relatively sustained and explicit inspirational motivation towards Conciliation as well as its collection and inter-connection of Conciliation terminology and principles in a single passage. Q.41:33 asks who is *aḥsanu qawlan* (better in speech) than the one who calls to God and *ʿamila ṣāliḥan* (acts righteously), beginning the passage with a reference to *iḥsān* in speech. This has been explained in more detail in Q.16:125, discussed in Chapter 3, where we also find four references enjoining *ṣabr* on the Prophet and his followers in two adjacent near-concluding verses at Q.16:126–127, and two references to *iḥsān* in the same passage at Q.16:125 and 128.

Q.41:34 continues by differentiating between good and evil conduct, and then instructing (the Prophet, according to Abdel Haleem): *idfaʿ bi 'llatī hiya aḥsanu fa idha 'lladhī baynaka wa baynahū ʿadāwatun ka annahū waliyyun ḥamīm* (repel evil with what is better and your enemy will become as close as an old and valued friend, Abdel Haleem). Nasr (p.1165) highlights, based on the commentary of Ibn Kathīr: 'Such conduct can lead to reconciliation, love and empathy.' Nasr also draws attention to the absence of an object after the imperative *idfaʿ*, providing examples of possible conduct which should be repelled (see also the similar verse Q.23:96 where the object *al-ssayyiʾata* (evil) is stated but deferred in the sentence). I would add that this *ḥadhf* (ellipsis) provides a powerful expansion in the scope of the command by rhetorical effect, as if to say 'no matter the type or greatness of the evil conduct you have suffered, repel it with what is better'. The same ellipsis also powerfully symbolises by its very grammatical omission, the evasion and overlooking of the harmful problematic conduct of the other and focusses the mind on the solution through one's personal conduct. The imperative verb *idfaʿ* (repel) is itself loaded with meaning, highlighting the need to protect one's character and the relationship between the parties from harm. At the same time, any retaliatory connotation in the word is nullified by the term *aḥsanu* (better).

The notion of reciprocating harm with good as a means of breaking vicious cycles of conflict, de-escalating and containing conflict, and even promoting a virtuous cycle of cooperation is a crucial principle in Conciliation and has been discussed extensively in Chapter 3. Although this principle is in itself counter-intuitive and thus remarkable, it has been encountered in other verses. What is therefore perhaps most remarkable in the above verse Q.41:34 is not only the principle of reciprocating harm with good but what follows. The ambitious assertion of the verse and the strategic reach of its explicit Conciliation objective is extraordinary. Through the implementation of one, albeit multi-dimensional, principle of reciprocating harm with good, the Qurʾan aims not only to limit harm to one's self or the other, or to contain a situation of conflict, but to transform a relationship which has deteriorated to a state of *ʿadāwatun* (enmity), to a relationship of reliable and lasting friendship. The noun *waliyyun* has connotations of providing assistance and support (see for example the reference to angels as *awliyāʾ* (allies, Abdel Haleem) at Q.41:31 three verses earlier) as well as mere companionship, whilst the adjective *ḥamīm* adds a sense of special proximity and intimacy to the relationship (see Q.70:10 for another notable use of the term drawing on this meaning).

Such transformation is not, however, lightly asserted and the ensuing Q.41:35 qualifies that the objective of such absolute Conciliation is only attained by those who persevere, demonstrating *ṣabr*: *wa mā yulaqqāhā illa 'lladhīna ṣabarū, wa mā yulaqqāhā illā dhū ḥaẓẓin ʿaẓīm* (but only those who are steadfast in patience, only those who are blessed with great righteousness, will attain to such goodness, Abdel Haleem). Al-Rāzī provides his customarily illuminating commentary at Q.41:34. Regarding the phrase *idfaʿ bi 'llatī hiya aḥsanu*, he elucidates: *yaʿnī idfaʿ safāhatahum wa jahālatahum bi 'l-ṭarīq alladhī huwa aḥsan al-ṭuruq, fa innaka idhā ṣabarta ʿalā sūʾ akhlāqihim* ***marratan baʿda ukhrā***, *wa lam tuqābil safāhatahum bi 'l-ghaḍab wa lā iḍrārahum bi 'l-iydhāʾ wa 'l-iyḥāsh* ***istaḥyū*** *min tilka 'l-akhlāq al-madhmūma wa tarakū tilka 'l-afʿāl al-qabīḥa* (meaning repel their foolishness and ignorance in the way that is the best of ways, for if you endure their bad manners **time after time**, having never countered their foolishness with anger nor their harm with injury or isolation, they will feel **ashamed** by such reprehensible manners and desist from such repulsive acts).

The phrase *marratan baʿda ukhrā* (time after time), used by Al-Rāzī, is particularly revealing. Demonstrating *iḥsān* is not an instant solution resulting in lasting Conciliation. Rather, Conciliation demands patience in the recurrent display of *iḥsān* over a protracted duration. It requires perseverance and a long-term perspective. It is only this recurrent *iḥsān* which results in others feeling ashamed by their actions. This sense of shame is the catalyst for the transformation in the relationship. Al-Rāzī elaborates further: *yaʿnī idhā qābalta isāʾatahum bi 'l-iḥsān, wa afʿālahum al-qabīḥa bi 'l-afʿāl al-ḥasana tarakū afʿālahum al-qabīḥa wa* ***inqalabū*** *min al ʿadāwa ila 'l-maḥabba wa min al-bighḍa ila 'l-mawadda* (meaning if you counter their harm with gracious conduct and their repulsive acts with acts of kindness they will desist from their repulsive acts and **turn** from enmity to affection and from hatred to love).

It is clear that such conduct requires the absorption of harm over a protracted duration without retribution and amounts to a significant feat of self-restraint. At the same time, it requires the individual to not lose heart and to persevere undaunted in their *iḥsān* despite having seen their positive conduct reciprocated by harm on multiple previous occasions. It is this unyielding inner strength of purpose and character which, in my view, is indicated by the phrase *dhū ḥaẓẓin ʿaẓīm* at Q.41:35. Yusuf Ali's 'persons of the greatest good fortune' and Nasr's 'those who possess great fortune' do not provide the correct emphasis, focussing on fortune rather than fortitude and even Abdel Haleem's 'those who are blessed with great righteousness' tends towards emphasising piety over fortitude and determination. Abdel Haleem and Badawi (2013, p.219) list two meaning of *ḥaẓẓ*, one meaning 'a fortunate person' and the other meaning 'an allocation'. Thus, the meaning of the term as used in the verse, immediately following a clear reference to patience, could be 'one who has been blessed with great fortitude'.

At Q.41:35, Al-Rāzī only briefly, as an afterthought, contemplates the phrase *dhū ḥaẓẓin ʿaẓīm* as indicating reward for patience in the Hereafter, instead leading with an alternative meaning which he shows preference by explaining it in detail as follows: *min al-faḍāʾil al-nafsāniyya wa 'l-darajat al-ʿāliya fi 'l-quwwa al-rūḥāniyya, fa inna 'l-ishtighāl bi 'l-intiqām wa 'l-dafʿ lā yaḥṣulu illā baʿda taʾaththur al-nafs, wa taʾaththur al-nafs min al-wāridāt al-khārijiyya lā yaḥṣulu illā ʿinda ḍuʿf al-nafs fa ammā idhā kānat al-nafs qawiyyat al-jawhar lam tataʾaththar min al-wāridāt al-khārijiyya* (with respect to qualities of disposition and a high level of spiritual strength, since being occupied with retribution and repulsion only comes about after the disposition is affected, and the disposition is only affected by external influences where there is weakness of disposition. As for the case where the disposition is intrinsically strong, it is not affected by external influences). Al-Rāzī's explanation not only supports my interpretation and emphasis but also dissects the notion of fortitude of character revealing the need for one party to remain uninfluenced by the harm of the other and thus disrupt a negative chain of causation which would otherwise lead to the inception and escalation of conflict.

In the above quotation from Al-Rāzī *al-quwwa al-rūḥāniyya* (spiritual strength) draws attention to the internal human struggle to choose the path of Conciliation promoted and prescribed by God, and overcome the incitement of Satan towards conflict and strife. Immediately after lauding those possessing *ḥaẓẓin ʿaẓīm*, Q.41:36 continues: *wa immā yanzaghannaka mina ('l)-shshayṭāni nazghun fa 'staʿidh bi 'llāhi* (if a prompting from Satan should stir you, seek refuge with God, Abdel Haleem). Notably, this exact formulation is repeated at Q.7:200, also immediately after another seminal Conciliation verse directed at the Prophet. It becomes clear that the entire passage Q.41:33–36, advocating perseverance in *iḥsān* and *ṣabr* over a protracted duration, is a motivation to the Prophet to persist in a struggle across two decades and the two environs of Mecca and Medina which would ultimately result in, and not jeopardise, an epic reconciliation with his people, also related to him by kinship, at the Conquest of Mecca. Narratives highlighting the *iḥsān* and *ṣabr* displayed by Joseph and Jacob and David's fortitude of character serve to support these direct enjoinders. Further on, Q.60:7 intimates towards the forthcoming reconciliation, declaring that God may yet bring about *mawadda* (love) between yourselves, apparently addressing the Prophet and his followers, and *alladhīna ʿādaytum* (your present enemies, Abdel Haleem). This verse demonstrates the aptness of Al-Rāzī's above use of the term *mawadda* in discussing the transformation of relationships from enmity to love at Q.41:33–36.

The term *mawadda* features again in the following sura at Q.42:23 where the Prophet is instructed to say that he seeks no recompense for his efforts to guide his people except: *mawaddata fi 'l-qurbā* (love amongst relatives). This expression has given rise to alternative interpretations in the various commentaries and translations which can be summarised through the analysis provided by Iṣlāḥī (vol.7, pp.165–67). He strongly supports an interpretation which can be paraphrased: 'except that I do this out of concern for you as my relatives', basing his view on Q.26:214 where the Prophet is commanded to warn his closest relatives. He also cites his mentor Farāhī's position which can be paraphrased: 'I only promote good relations between relatives for your benefit.' Iṣlāḥī dismisses another possible meaning, 'except that you maintain social ties with me as your relative' as 'weak' on the basis that this is itself a form of recompense, and dismisses another potential interpretation, 'except that you love those who are related to me', even more strongly as being deviant. Iṣlāḥī's analysis demonstrates the range of interpretations which he treats as exclusive but does not, in my view, place sufficient emphasis on the term *mawadda* itself as an indication of strong affection.

The grammatical use of a negation and exception construct, *lā . . . illā* (no . . . except), creates a powerful exemptive emphasis on the phrase which follows: *mawaddata fi 'l-qurbā*. The term *mawadda* also features at Q.60:7, mentioned just above, and is also used by Al-Rāzī to explain Q.41:34, with both references focussing directly on the transformation in relations between the Prophet and his Meccan opponents, from enmity to love. I would therefore argue that the Qurʾanic phrasing here is deliberately generic and concise such that it allows multiple layers and shades of meaning, without one interpretation excluding the other. Thus my translation of *mawaddata fi 'l-qurbā* as 'love amongst relatives' serves first and foremost as a common value: a mutually agreed principle specifically amongst the tribal Arabs which serves as a sound basis for Conciliation and provides an evocative sense of conciliatory appeal.

The above principle of 'love amongst relatives' accords with the general Qur'anic emphasis on maintaining kinship as a basic tenet of human relations, discussed in Chapter 3. From the Prophet's perspective, the same statement serves as a form of *salām* or reassurance of peaceful intentions and conciliatory endeavour: a desire to provide only benefit and not to instigate or reciprocate harm. There is, however, a sense of implied reproach: you are my kin, and it does not behove you to isolate me and distance me, when it is an intrinsic quality to love one's relatives. Finally, the phrase provides a sense of wistful anticipation that present enmities can one day be set aside and mutual, proximate relations of love between relatives can be restored.

An important conciliatory notion in the above process is that of forgiveness, rather than reciprocation, of harm suffered. The inter-relation between forgiveness of harm and the apparently competing concept of a desire for justice in the case of transgression, introduced in Section 5.1.1, is now discussed in the context of the ensuing Qur'anic discourse.

5.1.3 Patience, Justice and Forgiveness

Moving forward a few verses in the sura, Q.42:37–43 sheds light on the three important inter-related notions of transgression, justice and forgiveness, including an explicit reference to *iṣlāḥ* with the meaning of Conciliation (Q.42:40) and a concluding reference to *ṣabr*. The passage is at once instructional and motivational in style, following Q.42:36 which promises ever-lasting reward for those who believe and rely on God, who are then apparently portrayed aspirationally in the following verses for the emerging community of the Prophets' followers. The structure of the passage is also highly coherent and impactful according to my analysis. The descriptive verses in the passage open with the relative pronoun *alladhī* (those who) three consecutive times at Q.42:37–39. Two verses opening with the conditional *man* (whoever) at Q.42:4 and 43 present a human choice between retribution and forgiveness, respectively, in the face of transgression suffered. The remaining verses Q.42:40 and 42 have a declarative style which is suited to the statement of general principles. The opening two verses are more general and summative whilst the subsequent five verses deal specifically with the issue of retribution and forgiveness.

Amongst the qualities mentioned in the opening verses, most deal with God's rights, such as abstaining from sins, and worshipping him and spending in his cause. However, two relevant social behaviours are also highlighted. At Q.42:37, alongside restraint in abiding by God's prohibitions, specifically laudable behaviour includes restraint in social dealings: *wa idhā mā ghaḍibū hum yaghfirūn* (who forgive when they are angry, Abdel Haleem). The opening verse of the passage therefore throws anger management sharply into focus by concluding on this notion and ending specifically on the word *yaghfirūn* (they forgive). The second verse Q.42:38, which deals with the performance of prescribed behaviours, includes a reference to collaboration and consultation in societal affairs: *wa amruhum shūrā baynahum* (conduct their affairs by mutual consultation, Abdel Haleem). In my view, this alludes towards the resolution of disputes through inter-party dialogue, intervention and supportive consultation, as I will discuss further below.

The final verse of description provides the specific context for the operative five verses of the passage from Q.42:39–43. We are told of those who, *idhā aṣābahumu 'l-baghyu hum yantaṣirūn* (defend themselves when they are oppressed, Abdel Haleem, Q.42:39). The general concept of retaliation here is permissive rather than instructive as is clear from what follows. Furthermore, it is conditional on actual suffering of conduct amounting to oppression. Even syntactically, the Arabic *sharṭ* (condition) *precedes* the retaliation as well as occupying the majority of the verse, with only the final word of the sentence indicating a defensive response. This effect is rather lost in the translation presented by Abdel Haleem who leads with the defensive response to facilitate its reading in English. The reference to a retaliatory response in this verse is now expounded in what follows.

Q.42:40 declares a general principle of justice, coupled with a motivation towards forgiveness and Conciliation, and a concluding Divine reproach against transgression which could apply to both instigation or excessive retribution: *wa jazā'u sayyi'atin sayyi'atun* ***mithluhā****, faman* ***'afā wa aṣlaḥa*** *fa ajruhū 'ala 'llāh, innahū lā yuḥibbu ('l)-ẓẓālimīn* (Let harm be requited by an **equal** harm, though anyone who **forgives and puts things right** will have his reward from God Himself – He does not like those who do wrong, Abdel Haleem). This verse is particularly noteworthy in the passage as it deals explicitly with the inter-relation of all three of the central concepts and is itself the sequentially central verse in the passage. In law, retribution is permitted but only to the like extent of what has been suffered. From an ethical perspective, however, forgiveness and resolution of the dispute is a more favourable option and will be compensated by Divine reward. The conditional is used here to indicate a choice available to the wronged party. At Q.2:178, we have encountered a similar enunciation of a legal principle permitting retribution followed by a conditional clause allowing forgiveness by the wronged party, but avoiding a sense of duress to do so. Notably, to my mind, the coupling of forgiveness with *iṣlāḥ* suggests a resolution effected through one party not exerting his full legal rights. The notion of forgiveness is an important Conciliation concept and has been discussed in Chapter 2 in analysing Q.7:199 in particular.

Forgiveness as a means to Conciliation is very much the preferred path in this passage. Q.42:37, 38 and 39 present three consecutive verses which highlight forgiveness, consultation and retaliation, respectively. Of these, the passage leads with a commendation of forgiveness and only ends with retaliation as if it is a last resort. In between the two is the verse encouraging dialogue, thereby facilitating Conciliation. After these three verses, the option of retaliation is justified by a principle of justice which includes a caution against excessive retaliation at Q.42:40, and then bolstered by two verses Q.42:41–42 respectively absolving those who retaliate with justice of any wrongdoing and chastising those who *yaẓlimūna (ʻl)-nnāsa wa yabghūna fi ʻl-arḍi bighayri ʻl-ḥaqq* (oppress people and transgress in the land against all justice, Abdel Haleem). Of the two options of retaliation and forgiveness, however, it is forgiveness which is held aloft as exemplary, first through its leading reference in the passage, secondly by its promise of Divine reward in the central verse at Q.42:40, and finally by its strategic commendation in the conclusion of the passage at Q.42:43: *wa laman **ṣabara wa ghafara** inna dhālika lamin ʿazmi ʻl-umūr* (though if a person is patient and forgives, this is one of the greatest things, Abdel Haleem). This final verse recalls the pervasive Conciliation notion of patience which highlights forbearance and the absorption of harm, reinforcing the references to forgiveness at Q.42:37 and Q.42:40 and, as with Q.41:35 above, ends with an aspirational commendation of the fortitude of character and determination displayed by those who forego their just rights so that Conciliation may prevail.

Iṣlāḥī (vol.7, p.175) specifically highlights in his introductory comments to Q.42:37–43 that Q.42 was revealed immediately prior to the Prophet's migration and hence stylistically it heralds the impending openings of the Medinan period as well as reminding the Prophet and his followers of *un ke farāʾiḍ aur un kī zimmidāriyaun* (their duties and their responsibilities) during the challenges ahead and *un ko kyā rawayya ikhtiyār karnā hai* (what approach they should adopt) as they form an organised social and political community with the strength to defend themselves. At Q.42:40 he also stresses that Conciliation either between the parties or with the solicited or unsolicited assistance of third-party intervention is the Divinely preferred option but adds an apparently subjective qualification: *ʿām infirādī waqiʿāt mein* (in general personal situations, Iṣlāḥī (vol.7, pp.181–82)). Remarkably, he concludes his analysis of the passage with the assertion that the enjoinder towards patience at Q.42:43 relates to the circumstances faced by the Prophet's followers immediately prior to their migration when they had not yet formed an organised political force. In the Medinan period when they had formed such a community, he asserts that they were Divinely instructed to *kulliyyatan apnein tamām rawābiṭ munqaṭiʿ karlein* (entirely sever all their connections, Iṣlāḥī (vol.7, p.183)) with the Meccan Quraysh and to be at war with them until they accept defeat.

Iṣlāḥī's position above is worthy of significant criticism here in my view. Firstly, in a coherence-based commentary, his qualification and side-lining of the enjoinder towards Conciliation from the principle circumstances of opposition faced by the Prophet and his followers is unjustified, and results in an unacceptably disjointed reading of a clearly connected passage. By contrast, in explaining the reference to forgiveness and Conciliation at Q.42:40, Al-Rāzī specifically cites Q.41:34 above which explains how the Prophet may turn his enemy into a loyal friend. Secondly, the limitation of conciliatory teachings to the Meccan period of weakness in his conclusion contradicts his own introduction which talks of the conduct to be displayed by the believers as they form a strong and organised community, by obvious implication in the Medinan period. In addition, Q.45:14 specifically enjoins the believers to forgive those who do not anticipate God's days (of requital), with Al-Rāzī providing three potential *sabab al-nuzūl* (circumstances of revelation) where ʿUmar was diverted from retribution for insulting remarks, of which two out of three are apparently Medinan. Thirdly, the entire severance of all connections with the Quraysh, the Prophet's tribe, contradicts the Qurʾanic emphasis on maintaining ties of kinship and their fundamental importance in conciliatory appeal which have been highlighted above and in Chapter 3, even in situations of differences of faith (Q.31:15). Finally, as discussed in the remainder of this chapter, the historical circumstances demonstrate that the final resolution of the conflict between the Prophet and the Quraysh *en masse* came about through contractual Conciliation at Ḥudaybiya, and through forgiveness and recognition of kinship at the Conquest of Mecca, both without precondition of conversion to Islam, and not through a fight to the finish.

To put the matter further into context, the earlier discussed sura Q.39, which alludes to migration and is therefore likely to have been revealed at a similar time, declares at Q.39:53: *qul yā ʿibādiya 'lladhīna asrafū ʿalā anfusihim lā taqnaṭū min rraḥmati 'llāhi, inna 'llāha yaghfiru ('l)-dhdhunūba jamīʿā, innahū huwa 'l-ghafūru ('l)-rraḥīm* (Say, '[God says], My servants who have harmed yourselves by your own excess, do not despair of God's mercy. God forgives all sins: He is truly the Most Forgiving, the Most Merciful, Abdel Haleem). The extraordinary conciliatory reach of this verse and its multi-layered emphasis on mercy and forgiveness is self-evident. The enjoinder towards dialogue, the proximity created by the *ḥarf nidāʾ* (particle of direct address) *yā*, the use of the endearing term *ʿibādiya* (my servants), the comforting reassurance of the appealing *lā taqnaṭū* (do not despair), the limitless reach of *jamīʿā* (all), the multiple references to mercy, then forgiveness, then forgiveness again and then mercy again, are extraordinarily impactful and hope-inspiring.

Iṣlāḥī (vol.6, p.603) considers this verse to be directed at the polytheists and, although Al-Rāzī considers it in general as an address to believers, the several possible *sabab al-nuzūl* (circumstances of revelation) he cites also all relate to new entrants to the faith concerned about their actions prior to accepting Islam, including the example of Waḥshī, who killed the Prophet's uncle Ḥamza at Uḥud, which is clearly Medinan. The Divine promise at Q.39:53 of limitless forgiveness for pre-Islamic acts of enmity, delivered on the tongue of the Prophet himself, is far more plausible as an exemplar of forgiveness and Conciliation to the Prophet than as an accompaniment to a human severance of relations of kin and a state of continuing conflict, as Iṣlāḥī argues above. It should be noted that this discussion of Q.39:53 also supports and accords with my broad interpretation of Q.6:54 in Chapter 2 as a universal call to redemption directed at the Meccan audience at large.

After discussing the commendation of patience at Q.42:43 above, the final reference to patience to be discussed in this section arises at Q.46:35. My analysis identified the Conciliation theme of the suras discussed above to be centred around the important and pervasive notion of patience, and this is supported by the final verse of the Meccan sura cluster from Q.34–46, spanning some four *juz'* (parts) of the Qur'an, which concludes emphatically with the following enjoinder on the Prophet: *fa 'ṣbir kamā ṣabara ulu 'l-ʿazmi mina ('l)-rrusul* (be steadfast, like those messengers of firm resolve, Abdel Haleem). This pointed enjoinder to show patience like the patience of prophets before at the turning point of imminent migration, with a near-decade of endurance behind the Prophet and a near-decade of new challenges lying ahead before the resolution of conflict at the Conquest of Mecca in 8 A.H., is entirely apt and a fitting climax to the exposition of patience which pervades the Meccan sura cluster from Q.34–46.

The above enjoinder throws into focus the exemplary narratives of the patience of past prophets such as Joseph and now David. Although the principle of implementing justice when adjudicating disputes in a position of office is clearly established from the story of David, and the above passage Q.42:37–43 which grants a right of retribution in kind without excess, it is clear that the wronged party is given a choice between retribution and forgiveness. In this choice, it is those who forgive who are lauded and this is clearly the preferred option. Forgiveness is also directly coupled with the achievement of Conciliation, as well as being exemplified by the conciliatory appeal of limitless Divine mercy. For the Prophet, who is an exemplar for his followers, there is only one fitting course of action which is enjoined on him no less than 18 times: *iṣbir* (be patient). *Ṣabr*, as has been shown, is both a fundamental and rich conciliatory concept, incorporating forbearance, forgiveness, fortitude and perseverance. The Prophet is to show all these qualities and strive for and aspire to a complete reconciliation based on a common value of love for kin, the opportunity for which will only come to fruition after years of further struggle. The foundation for realising that opportunity for reconciliation at the end of the Medinan period is laid down in the Meccan period: Conciliation is a long-term endeavour and is only achieved by virtue of patience.

After concluding the Meccan sura cluster by distilling its central message to an enjoinder of patience at Q.46:35, the sequence of Qur'anic discourse moves across the 35-verse Medinan Q.47 providing a glimpse of the early period of military conflict already discussed in Chapter 2. Immediately after this, Q.48 opens with a dramatic and arresting declaration apparently referring to a peace agreement between the Prophet and the Meccans at Ḥudaybiya, and announcing the successful fulfilment of the protracted quest for Conciliation. The Qur'anic style of suspending narratives and inter-weaving-related themes has led to some fragmented interpretations of Q.48, as discussed in the following section. Figure 5.1 therefore provides a structural analysis of the sura content in which I separate the verses into functional categories based on their introductory particles in order to shed light on the sura's central theme and context. This structural outline should be referred to in conjunction with the ensuing discussion.

	Declarative (*inna, laqad*)	**Restrictive (*huwa 'lladhī*)**	**Purposive (*li*)**	**Contextual (*idh*)**	**Advisory (*sayaqūlu*)**
1	Grant of victory				
2–3			Divine blessings		
4		*Sakīna* (tranquillity) sent down			
5–7			Punishment and reward, God's power		
8	God's Messenger				
9			Belief in God and His Messenger and providing assistance		
10	Oath of allegiance				
11–17					Dealing with the hypocrites' contentions
18–23	Oath of allegiance and consequential remarks				

Figure 5.1: Sūrat Al-Fatḥ (Q.48) outline.

	Declarative (*inna, laqad*)	Restrictive (*huwa 'lladhī*)	Purposive (*li*)	Contextual (*idh*)	Advisory (*sayaqūlu*)
24–25		Restraint in the Valley of Mecca			
26				*Ḥamiyya* of disbelievers vs *Sakīna* of believers	
27	Dream of entering Mecca fulfilled				
28–29		God's Messenger and his companions			

Figure 5.1 (continued)

5.2 Conciliation in Practice: The Treaty of Ḥudaybiya

5.2.1 The Meaning of Victory

Q.48 (Sūrat Al-Fatḥ, The Sura of Victory) deals with the circumstances and implications of the historically renowned Treaty of Ḥudaybiya entered into in 6 A.H. between the Prophet and the Meccans. According to commentators, Sūrat Al-Fatḥ was revealed on the return from Ḥudaybiya to Medina, and indeed according to Iṣlāḥī (vol.7, pp.431–33) the significance of the sura can only truly be understood in this historical context. Although the entire historical context relates to Conciliation, it is remarkable that linguistic references to *ṣulḥ* or other terms obviously signifying Conciliation are conspicuously absent, rendering academic studies focussing purely on linguistic references to Conciliation incomplete.

Q.48.1 opens the sura with a resounding declaration of victory, giving its name to the sura: *innā fataḥnā laka fatḥan mubīnā* (Truly We have opened up a path to clear triumph for you [Prophet], Abdel Haleem). The declarative opening particle *innā* (truly We) incorporating the plural of majesty provides a grammatical emphasis and sense of Divine gift, whilst the *mafʿūl muṭlaq* (cognate accusative: *fataḥnā . . . fatḥan*) coupled with the adjective *mubīnā* (manifest) provides an echoing proclamation of triumph, the rhetorical effect of which is rather diluted in translation. As Al-Rāzī highlights, *laka* (for you) at Q.48:1

highlights the unique honour of such a 'victory' given to the Prophet *'ulū wujh ul-minna* (as a manifestation of (Divine) grace). The verse itself does not immediately explain what this victory is, giving rise to some debate amongst commentators, about what it might refer to. To understand the meaning of this 'manifest' victory, therefore, we must look further into the sura.

Immediately after explaining Q.48:1 at Q.48:2–3, Q.48:4 tells us specifically what God has bestowed: *huwa 'lladhī anzala ('l)-ssakīnata fī qulūbi 'l-mu'minīn* (He is the one who sent down tranquillity into the hearts of the believers). The use of restriction in the phrase *huwa 'lladhī* (He is the one who) distinguishes the grant of *sakīna* (tranquillity) as a particularly Divine gift. This reference is elaborated at Q.48:18, where it is contextualised by a reference to the believers' swearing of allegiance to the Prophet and this time *directly* coupled with the grant of *fatḥan qarībā* (an imminent victory). Further on, Q.48:26 appends the possessive pronoun *hū* (His) to the grant of *sakīna*, rendering it even more closely affiliated with God's Divine gift. The immediately following verse Q.48:27 proclaims that God has fulfilled His Messenger's vision: the Muslim pilgrims will undoubtedly enter the Sacred Precinct at Mecca in peace and God has granted, *min dūni dhālika* (besides this, Yusuf Ali), *fatḥan qarībā* (an imminent victory). To my mind, there is a notable parallel between the delayed yet ultimately successful fulfilment of the Prophet's vision and Joseph's dream, the story of which is presented as a lesson to the Prophet in Q.12.

Q.48 thus contains three references to a Divine gift of victory, the second at Q.48:16 connected to an Oath of Allegiance 'under the tree' (generally considered a reference to an oath of loyalty following rumours that the Prophet's emissary 'Uthmān had been killed by the Meccans) and the third at Q.48:27 to the fulfilment of the Prophet's vision regarding a pilgrimage to Mecca. The latter two are explicitly connected to the circumstances of Ḥudaybiya which, to my mind, suggests that the victory referred to in Q.48:1 is also a reference to the final outcome of the Treaty at Ḥudaybiya. This would have been clear to the audience through the circumstances and timing of revelation on the return journey and the first verse by its very omission of (to them) unnecessary detail would have had a powerful rhetorical and uplifting effect on the previously dejected morale of the Prophet's Companions. In addition, all three references to victory are connected, the second at Q.48:18 particularly closely, to one of three references to a Divine gift of *sakīna* (tranquillity). This suggests that the internal state of the Prophet and his followers was the means by which God's grant of victory was accomplished, as discussed further in the following section. Furthermore, it suggests that all three references to victory refer to a *single event* in which that gift of *sakīna* was instrumental, namely the Treaty at Ḥudaybiya.

The recurrent assertion of a Divine gift in this sura is also reinforced by another example of restriction at Q.48:24 which specifies: *wa huwa 'lladhī kaffa aydiyahum ʿankum wa aydiyakum ʿanhum bi baṭni Makkata min baʿdi an aẓfarakum ʿalayhim* (He is the one who restrained their hands from you and your hands from them in the Valley of Mecca after he gave you the advantage over them). The use of restriction to claim unique Divine credit for restraining the parties from conflict is particularly important because it indicates that this mutual restraint is the subject of the Divine gift referred to three times as a victory, as I have argued above. Q.48:27 notably specifies that although God will most certainly bring the Prophet's vision to reality, the entry to Mecca for pilgrimage will be non-confrontational and will avoid conflict and even the fear of conflict: *inshāʾ Allāhu āminīna . . . lā takhāfūn* (God willing, in peace . . . with no fear). This crucial element of the Divine scheme is achieved by means of the Treaty of Ḥudaybiya. The reference to *kaff* (restraint) also features at Q.48:20 where God's restraining of hands from the believers is described as an *āya* (sign) for the believers, and Yusuf Ali even translates the reference to *taqwā* at Q.48:26 as 'self-restraint'. This is significant because it indicates that such Conciliation between the Prophet's followers and the Meccans is a manifest priority in the Divine scheme. At Q.8:63, discussed in Chapter 2, the Qurʾan similarly claims unique credit for the unification of believers' hearts, with three emphatic references to the verb *allafa* (to unify).

As indicated above, there has been some debate about the meaning of 'victory' in the verses cited above. Both Ḥijāzī (1986, pp.184–95, esp. p.191, n.3, p.194) and Ṭāhā (2009, p.22) provide support from exegesis, biographies of the Prophet and classical scholarship for my position that Q.48:1 refers to the Treaty of Ḥudaybiya. Iṣlāḥī (vol.7, pp.436–37) is also adamant that the Treaty of Ḥudaybiya is the only possible interpretation of Q.48:1 given the Meccan's acceptance of the Muslims' right of access to the Kaʿba, their acknowledgement of the Muslims as equal opponents and the Meccans' reluctance to engage the Muslims in military conflict. However, he notes (pp.433, 458) that the Treaty was the prelude to the Conquest of Mecca. At Q.48:1, Al-Rāzī considers whether *fatḥ* means the Conquest of Mecca, the Conquest of Rome and other victories, the Treaty of Ḥudaybiya, the victory of Islam, or *fatḥ* with the meaning of *al-ḥukm* (a decision), concluding that the most preferred interpretation is the Conquest of Mecca, and then the Treaty of Ḥudaybiya, and then the victory of Islam by exposition and proof. He explains the use of the past tense in Q.48:1 whilst referring to the future Conquest of Mecca as indicating God's incontrovertible decree – a similar usage can be found at Q.48:27.

Although Al-Rāzī's view is plausible, it sits uncomfortably with the notion of a 'manifest' victory if the generally agreed circumstances of the sura's revelation are taken as accurate. The circumstances of the Conquest of Mecca were anything but 'manifest' at the time of the Treaty of Ḥudaybiya and it would have been hard to imagine such an enigmatic reference having the same uplifting effect on its audience as the description of the Treaty of Ḥudaybiya as a victory – in fact, future as yet unknown victories and particularly the Conquest of Mecca appear to be referenced by the suitably remote and vague term *ukhrā* (others) at Q.48:21, a point supported by Iṣlāḥī's commentary (vol.7, p.459). Furthermore, the opening verse Q.48:1 would become fragmented from the various factual circumstances of Ḥudaybiya mentioned elsewhere in the sura and both elements would therefore lose both significance and impact. In addition, Q.48 in the end is an entire sura devoted to the events at Ḥudaybiya, which proved a historical turning point: the parties went from being on the brink of war, to being on the brink of final reconciliation. The Qur'an does not provide such an entire sura devoted to the Conquest of Mecca, despite its obvious significance.

Al-Rāzī's view is also contradicted by Nasr (p.1248), referencing the *tafsīr bi 'l-riwāya* (narration-based exegesis) of Ibn Kathīr, who notes that the Companion Ibn Masʿūd is reported to have said, "You consider the conquering of Makkah to be the *victory*, while to us the *victory* is the treaty conducted at Ḥudaybiya." Nasr (pp.1246–47) explains that the sura was revealed on the return from Ḥudaybiya, described by the Prophet as "dearer to me than all over which the sun rises" indicating its momentous significance, but was also recited by the Prophet at the Conquest of Mecca. These narrations support my interpretation of 'victory' above. At Q.48:18, however, Nasr (p.1252) considers the 'victory' as most likely a reference to the Conquest of Khaybar shortly after the Treaty of Ḥudaybiya, despite quoting the Companion Al-Barāʾ bin ʿĀzib as considering the 'victory' to be the Oath of Allegiance at Ḥudaybiya. At Q.48:27, Nasr, based on Qurṭubī's exegesis, again takes the 'victory' to mean the Conquest of Khaybar, or the Conquest of Mecca, or the general victory of Islam as facilitated by the Treaty of Ḥudaybiya which allowed free movement between the Muslims and the Quraysh resulting in the doubling of the Muslim community in the two years after the Treaty. The last point seems to me very much to support the interpretation of the 'victory' throughout as a reference to the Treaty of Ḥudaybiya, given its implications for the success of the Prophet's propagation of faith (see also Q.110, probably a later revelation, which refers to a *fatḥ* (victory) resulting in mass acceptance of the new faith).

Al-Rāzī also takes the 'victory' at Q.48:18 to mean Khaybar, although he uncharacteristically fails to provide any elaboration or explanation. Iṣlāḥī (pp.458, 468) too takes the 'victory' at Q.48:18 to refer to Khaybar based on the subsequent reference to *maghānim* (gains/spoils, Q.48:19, 20) but then admits his subsequent divergence from other commentators and reverts to

Q.48:27 as a reference to Ḥudaybiya, despite the two verses using the same phrase *fatḥan qarībā* (an imminent victory), demonstrating the inconsistencies of a fragmented approach. This is at odds with his own methodology of identifying coherence in the structure of the Qur'anic discourse. The terminology used by Iṣlāḥī (vol.7, p.468) at Q.48:27 is also unsatisfactory as he describes *fatḥan qarībā* as an indication that Ḥudaybiya had paved the way for the *aṣlī* (true) but hidden victory of the Conquest of Mecca, which rather contradicts his own acknowledgement of Ḥudaybiya as a 'manifest' victory at Q.48:1.

Furthermore at Q.48:18, Iṣlāḥī has like Nasr, in my view unjustifiably, detached the phrase *fatḥan qarībā* from the reference to the Oath of Allegiance and even the descent of *sakīna* (tranquillity) to which it is *directly coupled*, and attached its significance to a reference to *maghānim* (gains/spoils, Q.48:19, 20) in the following verse, despite the fact that there is a clear temporal shift from the past tense in *athābahum* (reward**ed** them with, Abdel Haleem) referring to the 'imminent victory' and *ya'khudhūnahā* (you **will** attain) referring to the 'gains/spoils'. In addition, taking a mere reference to 'spoils' as automatically indicating a reference to Khaybar without further context appears a rather tenuous link, particularly since the term *maghānim* (spoils, Q.48:19, 20) is itself unclear, with Nasr (pp.1252–53) citing the exegesis of Qurṭubī and Ṭabarī as considering that the reference at Q.48:19 may even be to the future conquests of Persia and Byzantium, and at Q.48:20 to all conquests obtained by Muslims until the Day of Resurrection. Nasr also mentions that the term may refer to 'inner riches received by those who follow the spiritual path'. With such speculative divergence of views, it is difficult to argue that the choice of Khaybar is more justifiable than others in an apparently disparate selection. Instead, Yusuf Ali (p.1333, n.4895) provides an entirely plausible and straightforward explanation of the term *fatḥan qarībā*, noting that 'The Treaty of Ḥudaybiya itself was a "speedy victory": it followed immediately after the Bay'ah.'

Another connection to Khaybar is made by Lecker (2010, p.74), who draws on Hamidullah's research into the jurist Al-Sarakshī's (d. 483/1090) account that the Prophet strategically 'made a non-belligerency agreement with the people of Mecca in order to be secure from their side when he marches on Khaybar'. Lecker himself notes that Al-Sarakshī 'is not a specialist on Muḥammad's biography' and whatever the plausibility of his account, it is both speculative as to the Prophet's personal intentions and detached from the express content of the sura itself. The reference to Khaybar also introduces yet another variable into the already multifarious discussion of interpretations of 'victory' at Q.48:1, as well as further fragmenting the coherence of the various references in the sura to a 'victory'. At Q.12 in Chapter 3, I explained that taking different contextual meanings of the same term *muḥsinīn* (those who are gracious) in the same sura can retract from the true significance and impact of the term. In the same way, in this sura each reference to 'victory' would become divergent and open to subjective interpretation rather than each reference supporting the other in significance and rhetorical effect. Only Yusuf Ali (p.1328, n.4866, p.1333, n.4895, p.1336, n.4911) amongst the commentators reviewed takes a consistent position that all three verses Q.48:1, Q.48:18 and Q.48:27 mentioning 'victory' refer to the Treaty of Ḥudaybiya, thus supporting my above argument for a coherent interpretation in accordance with the content of the sura.

My interpretation of the three references to 'victory' as reinforcing each other and consolidating their significance and effect by emphasising the triumphal outcome at Ḥudaybiya is consistent with the emphatic style of the sura which returns again and again to the same notions, such as the grant of *sakīna* (tranquillity), the Oath of Allegiance and the restraining of the parties from conflict. The sura leads this account with an impactful triumphant opening proclamation which re-focusses its audience's minds from what they have *not* achieved at Ḥudaybiya to what they *have* achieved, and thus elevates their dejected spirits. In particular, Q.48:27 towards the conclusion of the sura declares that although they will indeed fulfil the Prophet's vision of pilgrimage, as transpired the following year in 7 A.H., they have also been granted a more imminent and significant victory. Rather than performing one pilgrimage at any cost, they have secured with contractual assurances and without conflict or casualties, both a long-term peace and future unfettered access to the Kaʿba.

As I argued in Chapter 2, the Prophet and his followers were permitted to fight only to prevent persecution and to preserve their freedom to worship. These very aims had now finally been 'manifestly' achieved at Ḥudaybiya peacefully and even at the behest of their arch-enemies who had visibly experienced a change of heart: their appetite for conflict clearly appeared to be exhausted, and the Muslims had been granted express contractual rights to live in peace and to worship in freedom. The process of being able to achieve these aims by peaceful negotiation with a party who was now willing to engage in dialogue was itself remarkable. As Cragg (p.93) perceptively remarks, 'Al-Hudaibiyyah was to prove a sort of diplomatic Badr. It established Islam as treating on equal terms with the prestigious Quraish whose own position it drastically weakened on the same count.' Ḥudaybiya was a turning point in relations between the Muslims and the Quraysh, and paved the way for the also peaceful Conquest of Mecca in 8 A.H. and final reconciliation between the parties, as discussed in Chapters 2 and 3.

The 'manifest' victory was experienced by the Muslims but was ultimately claimed by God. The sura stressed throughout that it was only through God's gift that this had been brought about, whilst immediately after Q.48:27 above, Q.48:28 declares that it was God who had sent His Messenger with *al-hudā wa dīni 'l-ḥaqqi liyuẓhirahū ʿala ('l)-ddīni kullih* (with guidance and the religion of Truth, for him to show that it is above all [false] religion, Abdel Haleem). Although Al-Rāzī refers to this as the abrogation of previous religions, its strategic concluding location between Q.48:27, extolling the victory at Ḥudaybiya, and Q.48:29, which commends the virtues of the Companions, suggests that it is a celebration of a landmark achievement in the establishment of Islam and the Muslim community. Ahmad (2009, pp.201–02) argues that Q.61:9, Q.48:28 and Q.9:33, near-identical verses, were revealed at three-year intervals commensurate with significant points in the establishment of the Islamic community. It is interesting to note that the second instance coincides with the Treaty of Ḥudaybiya and the third with the period surrounding the Conquest of Mecca.

The Qur'an abounds with narratives of prophets whose followers were few and whose opponents were often ultimately destroyed, with the notable exception of the people of Jonah. However, a mass reconciliation in the shape and on the scale of what unfolded at Ḥudaybiya, and the historical aftermath which it heralded, is unprecedented in the Qur'anic discourse. It is perhaps unsurprising therefore that an entire sura is devoted to its triumphant celebration.

5.2.2 A Test of Mettle

Section 5.2.1 discussed the triumphal outcome at Ḥudaybiya: the negotiation of a long-term contractual peace agreement, the religious freedom and security gained by the Muslim community, and their apparent elevation in negotiating power and prestige. All of these are remarkable exoteric achievements, observable by history and historians. It is perhaps for this reason that the Qur'anic discourse focusses attention on the less accessible esoteric achievements of Ḥudaybiya, revealing crucial insights as to the internal qualities and personal development required to achieve Conciliation. Central to this discussion is the thrice-reiterated notion of Divinely bestowed *sakīna* (Q.48:4, 18, 26), which has been translated above as 'tranquillity'. We will now examine this notion in more detail.

The notion of *sakīna* also features at Q.9:26 and 40 in the respective contexts of Ḥunayn and the Cave of Thawr during the migration, in both contexts coupled with the provision of Divine assistance through unseen forces, a notion which seems to be alluded to in the reference to *junūd* (forces, Abdel Haleem) at Q.48:4 also. In Q.48 itself commentators are substantially aligned but with slightly different emphasis in their explanations of the term *sakīna*. Abdel Haleem translates *sakīna* (Q.48:4, 18, 26) as 'tranquillity' in all three verses, as does Yusuf Ali, who adds to tranquillity, the notions of 'calmness and cool courage' in his annotation to Q.48:4 (p.1328, n.4869). Al-Rāzī also provides three explanatory notions: *al-sukūn* (calmness), *al waqār* (dignity) and *al yaqīn* (certainty), although noting that the latter two stem from the first. At Q.48:26, in explaining *sakīna*, Nasr (p.1254) contrasts 'the peace, patience and dignity that stand in direct opposition to "impassioned haughtiness"', the latter a reference to the *ḥamiyya* which describes the internal state of the Meccans in the same verse. The notion of 'patience', expounded at length in Section 5.1 as a vital Conciliation concept, emerges even more clearly in the commentary of Iṣlāḥī.

Iṣlāḥī (vol.7, p.441) first explains *sakīna* as the *ḥawṣala* (courage) of the Companions in accepting the Prophet's call to pilgrimage and rising above the dangers of facing the hitherto dominant Quraysh, who were on war-footing, with little in the way of armaments, against the example of the hypocrites who had backed out of what they considered a doomed mission (as indicated at Q.48:11–12). Iṣlāḥī highlights that such challenges are faced by believers as *īmān kī jānch* (a test of faith). After taking a similar meaning at Q.48:18 (p.458), Iṣlāḥī (vol.7, pp.464, 470) provides more detail at Q.48:26 yielding relevant insights: *sakīnatahū se murād yahan* ***ṣabr***, *ḥilm, razānat aur ḥikmat aw tadabbur hai* (what is intended by *sakīnatahū* here is **patience**, forbearance, sobriety, wisdom and foresight). He goes on to explain that in collective affairs there are severe tests of forbearance and foresight in which: *agar jamāʿat ḥarīf ke rawayya se mushtaʿal ho kar koī ʿājilāna qadam uthāde to is se aṣal maqṣad ke nā qābile talāfī nuqṣān pahonch jata hai* (if a group becomes provoked by the conduct of its opponent and takes a hasty step, then this causes irreparable damage to the true objective). Further on, Iṣlāḥī (vol.7, p.470) adds that the unfolding reality made clear to the believers that although they would eventually achieve hegemony, this would only be achieved *bi 'l-tadrīj* (gradually); accordingly, they should neither be hasty nor fall into despair.

Iṣlāḥī's above exposition of *sakīna* provides incisive detail which furthers our understanding significantly. The introduction of the notion of *ṣabr* itself provides a focus on 'patience' as a crucial internal attribute of the hearts of the Prophet and his Companions. This, in itself, provides an extraordinary correlation between the recurrent emphasis discussed in Section 5.1 on developing *ṣabr* in the Meccan period, and the very same quality being absolutely instrumental to the achievement of a historical political Conciliation in the late Medinan period. Indeed, even in the early Medinan period of apparent military conflict, Cragg (p.92) notes that Uḥud 'could be interpreted as salutary in underlining the necessity of that vital Muslim virtue of *ṣabr*', providing a further interim indication of the continuous significance of this quality. Even more tellingly, at Q.41:35 above, Al-Rāzī explained the reference to *dhū ḥaẓẓin ʿaẓīm* as indicating a strong disposition insulated from influence by the detrimental action of others. In the explanation of *sakīna* at Ḥudaybiya, we see Iṣlāḥī highlighting the same notion of remaining steadfast and showing fortitude of character and determination in achieving the over-arching objective of Conciliation, resisting any counter-productive impulse towards retaliation and conflict instigated by the actions of others.

More specifically, the additional terms such as *ḥilm* (forbearance) and *ḥikmat aw tadabbur* (wisdom and consideration of future consequences) provided by Iṣlāḥī shed light on the qualities of forbearance, foresight and fortitude which accompany the instilment of *ṣabr*. In the case of forbearance at Ḥudaybiya in particular, the Companions would have had to suppress their indignation at being denied pilgrim access to the Kaʿba which was accessible to all others, to overlook an attack on their camp apparently alluded to in Q.48:24 (the attackers were captured but later released as noted by Abdel Haleem), to concede to apparently unequal and demeaning terms in relation to the return of renegades, and to swallow their personal sense of outrage at the Meccans' insistence on removing the description of the Prophet as the Messenger of God from the text of the Treaty.

At the same time, it would have been crucial to maintain focus on the long-term benefits of establishing the Treaty and this appears from historical accounts to have been the Prophet's unrelenting focus throughout. Even when confronted with the immediate and obvious plight of the believer Abū Jandal, the son of the Meccan emissary Suhayl bin ʿAmr, who had fled persecution and torture to seek refuge with the Prophet, the Prophet enjoined Abū Jandal to patience and returned him to the Meccans in accordance with the Treaty, demonstrating his commitment to what had been agreed (Hamidullah, 1945, p.269). The Prophet is also reported to have personally removed the reference to himself as the Messenger of God, when ʿAlī had apparently been unable to bring himself to perform this task (Iqbal, 1965, p.34).

Apart from the diplomatic and personal forbearance and fortitude indicated above, the internal resolve of the Muslims was also tested militarily. Initially, as Iṣlāḥī highlights, they were asked to show courage and venture into the mouth of their enemy's heartland with the lightest of armaments for pilgrimage. After this, they came under attack at Ḥudaybiya but showed restraint by taking prisoners who were apparently later returned unharmed (Abdel Haleem, 2005, p.336). They were then called in an instant to assume a state of battle-readiness and take an Oath of Allegiance in response to the rumour of their envoy's assassination and then again to climb down from this state of heightened passion to a state of restraint from conflict, allowing negotiations to proceed and progress despite their distaste for the terms of the settlement. An important point should be noted in this regard that the Muslims were enjoined to fight to defend their fundamental freedoms at the time of their weakness in the early days of the Medinan period, but were inspired to show restraint from fighting at the moment of their relative strength in the late Medinan period both at Ḥudaybiya and at the Conquest of Mecca. In both cases, they had to demonstrate an ability to overcome their personal natural inclination and to work towards a higher objective that would benefit their collective cause of living and worshipping peacefully in the long term.

This internal test of the inner resolve of the believers is sharply contrasted with the conduct of the hypocrites who at Q.48:11–12 are accused of insincerity in excusing themselves from a spiritual expedition which they considered perilous, whilst subsequently coming forward to join later expeditions where they anticipated greater financial gain from battle spoils (Q.48:15). At Q.48:16, we are told of a future call to an expedition against *qawmin ulī ba'sin shadīdin tuqātilūnahum aw yuslimūn* (a people of great might in war and to fight them, unless they surrender, Abdel Haleem). Iṣlāḥī (vol.7, p.456) argues that the foe referred to here is the Quraysh, who were given only two options: to accept Islam or face the sword, a position he also adopts in his earlier commentary of Q.47:4 (vol.7, p.398). As I have consistently argued, this position contradicts the principle of non-compulsion discussed in Chapters 2 and 4 and is also contradicted by history: The Prophet made peace with the Meccans both at Ḥudaybiya and at the Conquest of Mecca, without any condition of their conversion to Islam. At the Conquest of Mecca, those who merely confined themselves indoors (rather than coming out to fight) were apparently promised security (Iqbal, 1965, p.42). It should be added here that Iṣlāḥī is at pains to limit his position on conflict to the Quraysh, specifying both that peaceful relations with non-Muslims in general could be maintained under treaty (vol.7, p.398) and in everyday situations (vol.7, p.472).

In any event, it makes little sense to describe the Quraysh, whose dominance was clearly dwindling to such an extent that they had sued for peace, as a 'people possessed of great might'. Q.48:25 also highlights an important aspect of Conciliation – the need to protect innocent bystanders; specifically that the Muslims had been restrained from attacking the Meccans, despite their obstruction of the pilgrimage, to avoid harm to the believers in Mecca who might unknowingly be trampled under-foot. Nasr (p.1251) clarifies at Q.48:16 that the battles referred to may be one of several battles with the surrounding tribes either immediately or significantly after the Conquest of Mecca or even the later conflicts with the Byzantine or Persian armies. He also clarifies that the reference to *tuqātilūnahum aw yuslimūn* simply indicates the two options to fight or 'submit' given to their opponents 'when confronted by' the Muslim army. In this case, an opportunity for extrication would be provided even in a situation of imminent conflict on the battlefield. In Chapter 2, I also discussed the reference by Watt (pp.219–20) to a '*pax Islamica*' where minority tribes who agreed not to fight were even effectively put under the protection of the Muslim army.

In short, relations with the Quraysh were never intended to end with a fight to the finish or a clash of swords, but with progressive phases of Conciliation. In Mecca, the Prophet and his followers were meticulously taught to develop a patience that would develop a sense of forbearance and fortitude that would prepare them for the demands of that Conciliation, in a distant future they might have found difficult to even contemplate at that time. In Medina, they were initially taught to overcome their military inferiority and to match the Meccans on the battlefield until their fundamental freedoms were recognised. Once they had acquired a critical mass, however, and were recognised as a negotiating party, they were delivered the inner resolve to exercise restraint from military conflict and to submit to a contractual peace settlement, even against the impulse of their natural emotions and sentiments. In the end, Ḥudaybiya and its aftermath was never intended to be a test of metal, but a test of *mettle*. It signified that Conciliation would ultimately prevail over conflict, and the tide of relations between the Prophet and the Quraysh had now turned.

Verse	Actual/potential cause of conflict	Conciliation mechanism	Literary technique (cumulative no. of references to concept)
1	Disunity in decision-making	Unqualified prohibition on preceding God and His Messenger	– Address by faith (1) – Prohibitive *lā* (do not) (1) – Declaration of God's knowledge (1) – Enjoinder of *taqwā* (God-consciousness) (1)
2–5	Lack of respect for the Prophet's status and leadership	Prohibition on raising the voice over the Prophet's or to call him and incentive of forgiveness and reward for lowering the voice in the Prophet's presence	– Address by faith (2) – Prohibitive *lā*, twice at v.2 (3) – Sanctions: ruination of accumulated deeds – Hearts tested for *taqwā* (2)
6	Unwarranted harming of others based on rumours	Verify information from unreliable sources	– Address by faith (3) – Use of *fāsiq* (troublemaker) to condemn perpetrator of rumours – Reference to action based on ignorance and consequential regret

Figure 5.2: Sūrat Al-Ḥujurāt (Q.49) summary analysis.

Verse	Actual/potential cause of conflict	Conciliation mechanism	Literary technique (cumulative no. of references to concept)
7–8	Disunity in decision-making	Unqualified prohibition on preceding God and His Messenger	– Warning that people would often suffer if the Messenger of God were to take their lead – Love for faith, beautified in hearts; disbelief, wilfulness and disobedience made detestable – Declaration of God's knowledge (2)
9–10	Any conflict between groups of believers	Third party intervention to conciliate with justice and prevent transgression	– *aṣliḥū* (reconcile) (3) – Conciliation described as *amri 'llāh* (God's command) – Justice (3); God loves the just – Brothers (2) – Enjoinder of *taqwā* (3) to obtain Divine mercy
11	Public insulting of others	Prohibition on mockery, defamation and derogatory nicknames	– Address by faith (4) – Prohibitive *lā* three times (6); plus one to specifically include women (7) – Condemnation of wilfulness after faith, and transgression on failure to repent
12	Attacking the reputation of others in private	Enjoinder to eschew suspicion, and mutual spying and back-biting	– Address by faith (5) – Reference to suspicion potentially amounting to *ithm* (sin) – Prohibitive *lā*, twice (9) – Metaphor of consuming dead brother's (3) flesh to inspire revulsion – Enjoinder of *taqwā* (4)

Figure 5.2 (continued)

Verse	Actual/potential cause of conflict	Conciliation mechanism	Literary technique (cumulative no. of references to concept)
13	Arrogance and alienation over differences	Diversity of creation presented as a call to mutual interaction and awareness	– Address by genus – Divine honouring of those highest in *taqwā* (4) – Declaration of God's knowledge (3)
14–18	Failure to internalise faith	Obedience to God and His Messenger, certainty of faith, striving in God's way	– Declaration of God's knowledge twice at vv.16, 18 (5)

Figure 5.2 (continued)

The significance of the strong Conciliation theme in Q.48 is accentuated by its collocation with the ensuing Q.49 which contains a vast quantity of Conciliation content, as we shall now see in the next section. Figure 5.2 provides a summary analysis of this material which is now discussed in Section 5.3.

5.3 A Complete Conciliation Paradigm: Sūrat Al-Ḥujurāt (Q.49)

In this chapter, the concentration of material addressing Conciliation has increased to the point that the current sura Q.49 is so replete with Conciliation content that I have produced a table (Figure 5.2) detailing the actual and potential causes of conflict which the sura addresses in its entirety, how it regulates these through Conciliation and the literary techniques through which the importance of the Conciliation theme is reinforced. From this material, I discuss three principle themes in the three subsections below which I will argue form a complete Conciliation paradigm in this sura: The Call to Internal Transformation, the Duty of Reconciliation and the Prohibition of That Which Leads to Conflict. The depth and range of material belies the brevity of the 18 verse sura, which contains a notably high concentration of commands and prohibitions, even within a single verse, giving a clearly legislative style to the sura and emphasising the importance of its subject matter.

In my view, Q.48 and Q.49 form a manifest closely coupled pair of suras focussing almost exclusively on the practice and theory of Conciliation, which has quite discernibly now burgeoned into the central theme of the current Qur'anic discourse. Q.48 deals with Conciliation between the Muslim community and their opponents, which can be seen as an example of international relations, and Q.49

deals with Conciliation between believers, which can be seen as representative of social cohesion within a community. Al-Rāzī also notes at Q.49:1 a natural coherence between the believers' need to overcome their own contrary inclinations and fall into line behind the Prophet's propensity towards Conciliation in Q.48, and the general reminder to give precedence to God and His Messenger in the opening line of Q.49. This highlights the importance of authoritative leadership and discipline, both as a means of ensuring internal unity in a community and facilitating negotiations to achieve Conciliation with external parties.

Structurally, Iṣlāḥī (p.479) considers Q.49 to be an addendum to Q.48, constituting an exegesis of Q.48:29 in which the Prophet is described as the Messenger of God and his followers are described as *ruḥamāʾu baynahum* (compassionate towards each other, Abdel Haleem). I consider this a rather restrictive and limited understanding of the sura's manifest importance and independent standing in the central Qurʾanic discourse. In content, however, Iṣlāḥī acknowledges that the sura's commandments and admonishments are concerned throughout with the *iṣlāḥ* (reform) of society and particularly the mutual rights of the Prophet and the Muslims, a subject of obvious importance in ensuring Conciliation and unity. In his seminal work *Dalāil Al-Niẓām* (1970, p.91), Al-Farāhī argues that the Medinan content supplements and expounds the foundational Meccan content, which indicates a closely connected and possibly more sophisticated or complete exposition of the Conciliation theme in the Medinan content as compared to the fundamental Conciliation theory in the Meccan content. This accords with my discussion of the closely connected notions of *ṣabr* and *sakīna* at Section 5.2.2 in particular, and with the comprehensive Conciliation content of Q.49 apparent from Figure 5.2.

I have previously highlighted the importance of the below theme of internal transformation, particularly by reference to the notions of *birr* (dutiful conduct) and *taqwā* (God-consciousness) at Q.2:177 in Chapter 1, as a call to unity based on *īmān* (faith) at Q.8:1 in Chapter 2, and in various other places including this chapter. I will now examine this notion of internal transformation in relation to Q.49. Contextually, Yusuf Ali suggests that the sura was revealed in 9 A.H. when many deputations came to Medina to accept Islam, in the year after the Conquest of Mecca, and this is relevant to its admonishment of those who have not yet internalised their faith.

5.3.1 The Call to Internal Transformation

From the outset, Q.49:1 begins: *yā ayyuha ʿlladhīna āmanū* (O you who believe). This term of address is used to open a verse no less than five times in this sura at Q.49:1, 2, 6, 11 and 12, indicating that the entire context of the sura is a rendition of conduct, namely the prompt reconciliation of disputes and abiding by God's prohibitions on what leads to conflict, which constitutes and demonstrates true internal faith. Linking Conciliation in such an instructive way with the fundamental notion of faith highlights both its integral role at the core of Qur'anic teachings, and its call towards inner transformation. The specific verses mentioned command, respectively, obedience to God and His Messenger, reverence for the Prophet, verification of rumours to avoid harming people, and a prohibition on hurting the reputation of others either in public or in private. In terms of Conciliation, this ensures God's pleasure in Divine–human relations, unity of leadership and purpose as a community, and prevention of group or individual social disputes based on false rumour or injury to feelings. Figure 5.2 provides a more detailed analysis of the Conciliation mechanisms and supportive literary techniques used to promote the resolution and prevention of conflict.

As well as stipulating precisely the intricate conciliatory obligations relating to conduct, speech and even thoughts and feelings, which are associated with belief, the sura reprimands those who fail to live up to these standards. After rebuking the conduct of people who had apparently called out to the Prophet invading his privacy at Q.49:4–5 (Iṣlāḥī (pp.486–91) refers to recent Bedouin converts around Medina), Q.49:14 rounds on the 'desert Arabs', disputing their claim to faith: *qūlū aslamnā wa lammā yadkhuli 'l-īmānu fī qulūbikum* (say 'We have submitted' for belief has not yet entered your hearts, Nasr). Nasr (p.1262) suggests this admonishes all forms of religious pretension but may be a reference to the Banū Asad who had moved to Medina after a drought and had come seeking charity with an overbearing sense of entitlement, a narration also cited by Al-Rāzī although with the less affirmative *qīla* . . . (it is said . . .). This highlights that mere formal testimony is considered insufficient to claim faith, in the absence of conciliatory conduct. Al-Rāzī also mentions the Bedouin's tendency to self-aggrandisement based on lineage which may have been considered a violation of Q.49:13. In any event, the apparent failure to internalise faith is contrasted at Q.49:15 with *mu'minūn* (believers) who are unwavering in faith and fully exert themselves in God's way. There is also a notable contrast here with the Oath of Allegiance at Ḥudaybiya which earned God's pleasure at Q.48:18 based on His knowledge of what was in their hearts.

The notion of God's knowledge is also stressed repeatedly in Q.49 and indicates the Divine reach encompassing both public and private conduct and the sentiments of the heart. God is described as 'All-Hearing, All-Knowing' at Q.49:1, 'All-Knowing' again at Q.49:8, and 'All-Knowing, All-Aware' at Q.49:13. In the context of internalising faith, Q.49:16 specifically affirms God's complete knowledge of all that is in the heavens and the earth, with Q.49:18 declaring that this includes what is *ghayb* (hidden), and that God sees all that you do. The notion of God's complete knowledge is further reinforced through the internal spiritual notion of *taqwā* (God-consciousness), which is enjoined at Q.49:1 in relation to obedience to God and His Messenger, at Q.49:10 in relation to conducting reconciliation between disputing parties and at Q.49:12 in relation to the prohibition of private attacks on another's character.

Q.49:3 further declares regarding those who lower their voices (out of reverence) in the presence of the Prophet: *(i)mtaḥana 'llāhu qulūbahum li(l)-ttaqwā* (God has tested their hearts for *taqwā*). Al-Rāzī highlights that reverence for God's Messenger and God's commands are both from *taqwā* (God-consciousness). In this sense, following the Prophet's lead towards Conciliation at Ḥudaybiya, unifying behind his spiritual and diplomatic leadership, and abiding by God's prohibitions of that which leads to conflict in Q.49, all signify the internalisation of faith. Q.49:13, which emphasises the internal recognition of human equality and diversity, also declares that the most honourable in God's eyes are those who are highest in *taqwā* and not, by implication, those who consider themselves superior based on external characteristics. Knowing God to be omnipresent and omniscient is in this sense a constant fetter on the conduct of the believer and a powerful motivation towards sincere and total obedience to His commands from the exterior through to the core.

The entire notion of unwavering sincere obedience to the command of God and His Messenger is treated as an expression of faith in the heart. It is notable that Q.49 so powerfully and persuasively drives home this notion in the context of a sura whose commands and prohibitions so comprehensively relate to Conciliation and the prevention of conflict. Q.49:7 declares that God has ***ḥabbaba ilaykumu 'l-īmana*** *wa zayyanahū fī qulūbikum wa* ***karraha ilaykumu*** *'l-kufra wa 'l-fusūqa wa 'l-ʿiṣyān* (God has **endeared faith to you** and made it beautiful to your hearts; He has made disbelief, mischief and disobedience **hateful to you**, Abdel Haleem). As an example of faith, the term *mu'minūn* (believers) is used to positively reference those who reconcile disputes at Q.49:9–10, with both the disputing parties and the intervening third party referred to as 'brothers' and hence *mu'minūn* (believers), given the equational use of these two terms at Q.49:10. The form II intensifying verbs *ḥabbaba* (he endeared), *zayyana* (he made beautiful) and *karraha* (he made hateful) indicate the Divine claim to inspire emotions impacting the very hearts of believers, causing them to be attracted and drawn towards conciliatory conduct and repelled from that which leads to conflict. This is reflected in both the emphasis on *sakīna* (tranquillity) as a means to ultimate Conciliation in Q.48 and the emotive and persuasive language used in Q.49 (see Figure 5.2 for examples), of which more will be discussed below.

In this relatively brief first subsection, I have highlighted how Q.49 associates the fundamental notion of internalising faith with both the command to conciliate and the prohibition of what leads to conflict. In the following subsections I will discuss these two concepts in more detail, commencing with the Duty of Reconciliation.

5.3.2 The Duty of Reconciliation

Q.49 adopts a largely prohibitive and declarative style with recurrent use of the particles *lā* (do not; which occurs nine times, see Figure 5.2) and *inna* (Q.49:1, 3, 4, 10, 12, 13, 14, 15 and 18) often translated as 'surely' or simply omitted for declarative effect. However, on two occasions at Q.49:6 and Q.49:9 the particle *in* (if) is used to introduce two conditional clauses dealing with potential and actual conflict, respectively, both including an imperative command as to what is to be done in the event specified. In the case of being approached with news by an unreliable person, Q.49:6 commands: *fatabayyanū* (verify, Q.49:6; there is a variant reading which also has a similar meaning), clearly imposing a positive duty of investigation and corroboration, and by corollary a duty not to rely or act upon unverified information from an unreliable source. The verse explains this duty as aiming to avoid harm to others and regret to the self: *an tuṣībū qawman bijahālatin fatuṣbiḥū ʿalā mā faʿaltum nādimīn* (in case you wrong others unwittingly and later regret what you have done, Abdel Haleem). The phrase *tuṣbiḥū . . . nādimīn* (you become . . . regretful) uses an active participle which grammatically conveys a sense of everlasting regret.

Nasr (p.1259) places this verse in the context of a near conflict between the Muslims of Medina and the Banū Muṣṭaliq tribe based on unverified information. Iṣlāḥī vehemently rejects this report listing numerous objections (vol.7, pp. 495–97), and instead mentions as context (vol.7, p.492) the Bedouin practice of trying to influence the Prophet and Companions against their opponents to secure the support of the central government in their tribal disputes. At Q.49:6, Al-Rāzī cites the *sabab al-nuzūl* (circumstances of revelation) of the Banū Muṣṭaliq account but is sceptical of some aspects and stresses that the verse establishes a general principle. Whatever the historical context, Q.49:6 clearly aims to prevent harm to innocent third parties caused by the incorrect reports of an unreliable source, enjoining the duty of verification as a conflict prevention mechanism.[14]

14 Q.49:6 is also of particular importance, being the seminal verse on the admissibility of testimony from unreliable witnesses in Islamic legal matters and the classification of Ḥadīth

Al-Rāzī highlights at Q.49:6 an important aspect of the arrangement of the sura, considering after what pertains to God and then His Messenger, Q.49:6 has been foregrounded in preference to Q.49:11–12 due to its greater importance and greater potential for conflict resulting from unfounded allegations: *thumma dhakara mā yufḍī ila 'l-iq**ti**tāl bayna ṭawā'if al-muslimīn bi sabab al-iṣghā' ilā kalām al-fāsiq wa 'l-i'timād 'alayh, fa innahū yadhkuru kulla mā kāna ashadda nifāran lil-ṣudūr* (then He mentioned that which leads to fighting between groups of Muslims due to attention given to the speech of a troublemaker and reliance upon it, so He mentions all that is most strongly divisive of hearts).[15] Al-Rāzī goes on to explain that the hurt caused to a believer in his presence or the insult to him in his absence pursuant to Q.49:11–12 does not cause such severe harm as to cause *al-qatl* (killing) whereas Q.49:6 is closely succeeded by *āyat al-iqtitāl* (the 'Fighting Verse', Q.49:9) – Al-Rāzī considers the conflict referred to at Q.49:9 as following directly from the reliance on unverified information cautioned against at Q.49:6.

Whilst I agree with the importance Al-Rāzī gives to Q.49:6, it is difficult to underestimate the effect of damage to reputation and dignity on an individual, and the harm caused to their mental and physical health. This is indicated by the modern-day phrase 'character assassination' and can certainly result in a person's life becoming 'not worth living'. This gravity is fully recognised in the tone of Q.49:11–12 and the metaphor in Q.49:12 as I discuss below. I do agree with Al-Rāzī that there is a hierarchical arrangement to the sura but I would argue that this is based on a top-down ordering ranging from the most public to the most private actions, and not based on the level of harm caused which varies from context to context.

Shortly after the above duty to investigate unreliable reports to prevent conflict, Q.49:9 stipulates a second duty, this time a duty of reconciliation in the case of actual conflict: *wa in ṭā'ifatāni mina 'l-mu'minīna 'qtatalū fa aṣliḥū baynahumā* (if two groups of the believers fight, you [believers] should try to reconcile them, Abdel Haleem). Once again, as for the first duty, the conditional particle *in* (if) is used to introduce this second duty, a point which Al-Rāzī considers cautionary, as *ishāra ilā annahu yanbaghī an lā yaqa'a illā* ***nādiran*** (an indication that it is necessary that it does not occur except **rarely**). Indicating further Divine disapproval of conflict, Al-Rāzī notes that the address to the believers at Q.49:6 has shifted into a third-person reference to believers at Q.49:9

narrators as reliable or unreliable in assessing the authenticity of Ḥadīth. Iṣlāḥī (vol.7, pp. 500–03) discusses the merits and alternative approaches within this genre at length.

15 The bold letters indicate an erroneously omitted letter *ta* in *iq**ti**tāl* on al-tafsir.com.

tanbīhan ʿalā qabḥ dhālik wa tabʿīdan lahum ʿanhum (as a warning of the ugliness of (fighting between believers) and as a way of banishing them from (other believers)). After adding that the reference to *al-muʾminīna* (the believers) has been advanced before the verb as a further means of necessitating the absence of conflict between them, Al-Rāzī highlights that the verb *iqtatalū* (they fight) has been used in the past tense *lianna ṣīghat al-istiqbāl tunabbiʾu ʿani ʻl-dawām wa ʻl-istimrār* (because the future form indicates continuity and permanence). It is quite obvious from Al-Rāzī's careful dissection of the above *sharṭ* (conditional clause) that conflict in this fundamental Qurʾanic discourse is considered an abnormal, undesirable and anomalous state of affairs.

The *jawāb al-sharṭ* (result clause) *fa aṣliḥū baynahumā* (reconcile the two) then provides an imperative command which stipulates the actual Duty of Reconciliation. The active form IV verb is a call to action whilst the collective plural address *aṣliḥ**ū*** creates an unrestricted general duty. Ṭāhā (2009, pp.1, 30) concludes that the duty to conciliate is *farḍ al-kifāya* (a collective obligation). The root *ṣ-l-ḥ*, conspicuously absent in Q.48 and manifest in the sense of reform in obedience to God and preservation of Divine order in the form IV *maṣdar* (verbal noun) *iṣlāḥ* in Chapter 2, is here used in the clear sense of reconciliation between people, as in Q.2:224 and Q.4:114. Al-Rāzī notes that the plural used at Q.49:9 to indicate an outbreak of general fighting in *ʻqtatal**ū*** above, despite the earlier reference to two disputing parties, is now again referred to in the dual form in *bayna**humā**,* indicating the restoration of two orderly parties in the agreement of a reconciliation.

Having stipulated a general duty to conciliate, the question arises as to what should be done to discharge that duty if the parties themselves refuse to negotiate and continue fighting. It soon becomes clear that the command to conciliate has teeth, prescribing sanctions which raise fundamental questions about the interrelation of Conciliation and conflict in the Qurʾan. Another condition–result pair follows the first, clarifying the course of action to be taken in this event: *fa **in baghat** iḥdāhumā ʿala ʻl-ukhrā **fa qātilu** ʻllatī tabghī **ḥattā** tafīʾa ilā **amri ʻllāh*** (if one of them is [clearly] **oppressing** the other, **fight** the oppressors **until** they submit to **God's command**, Abdel Haleem). We see here an extraordinary juxtaposition of Conciliation and conflict. At the heart of perhaps the most explicit and far-reaching direct command to conciliate in the entire Qurʾan, we find an actual command to fight. Neither Cragg's argument of increased belligerence in the Medinan period, nor Iṣlāḥī's argument of continuous conflict with the Meccans until they submit to Islam, is sufficient to explain this command. This is not even a command of conflict between believers and disbelievers. The command is for believers to fight believers, including the very people whom they are commanded to reconcile.

There are, however, two important defining parameters on this command which must be analysed carefully to understand the scope of the conflict enjoined here. The first is a pre-condition that one party must be oppressing the other for the fighting to be permissible in the first instance, and the second is a restriction that the fighting must end when the oppressor submits to God's command. Al-Rāzī stipulates that the fighting indicated is purely defensive: *hādha 'l-qitāl li dafʿ al-ṣāʾil* (this fighting is to drive back an attacker). He considers 'God's command' could mean either obedience to God's Messenger and those in authority, or Conciliation, or the fear of Allah which prohibits harbouring enmity against anyone other than Satan. To my mind, the only satisfactory explanation of 'God's command' in this verse is the command *fa aṣliḥū baynahumā* (reconcile between them). This is clear from the *siyāq al-naṣṣ* (textual context) and is the directly preceding Divine command. The use of the term *amri 'llāh* (God's command) heightens the gravity of the command to conciliate in the eyes of the parties, thus reinforcing the initial command. It is also a clear indication of the importance of Conciliation in the Qurʾan as God's own command and the priority given to it: *fa aṣliḥū* is repeated no less than three times in Q.49:9–10. In my view, therefore, the above language indicates that fighting should only be used defensively against a party who persists in attacking the other upon being enjoined to conciliate, and only up to the point that the attacker desists and agrees to come to the negotiating table.

Iṣlāḥī advocates a rather more robust approach to the enforcement of reconciliation based on the above language, suggesting (vol.7, p.480) in summary that the Muslims should attempt a just reconciliation, and that once the just course of action has been established, any party which refuses to submit to it should be forcibly made to do so. He clarifies further on (pp.498–99) that if either party refuses to conciliate (he only later adds 'and insists on war'), or violates the terms of reconciliation, or even self-servingly presents terms which are against justice, then that party should be forcibly made to submit to the terms of reconciliation. Iṣlāḥī regards the reconciliation terms as a *fayṣala* (adjudication) made by the 'conciliators' on the basis of justice meaning with full compensation to the party who has incurred loss. He qualifies that the above applies where there is a strong central government who can intervene between two groups of Muslims who are in conflict, whilst in modern international affairs where two countries are at war, active intervention by others may cause greater complications although negotiation efforts should still be maintained.

Iṣlāḥī's position raises three important questions. The first is whether a party can be fought on the basis of a mere refusal to negotiate, presentation of unreasonable terms or breach of reconciliation terms. In my view, Al-Rāzī's position of fighting being permitted only to drive back an aggressor indicates that only a party who insists on attacking the other can be fought against. It would be quite absurd for a provision which manifestly aims to *end fighting* between two parties to instruct a third party to instigate fighting where there is no fighting already in progress. The sequence of the conditional clauses at Q.49:9 indicates that 'fighting' should be responded to with Conciliation. 'Transgression' should be responded to with fighting. This accords with Q.42:39–41 in Section 5.1 which established the principle that retaliation was permitted in response to transgression. The transgression referred to in Q.49:9 appears to be an insistence on fighting after the other party has agreed to cease fighting and negotiate, since when both parties were fighting the word transgression was not used to describe their conduct.

Secondly, should a settlement be imposed or negotiated by consent? I would argue that where the Qur'an intends an imposed adjudication, it uses the root *ḥ-k-m* as in Q.4:65 and Q.5:42 (however, see the debate regarding Q.4:35 in the early section on Definitional Scope of *Ṣulḥ*). Commentators also generally distinguish negotiated contractual *ṣulḥ* (Conciliation) based on the parties' agreement to the terms, from arbitration where the parties agree to be bound by the arbitrator's decision (Alsheikh, 2011, pp.378, 399). Given that the third party intervening here is not an appointed adjudicator or arbitrator but the general body of Muslims (or potentially a Muslim authority), the use of the phrase *aṣliḥū baynahumā* (reconcile the two) clearly indicates, to my mind, third-party facilitation of negotiation of terms agreed by consent with both parties. Q.42:38 above also commended the use of mutual consultation in matters two verses before an explicit reference to *ṣulḥ* at Q.42:40, and this points more to the promotion of negotiation than to the imposition of a forced settlement.

Thirdly, are the settlement terms themselves required to be fair and just? As mentioned, in a quasi-judicial process or binding arbitration, the settlement would often be guided by legal principles, and in the absence of agreement by the parties to the terms, it would be for the adjudicator or arbitrator to ensure that justice is done to both parties (Bouheraoua, 2010, p.3). However, in a Conciliation process one would expect more scope for latitude in this requirement, since arguably whatever the parties agree to might be considered 'fair', subject to their equal bargaining power and an absence of actual or perceived duress. Othman (2007, pp.73–81) discusses the question raised by classical jurists as to the validity of *ṣulḥ al-inkār* (disputed claim) in cases where there are disputes of fact and hence a risk of injustice, with Ibn Al-Qayyim apparently arguing that all settlements should be *ṣulḥ ʿādil*, meaning a settlement which is subject to a test of fairness. This may be more arguable in a case where the judge is acting in a quasi-judicial pre-litigation Conciliation procedure.

In Section 5.1, however, we saw that Q.42:40 indicates that damage may fairly be requited but that forgiveness and reconciliation are rewarded by God, indicating that Conciliation sometimes requires the gracious approach of forgiveness for past wrongs, with compensation reserved for the Hereafter. I would therefore argue that Conciliation often requires concessions and forgiveness of past wrongs– indeed some wrongs are such that they can never be requited. Furthermore, in a case where the facts are disputed, fairness is entirely subjective. In the end, the definitive argument must be the apparently ignominious terms accepted by the Prophet at Ḥudaybiya – if the parties are willing to agree, it seems that peace can be bought at any cost. Structurally, the arrangement of Q.48 and Q.49 as a closely coupled pair also indicates to me that Q.49:9 advocates a negotiated Conciliation rather than an arbitration, a point which is crucial to the question of whether the settlement terms must be fair and just – in a Conciliation process, the parties' consent is paramount not the ostensible 'fairness' of the terms.

Q.49:9 itself addresses the issue of justice by prescribing a third condition–result pair: *fa in fāʾat fa aṣliḥū baynahumā bi ʿl-ʿadli wa aqsiṭū, innAllāha yuḥibbu ʿl-muqsiṭīn* (if (that party) submits (to God's command) then reconcile the two with justice and be equitable, God loves those who are equitable). This command for the conciliators to be just and equitable is, in my view, best understood as a command to follow due process and to be even-handed and impartial between the parties. This argument was also made in Fazaluddin (2016, p.350), where it was noted that this position is supported by Al-Bayḍāwī's exegesis which suggests that there is a likelihood of unfairness due to the prior conflict. The purpose of the enjoinder to justice at this juncture is particularly pertinent since the conciliators have been *embroiled in conflict* with the transgressing party and are now required to resume their role as fair and impartial conciliators, a point which therefore now requires explicit emphasis. Q.5:8 is most instructive on this issue, stating: 'You who believe, be steadfast in your devotion to God and bear witness **impartially**: do not let *hatred of others* lead you away from **justice**, but adhere to **justice**, for that is closer to awareness of God. **Be mindful of God**.' (Abdel Haleem). This verse refers to ***qisṭ***, ***ʿadl*** and ***taqwā***, respectively. Similarly, Q.49:9 refers to the first two and Q.49:10 to the latter concept.

Al-Rāzī argues an intermediate position between that of Iṣlāḥī and myself, which is nonetheless problematic in my view as explained below. He distinguishes the two commands to conciliate in Q.49:9, since the first before intervention with force makes no mention of justice, and the second after such intervention stipulates the requirement of justice. He argues that in the first instance, Conciliation is achieved by putting an end to the fighting either by advice, threat, prevention or punishment. In the second instance, he argues that Conciliation is through removing the harmful effect of the conflict, by following the end of fighting with a just adjudication so as to prevent a future outbreak of conflict between the parties. At Q.49:10, Al-Rāzī then appears to interpret the third command to conciliate as encouraging, but *not mandating*, the mediation of a reconciliation in private disputes which fall short of an open outbreak of fighting. These three different interpretations of the exact same phrase *aṣliḥū baynahumā* at Q.49:9–10 are, in my view, highly subjective and at odds with the consistency of the language used in the verses, as well as diluting the emphatic effect of their recurrence.

Al-Rāzī's customarily thoughtful and nuanced analysis deserves acknowledgement. Nonetheless, I would argue that his perspective on the Conciliation processes indicated at Q.49:9–10 fails to achieve reconciliation in a number of circumstances, which undermines his position. In the first instance of *aṣliḥū baynahumā* at Q.49:9, this phrase according to Al-Rāzī would mean simply 'make peace', without resolution of the underlying issues and therefore without achieving actual reconciliation. Can the Duty of Reconciliation be discharged simply by ending the fighting without facilitating the negotiation of a lasting settlement? In the second instance at Q.49:9, the exact same terminology *aṣliḥū baynahumā* with the simple addition of a reference to justice is interpreted by Al-Rāzī as a command to *adjudicate*, rather than mediate, and thus to impose an arbitrary settlement on the parties which *both* may be dissatisfied with. This seems to me at odds with the actual meaning of 'reconcile the two'. In addition, given that Q.49:9 imposes a *general duty* to reconcile, it is more reasonable to interpret this as a duty to mediate, since adjudication is more onerous on the intervenor and the parties themselves and necessarily demands the appointment of a *specific* third party.

Overall, I remain unconvinced that a simple reference to justice can imply a complete change of process in the above two situations at Q.49:9. Circling back to the earlier narrative of David from Section 5.1 to shed further light on the significance of the reference to 'justice,' it will be recalled that David was enjoined at Q.38:22 to adjudicate with justice between two disputants with one alleging transgression using the same term *baghā*. It can also be seen that the command at Q.38:22 uses the verb *ḥa-ka-ma* in the imperative form to indicate adjudication. Notwithstanding the use of *ḥaqq* to reference the notion of justice in that verse, it is clear from the story that in his zeal to end transgression and achieve fair terms, David does not give the party who is accused of transgression a fair hearing and appears completely swayed by the allegation of transgression and ostensible unfairness of conduct by the defendant, passing prompt judgement against the defendant.

At this point in the analysis of Q.49:9, it appears to me to be this inclination and leaning of David's which is referred to as *hawā* (desires, Abdel Haleem) at Q.38:26, David's apparent fault in the story. This is in line with the point noted in Section 5.1.1 that some commentators had considered David's hastiness in judgement to be the point for which he seeks forgiveness, although my focus here is on his following of his *inclination* towards the plaintiff and *consequent failure* to hear the defendant, perhaps also affected by the informal nature of the disputants' approach and the setting – he was not sitting in court at the time. Justice at both Q.38:22 and Q.49:9, in my view, means impartiality and due process and not an imposed adjudication on what an arbitrary third party considers 'fair' terms.

Before closing off this involved discussion of the central verse Q.49:9 on the theme of Conciliation, it is also worth reflecting on the scope of conflict permitted here and in other contexts. I would argue that there is a clear parallel between the use of force limited to the purpose of terminating an existing conflict and in response to transgression in Q.49:9 and the use of force permitted elsewhere in the Qur'an. Thus in Q.48, the Prophet and his followers were permitted to use force when they initially thought that their emissary had been wrongfully assassinated. At the Conquest of Mecca, the Prophet and his followers came in force in response to a breach of peace treaty. In the early Medinan period they were permitted to fight when their nascent community faced annihilation from overwhelming opposition.

However, at Ḥudaybiya the Muslims were not permitted to fight once the opposition had solicited peace, even on apparently unfair terms. At the Conquest of Mecca, they did not fight once the Meccans confined themselves indoors demonstrating their non-combative intentions. In both the early and late Medinan periods, it is clear from Q.8:61, Q.8:72, Q.9:4 and Q.9:7, discussed at length in Chapter 2, that once the Meccan opponents incline to peace, the Muslims should also do so and that they should abide by peace treaties which have not been breached. This demonstrates a consistent approach to the inter-relation of Conciliation and conflict in different times and contexts, and irrespective of whether the opposing party is Muslim or not. Indeed, conflict in all of these contexts is used to end the opponent's overbearing inclination to persist in conflict and to bring them to the negotiating table or an inclination towards peace, at which point the permission to fight is terminated.

We can see now that the theory of Conciliation is outlined in the Meccan suras of Group 5, as demonstrated in Section 5.1. In the Medinan suras, the limited use of force to end conflict and in response to transgression is permitted in Q.47. The use of peace treaties to end conflict as soon as the enemy inclines to it, even on the basis of unfair terms, is demonstrated in Q.48. These stages of Conciliation are presented in concise definitive summary form at Q.49:9 in three remarkable successive condition–result clauses. Figure 5.3 presents a Logic Diagram of the central Conciliation process at Q.49:9 within the surrounding Conciliation Paradigm of Q.49.

Q.49:10, the next verse, continues: *innama 'l-mu'minūna ikhwatun fa aṣliḥū bayna akhawaykum wa 'ttaqu 'llāha la'allakum turḥamūn* (the believers are brothers, so make peace between your two brothers and be mindful of God, so that you may be given mercy, Abdel Haleem). We see here a declarative statement establishing a principle of brotherhood as a basis for the unity of believers. I have

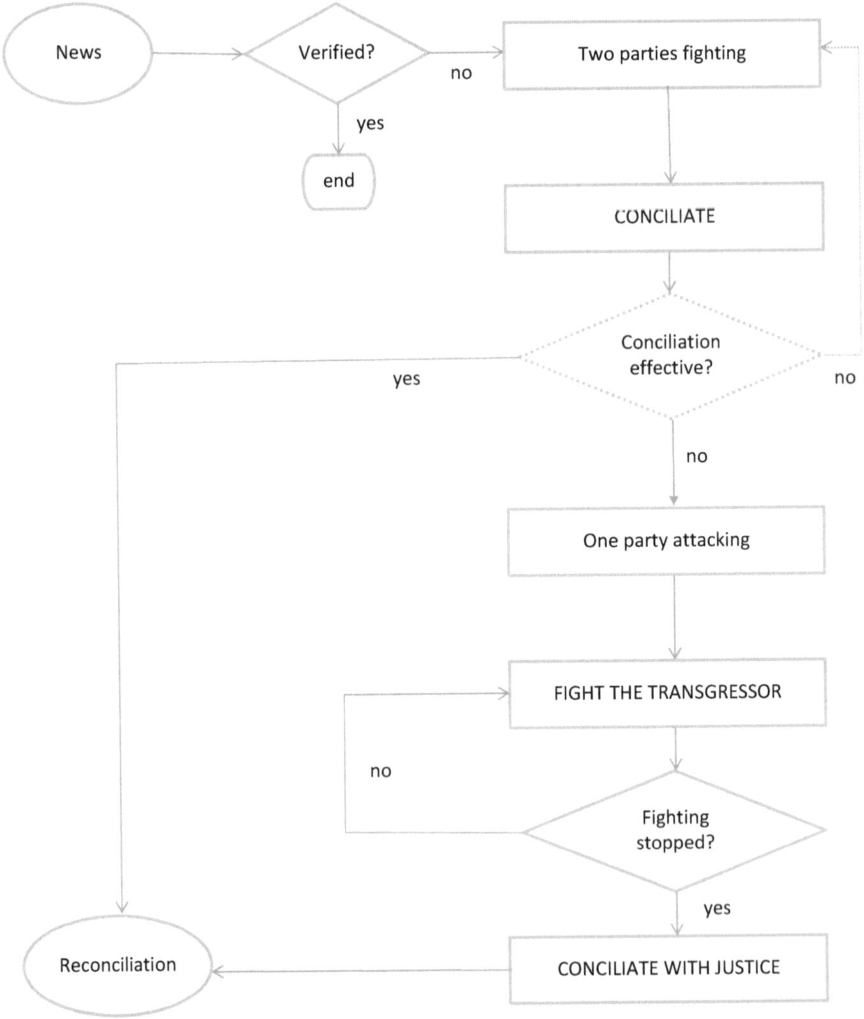

Figure 5.3: Q.49:6 and Q.49:9 Conciliation procedure.

drawn attention at Q.3:103 in Chapter 1 and Q.15:47 in Chapter 3 (see also Q.59:10 which refers to 'brothers in faith') to brotherhood as a key notion in Conciliation used to engender close relationship ties, particularly in the context of developing a sense of community between the newly formed body of believers. Al-Rāzī even likens Islam to a father. This is another example of the Qur'an's use of evocative terminology to arouse emotional bonds and highlighting commonalities to facilitate conciliatory relationships.

The concluding reference to believers as brothers reunites the broken bonds indicated at the opening of Q.49:9, healing the emotional wounds caused to the warring factions by the conflict. The injunction to 'make peace between your two brothers' reinforces the message of impartial and balanced treatment of the two parties, as well as reuniting the conciliating party with any 'transgressing' party which has been fought against. In combination the two references to brotherhood reinstate a triangle of close relationships between the originally conflicting parties, and the conciliating party and each of them, as if symbolising a successful multi-party reconciliation. The concluding reference indicates that those who are mindful of the Divine injunctions towards just reconciliation shall be rewarded with Divine mercy.

We now move to a discussion of the prohibition of that which leads to conflict, including the ensuing Q.49:11–12, and finally concluding this chapter with a discussion of Q.49:13 which provides a powerful climax to both the sura's and the Qur'an's Conciliation discourse.

5.3.3 The Prohibition of That Which Leads to Conflict

At Q.49:9–10 above, we saw repeated use of the imperative form to command Conciliation three times: *aṣliḥū* (reconcile, Q.49:9–10). Conversely, the sense of prohibition and disapproval of all that leads to conflict in Q.49 is palpable. This effect is garnered progressively through the sura through a range of literary features. From the outset, the attention of the reader is seized, at Q.49:1–2, with the prohibitive *lā* used *three times* in two verses in connection with duties of obedience and reverence to God and His Messenger. Immediately after the command to conciliate, the prohibitive *lā* features a further *six times in two verses*, at Q.49:11–12, to prohibit public or private attacks on the reputation of another. This high frequency and concentration of the prohibitive particle in connection with conduct leading to conflict in Divine–human and social relations provides a fitting complement to the thrice-repeated emphatic command to conciliate at Q.49:9–10.

As discussed in Section 5.3.1, the repeated term of address (Q.49:1, 2, 6, 11 and 12) calling for inner transformation, and the pervasive references to *taqwā* (God-consciousness, Q.49:1, 3, 10, 12 and 13) provide another complementary message of *targhīb* (motivational appeal) and *tarhīb* (warning), a common stylistic feature in Qur'anic discourse. The second of these is in my view the stronger feature in this sura which adopts a robust style, allowing no room for dissension. Explicit and severe sanctions, the destruction of all one's accumulated deeds, are threatened at Q.49:2 for raising one's voice over that of the Messenger of God or even addressing him aloud in a familiar manner. At Q.49:11, those who insult others in public are referred to as *ẓālimūn* (evildoers, Abdel Haleem), if they fail to repent. Al-Rāzī highlights that: *iẓhār al-nadm ʿalayhā mubāligha fī ʾl-taḥdhīr wa tashdīdan fī ʾl-zajr* (the demonstration of remorse (for such conduct) is the utmost expression of admonition and (indicates) severity in prohibition). Another reference to sinfulness occurs at Q.49:12 where even some *ẓann* (supposition), a mere state of mind, is described as *ithm* (sin) indicating both gravity of conduct and severity of sanction. The accompanying command *ijtanibū* (eschew, Q.49:12), which enjoins the avoidance of such supposition, is a positive command but semantically has the effect of a prohibition. The same command is used at Q.5:90–91 in connection with alcohol and gambling, on the explicit basis that they are a cause of conflict, indicating a similar usage here.

Highly charged terminology is also used to indicate prohibition and reprimand. The term *fāsiq* is used to describe an unreliable rumour-monger who incites conflict at Q.49:6, whilst those insulting others in public at Q.49:11 through mockery, defamation or derogatory nicknames are themselves in turn given a 'bad name': *biʾsa lismu ʾl-fusūqu baʿda ʾl-īmān* (how bad it is to be called a mischief-maker after accepting faith! Abdel Haleem). Abdel Haleem and Badawi (2013, p.710) define the root *f-s-q* as meaning 'acting outside moral and social norms in general and violating Islamic teachings in particular', with derivative meanings including 'deserting the community'. *Fasaqa* is even used at Q.18:50 to describe Satan's original rebellion against God, highlighting the gravity of its usage. At Q.49:11, the Dictionary defines *fusūq* as an 'ungodly act'. Whilst the Dictionary defines *fāsiq* at Q.49:6 as 'unreliable' and a 'troublemaker', to my mind there is a connotation almost tantamount to sedition or creating unrest in the use of this term at Q.49:6, indicating rebellion against God's order, breaching His peace and inciting others to do the same: the Dictionary's alternative meanings of the term *fāsiq* include rejection of God, His religion and His law. Although the 'everyday' context at Q.49:11 may indicate a milder interpretation of the term, the use of such a potentially severe term itself conveys a sense of gravity and reprimand for what might otherwise be considered relatively trivial conduct.

Another striking feature of the sura indicating censure is the use of metaphor at Q.49:12. Immediately after the command *lā yaghtab baʿḍukum baʿḍā* (do not back-bite one another), the narrative continues: *ayuḥibbu aḥadukum an yaʾkula laḥma akhīhi maytan fa karihtumūhu, wa ʾttaqu ʾllāh* (would any of you like to eat the flesh of your dead brother? No, you would hate it. So be mindful of God, Abdel Haleem). The metaphor is repulsive on multiple levels. The close ties between believers are described as brotherhood at Q.49:10, indicating reproach against back-biting one who is a 'brother'. Carrion is specifically rendered unlawful at Q.5:3 and humans are also specifically honoured at Q.17:70 and Q.95:4, compounding the sense of detestable conduct – Al-Rāzī terms it:

ghāyat al-qubḥ (the height of repulsiveness). The reference to love and hate in connection with this metaphor recalls to mind Q.49:7 in which faith was claimed to have been endeared and disbelief, *fisq* (wilfulness) and disobedience made detestable in the hearts of believers. This indicates that the repulsion inspired against back-biting, an example of inter-personal conflict, is a specific part of this general effort to root out all forms of conflict in opposition to the Divine will and to instil conciliatory attitudes and conduct which reflect genuine faith.

The far-reaching scope of the effort to uproot conflict of all types is clearly evident at Q.49:11–12, with even oral 'attacks' subjected to scrupulous censure. Q.49:11 prohibits three specific behaviours: mocking others, defaming others and addressing others by derogatory nicknames. All of these are public in the sense that they are (often) sensed by the victim causing him/her direct injury to feelings and a sense of being demeaned, which in turn can lead to further conflict. This indicates that the Qurʾan aims not only to prevent conflict which involves physical fighting as in Q.49:9 but also conflict which involves the use of the tongue to injure the feelings and dignity of another. It is notable that, in each case, the Qurʾan defends the victim, saying 'they may be better than you' in the first case, turning the defamation on the defamer in the second case by saying 'do not defame yourselves', and giving the perpetrator a 'bad name' in the third case.

Q.49:12 on the other hand prohibits negative supposition, spying and mutual back-biting. These three behaviours are private in the sense that the victim often remains, at least initially, unaware whilst his/her faults are wrongfully suspected, sought out or publicised. Here, the prohibition aims to control the tongue, the senses and even the *mind* to prevent either indirect harm to the reputation of another or even *potential* harm which might only crystallise in the future. It can be seen that the sura encompasses both a broad range of harmful or potentially harmful conduct and a broad range in the type of harm caused or potentially arising. Al-Farāhī (1970, p.91 (footnote)) explains the progressive censure of conflict and its causes: *baʿda sadd abwāb 'al-baghy wa 'l-fasād dhakara asbābahu wa sadda abwābahā, fa manaʿa ʿani 'l-sukhr wa 'l-lamz wa nabz al-alqāb wa sūʾ al-dhann wa 'l-tajassus wa 'l-ghība wa 'l-fakhr* (after closing the doors of transgression and disorder, He mentioned its causes and closed their doors, thus He prohibited mockery, defamation, using derogatory nicknames, negative supposition, spying, back-biting and pride),[16] going on to state that the Prophet had captured

16 The text contains *nabdh/nabadha* (renunciation/he renounced) rather than *nabz* which would render a slight difference of translation though not of overall meaning; on reflection I have assumed there is a typing error here given the terminology *tanābazū* used in Q.49:11 and the lack of obvious explanation for changing the verb of prohibition from *manaʿa* to *nabadha* mid-sentence.

these sentiments in his Final Sermon (during the *ḥajj* pilgrimage in 10 A.H.). At Q.49:10, Al-Rāzī also cites a Prophetic narration which encapsulates this sense to some extent: *al-muslimu man salima 'l-nāsu min lisānihī wa yadihī* (a Muslim is one from (the harm of) whose tongue and hand people are safe). The use of *nās* in this narration indicates that these social teachings are of general application, although in context addressed to believers at Q.49.

It can be seen that many of the above behaviours stem from diseases of the heart such as envy, malice, rancour and arrogance. This is not the subject of this study but is a field of study in itself (see Al-Ghazālī's *Al-Iḥyā' 'Ulūm Al-Dīn* (2011) for further reading on the subject). It is, however, worth reflecting that the seed of conflict can originate in one heart but its growth can spread through society through the kind of thoughts, speech and conduct regulated above, if not promptly weeded out. Iṣlāḥī (vol.7, p.507) highlights that the desire to elevate the self and demean the other can have far-reaching societal effects whose effect can last for generations. In particular, he notes that the Arabs had a pre-Islamic poetic tradition of boasting about their own tribes and demeaning the tribes of others, which he considers to have been an obstruction to their unification prior to the advent of Islam.

Arrogance, the elevation of one's worth over that of others, is the root of many of the behaviours prohibited above which seek to demean and humiliate others, a connection which Al-Rāzī reflects on in his analysis of Q.49:11. At Q.7:12, Satan's arrogance is reflected in the seemingly innocuous statement: *ana khayrun minhu, khalaqtanī min nārin wa khalaqtahū min ṭīn* ('I am better than him: You created me from fire and him from clay,' Abdel Haleem). This one statement delivers Satan into a state of eternal conflict with God and a devastating fall from grace. As discussed in Chapter 2, Satan represents the archetypal model of arrogance, and man's sworn enemy. It is his example of arrogance which is to be avoided at all costs in the Qur'anic narrative. Time and again, we have seen an incitement to conflict associated with Satan (Q.5:91, Q.7:200, Q.41:36).

Having presented a comprehensive top-down paradigm of conflict prevention measures and enjoinders to Conciliation, dealing with obedience to God, reverence for the Prophet and mutual respect for others, Q.49:13 now addresses the fundamental issue of social equality as a remedial cure for arrogance. After this, the sura concludes with a context-specific address which I have dealt with in Section 5.3.1. I regard Q.49:13 as the **paramount Conciliation verse** in this sura, and arguably in the Qur'anic discourse: a universal statement of mankind's social equality and a celebration of their diversity as a means of mutual increase in knowledge and respect of others, rather than ignorance and division. It is a principle which, as Levy (1969, p.55) describes, 'although judged by modern critics to have been revealed at a comparatively late date in the career of the Prophet, voices what must have been an essential doctrine from the beginning.' Levy notes that the verse was reported to have been recited by the Prophet on his entry to the Kaʿba in 8 A.H./630 C.E., the year of the Conquest of Mecca.

Q.49:13 directly addresses all of humanity: ***yā ayyuha (ʾl)-nnāsu innā khalaqnākum min dhakarin wa unthā wa jaʿalnākum shuʿūban wa qabāʾila li taʿārafū, inna akramakum ʿinda ʾllāhi atqākum, inna ʾllāha ʿalīmun khabīr*** (People, We created you all from a single man and a single woman, and made you into races and tribes so that you should recognize one another. In God's eyes, the most honoured of you are the ones most mindful of Him: God is all knowing, all aware [translator's note: of people's true worth and the thoughts they harbour (see also Q.50:16)], Abdel Haleem). The verse is stylistically emphatic and dramatic, a direct address in the plural of majesty from the professed Creator to all mankind in creation, without discrimination of gender, race or faith. All such diversity of creation is equalised through commonality of origin in the verse before being joined together through the *lām al-taʿlīl* (*lām* of purpose) followed by a simple enjoinder in the mutual form VI grammatical form: ***li taʿārafū*** (so that you should recognize one another). The verse continues by signalling that true worth in God's eyes is based on internal mindfulness of God, and God's all-encompassing knowledge. The whole verse is a manifestation of the Qurʾan's extraordinary conciliatory reach, its recurrent highlighting of commonalities as a basis for mutual engagement and its commanding employment of literary techniques to provide impact to its central Conciliation discourse.

Summary Table: Group 5 Conciliation Themes Map by Sura and Verse

	Conciliation through patience	A historical Conciliation	Conflict prevention and resolution
Q.38	17 David as an exemplar of fortitude		
Q.39	10 withdrawal from conflict and Divine reward 53 God's limitless mercy		
Q.41	34–35 recurrent *iḥsān* and transformation of enmity into lasting friendship 36 Satan's incitement		

(continued)

	Conciliation through patience	A historical Conciliation	Conflict prevention and resolution
Q.42	23 maintaining love for relatives 40 justice, forgiveness and Conciliation, transgression 43 patience and forgiveness		
Q.46	35 Enjoinder to emulate the patience of past prophets		
Q.48		1, 18, 27 Conciliation as a victory 5, 18, 26 internal *sakīna* (tranquillity) 18, 29 mutually satisfactory relations with God 24 mutual restraint 25 protection of innocents 27 objective met peacefully	
Q.49			1–5 unity through obeying God and honouring the Prophet 6–10 verify rumours and reconcile group disputes with justice, based on brotherhood 11–12 prohibition of mockery, defamation, derogatory nicknames, suspicion, spying and back-biting 13 equality of mankind and honour only through *taqwā* (God-consciousness)

Conclusion

In assessing the pervasiveness of Conciliation in Group 5 suras, the Meccan content from Q.34–Q.46 is best described as intermittent but highly significant, coherent and instructive. The Medinan content of Q.47–Q.49, on the other hand, is so replete with Conciliation material as to justify, in my view, the conclusion that Conciliation is the paramount theme of the Qur'anic discourse at this juncture. Q.48 and Q.49 provide the central platform for this theme in Group 5 addressing the practice and theory of Conciliation, with the incremental Meccan content closely correlating with and supporting the sustained focus of the Medinan suras. Q.49:13 provides the apex to the comprehensive Conciliation paradigm presented in Q.49. The high level of semantic correlation between the Conciliation content of the two time periods demonstrates a clear consistency and continuity of emphasis on Conciliation between the Meccan and Medinan periods, rather than a disjointed approach during the two periods as suggested by Cragg and others. Also contrary to the views of such commentators, it is the *Medinan content* which takes the lead between the two, presenting a sustained thematic focus, and a profound and sophisticated Conciliation paradigm coupled with a notable and exemplary historical context.

The range of Conciliation concepts in Group 5 is especially comprehensive and diverse yet in no way disparate. Rather it indicates an advanced state of development and consolidation in the concepts presented. In the Meccan period, the previously encountered conciliatory basis of *iḥsān* (gracious conduct) is now developed into a successful Conciliation mechanism through the notion of *ṣabr*, loosely translated as patience, but signifying the crucial qualities of forbearance and fortitude. Forbearance requires an ability to withstand the harm caused by others and to make sacrifices even to the point of emigration. Fortitude requires perseverance and recurrent reciprocation of harm with good conduct, with the ultimate aim of transforming enmity into deep friendship. This includes both a strength of character which remains uninfluenced by the recurrent harm of the other party and thus breaks the chain of causation of conflict, and a determination which ultimately leads to a sense of shame and consequent internal transformation in the other party's attitude, resulting in Conciliation. Past prophets exemplify these qualities of *ṣabr* demonstrating the laudability of Conciliation, whilst Satan conversely provides the archetypal model of incitement away from such fortitude and hence towards conflict. The Prophet, himself a pre-eminent role model for his followers, is instructed to show *ṣabr* on 19 occasions in the Qur'an, including notably in Group 5 with reference to the example of past prophets.

At Q.48 in the Medinan period, Conciliation features externally as a momentous peace treaty between the Prophet and his arch-enemies, the disbelieving leaders of Quraysh. It is this peace agreement and its historical aftermath, rather than any military outcome, which is significantly termed on three occasions a manifest and imminent victory, clearly challenging and refuting Iṣlāḥī's assertion of a fight to the finish between the two parties, and establishing Conciliation as the ultimate desideratum. Yet the Qur'anic narrative of Q.48 does not even mention the terms *ṣulḥ* (reconciliation), *salm* (peace agreement) or any other contractual terminology which references the agreement itself. Purely linguistic studies of such terms without reference to historical and textual context are therefore incomplete as a study of Conciliation. Instead Q.48 focuses inwards on the thrice-recurrent notion of *sakīna* (tranquillity) in the hearts, which includes forbearance and fortitude as advocated in the Meccan period, and the need for foresight. This provides a close correlation with the notion of *ṣabr*. Conciliation is a long-term endeavour for which the Meccan period provides only the instructive preparation, the early Medinan period providing the impetus to fight for survival at a time of weakness, and only the late Medinan period eventually culminating in an end to conflict and a final reconciliation of hearts. The restoration of *mawadda* (love) between relatives is maintained throughout as a basis for Conciliation between the estranged kin.

Q.49 builds on the Conciliation theme of its predecessor, providing what I perceive as a complete Conciliation paradigm. Hierarchically, it descends from Divine–Human Conciliation through obedience to God and then reverence for His Messenger, to Social Conciliation through respect for leadership, then mutual reconciliation and then mutual respect. At the same time, laterally, Conciliation penetrates from the exterior to the core of both society and individuals, an essential and explicit pre-requisite to the instilment of internal faith. As a collective, discipline and unity is ensured through respect for leadership and authority, fragmented groups are united through reconciliation processes, and everyday social relations are tightly regulated to address the root causes of conflicts and avert conflict at source. Actions, speech and even thoughts and feelings are regulated.

Linguistically, at Q.49, we find nine recurrences of the prohibitive *lā* (do not) with a notably legislative style employed to restrict both actual and potential causes of conflict. These include any form of oral challenge to the Prophet's Divinely gifted authority, or any injury through the spoken word or related conduct to the feelings or reputation of another, with or without their knowledge. The notion of brotherhood is utilised in this sura, as in past sura groups, to heal wounds and re-unite fragmented relationships, whilst the pervasive injunction towards *taqwa* (God-consciousness) provides a perpetual reminder of Divine reach and future accountability for the instigation of conflict.

Of all the sura groups reviewed, Group 5 provides the most coherent exposition and development of the Conciliation theme. At the core of this exposition is the integral coupling of Q.48 and Q.49, an impactful collocation, which provide a complementary focus on the practice and theory of Conciliation. The apparent weakness in pairing of these suras in Iṣlāḥī's schema can, in fact, be addressed by considering Q.48 and Q.49 a formal pair with the central theme of Conciliation. The central importance of Q.49 goes well beyond Iṣlāḥī's limited perception of the sura as an explanatory appendix to Q.48. Similarly, the Meccan content provides a preparatory theoretical platform for the practical Medinan implementation of Conciliation, with the internal notions of *ṣabr* and *sakīna* (tranquillity) demonstrating a notable correlation. The systematic development of a Conciliation theory in the Meccan content, the sustained engagement with a historical Conciliation in Q.48 and the complete Conciliation paradigm in Q.49 all indicate a high level of coherence in the progressive development of the Conciliation theme in this sura Group. Ironically, it is Iṣlāḥī's ostensibly coherence-based exegesis which masks this very coherence most, by a misplaced insistence on lasting enmity with the Quraysh in interpreting the Meccan content, fragmented interpretations of the recurrent references to 'victory' in Q.48, and downplaying the structural importance of Q.49 in his schema.

Group 5 provides clarity on the relationship between Conciliation and the related notions of forgiveness and justice. Q.42:37–43 provide an explicit and sustained emphasis on the notion of restraint and forgiveness. A delicate conditional phrase at Q.42:40 and Q.42:43 is used to incentivise and prefer forgiveness over the exertion of the right to just requital of transgression suffered, whilst Q.39:53 provides a Divine exemplar of expansive and emphatic forgiveness. This inviting call to Divine–Human Conciliation is realised by the apparently multitudinous entrants to the new faith after the manifest victory signified in Q.48, whilst the internal resolve of the Prophet's Companions is also rewarded with the assurance of Divine pleasure.

Justice, however, also has an important role to play in Conciliation and is emphasised three times in the central Conciliation verse at Q.49:9. Whilst this reference to justice has led Iṣlāḥī to argue that Q.49:9 justifies the imposition of a 'fair adjudication' by force, and Al-Rāzī to interpret Q.49:9–10 as providing three alternative processes with only the second being a 'fair adjudication', I have argued for a quite distinct interpretation. In my view, *aṣliḥū* (reconcile) means the mediation of a settlement by *consent* between the parties and is repeated three times in typically emphatic Qur'anic style. In this context, the insistence on a fair hearing and impartial treatment for all parties, even an apparent transgressor, is a principle established by the story of David and other Qur'anic verses. In addition, true resolution of disputes can only be attained by the parties' agreement to the terms of settlement, whose fairness is an entirely subjective matter to be assessed by each party based on their own perspectives and priorities.

6 Prophetic Disengagement and Social Justice

Overview: Groups 6 & 7 Suras – Q.50–Q.114

This chapter concludes the research with an analysis of the final two groups, Groups 6 (Q.50–Q.66) & 7 (Q.67–Q.114), of the Farāhī-Iṣlāḥī schema. These relatively shorter groups even together form only a little over four juz᾽ (parts) of the Qur᾽an and have therefore been addressed jointly to provide a Qur᾽anic segment broadly consistent in size with earlier chapters. In its subject matter, the at-once motivational and warning style of the Qur᾽an reaches a notable climax in this final component of the Qur᾽an with graphic eschatological portrayals of Heaven and Hell, highlighting the ultimate consequences of choosing either belief or disbelief. Pervading the theatrical splendour of this ethereal backdrop, however, is a persistent enjoinder towards social justice in this world, a theme also previously discussed in Chapter 4.

In the Farāhī-Iṣlāḥī schema, the theme of Group 6 is the Hereafter, whilst the theme of Group 7 is Warning the Disbelievers. Sura themes include the Final Cataclysm (Al-Qiyāma), God's Kingdom, the Promise of Victory, Enjoining the Prophet to Patience, Warnings to the Disbelievers and the Unity of God. The suras largely form binary pairs of which some are less formal, with the exception of a loose grouping of Q.54–Q.57 and an apparent isolation of Q.60. Group 6 is relatively balanced between Meccan and Medinan suras, consisting of 7 Meccan suras (Q.50 Sūrat Qāf, Q.51 Sūrat Al-Dhāriyāt, Q.52 Sūrat Al-Ṭūr, Q.53 Sūrat Al-Najm, Q.54 Sūrat Al-Qamar, Q.55 Sūrat Al-Raḥmān and Q.56 Sūrat Al-Wāqi῾a) and 10 Medinan suras (Q.57 Sūrat Al-Ḥadīd, Q.58 Sūrat Al-Mujādila, Q.59 Sūrat Al-Ḥashr, Q.60 Sūrat Al-Mumtaḥina, Q.61 Sūrat Al-Ṣaff, Q.62 Sūrat Al-Jumu῾a, Q.63 Sūrat Al-Munāfiqūn, Q.64 Sūrat Al-Taghābun, Q.65 Sūrat Al-Ṭalāq and Q.66 Sūrat Al-Taḥrīm).

Group 7 has a predominantly Meccan component of 43 suras (Q.67 Sūrat Al-Mulk, Q.68 Sūrat Al-Qalam, Q.69 Sūrat Al-Ḥāqqa, Q.70 Sūrat Al-Ma῾ārij, Q.71 Sūrat Nūḥ, Q.72 Sūrat Al-Jinn, Q.73 Sūrat Al-Muzzammil, Q.74 Sūrat Al-Muddaththir, Q.75 Sūrat Al-Qiyāma, Q.76 Sūrat Al-Dahr, Q.77 Sūrat Al-Mursalāt, Q.78 Sūrat Al-Naba᾽, Q.79 Sūrat Al-Nāzi῾āt, Q.80 Sūrat ῾Abasa, Q.81 Sūrat Al-Takwīr, Q.82 Sūrat Al-Infiṭār, Q.83 Sūrat Al-Muṭaffifīn, Q.84 Sūrat Al-Inshiqāq, Q.85 Sūrat Al-Burūj, Q.86 Sūrat Al-Ṭāriq, Q.87 Sūrat Al-A῾lā, Q.88 Sūrat Al-Ghāshiya, Q.89 Sūrat Al-Fajr, Q.90 Sūrat Al-Balad, Q.91 Sūrat Al-Shams, Q.92 Sūrat Al-Layl, Q.93 Sūrat Al-Ḍuḥā, Q.94 Sūrat Al-Inshirāḥ, Q.95 Sūrat Al-Tīn, Q.96 Sūrat Al-῾Alaq, Q.97 Sūrat Al-Qadr, Q.98 Sūrat Al-Bayyina, Q.99 Sūrat Al-Zilzāl, Q.100 Sūrat Al-῾Ādiyāt, Q.101 Sūrat Al-Qāri῾a, Q.102 Sūrat Al-Takāthur, Q.103 Sūrat

https://doi.org/10.1515/9783110747348-008

Al-ʿAṣr, Q.104 Sūrat Al-Humaza, Q.105 Sūrat Al-Fīl, Q.106 Sūrat Quraysh, Q.107 Sūrat Al-Māʿūn, Q.108 Sūrat Al-Kawthar and Q.109 Sūrat Al-Kāfirūn) and only 5 short Medinan suras (Q.110 Sūrat Al-Naṣr, Q.111 Sūrat Al-Masad, Q.112 Sūrat Al-Ikhlāṣ, Q.113 Sūrat Al-Falaq and finally Sūrat Al-Nās Q.114).

Divine–Human and Social Conciliation are closely inter-woven once more in this chapter, with Divine eschatological rewards offered as recompense for earthly assistance provided to those in need. The first section of the chapter, 'The Holistic Conciliatory Conduct of the *Muḥsinīn*', introduces this connection, once again formulated in the Qur'anic terminology of *iḥsān* (gracious conduct). The second section, 'Disengagement by the Prophet: A Means to Conflict or Conciliation?' explores the recurrent enjoinders to the Prophet to disengage from his adversaries, and engages critically with the Qur'anic exegesis to assess the conciliatory effect of these enjoinders.

The third and final section, 'The Qur'an Closes by Return: Human Kindness in the Notion of *Birr*', builds on the first section, highlighting the remarkable emphasis on social justice in the concluding segment of the Qur'an and its integral, foundational importance in the Qur'an in general and in the thematic study of Conciliation in particular. Although entirely unanticipated at the commencement of the research, this entire study of Conciliation in the Qur'an ends with the same notion of *birr* (dutiful conduct) first examined in Chapter 1, providing an illuminating insight into the structural coherence of the Qur'an.

Key Conciliation verses analysed in this chapter include Q.51:16–19 on the subject of social justice and Divine pleasure, Q.53:29 and Q.60:1, 4 and 7–8 regarding Prophetic disengagement, and finally the notion of *birr* (dutiful conduct) at Q.76:8–9 and Q.89:12, 17–20.

6.1 The Holistic Conciliatory Conduct of the *Muḥsinīn*

In earlier chapters, there has been extensive discussion of the notion of *iḥsān* (gracious conduct) and the *muḥsinīn* (those who engage in *iḥsān*). Q.3:134 in particular elaborated that the *muḥsinīn* provide benefit to others, exercise self-restraint by controlling anger, and are forgiving towards others, all of which is recompensed by a declaration of God's love for the *muḥsinīn*. In this closing segment of the Qur'an, we find a narrower and more sustained focus on the first of these three aspects of gracious conduct, namely spending on others, as illustrated in this section and in Section 6.3. This throws into particular focus the theme of social justice introduced in Chapter 4, highlighting its essential importance in the Qur'an's societal paradigm. Furthermore, unlike the sustained enjoinders to *iḥsān* and the aspirational presentation of exemplary models of *iḥsān* provided in Chapters 3 to 5,

Groups 6 & 7 demonstrate a notable focus on the eschatological reward of those who have engaged in *iḥsān* on earth. This creates a sense that the Qurʾanic narrative is drawing to its conclusion, with a final portrayal of eschatological consequences for choices made regarding conduct on earth.

Q.50 opens Group 6 with a forceful rendition of the certainty of resurrection and accountability on the Day of Judgement. Q.51 takes up the same theme before focusing on the people of Paradise. Q.51:16 effectively juxtaposes their ethereal and worldly state: ***ākhidhīna*** *mā ātāhum rabbuhum, innahum kānū qabla dhālika* ***muḥsinīn(a)*** (they will receive their Lord's gifts because of the good they did before, Abdel Haleem). The unmistakable acoustic resonance of the accusative grammatical forms *ākhidhīna and muḥsinīna* at the two ends of Q.51:16, one active participle indicating a state and the other forming a predicate of the verb *kāna* (to be), highlights the bestowal of Divine gifts in Paradise on those who have shown generosity to others on earth, the latter point being explicitly specified at Q.51:19, discussed below.

Like the *ʿIbād Al-Raḥmān* (the Servants of the Lord of Mercy) of Q.25:63 onwards, discussed in Chapter 4, Q.51:17–18 highlight that the *muḥsinīn* are to be found sacrificing their nightly repose for the pleasure of God, this time habitually imploring His forgiveness at the early hours of dawn. This earnest penitence for any shortcomings in the fulfilment of their duty to God, following the example of their forefather Adam at Q.7:23, demonstrates their regard for His Divine right over them to be worshipped and obeyed, as specified further on at Q.51:56. Their efforts to make peace with God and reconcile the Divine–human relationship are also balanced by their fulfilment of human rights as described at Q.51:19 below, together forming a holistic Conciliation model both embodied by the *ʿibād Al-Raḥmān* and espoused by the sage Luqmān at Q.31:17 and its surrounding verses, as discussed in Chapter 4. In his commentary of Q.51:19, Al-Rāzī reminds us he has frequently highlighted that God mentions compassion towards His creation after mentioning His own veneration. In Chapter 3, it was noted that in his commentary of Q.16:90 and elsewhere, Al-Rāzī explains *iḥsān* as: *al-taʿẓīm li amri ʾllāhi taʿālā wa ʻl-shafaqa ʿalā khalqi ʻllāh* (honouring the command of God the Exalted and compassion towards God's creation).

Regarding compassion towards creation, Q.51:19 lauds the meritorious conduct of the *muḥsinīn*, in providing from their wealth for those in need: *wa fī amwālihim* ***ḥaqqun*** *li (ʻl)-ssāʾili wa ʻl-maḥrūm* (giving a **rightful** share of their wealth to the beggar and the deprived, Abdel Haleem). Crucially this generosity is based on the *ḥaqq* (right) of those in need whether they solicit help or not and without considering such charity a favour, an attitude criticised at Q.2:262 and Q.2:264. This indicates the *entitlement* of such people to social assistance from the resources that God, explicitly referred to as the ultimate Provider at

Q.51:58, has bestowed upon mankind. In Chapter 3, I criticised Iṣlāḥī for misdirecting two references, at Q.12:90 and Q.16:128, to *iḥsān* in the context of social dealings, towards worship. At Q.51:19, the text is so explicit that Iṣlāḥī this time appreciates the social dimension of *iḥsān*, like Al-Rāzī above. Iṣlāḥī (vol.7, p.594) states*: ye muḥsinīn jis ṭaraḥ khudā kā ḥaq pehchān-ne wāle hein isī ṭaraḥ is ke bandon ke ḥuqūq bhī adā karne wāle hein* (these *muḥsinīn*, just as they recognize God's right, so they are also those who fulfill the rights of His servants).

Fair distribution of wealth and opportunity, or social justice, is an important Conciliation concept, as previously discussed in Chapter 4. Pharaoh is condemned as a perpetrator of *fasād* (disorder) at Q.28:4 for implementing social *injustice*, elevating himself and his people over the downtrodden and enslaved Banī Isrā'īl. In Chapter 5 also, the message that all humans were created equal and classified into tribes only to know one another was encapsulated by the memorable verse Q.49:13, to address the underlying issue of conflicts arising from the arrogance of some towards others. The Qur'an thus recognises that human equality and fair distribution of resources are a means to societal order and Social Conciliation. By isolating and thus highlighting social assistance as a noteworthy worldly behaviour of those who are rewarded with the gifts of Paradise, and juxtaposing it with the act of seeking Divine forgiveness, the Qur'an also emphasises that human rights and Divine rights are both fundamental tenets of its teachings.

The attainment of Divine–Human Conciliation, indicated here by entry to Paradise, is achieved by asking God's ***forgiveness*** for any shortcomings in His worship and obedience, and by ***fulfilling the rights*** of His people. Several verses from Groups 6 & 7 make it clear that entry to Paradise indicates the attainment of Divine–Human Conciliation. Q.58:22 declares that those who believe in God and the Day of Judgement do not love those who oppose Him and His Messenger. Immediately after promising the believers entry to Paradise, Q.58:22 continues: *raḍiya 'llāhu ʿanhum wa raḍū ʿanhu* (God is well pleased with them and they with Him, Abdel Haleem). In a later sura, Q.89:27–30 invite the 'contented soul' to return to its Lord *rāḍiyatan marḍiyya* (well pleased and well pleasing, Abdel Haleem), continuing by inviting it to enter God's Paradise, included in His elect servants: *ʿibādī* (My servants, Q.89:29).

Importantly, Paradise also represents the abode of Divine recompense for human *iḥsān*, a point made in Chapter 3 in the discussion of Q.10:26. In Group 6, Q.53:31 mentions God's dominion over the heavens and the earth and His ultimate design of just requital for those who engage in evil actions and gracious reward for those who have demonstrated excellent conduct on earth: . . . *wa yajziya 'lladhīna aḥsanū bi 'l-ḥusnā* (. . . and reward, with what is best, those who do good; Abdel

Haleem). Al-Rāzī, who seemingly takes *bi 'l-ḥusnā* as a reference to (God's reward of) *the best* actions of those who do *iḥsān*, explains this highest form of earthly good conduct as indicating *al-karam wa 'l-ṣafḥ* (benevolence and forgiveness), apparently in light of the enjoinder to the Prophet at Q.53:29 to turn away from those who deny the Day of Judgement, a point discussed further in Section 6.2.

Further on in Group 6, Q.55:60 in the celebrated *Sūrat Al-Raḥmān* follows a lengthy and vivid description of the delights of Paradise by asking rhetorically: *hal jazā'u 'l- iḥsāni illa 'l-iḥsān?* (shall the reward of good be anything but good? Abdel Haleem). Al-Rāzī remarks that this is one of three verses in the Qur'an about which it is said that there are a 'hundred narrations', which demonstrates how renowned this verse is amongst commentators of the Qur'an. Iṣlāḥī (vol.8, p.148) highlights that the word *iḥsān* can mean both a good action and a good reward and features eloquently with both meanings in this verse. To my mind, this usage of paronomasia provides a powerful rhetorical effect, indicating that gracious conduct by humans towards others will be directly recompensed by God's Divine grace towards them in Paradise. Social assistance will be rewarded by Divine gifts, and forgiving others will be rewarded by Divine forgiveness.

As indicated in the discussion of Q.53:31 above, Section 6.2 now turns from a general discussion of *iḥsān* to the Prophet's specific situation and the numerous Qur'anic enjoinders in Groups 6 & 7 towards patience and disengagement, a subject previously discussed in Chapter 2 on the subject of faith propagation and the Prophetic exemplar.

6.2 Disengagement by the Prophet: A Means to Conflict or Conciliation?

The suras of Groups 6 & 7 display a notable emphasis on enjoining the Prophet to patience and disengagement in the face of rejection and ridicule endured in the course of his faith propagation, to a level which prompted Saleh (2010, p.34) to comment, based on the paucity of the Prophet's followers after a decade of preaching, 'there is no escaping the conclusion that Muḥammad's mission in Mecca was a failure.' The disbelievers' incredulous reaction to the ultimate resurrection of bodies after their decomposition in the earth is remarked upon at Q.50:2–3, whilst their slanderous accusations that he is a fortune-teller, deranged or a poet, are repudiated by the Qur'an at Q.52:29–30.

In response, the Prophet is instructed at Q.50:39: *fa 'ṣbir 'alā mā yaqūlūna wa sabbiḥ bi ḥamdi rabbika* (so [Prophet], bear everything they say with patience; celebrate the praise of your Lord, Abdel Haleem). Q.52:48 likewise states:

wa 'ṣbir li ḥukmi rabbika fa innaka bi a'yuninā wa sabbiḥ bi ḥamdi rabbika ḥīna taqūm (Wait patiently for your Lord's judgement: you are under Our watchful eye. Celebrate the praise of your Lord when you rise, Abdel Haleem). Both the verses Q.50:39 and Q.52:48 encourage the Prophet to tolerate the hurtful speech of his adversaries and to occupy his own thoughts and speech in response only with the praise of God, on whom he is to rely for his safety from their harm. This absorption and non-reciprocation of harm invokes the conciliatory model conduct of the *'Ibād Al-Raḥmān* (the Servants of the Lord of Mercy) of Q.25:63, and Q.52:49 goes on to enjoin the Prophet to night worship, another hallmark of their exemplary conduct.

The Prophet is also taught the limitation of his duty of faith propagation: he is merely to deliver his message but leave the choice of acceptance to the recipient, without any form of insistence. Q.50:45 reminds the Prophet: *wa mā anta 'alayhim bi* ***jabbār****, fa dhakkir. . .* (you [Prophet] are not there to force them, so remind. . .), Abdel Haleem). A later sura also reiterates the point at Q.88:21–22: *fa dhakkir, innamā anta mudhakkir; lasta 'alayhim bi* ***muṣayṭir*** (so [Prophet] warn them: your only task is to give warning, you are not there to control them, Abdel Haleem). These verses are explicit and clear in denoting that the Prophet's religious mission was limited to a conciliatory approach, and precluded any form of compulsion in faith conversion which would have resulted in confrontation, a point on which I have taken issue with Iṣlāḥī in Chapter 2 and subsequently. Although both of these suras are Meccan, I have also argued in Chapter 2, against Cragg (2001, pp.90, 95), that Conciliation remained paramount even in the Medinan period and that conciliatory Meccan verses in Group 2 suras were emphatically worded and not abrogated by later Medinan verses granting permission to fight. Both the terms *jabbār* (compeller) and *muṣayṭir* (controller) in the above verses are active participles, indicating the Prophet's ongoing function, rather than his transient actions at a specific instance in time. I have also noted previously that the seminal verse establishing the principle of non-compulsion in faith at Q.2:256 is Medinan. This sacrosanct principle of free choice is a cornerstone of the Divine scheme, providing an essential prelude to eschatological reward and punishment, as I discussed in detail in Chapter 4.

In his commentary of Q.88:22, Al-Rāzī fleetingly remarks: *qālū: thumma nasakhathā āyat al-qitāl, hādhā qawlu jamī' al-mufassirīn* (they said: [the verse] was subsequently abrogated by the 'Sword Verse' (Q.9:5), this is the position of all commentators). Viewed in isolation, this might be taken to indicate Al-Rāzī's position on the verse. However, I have discussed in Chapter 2, Al-Rāzī's frustration with those who unnecessarily argue for abrogation, and the fact that Al-Rāzī's encyclopaedic approach compels him to relay the narrations of commentators he does not necessarily agree with. In Groups 6 & 7, his commentary on other related verses provides insight into his own perspective.

Q.53:29 enjoins the Prophet to disengage from those who reject his message: *fa aʿriḍ ʿan man tawallā ʿan dhikrinā* (so [Prophet] ignore those who turn away from Our revelation, Abdel Haleem). Al-Rāzī explains: *ay utruk mujādalatahum* (meaning leave their arguing), clearly indicating an avoidance of disputation and conflict. He goes on to say that most commentators say that everything in the Qur'an saying *fa aʿriḍ* (ignore) is abrogated by the 'Sword Verse', to which he responds: *wa huwa bāṭil* (and this is invalid), arguing that the two are compatible. He elucidates that the Prophet was commanded at Q.16:125 to call people with good judgement and rational discourse, and then to debate courteously in response to their objections, as discussed in Chapter 3. If they remain heedless, then the Prophet is now told to disengage from further pointless debate or disputation, as indicated by the reference to 'those who turn away from Our revelation' in Q.53:29. Q.54:6 similarly directs: *fa tawalla ʿanhum* (so [Prophet] turn away from them, Abdel Haleem). Al-Rāzī again rejects the commentators' claim that this command is abrogated, again interpreting it as a command to terminate oral disputation.

Despite his aversion to the use of abrogation as a technical point, Al-Rāzī does appear to assert a relatively robust approach to dealing with the polytheists, similar to that which I pointed out in Chapter 2. He declares at Q.53:29 that the Prophet was *ṭabīb al-qulūb* (a physician of hearts). As such, Al-Rāzī says he offered progressively stronger cures, first the remembrance of God as a means of attaining spiritual peace, second demonstrative proofs and finally warnings and threats. When these failed to provide any benefit, he disengaged from cure and cut off the corrupt so that it might not corrupt the sound. *Aʿriḍ* (ignore) in this sense commands a metaphoric amputation, a severance of dialogue and any hope of consensus.

This apparently divisive approach based on the above Meccan suras may also be considered supported by some verses in the Medinan suras. Q.60:1 opens the sura by commanding the believers not to befriend or (secretly) offer their *mawadda* (friendship, Abdel Haleem) to those who are God's enemies and enemies of the believers, having rejected the message of Truth and driven out the Prophet and his followers solely on the basis of their belief. Q.60:4 continues in the same vein, declaring that an excellent example for the believers is to be found in Abraham and his followers who renounced their people, declaring their lasting *ʿadāwatu wa 'l-baghḍāʾu* (enmity and hatred, Abdel Haleem) until such time as their people believed in One God, with the exception of Abraham's prayer for his father. Iṣlāḥī (vol.8, pp.319, 324) states that this sura commands *qaṭʿe taʿalluq* (cutting ties) of all kinds with the polytheists in general, particularly ties of kin and friendship or appeasement of the Meccan leadership, which some emigrants had maintained with the Meccans in the hope of their future conversion to Islam. However, Iṣlāḥī's own subsequent analysis of Q.60:8 below demonstrates some internal inconsistency with the scope of his comments under Q.60:1, rather undermining his coherence-based approach.

In my view, as I have argued in Chapter 2, Iṣlāḥī's assessment of the hostilities advocated by the Qur'an is exaggerated and thus he frequently encounters verses which contradict his stance and undermine the consistency of his position. A striking example is Q.109:6, where Iṣlāḥī (vol.9, p.611) takes a verse which merely states *lakum dīnukum wa liya dīn* (for you is your religion, and for me is mine), and which he acknowledges is understood by most as an indication of *rawādārī* (non-compulsion or tolerance), as indicating *abadī mufāraqat aur iʿlān-e-jang* (perpetual separation and proclamation of war) with the disbelievers on the model of Abraham at Q.60.4. The terminology of 'war' in particular is premature in a Meccan sura and the reference to perpetual separation is contradicted by Q.60:7 below which promises future reconciliation. At the same time, Iṣlāḥī (vol.9, p.28) cannot ignore verses such as Q.73:10 *wa 'ṣbir ʿalā mā yaqūlūna wa 'hjurhum hajran jamīlā* (bear patiently that which they say and take leave of them in a beautiful manner, Nasr) which he acknowledges as indicating compassion rather than anger and abuse, in the manner of a concerned parent towards an unruly child, and a dignified conduct which inclines the other towards self-reflection. Surprisingly, he continues by again suggesting that once a prophet departs and proclaims his riddance of his people it is a prelude to their death. In fact, the Prophet was ultimately reconciled with the Meccans at the Conquest of Mecca in 8 A.H., with vast numbers apparently entering Islam.

Despite the apparently hostile relations indicated in Q.60:1 and Q.60:4 above, as interpreted by Iṣlāḥī in particular, these verses do not, in my view, establish a general principle of hostile relations, particularly on the basis of difference of faith. Al-Rāzī mentions an apparently limiting *sabab al-nuzūl* (circumstances of revelation) of Q.60:1 which indicates that the provision only restricts the offering of secret assistance to the enemy in war. Al-Rāzī narrates that a particular individual Ḥāṭib bin Abī Baltaʿa had secretly attempted to divulge to the Meccans the Prophet's intention to march on Mecca, professing his desire to thereby preserve his financial interests and familial connections in Mecca. He was intercepted by the Companions of the Prophet, and ʿUmar's impulsive desire for retribution was quenched by the Prophet. Although Iṣlāḥī (vol.8, p.326) takes pains to point out that this *sabab al-nuzūl* should not be taken as limiting the general application of the verse which he applies to a wider context, the explicit ensuing verses of the same sura are so definitive in establishing a general principle of conciliatory conduct that both Al Rāzī and Iṣlāḥī appreciate their import, as discussed below.

Q.60:7 explicitly encourages maintaining the hope of future reconciliation even with the currently hostile Meccans, declaring: *ʿasa ʻllāhu an yyajʿala baynakum wa bayna ʻlladhīna ʿādaytum minhum mawadda* (God may still bring about affection between you and your present enemies, Abdel Haleem). As discussed in Chapter 5 at Q.41:34, this ultimate reconciliation was to be the fruit of perseverance in *iḥsān* over a prolonged period, turning enmity into close friendship. Al-Rāzī confirms that future reconciliation with present enemies in Q.60:7 refers to the Meccans: *ay min kuffari Makka* (meaning with the disbelievers of Mecca). He then cites a narration that the Prophet married Umm Ḥabība, daughter of the Meccan chieftain Abū Sufyān, after her conversion to Islam and the demise of her husband, *fa lānat ʿinda dhālik ʿarīkat Abī Sufyān, wa ʻstarkhat shakīmatuhu fi ʻl-ʿadāwa* (as a result of which, Abū Sufyān's disposition softened, and his staunch enmity relaxed).

Al-Rāzī also takes *ʿasā* in Q.60:7 as a *waʿd* (promise) from God, rather than a possibility as Abdel Haleem indicates above, referring to the large numbers embracing Islam after the Conquest of Mecca, including Abū Sufyān and the chief Meccan negotiator at Ḥudaybiya, Suhayl bin ʿAmr. Referring to the description of God in Q.60:7 as all powerful, forgiving and merciful, Al-Rāzī declares that God is *qādirun ʿalā taqlīb al-qulūb* (capable of transforming hearts), and forgiving and merciful towards those who repent and submit and return to His presence. The Divine transformation of hearts towards Conciliation has also been remarked on in Chapter 2 at Q.8:63. The juxtaposition of this notion alongside God's own merciful embrace here creates a holistic paradigm of Social and Divine–Human Conciliation, which appears to signify the ultimate outcome of the Prophet's multifarious engagement with the Meccans over time.

Next, Q.60:8 expressly limits the scope of Q.60:1, just as the verses regarding military conflict were habitually limited in Chapter 2, and in fact goes on to positively prescribe kindness and justice towards those who have not engaged in direct religious persecution: 'and He does not forbid you to deal kindly and justly with anyone **who has not fought you for your faith or driven you out of your homes**: God loves the just (Abdel Haleem).' Q.5:8 in Chapter 1 similarly establishes a general principle of justice even against enemies. Notably, Q.60:8 and Q.5:8 are Medinan, yet both verses emphasise fair treatment and conciliatory conduct despite differences of faith and even animosity. Q.60:9 goes on to reiterate the qualification indicated in bold once again, this time beginning with the limiting *innamā yanhākum* (He only forbids you. . .) for further emphasis of the limited scope of the restriction on friendship.

Iṣlāḥī (vol.8, p.332) acknowledges that there is no restriction on *iḥsān aur inṣāf* (gracious conduct and justice) with those who have not engaged in the aforementioned *ziyādatī* (oppressive conduct). He goes on (vol.8, p.334) to confirm that the prohibition (in Q.60:1) is in fact not on justice and gracious conduct with disbelievers but only on *mawālāt* (allying), and even then only with those disbelievers who have fought the believers or driven them out as a form of *religious persecution*. This is consistent with the scope of the restricted permission to fight discussed in Chapters 2 and 5. The insistence on repeatedly qualifying the restriction on friendship and the reminder of good conduct and justice as a transcendent principle highlights the Qur'anic principle of Differentiation, discussed in Chapter 2. This principle avoids tarnishing all members of a group due to the actions of a few, or entirely severing a relationship on the basis of one aspect of difference, thus limiting the scope of potential conflict.

Al-Rāzī mentions several narrations regarding Q.60:8. The majority of commentators, including Ibn ʿAbbās, the two Muqātils and Kalbī, considered this verse as referring to those who had made a pact with the Prophet that they would not fight or persecute him, such as the Khuzāʿa. The Prophet *amara... bi 'l-birr wa 'l-wafā' ilā muddat ajalihim* (ordered dutiful conduct and honouring the duration of their term [of agreement]). Abdullāh bin Zubayr narrated that it referred to Asmā' bint Abī Bakr who refused to welcome her polytheist mother's visit and was commanded by the Prophet to welcome her, honour her and to treat her with *iḥsān*, supporting my argument in Chapter 3, against Levy (1969, pp.195, 196), that good conduct towards parents is incumbent on their offspring irrespective of faith based on Q.31:15.

Ibn ʿAbbās considers the command *tuqsiṭū* ([you] treat justly) in Q.60:8 a reference to maintaining ties of kinship. All of these examples highlight again the importance of maintaining peace treaties as discussed in Chapter 2, honouring parents, and justice, including maintaining ties of kinship. Yet the crucial point here is that all of these social teachings are upheld in the context of the Prophet and his followers' relations with the disbelievers and polytheists, showing they are fundamental principles of general human conduct espoused by the Qur'an, maintaining a standard of conciliatory conduct irrespective of differences of faith and without the pre-requisite of conversion to Islam. Al-Rāzī highlights that the *ahl al-ta'wīl* (interpeters of the Qur'an) said: *hādhihi 'l-āya tadullu ʿalā* ***jawāz al-birr*** *bayna 'l-mushrikīn wa 'l-muslimīn* (this verse evidences **the permissibility of dutiful conduct** between polytheists and Muslims).

Given the response of *ṣabr* (patience) initially enjoined above and the curbing of the Prophet's zeal in faith propagation by the reminder of non-compulsion, I would argue that the Qur'an advocates a conciliatory response to rejection by the Prophet's adversaries. The enjoinder *aʿriḍ* (ignore) signifies disengagement, meaning a mandate to cease remonstrating against a non-receptive audience and the cessation of argument to avoid confrontational dispute and escalation, a point supported by Al-Rāzī above. Despite a specific restriction on divulging secret information in the context of war, however, there does not appear to be any encouragement of the general cutting off of ties of kinship as initially suggested by Iṣlāḥī at Q.60:1. Instead, it is clear that the Qur'an, both explicitly and in the view of commentators, encourages the maintenance of peaceful relations in the absence of their open hostility, and the fulfilment of basic human rights, particularly the rights of kinship, even with the disbelievers.

As I argued in Chapter 3, this kinship was the core of the Prophet's lasting conciliatory appeal to the Meccans of *mawaddatan fi 'l-qurbā* (love amongst kin). It is unsurprising therefore that explicit injunctions towards *birr* (dutiful conduct) or basic human kindness, and justice or fulfilment of human rights are emphatically and repeatedly preserved at Q.60:8–9, even in the context of a restriction on secret alliance in a war context. Q.60:7 is explicit in describing the ultimate aim, in Al-Rāzī's view a promise rather than a possibility, of the Divine instilment of *mawadda* (love) in the hearts of present enemies, signifying ultimate reconciliation.

In Chapter 3, the specific example of Abū Bakr's orphan nephew Misṭaḥ was presented. Even in the context of a highly emotive dispute, the Qur'an enjoined the maintenance of ties of kinship and social assistance to those in need. The inclusion of the family of the Prophet's closest Companion and direct successor Abū Bakr in this example and in Q.60:8 above provides a highly exemplary illustration for the Prophet's followers of basic conciliatory conduct to be maintained even during disputes or where there are differences of faith. The significance of maintaining ties of kinship in conciliation has been discussed above. The fundamental importance of *birr* (dutiful conduct) and the provision of social assistance are now explored further in the ensuing section.

6.3 The Qur'an Closes by Return: Human Kindness in the Notion of *Birr*

In Chapter 1, the notion of *birr* (dutiful conduct) was discussed extensively by reference to Q.2:177. In this verse, *birr* is defined as a quality of those who: 'believe in God and the Last Day, in the angels, the Scripture, and the prophets; who give away some of their wealth, however much they cherish it, to their relatives, to orphans, the needy, travellers and beggars, and to liberate those in bondage; those who keep up the prayer and pay the prescribed alms; who keep pledges whenever they make them; who are steadfast in misfortune, adversity, and times of danger (Abdel Haleem).' It can be seen from this list of encouraged conduct that a great deal of importance is attached to social assistance, the fulfilment of the needs of others and to the preference of the needs of others over one's own. Social justice has been discussed as an important Qur'anic theme in Chapter 4. In the concluding section of the Qur'an, which is mostly Meccan, this theme manifests a consistent recurrence and insistence which makes clear that social justice is a central tenet of the Qur'anic societal vision and the new teachings advocated before the Meccan audience.

Q.4:114, mentioned in Chapters 1 and 2, previously criticised secret counsels other than those enjoining charity, good conduct or reconciliation between people. In Group 6, Q.58:9 makes a similar point prohibiting secret discussions regarding *ithm* (sin), *ʿudwān* (hostility) and *maʿṣiyati (ʻl)-rrasūl* (opposing the Prophet), and enjoining such discussions regarding *birr* (dutiful conduct) and *taqwā* (God-consciousness). A similar oppositional construct of these same notions is found at Q.5:2, referred to in Chapter 1. Al-Rāzī clarifies that *birr* is the opposite of *ʿudwān*. This linguistic insight indicates that the various references in Chapters 1 and 2 and in this chapter promoting *birr* are, in fact, promoting good relations through the fulfilment of rights and also opposing hostility and therefore conflict. *Birr* is therefore, as I have argued, an important conciliatory notion which is recurrently promoted in the Qur'an.

An important example of *birr*, which also highlights the notion of social assistance, features at Q.76:8–9. Following the format discussed in Section 6.1 of eschatological scenes embedded with a rendition of meritorious earthly conduct, Q.76:5–22 provides a remarkable and evocative lengthy description of the rewards of Paradise. Into this inspirational description is embedded a reference to the *ʿibādu ʻllāh* (servants of God, Q.76:6), the term *ʿibād* indicating obedience to God, as it does in the phrase *ʿibād Al-Raḥmān* (Q.25:63) and *ʿibādī* (Q.89:29) above. After lauding their fulfilment of vows and fear of the Day of Judgement at Q.76:7, Q.76:8 continues: *wa yuṭʿimūna (ʻl)-ṭṭaʿāma ʿalā ḥubbihī miskīnan wa yatiman wa asīrā* (they give food to the poor, the orphan, and the captive, though they love it themselves, Abdel Haleem). Q.76:9 adds that this preference of those in need over their own personal needs is purely out of a desire to please God and not for any earthly reward or thanks from the beneficiaries of their actions. The phrase *ʿalā ḥubbihī* (despite their love of it) is taken by Al-Rāzī as a reference to love of what is given, a reference to personal need, in light of Q.2:177 and Q.3:92 and Q.59:9, although he also cites Al-Fuḍayl bin ʿIyāḍ as considering it a reference to love for God. I concur with Al-Rāzī's position based on other examples criticising worthless gifts and the love of wealth, at Q.2:267, Q.89:20 and Q.100:8. The conduct of providing social assistance in Q.76:8 is clearly an example of *birr*, both based on the above explicit definition of *birr* at Q.2:177, and based on Al-Rāzī's citation of Q.2:177 and Q.3:92 (which both explain *birr*) in his commentary of Q.76:8.

Al-Rāzī ascribes the fulfilment of vows at Q.76:7 to the 'honouring of God's command', and the feeding of people at Q.76:8 to 'compassion towards God's creation', another reference to the now familiar explanation of *iḥsān*, or what Al-Rāzī describes here as the distillation of all forms of obedience. He cites a number of sources who attribute the revelation of the verse particularly to the conduct of the Companion and son-in-law of the Prophet, ʿAlī. Others attributed a more general meaning to the verse and considered feeding an example of *kināya* (metonymy, see Chowdhury (2015, p.130)), alluding to *iḥsān* of any kind, of which feeding is merely a fundamental example. As well as the highlighting of social assistance as a means to eschatological redemption, and the close pairing of Social and Divine–Human Conciliation once again in this reference, a crucial point is the reference to feeding captives. Al-Rāzī leads his commentary on the term *asīrā* (captive) by citing Ibn ʿAbbās, Al-Ḥassan and Qatāda who consider this a reference to polytheists who are captured. In my view, this is yet another indication that basic human rights are maintained in the Qurʾan regardless of difference of faith, even in a situation of actual military conflict. Far from indicating a complete cutting off of ties and a proclamation of war against the Meccans, this verse places polytheist captives under the explicit care and protection of their Muslim adversaries. Q.9:6 in Chapter 2 also provides for the offering of sanctuary and Q.47:4 in Chapter 5 provides for the release of captives.

Moving on to Q.89:12, a reference to the punishment of past nations, refers to their conduct as *fasād* (disorder). This notion has been discussed extensively in Chapter 2, together with its Qurʾanic opposite *iṣlāḥ* (order), and its linguistic opposite *ṣalāḥ* (a thriving state of affairs). At Q.89:12, Al-Rāzī elucidates that *ṣalāḥ* encompasses all forms of *birr*, whilst *fasād* incorporates all forms of *ithm* (sin), thus directly linking the conciliatory notion of *iṣlāḥ* from Chapter 2 with the conciliatory notion of *birr* from Chapters 1 and 6. It would seem from Al-Rāzī's comment here that *birr* signifies various types of dutiful conduct in particular relationships, whilst *ṣalāḥ* is a global state of affairs achieved when such *birr* is universally maintained. Al-Rāzī continues: *fa man ʿamila bi ghayri amri 'llāh wa ḥakama fī ʿibādihī bi 'l-dhulm fa huwa mufsid* (thus whoever acts against God's command and governs His servants oppressively is one who creates disorder). This expression, which appears to reverse Al-Rāzī's familiar definition of *iḥsān* as 'honouring God's command and showing compassion to God's creation', discernibly links the conciliatory notions of *iḥsān* and *iṣlāḥ* through the explanation of *fasād*.

Apparently supporting Al-Rāzī's linkage of *birr* and *ṣalāḥ* above, the reference to the *fasād* (disorder) of past nations at Q.89:12 is closely followed up by a specific berating at Q.89:17–20 of those who fail to honour the orphan and encourage the feeding of the needy, and who devour inheritance (possibly of orphans) and excessively love wealth. The love of wealth here contrasts powerfully with the dutiful conduct of those who assist others *ʿalā ḥubbihī* (despite their love of it), overcoming their own desire for its use. Although not anticipated when identifying the notions of *birr, iḥsān* and *iṣlāḥ* as conciliatory notions in the various chapters of this work, Al-Rāzī's commentary on Q.89:12 above provides substantive and cohesive linkage between these three fundamental notions corroborating the findings of this research.

The following sura again forcefully reiterates the eschatological reward and importance of social assistance. Q.90:6–7 chastise those who squander wealth, without regard to future accountability. After this, Q.90:8–10 highlight the Divine gift of man's senses of sight and speech and the choice offered to him between two paths. Nasr and Abdel Haleem suggest these are good and evil but, in context, perhaps it means more specifically squandering wealth or providing social assistance. Q.90:11 berates man for not attempting the 'steep path', which is: 'to free a slave, to feed at a time of hunger an orphaned relative or a poor person in distress, and to be one of those who believe and urge one another to steadfastness and compassion' (Abdel Haleem, Q.90:13–17). Q.90:12 describes people who choose this path as People of the Right, indicating those whose accounting on the Day of Judgement will be successful and who will enter Paradise. At Q.90:13, Al-Rāzī supports the position of Abū Ḥanīfa that freeing a slave is the best form of charity, on the basis of its foregrounding in the conduct listed in this verse.[17]

Iṣlāḥī (vol.9, pp.375–77) makes a number of important points in his commentary on the above verses from Q.90. He considers the two choices given to man are between gratitude and ingratitude, which supports my interpretation of expenditure in accordance with God's will or squandering of wealth without fear of accountability. He considers the path of gratitude to be that which man intuitively knows to be right but has to overcome his desires to embark upon. This certainly puts into context the references to spending wealth on others despite personal love of that wealth. He summarises the example conduct which lies on the *ʿaqaba* (steep path) as *hamdardī-e-khalq aur bandagī-e-rabb* (compassion towards creation and service of God), echoing Al-Rāzī's recurrent explanation of *iḥsān* and conclusively bringing the two exegetes, despite their different methodologies, focus, language and era, into alignment in emphasising these two

---

17 Iṣlāḥī (vol.9, p.376) explains at length that from the outset of its invitation, the Qurʾan advocated social assistance in general and the gradual elimination of slavery in particular within its system, rather refuting Levy's suggestion that slavery was accepted in Islam (1969, p.73). For further discussion on the subject, see Brown (2019).

fundamental Qur'anic notions which together form a unified call to both Social and Divine–Human Conciliation. Although Iṣlāḥī considers the subsequent references to mutual enjoining of *ṣabr* (patience) and *marḥama* (compassion) at Q.90:17 refer to determination and compassion, respectively, whilst Al-Rāzī considers they refer again to 'honouring God's command' and 'compassion towards creation', respectively, it is not unreasonable to view the two positions as fully aligned on the basis that the determination to pursue the difficult path of assisting others in preference to one's own needs arises from a desire to please God and to honour His command.

The final sura examined in this research is Q.107, which by its very title Al-Mā'ūn (Common Kindnesses, Abdel Haleem) highlights the theme of social assistance, bringing it to the fore of the Qur'anic narrative. The sura once again links the two central tenets of prayer and social assistance, one 'honouring the command of God' and the other showing 'compassion towards creation', as Al-Rāzī highlights at Q.107:4. Structurally, the sura opens by referring to those who deny the Day of Judgement and hence accountability before moving on to condemn their repelling of orphans and failure to encourage others to feed the poor. After this it condemns their outward show but internal heedlessness in prayer, and finally their failure to provide everyday assistance (such as to neighbours, whose rights were also mentioned in Q.4:36).

The first three verses Q.107:1–3 begin the sura by highlighting an essential nexus between accountability before God and fulfilment of the provision of social assistance: *ara'ayta 'lladhī yukadhdhibu bi ('l)-ddīn, **fa** dhālika 'lladhī yadu''u 'l-yatīm wa lā yaḥuḍḍu 'alā ṭa'āmi 'l-miskīn* ([Prophet], have you considered the person who denies the Judgement? It is he who pushes aside the orphan and does not urge others to feed the needy, Abdel Haleem). Al-Rāzī highlights that the particle *fa* is *sababiyya*, indicating that the disbeliever's denial (of reckoning in the Hereafter) is the *sabab* (cause) of their failure to provide social assistance. The clear implication is that providing social assistance is a fundamental duty and a central tenet of the religion which is incumbent on all those who recognise their accountability in respect of this duty on the Day of Judgement.

Iṣlāḥī (vol.9, pp.579–85) provides additional context and credible insights into the background of this sura. Whereas Al-Rāzī takes the sura to describe the conduct of hypocrites at Q.107:4, Iṣlāḥī attributes the entire sura to the Meccans as failed custodians of the Ka'ba. He argues that the Ka'ba was established for two fundamental purposes: the worship of One God and the provision of social assistance to the needy. The Quraysh, he argues, had failed to live up to these founding principles, their prayer at the Ka'ba amounting to mere pretence and the conduct of people such as Abū Lahab, the Treasurer of the Ka'ba, demonstrating a hard-heartedness towards the plight of those in need of assistance. Referring in his introduction of the sura to the reminder of God's generous provision for the Quraysh in the previous sura Q.106, Iṣlāḥī goes on to argue that the true spirit of prayer is *shukr* (gratitude), which demands generosity towards others from what God has provided.

Iṣlāḥī concludes (vol.9, p.585): *falsafa-e-dīn ke iʿtibār se jazba-e-shukr kī teḥrīk se sab se pehle namāz wujūd mein ātī hai aur phir namāz infāq ke liye muḥarrik bantī hai aur phir inhī do chīzon par sharīʿat ka pūra niẓām qa'im hai* (from the perspective of the philosophy of religion, the stirring of the sentiment of gratitude first of all brings the prayer into being, and then the prayer initiates [social] expenditure, and then on these two things, the entire system of Islamic Law (the *Sharīʿa*) is established). This quotation renders Iṣlāḥī's perspective aligned with Al-Rāzī's position at Q.76:8: *iʿlam anna majāmiʿ al-ṭāʿāt maḥṣūra fī amrayn:* ***al-taʿẓīm li amri 'llāhi taʿālā. . . wa 'l-shafaqa ʿalā khalqi 'llāh*** (know that all forms of obedience converge within two essentials: honouring the command of God the Exalted and compassion towards God's creation). It is my argument that these two central tenets of the faith build relations with God and relations with people, respectively, providing the basis for Divine–Human and Social Conciliation in Qur'anic discourse. As such, Conciliation is of paramount importance in the Qur'an.

Summary Table: Groups 6 & 7 Conciliation Themes Map by Sura and Verse

	Conciliatory conduct of the *muḥsinīn*	Disengagement by the Prophet	The notion of *birr* and social justice
Q.50		39 patience 45 non-compulsion	
Q.51	16–19 seeking Divine forgiveness and providing social assistance		
Q.52		48 patience	
Q.53	31 Divine reciprocation of human *iḥsān*	29 disengagement	
Q.54		6 disengagement	

(continued)

	Conciliatory conduct of the *muḥsinīn*	Disengagement by the Prophet	The notion of *birr* and social justice
Q.55	60 Divine reciprocation of human *iḥsān*		
Q.58			9 counselling towards *birr* not enmity
Q.60		1 restriction on friendship with enemies 7 future reconciliation: *mawadda* (love) 8–9 limitation of restriction on friendship; maintaining ties of kinship	8 maintaining *birr* between Muslims and disbelievers
Q.73		10 disengagement without confrontation	
Q.76			8 feeding the poor, orphans and captives
Q.88		22 non-compulsion	
Q.89			12 ('*ṣalāḥ* encompasses all forms of *birr*') 17–20 criticism of those who fail to provide social assistance and love wealth excessively
Q.90			13–17 social assistance and compassion
Q.107			1–3 fundamental belief in the Hereafter intrinsically linked to social assistance

Conclusion

The content and style of Groups 6 & 7 suras indicate a sense of conclusion, only summatively referencing concepts elaborated more effusively previously in the Qur'an, but with a motivational and recurrent emphasis. In keeping with this general concision, Conciliation verses are quantitatively relatively less recurrent and fragmented compared to the frequency and concentration of Conciliation material examined in many other sura groups, which accounts for the relative brevity of this concluding chapter. As such, it may be considered an overstatement to consider Conciliation *pervasive* in Groups 6 & 7. Nonetheless, the isolation and embedding of essential Divine–human and social conciliatory conduct into the motivational accounts of Paradise, which are integral to the central discourse, lend the distilled Conciliation content an unmistakable focus and prominence. Whilst the majority of content in these two groups is Meccan, the Medinan content of Q.57–66 also provides brief but crucial references to the fundamental conciliatory notion of *birr* (dutiful conduct).

In this chapter, Conciliation features in the early description at Q.51 of the *muḥsinīn* (those who are gracious), who seek Divine forgiveness for their shortcomings in fulfilling the rights of God and who provide social assistance in recognition and fulfilment of the rights of creation. This holistic paradigm of Divine–Human and Social Conciliation notably recurs again at Q.76 and Q.107 and is a point of remarkable concurrence between both the key exegeses utilized in this research. A crucial point to highlight is the explicit Qurʾanic preservation of *birr* in dealings with the polytheists at Q.60:8 and the specific examples cited in the exegesis of the ties of kinship maintained with the Meccans outside of the specific context of military engagement, and their effect on the ultimate softening of relations. I have argued above that the recurrent Qurʾanic injunctions towards patience, non-compulsion and disengagement by the Prophet and his followers in the face of opposition are enjoinders towards non-confrontation rather than the total severance of relations with the Meccans consistently argued by Iṣlāḥī. This is supported by the promise of future reconciliation to the point of *mawadda* (love) between the believers and their present enemies in the Medinan verse Q.60:7, which is particularly inspirational and remarkably optimistic.

From a literary perspective, emphasis is provided in this chapter by the reinforcement of positive messages with a corresponding negative, such as the description of the Prophet's limited role as a warner coupled with a negation of his being a compeller at Q.88:21–22. Q.60:8–9 provide another balanced couplet delivering an emphatic repetition of the limited scope of the prohibition on friendship with the Meccans at Q.60:1. This chapter closes the Qurʾanic discourse by return, reinstating the fundamental importance of the notion of *birr* and encompassing within its scope the rights of the socially disadvantaged such as orphans, the needy, captives, slaves and neighbours requiring assistance.

The Conciliation content in Groups 6 & 7 demonstrates a good level of coherence, highlighting an essential linguistic and semantic connection between the fundamental conciliatory notions of *birr* (dutiful conduct), *iḥsān* (gracious conduct) and *ṣalāḥ* (a thriving state of affairs). The frequent injunctions to the Prophet to show patience and restraint, and the recurrent commendation of social justice and corresponding chastisement of failure to provide social assistance, demonstrate a sustained and coherent Conciliation narrative. The holistic paradigm of Divine–Human and Social Conciliation and the essential nexus between the two notions are neatly encapsulated in the promise of Divine eschatological *iḥsān* (grace) as a recompense for temporal human *iḥsān* (gracious conduct) towards others. This is most powerfully conveyed at Q.55:60 through an eloquent rhetorical question which also uses paronomasia to enhance its semantic import.

This chapter provides a fitting conclusion to the examination of Conciliation in this research. The recurrent notion of *iḥsān*, situated in a motivational eschatological context for added impact, is followed by an evaluation of the conciliatory effect of the repeated enjoinder to the Prophet towards disengagement. The chapter concludes with a return to the fundamental notion of *birr* which opened the discussion in Chapter 1.

Summary Table: Groups 1–7 Conciliation Map of Key Themes

	GROUP 1	GROUP 2	GROUP 3	GROUP 4	GROUP 5	GROUP 6 & 7
BIRR	Medinan (primary)					
CONFLICT MGMT						
JUSTICE		Meccan (secondary)				
UNITY						
DISENGAGEMENT		Meccan (primary)				
FORGIVENESS						
IṢLĀḤ						
PEACE TREATIES	Medinan (secondary)					
IḤSĀN						
KINSHIP						
GOOD SPEECH						
NON-COMPULSION						
SOCIAL JUSTICE						
PATIENCE						

The table illustrates the range of Conciliation themes and their distribution through the sura groups. Meccan and Medinan content is distinguished by colour (green and blue respectively), with darker shading indicating a primary theme with several important verses or a sustained engagement with a subject, and lighter shading indicating a secondary theme with occasional or ancillary content. Two 'split' boxes indicate shared Meccan and Medinan content across one theme in a sura group.

https://doi.org/10.1515/9783110747348-009

Final Conclusion

As explained in the Introduction, this study aims to analyse, and evaluate the importance of, Conciliation in the Qurʾan to provide a more balanced and complete understanding of the Qurʾan's perspective on social relations. In doing so, it views Conciliation as a holistic concept and asks four specific research questions. These questions are set out and answered in sections 1 to 4 below, based on the substantive analysis in Chapters 1 to 6, and the individual Chapter conclusions. Answers to key questions raised in the early discussion on Conciliation in Context are also provided based on my analysis. Section 5 then answers the central question of the research, providing a critical evaluation of the importance of Conciliation in the Qurʾan. The principal research sources, namely the exegesis methodologies of Al-Rāzī and Iṣlāḥī, are critically evaluated in the next section, which is followed by some insights into the limitations of the research. Finally, the theoretical and practical implications of the research are discussed, and opportunities identified for further research.

Before embarking on a detailed outline of the research findings in sections 1 to 4, the original contribution of this research to the field of Qurʾanic Studies is highlighted below, with reference to the relevant literature.

Original Contribution of the Research

As highlighted in the Introduction, Conciliation in the Qurʾan is an under-researched field of study, with limited and fragmented existing literature, a lacuna which this thematic study has aimed to address. Through extending the temporal range of this analysis to include pre-dispute mechanisms, considering the causes as well as the manifestations of conflict, extending the analysis to include a range of Qurʾanic terms, and taking into account both theoretical and practical examples of Conciliation, the thematic analysis of Conciliation in the Qurʾan compared to previous studies has been significantly extended through this research. In particular, a historical and contemporary linguistic restriction of the study of Conciliation in the Qurʾan to references including or focussed on the term *ṣulḥ* (reconciliation, settlement) has been addressed in this study by examining Conciliation as a holistic concept. ***Iḥsān*** (gracious conduct) is the most prominent of five key Qurʾanic terminologies identified in this study, as a result of this non-restrictive approach, which provide a focus for the recurrence of the Conciliation theme. The other four terms are: ***birr*** (dutiful conduct) in Groups 1 and 6 & 7; ***iṣlāḥ*** (order) in Group 2; ***ṣabr*** (patience) in Groups 3, 5, and

https://doi.org/10.1515/9783110747348-010

6 & 7 and ***i'rāḍ*** (disengagement) in Groups 2, 4 and 6 & 7. These five notions are not included in the brief list of ten words with similar meanings to *ṣulḥ* provided by ʿAbd Al-Quddūs (1999, p.195).

A particularly notable original contribution of this research is the identification and extensive analysis of the central Conciliation theme of *iṣlāḥ* (order) in Chapter 2, addressing an apparent lacuna in the understanding of coherence in the Meccan narratives of Q.7 identified by Welch (2000, p.85). According to my analysis of this key concept, *iṣlāḥ* is the central axis around which equilibrium is maintained in the Divine world order, a process of Divine education in the form of revelation and prophetic instruction, which prevents and contains disputes and directly aims to address the angelic complaint, at man's creation, of *fasād* (disorder) and bloodshed on the earth. I have argued that *iṣlāḥ* is the true opposite of *fasād* in the Qurʾan, distinguishing my position somewhat from the analysis of Neuwirth (2000, pp.13, 15) who juxtaposes *fasād* with *īmān* (faith). I have argued that *iṣlāḥ* is integrally embedded in the Qurʾanic discourse and appears to be the primary responsibility of man as God's vicegerent. I consider justice, which Amadu (2015, p.185) considers man's primary responsibility, to be one example of *iṣlāḥ*.

As can be unmistakably appreciated by reference to the Groups 1–7 Summary Table above and the content of this research, the notion of *iḥsān* has been the single most pervasive, recurrent and comprehensive term in this study of Conciliation. It has featured through every chapter of this book encompassing every group of suras, providing an invaluable depth and range of insights into the nature of, and the conduct required to achieve, both Divine-Human and Social Conciliation. The notion of *iḥsān* is, however, a somewhat nebulous concept in the Qurʾan, featuring in a range of linguistic forms, as well as both social and theological contexts. As such, it is susceptible to a misplaced emphasis on excellence in the worship of God rather than gracious conduct in social relations, a point on which I have criticised Iṣlāḥī in particular. The notion of *iḥsān* is also susceptible to loss of impact due to the use of variable and generic terms in translations, such as Abdel Haleem's, and under-appreciation in past studies on *ṣulḥ*, such as that of ʿAbd Al-Quddūs (1999). It is hoped that the analysis in this research has made a valuable contribution towards an appropriate understanding of the importance of this notion as a medium of Conciliation in social relations.

In relation to my organisational framework, I have highlighted that Iṣlāḥī's otherwise detailed schema shows a significant weakness in failing to pair Q.49 or to adequately appreciate its thematic significance, a point highlighted by Mir (1986, pp.76, 81). Based on my extensive and detailed analysis, and tabulated and diagrammatically represented data, I have addressed this issue and brought to light the full extent of sustained focus on Conciliation, foregrounded in a strong sura pairing at Q.48–Q.49. As argued in this work, the Meccan suras of Group 5 provide informative and detailed insights into the Qur'anic theory of Conciliation, which crystallises into a powerful practical example of steadfast resolve resulting in Conciliation at Ḥudaybiya in the Medinan Q.48, and a paradigm of conciliatory conduct and universal human equality and affinity in the Medinan Q.49. In this Group more than anywhere else in the Qur'an, I have demonstrated that Conciliation becomes the primary theme of the Qur'anic narrative, identifying Conciliation as a central theme in the Qur'anic discourse as a whole.

In the introductory chapters of this book, I pointed out the significant lag in the systematic study of Medinan suras as compared to Meccan suras, a point highlighted by Neuwirth (n.d., "Types of Medinan suras") as an 'urgent desideratum'. My relatively thorough analysis of Q.48 and Q.49, as well as my less comprehensive analysis of other Medinan suras, represents a significant though limited contribution towards this effort and is comparable with the similar contributions of other writers such as El-Awa (2006) and Locate-Timol (2009).

I have highlighted in the Introduction that coherence in the Qur'an and thematic studies of the Qur'an have hitherto been viewed as separate areas of research, with Iṣlāḥī's exegesis largely discussed at a structural level in the former of the two fields. This research has offered significant new insight into this monumental work through extensive analysis. From a methodological perspective, the original use of coherence in this research, not as an independent field of study but as an inherent part of the methodology of a thematic study, has provided a valuable analytical framework and hermeneutic device. The role of conflict, read coherently alongside the Conciliation narrative, has been properly delineated into its historical and textual context. Coherence has also provided an essential guide to proper interpretation and translation of key terms, such as *iḥsān* (gracious conduct).

In addition, the significance of *iṣlāḥ* as a binding theme at the sura level in Q.7 and the significance of Conciliation in Q.48–Q.49 as a central theme at the Qur'anic text level have been appreciated primarily as a result of forensic historical or textual context-based interpretation, and reference to other coherence indicators, such as recurrent keywords. Without commenting on the overall level of coherence in the Qur'an, which remains an area of analysis as indicated by Rippin (2013), my answer to question 4 below reveals a significant level of thematic coherence in the Qur'an in relation to Conciliation. This perspective on thematic Qur'anic coherence complements debates around the coherence of structural units such as verses (Abdul-Raof, 2003), suras (Neuwirth, n.d.) and the text as a whole (Iṣlāḥī's schema).

The correlation of Qur'anic notions of Conciliation in this thematic study to various contemporary Conciliation theories, whose authors are referred to in the research and the conclusions below, is another notably original contribution which extends the findings of my earlier research (Fazaluddin, 2016). This enhances the study of Conciliation generally and facilitates cross-over with Qur'anic Studies, supporting the contemporary application of the research findings outside of a limited religious context.

Finally, it should be highlighted that, in conducting a detailed study of Conciliation in the Qur'an, this research has also yielded important original insights into the restrictive parameters of conflict in the Qur'an, particularly by reference to Q.8–9 and Q.49, about which more will be said at the conclusion of the answer to research question 5 below.

Each research question will now be listed and answered in turn as mentioned above.

1 Is Conciliation Pervasive in the Meccan and Medinan Qur'an?

A close study of Conciliation in the Qur'an has demonstrated that Conciliation features substantively in each of the sura groups examined, indicating a sense of sequential continuity through the entire Qur'an. The manifestation of a range of diverse individual themes in each sura group indicates a sustained, collective thematic importance throughout. The Groups 1–7 Summary Table illustrates the recurrence of Conciliation themes across several sura groups, sometimes coming to the fore as a primary theme of greater significance, and at other times providing supportive references alongside other themes which predominate in a sura group.

The Groups 1–7 Summary Table further illustrates that Conciliation in the Qur'an, analysed in the holistic manner described in the previous section, is pervasive in the Qur'anic discourse, featuring extensively in both the Meccan and Medinan discourse. Of the 40 boxes populated in the Summary Table, 21 are wholly and 2 partially Meccan (17 primary and 6 secondary) and 17 wholly and 2 partially Medinan (12 primary and 7 secondary). Whilst quantitative analysis of this data, which includes qualitative assessments, has its limitations, some general insights can be obtained. Conciliation content in the Meccan and Medinan Qur'an appears to be consistent with the proportion of Meccan and Medinan content in the Qur'an, which is around 60%/40% (based on Noldeke; Robinson, 2003, p.196), indicating a balanced distribution between the two periods. Although the Meccan content might appear, from the individual chapter Summary Tables, to display a greater recurrence of Conciliation concepts and to be distributed across a much greater number of suras, the Medinan content is generally more concentrated and detailed when it occurs, providing overall balance in the level of Conciliation content. Groups 1, 2, 5 and 6 & 7 all feature important concrete, detailed and ambitious Medinan Conciliation provisions relating to both relations between believers, and between believers and disbelievers. Groups 1 and 5, in particular, display a strong core of Medinan Conciliation content across an exceptionally broad range of themes.

Viewed at this comprehensive, macro-level, it is difficult to see a disjunct between the emphasis on Conciliation in the Meccan and Medinan periods, as suggested by Cragg (2001, pp.90, 95). Indeed, the Medinan provisions appear to be in general more sophisticated and practical, often based on binding contracts and quasi-legal processes, whilst the Meccan provisions appear to be predominantly ethical, relating to the development of conciliatory values and conduct. 'Primary Conciliation Verses', detailing the Qur'an's fundamental Conciliation philosophy as described further below, feature equally in both the Meccan and Medinan periods. Notably, it is in the Medinan Qur'an, at Q.48–Q.49 in Group 5, that Conciliation features as the primary theme of the Qur'anic discourse, continuously pervading these two suras in their entirety. Similarly in Group 1, which is also Medinan, the focus of the Qur'anic discourse, as indicated by the group theme in the Farāhī-Iṣlāḥī schema, is Islamic Law. This discourse reflects a significant emphasis on conflict management processes and justice, providing a strong association with dispute resolution. Historically too, the most widely reported instances of Conciliation featured in the Medinan period at Ḥudaybiya and subsequently at the Conquest of Mecca. I have argued in this research that Conciliation in the Meccan period was essentially a preparatory development process for the crystallisation of these ultimate reconciliation opportunities in the Medinan period. All of this suggests a consistent progression of conciliatory teachings across the two periods, climaxing in the Medinan period.

2 What Are the Range of Aspects of Conciliation in the Qur'an?

The range of aspects of Conciliation in the Qur'an is vast. Many of these have been obscured by the narrow focus of past studies, and this study has aimed to bring to light the true richness of the notion of Conciliation, as now discussed. The Groups 1–7 Summary Table demonstrates a hierarchical panoply of Conciliation themes, reflecting the different levels of society at which the Qur'an interjects to effect change and instil a conciliatory framework. At the micro-level, the personal responsibilities and values inspired and encouraged include *birr* (dutiful conduct), *iʿrāḍ* (disengagement) from conflict, forgiveness, *iḥsān* (gracious conduct), good speech and *ṣabr* (patience). At the intermediate level, intra-societal conflict management systems include the stipulation of allocated financial shares in inheritance matters, the injunction to record financial contracts in writing to avoid disputes as to the precise terms, processes for the appointment of mutual arbiters in matrimonial disputes, and third-party intervention to contain and resolve group disputes. At the macro-level, inter-society or universal values include justice, unity, *iṣlāḥ* (order), peace treaties, kinship, non-compulsion in faith and social justice. These universal values are pervasively promoted and espoused by the Qur'an, often using legislative language or eschatological reward and sanction to emphasise their sanctity. The Conciliation themes identified range from the personal to the universal and the style of engagement becomes progressively more didactic as it moves from the personal to the universal, societal level.

The above hierarchical levels in the Qur'an are apparent from the outset in Group 1. The Qur'an promotes Conciliation through principles and processes. Principles such as *birr* (dutiful conduct), commonality of faith and sanctity of kinship in Group 1 promote change at the personal and universal levels and are expounded further below. Conciliation processes address practical issues at the intermediate level, and are explicitly mentioned in Q.2 and Q.4 in legal and quasi-legal civil and criminal law contexts, such as marriage, testatory matters and homicide, resurfacing in the context of group disputes at Group 5 in Q.49. These processes have been discussed in a fragmented fashion in existing literature. This research, however, has examined further legal material in Group 1, adopting a purposive construction of provisions stipulating pre-allocated shares in inheritance and detailed formality requirements for the recording of commercial contracts in Q.2 and Q.4 to identify anticipatory dispute avoidance mechanisms. These mechanisms are designed to address uncertainty in contractual terms and rights which might result in financial disputes. Indeed, it has been argued that the root causes of disputes arising from each of the *Maqāṣid Al-Sharīʿa* (underlying aims of Islamic Law) are addressed in these suras.

The Medinan suras of Group 2 have formed the core basis of extensive academic study and media coverage of the subject of conflict in the Qur'an, often dominating the narrative around these suras. Verses such as Q.9:5, sensationally referred to classically and in contemporary literature as the 'Sword Verse', have achieved notoriety and sometimes been granted an abrogating status by certain commentators, which the analysis in Chapter 2 has demonstrated to be unwarranted by the textual analysis. This research has argued for a balanced appreciation of the import of these suras (Q.8 and Q.9), bringing to light firstly the preceding Meccan content advocating disengagement and non-confrontation which provides essential interpretive context, and secondly the recurrent punctuation of conflict verses by emphatic enjoinders promoting and preserving peace treaties. These binding, legal agreements provide a concrete and robust manifestation of Conciliation whose importance in the Qur'anic narrative is undeniable, particularly in light of the historical circumstances of Ḥudaybiya highlighted at Q.48. The parameter of conflict envisaged in the Qur'an is discussed further below. The analysis of Group 2 also reveals the essential conciliatory notion of *iṣlāḥ*, which has been detailed in the Original Contribution section above.

Another fundamental conciliatory notion, *iḥsān* (gracious conduct), dominates and pervades the core themes and suras of Group 3, constituting two of Iṣlāḥī's central sura themes at Q.12:90 and Q.16:30. In Chapter 1, *iḥsān* featured at Q.4:36, emphasising good conduct in a host of human relationships and featuring alongside *birr* (dutiful conduct) in the maintenance of social cohesion. This was followed up in Chapter 2, where the conduct of *iḥsān* was apparent in the Qur'anic shaping of the Prophetic exemplar in maintaining relations with those who have cut off relations and showing forgiveness. Chapter 3 introduced the 'definition' of *iḥsān* at Q.3:134, providing benefit and showing restraint and forgiveness, and demonstrated this exemplary conduct through the Story of Joseph in Q.12, as well as highlighting *iḥsān* in good speech through rational and courteous (theological) debate. In Chapter 4, the conciliatory models of the *ʿIbād Al-Raḥmān* (the Servants of the Lord of Mercy), Luqmān's ideal and the story of Moses highlighted *iḥsān* in the reciprocation of harm with goodness, whilst Chapter 5 emphasised the need for fortitude and perseverance in the sustained maintenance of *iḥsān*, to effect a change in the other party and ultimately bring about a complete reconciliation between former enemies. Chapter 6 again brought to the fore the twin notions within *iḥsān* of ***al-taʿẓīm li amri 'llāhi taʿālā wa 'l-shafaqa ʿalā khalqi 'llāh*** (honouring the command of God the Exalted and compassion towards God's creation) and highlighted the Divine eschatological reward of earthly human *iḥsān*.

In Group 4, I have argued that the Qur'an espouses disengagement from conflict even to the extent of migration, provides exhaustive rational proofs which are explicitly referred to by commentators as *itmām al-ḥujja* (completion of proof), and delivers an unprecedented level of cross-layered appeals. In my view, therefore, the Group 4 suras not only demonstrate *itmām al-ḥujja* but also '*itmām al-iʿrāḍ*' (completion of disengagement) and '*itmām al-ighrāʾ*' (completion of appeal). In these three notions, Conciliation in Group 4 suras is not only absolutely central to the Qur'anic discourse but is also expounded to the ultimate level of persistence. This insistence on dialectic and appeal, and its essential nexus with accountability in the Hereafter through the notion of freewill, has been discussed at length because it provides essential context to the discussion of Conciliation and Conflict in Chapter 2 of this book. The Qur'anic approach highlighted in

Chapter 4 exemplifies and validates the enjoinders towards the Prophet in Chapters 2, 3 and 6 in particular to engage only in rational and courteous debate in faith propagation, to avoid confrontation and compulsion, and to disengage to the point of migration from non-constructive disputation, leaving the Meccans entirely free to choose whether or not to accept the new faith. This is consistent with the declared principle of non-compulsion in faith at Q.2:256 of the Qur'an.

It is my argument that this approach negates any suggestion that the Prophet was mandated by the Qur'an to engage in military conflict in order to compel the Meccans to accept Islam. This is an idea which is sometimes promoted by the views of certain classical commentators cited by Al-Rāzī who exaggerate the scope and effect of the 'Sword Verse' far beyond its textual capacity, by contemporary Islamic exegetes such as Iṣlāḥī who make the argument that military conflict with the Meccans was espoused until they accepted Islam, and by contemporary Western writers such as Cragg and others who again over-state the role of conflict in the Medinan period. In fact, peace treaties suspending conflict and considered sacrosanct and inviolable were permitted in Groups 2 and 5 despite differences of faith, whereas limited conflict was permitted in Group 5 even against fellow believers, in the specific case of defence against transgression.

Another important notion in Group 5 is *ṣabr,* enjoined no less than 18 times upon the Prophet. Although this term is frequently translated merely as 'patience', I have argued that its true import as a means to Conciliation far exceeds a momentary act of modest self-restraint. Q.41:34–36 in Group 5 provide detailed insight into the theory behind Qur'anic Conciliation. Here, the Qur'anic doctrine of *iḥsān* (gracious conduct) is closely coupled with the related notion of *ṣabr*, demonstrating much affinity with contemporary notions of the ingredients of effective reconciliations. In particular, the reciprocation of harm with good conduct provides a limitation on the escalation of conflict and promotes virtuous cycles of cooperation, identified by Allred (2005, p.95) in contemporary Conciliation theory. Sustained fortitude and forbearance over a protracted period can ultimately effect a change of heart, turning enmity to mutual affection, consistent with the contemporary importance of harnessing emotions in reconciliation highlighted by Shapiro (2005, pp.74–75). Crucially, a strong personal disposition, uninfluenced by the harm of the other, breaks the chain of causation which would lead to conflict actualisation and escalation.

Throughout the above process, dialogue is to be maintained based on a common value which appeals to the other and draws them towards the path of Conciliation. *Mawadda* (love) between kin, a common Arab value and irrefutable biological connection, is the central appeal which the Qur'an enjoins the Prophet to present to his adversaries as a basis for ultimate reconciliation at Q.42:23, again mirroring contemporary Conciliation theory by appealing to Explicit values in Greenhouse's model (1985, pp.91–92, 98–107). The earthly recompense promised for this effort is a lasting and complete reconciliation, whilst the eschatological recompense promised is a heavenly reward from God. Although the Meccan response to this call is not within the Prophet's control, the call to kinship and *iḥsān* (gracious conduct) is reversed at the Conquest of Mecca from the Meccans to the Prophet, who now responds affirmatively to this conciliatory appeal, bringing about a momentous final reconciliation, considered by Watt to be the Prophet's greatest achievement.

Another important Conciliatory notion in Group 5 is forgiveness, and its relationship with justice, one of the fundamental social duties included within *iṣlāḥ* (order). Injustice is an important example of *fasād* and potentially leads to disputation, with Al-Rāzī arguing that any corruption of the *maqāṣid* (aims) of the *Sharīʿa* constitutes *fasād*. Justice is explicitly enjoined at Q.5:8 as a sacrosanct principle to be preserved irrespective of past enmity with the Meccans. The Prophet is also enjoined in the Medinan period to adjudicate in disputes with justice. Yet both the homicide provisions of Q.2:178 and the provisions of Q.42:40 and Q.42:43 emphasise the laudability of forgiving one's legal rights in order to bring about an end to conflict. Whilst delicate persuasive wording is used to show sensitivity to the victim or claimant's right to justice in these cases, as a role model, the Prophet is held to a higher standard and instructed to forgive both believers and disbelievers (Q.3:159, Q.7:199). These examples all demonstrate that forgiveness can prevail over justice with the ultimate aim being the attainment of a peaceful outcome. The crucial objective of Qurʾanic Conciliation which aspires to reunite hearts is beyond the reach of imposed justice and judicial process, a well-known cause of rancour amongst litigants.

Justice is emphasised in the context of reconciliation between disputing groups in Q.49. However, I have argued that the emphasis is on due process and impartiality in dealings with the two disputing parties. I have argued against Al-Rāzī and Iṣlāḥī that a reconciliation settlement itself is not required to be objectively fair and just, provided that the two disputing parties are in agreement in accepting its terms. This provides crucial insight into the Qurʾanic perspective on an issue debated by Islamic jurists, as noted by Othman (2007, pp.73–81). It also supports the distinction made by Alsheikh (2011, pp.378, 399) between arbitration and *ṣulḥ* (Conciliation), the latter being a binding contract based on agreement between the parties, with concession of rights. Conciliation of disputes may necessitate the concession of rights and the forgiveness of wrongs, both to create solutions as indicated by Gopin (2001, pp.93–97), and to provide sustainable conclusions to conflicts (Derin, 2005, pp.1–2, 7–10). A crucial distinction to highlight is that, although the fulfilment of rights may *prevent* disputes from arising by addressing their root cause, as discussed in relation to *birr* (dutiful conduct) and inheritance, the *resolution* of existing disputes may necessitate the concession of rights, as discussed in relation to homicide and group disputes.

Ultimately, the Qur'anic Conciliation discourse encourages individuals to protect their own hearts from alienation and empowers them to transform the hearts of erstwhile enemies, inclining them towards reconciliation. Many examples have been seen of Qur'anic instructions towards internal transformation, such as Q.2:177 and several verses in Q.49, and also towards conduct which would lead to internal transformation in others, such as Q.3:64 and Q.16:125 in relation to inter-faith dialogue. What is particularly remarkable, however, is that the Qur'an makes a point of claiming Divine credit for the reconciliation of hearts, highlighting this as a Divine blessing (Q.3:103), a Divine miracle (Q.8:63), a Divine purification in Paradise (Q.15:47), the grant of a beneficent Lord (Q.19:96), a Divinely inspired means to victory (Q.48:4), and a symbol of God's power to transform past enmity to love (Q.60:7). In the Qur'anic schema, it appears that whilst conciliatory conduct and systems are also important, it is the hearts which are seen as the drivers of change and the seat of Divine influence.

The preservation of courteous dialogue and human ties appears to be absolutely essential to the achievement of long-term reconciliation. Speech is regulated in Group 3 in the context of faith propagation, again in Group 3 in relation to an instance of slander, and in Group 5 in the context of unverified rumours and public or private defamation or ridicule which might lead to conflict. These textual passages, contexts and related analysis highlight the capacity of derogatory or insulting speech to give rise to negative emotions and to initiate and escalate conflicts. In Group 3, the Prophet is required to debate rationally and courteously in his efforts to impart faith, whilst ties of kinship are exemplified by the story of Joseph and emphasised repeatedly throughout the Group, both temporally and eschatologically. Also in Group 3, the Prophet's close friend Abū Bakr is required to preserve ties of kinship and social assistance, despite the obvious affront to his honour resulting from the casting of aspersions against the honour of his daughter. In Group 5, good speech is enjoined at Q.49:11–12 and immediately followed at Q.49:13 by a seminal verse promoting common kinship and equality between all humans. This collocation indicates that courteous, honorific dialogue is both an entitlement and an obligation of mutual equality and proximity and a means to mutual knowledge and Conciliation.

In Groups 6 & 7, the maintenance of ties of kinship and *birr* (dutiful conduct) with the Meccan disbelievers is specifically and emphatically encouraged with those who have not shown hostility, contrary to Levy's suggestion that such duties appear to apply only between believers. The Qur'an even promises future *mawadda* (love) at Q.60:7, signifying reconciliation between the believers and the Meccan disbelievers. Reconciling of hearts is also emphasized in the context of relations between the Medinan believers at Q.3:103 and Q.8:63. I have argued in Groups 6 & 7 that *iʿrāḍ* (disengagement), advocated in this and earlier groups such as Group 2, is a means to non-confrontation rather than a means to severance of relations or perpetual conflict. In both the opening and closing sura groups of the Qur'an, there is a notable focus on the notion of *birr* (dutiful conduct) imbuing a sense of personal responsibility which redirects the focus of religion from mere rituals and underpins social justice. This fulfilment of human needs is an apparent means to avoiding social conflict, a point also made by Abu-Nimer (2003, p.9) in contemporary Conciliation theory, and applies irrespective of differences of faith.

Much of the discussion above relates to Social Conciliation and indeed this is by far the richer notion in the Qur'anic discourse. Nonetheless, Divine-Human Conciliation features in virtually every group of suras, providing reminders of God's Divine mercy as an exemplar for human forgiveness, promising eschatological rewards as a motivational incentive for human *iḥsān*, and defining aspirational holistic Conciliation models of those who engage in both Social and Divine-Human Conciliation through the fulfilment of rights and the seeking of Divine forgiveness for their shortcomings. In contrast with these models of humility and Conciliation, Satan epitomises arrogance, conflict and rebellion against God, a model emulated by the likes of Pharaoh and Qārūn. What has come to light in this thematic study of Conciliation, after much analysis and reflection at the focal point of Q.49, is that arrogance is not only a fundamental source of conflict in Divine-human relations but also in social relations. Arrogance, which results in self-elevation and the distancing and abandonment of others, is directly countered through the crucial verse Q.49:13 which delivers a universal address advocating human equality.

3 What Literary Techniques Are Used to Emphasise Conciliation in the Qur'an?

In the individual chapters and chapter conclusions above, a number of specific literary techniques utilised in the respective sura groups have been highlighted. Viewing the research as a whole, it can now be seen that a number of these literary techniques are a recurrent feature across multiple sura groups or are of particular significance within the overall Qur'anic discourse in emphasizing the importance of Conciliation. These literary techniques are discussed below.

A trinity of seminal Conciliation verses in Group 1, at Q.3:64, Q.3:102–103 and Q.4:1 respectively, address inter-faith dialogue, intra-faith brotherhood and universal human kinship, providing an over-arching canopy of unifying principles which each emphasise social cohesion and denounce social division. These notions recur in the following sura groups with brotherhood featuring motivationally again in the context of harmonious eschatological relations in Paradise at Q.15:47 in Group 3 and on earth in the explicit context of reconciliation at Q.49.9 in Group 5. Universal kinship is also most notably emphasised again at Q.49:13. Within these notions, the Qurʾan leverages commonalities, such as the common reception of Divine scripture, commonality of faith and belief, ties of blood and common parentage, and universal humanity, to instil a sense of mutual proximity and invoke unifying values and ties.

Q.3:64, Q.3:102–103 and Q.4:1 are examples of what I would term 'Primary Conciliation Verses'. These verses advocate universal conciliatory principles as detailed above, which provide the foundational theoretical basis of the Qurʾanic Conciliation philosophy. Other such principles derived from Primary Conciliation verses, whose fundamental reach has been individually highlighted in the body of this research, include: internal change (Q.2:177), non-compulsion (Q.2:256), peaceful relations (Q.2:208), maintaining the Divine order (Q.7:56), forgiveness and disengagement (Q.7:199), fulfilment of rights and gracious conduct (Q.16:90), rational and courteous theological debate (Q.16:125) and human equality and proximate relations (Q.49:13). These Primary Conciliation Verses are often signalled by appealing terms of address, grammatical signals such as the emphatic foregrounding of key terms in the accusative case, or commanding use of the imperative form. What is discernable in these verses is the direct and authoritative proclamation of principles advocating Conciliation in the Divine voice, drawing attention and delivering impact.

In Group 2, the mutual dependency and reciprocity integral to contractual peace treaties is indicated through two Medinan symmetrical constructs at Q.8:61 and Q.9:7, both of which explicitly use an imperative form to command the establishment and maintenance respectively of peace treaties between the believers and the Meccan disbelievers. The fundamental importance of Conciliation in the Meccan period is also clearly evidenced by the terminology and image of the *ṣirāṭ*, the 'path' to salvation, also referred to as the Prophet's way and God's way, to describe conciliatory behaviours which constitute *iṣlāḥ*. These behaviours are encapsulated by the essential theological doctrine of God's unity, again emphasising their fundamental and integral nature within the Qurʾanic discourse, whilst behaviour leading to conflict is associated with the Divinely rejected Satan. This oppositional duality between the way of God and the Prophet and the way of Satan manifestly highlights Conciliation as the ideal endorsed by the Qur'an, and conflict as its repugnant antithesis.

Satan is portrayed as the recurrent inciter of social conflict across Groups 1, 2, 3 and 5 in particular in a remarkable number of verses: Q.2:208, Q.5:91, Q.7:200, Q.12:100, Q.17:53, Q.24:21, Q.28:15 and Q.41:36. In doing so, the Qur'an appears to both indicate the repulsive nature of choosing the path of conflict and to draw the source of hostility away from the parties, resulting in 'Externalisation' of the conflict and facilitating their mutual reconciliation. This approach, which entails forgiveness and non-retribution, is specifically modelled by Joseph at Q.12:100 and presents a clear exemplar for the Prophet's own demonstration of gracious conduct towards his kin at the Conquest of Mecca, opening the way for a final reconciliation with the Meccans, as discussed in Chapter 3.

The origination narrative of Adam and Satan is embedded within the discourse on *iṣlāḥ* in Group 2, once again highlighting its fundamental importance. This narrative employs the recurrent term of address 'O Children of Adam' four times from Q.7:26–35 to provide a clear sense of universal and timeless appeal, appealing to mankind to prefer the Qur'anic teachings and reject the call of Satan. At Q.20:94 in Group 3, Aaron uses a term of address *ya'bna umma* (O son of my mother) which is remarkable for its unusually indirect reference to their sibling relationship. The invocation of a common mother and the associated memories of a merciful relationship maximise the conciliatory appeal. Terms of address are also used in Group 1 in each of Q.3:64, Q.3:102–103 and Q.4:1 respectively to unify and appeal, directly and collectively, to all those sharing the commonality invoked in each instance: *yā ahl al-kitāb* (O People of the Book), *yā ayyuha 'lladhīna āmanū* (O you who believe), *yā ayyuha ('l)-nnās* (O Mankind). The latter address *yā ayyuha ('l)-nnās* (O Mankind) is again invoked at Q.49:13 in Group 5 in a binding declaration of human unity and equality. These three terms of address collectively indicate that Conciliation pervades the Qur'anic discourse at multiple levels: inter-faith, intra-faith and at a universal human level, and is not, for example, restricted to relations between believers only.

Divine *iḥsān* serves as an aspirational exemplar for human *iḥsān* in Groups 3 and 6 in particular. The enticing promise of Divine reward for human *iḥsān* in these groups, most famously in Q.55:60, also engenders a strong motivational effect, promising rich eschatological recompense for gratuitous temporal benefit offered to others or forgiveness of their wrongs. Notably, relations with God are invoked to stimulate better relations between people. In Group 1, I coined this a "Conciliation Relationship Triangle" by reference to the three notions of *birr* (dutiful conduct), *taqwā* (God-consciousness) and *iṣlāḥ bayn al-nās* (reconciling between people).

As well as the Divine exemplar, the Qur'an also provides exposition of the narratives of Joseph and Abraham in Group 3, the *ʿIbād Al-Raḥmān*, Luqmān and Moses in Group 4, and David in Group 5. Each of these narratives serves as an aspirational human exemplar of conciliatory conduct, such as *iḥsān* (gracious conduct), *iʿrāḍ* (disengagement) and *ṣabr* (patience). The Qur'an often explicitly invokes these narratives primarily for their exemplary and motivational effect in encouraging the Prophet to maintain a conciliatory approach to his dealings with the Meccans in the face of protracted and significant opposition. Given the Prophet's own exemplary status relative to his followers, as highlighted in Groups 2 and 4 in particular, the employment of these narratives also has a significant secondary impact on the followers of the Prophet, vastly extending the popular reach of these conciliatory teachings. From the Divine exemplar to the exemplar of past prophets, and then the Prophet himself, this provides an incremental cascade of conciliatory exemplification.

Yet further motivation towards *iḥsān* and Conciliation is provided through the profound antithesis of harmonious familial relations in Paradise in Group 3, and the internal conflict endured by the inhabitants of Hell. In stark contrast, the plight of those in Hell is heightened by their mutual recriminations and estrangement, indicated in Groups 2, 3 and 5 at Q.7:38–39, Q.23:101, Q.40:47 and Q.43:67. The Qur'an frequently employs the use of *ṭibāq* (antithesis) to maximise the impact of its message. In Group 1, two metaphors at Q.3:103 powerfully contrast a possible ascension relying on the security of the 'rope' of unity with the danger of descent into the fiery abyss of enmity and strife. In Group 4 also, the humility and altruism of the *ʿIbād Al-Raḥmān* provides a notable contrast with the arrogance of Pharaoh and the social injustice perpetrated by him. In each case, antithesis enhances the impact of the Qur'anic discourse through a vivid and oppositional contrast of representations of Conciliation and conflict.

The use of sustained teleological and cosmological arguments in Group 2, and the sustained recurrence of dialogical and rhetorical indicators on multiple occasions in Group 4, signals the Qur'an's interactive engagement with its contenders, evoking a sense of urgency and presence. The use of recurrent motifs also provides rhetorical impact to the Qur'anic argument in Group 4, accentuating its rational and sensory appeal. Despite its apparent transcendence, the Qur'an devotes much textual capacity to addressing the contentions of its opponents, consistent with its declared insistence on the use of persuasion rather than compulsion. This is manifest in the notion of *itmām al-ḥujja*, based on the exhaustive enumeration of natural phenomena and historical narratives, as *āyāt* (signs). In the suras of this group there is also a palpable sense of progressive appeal, with the style of argument developing from a defensive response to an informative assertion, and finally climaxing with a challenging interrogative style, demanding an intellectual or sensory response.

We see perhaps the most explicit command to conciliate in the entire Qur'an in Group 5 at Q.49:9–10, with the arresting imperative ***aṣliḥū* (reconcile)** repeated emphatically three times, in the context of group disputes, and still further elevated by being referred to as 'God's command'. A triple repetition of the same notion and grammatical root indicating matrimonial Conciliation is also found at Q.4:128 in Group 1, whilst in Group 2 another triple repetition *allafa* (He united) emphasises the Divine unification of the hearts of the believers at Q.8:63. The use of *takrār* (repetition) and *tawkīd* (emphasis) in the Qur'an is well known. This can sometimes manifest, for example, in the recurrent employment of a narrative at different junctures in the case of *takrār*, or the use of a grammatical particle in the case of *tawkīd*. In the instances of repetition of a term indicating Conciliation highlighted here, there is an immediate and combined repetition *and* emphasis which is both rhetorically eloquent and semantically effective.

Q.49 utilises a manifestly evocative style, repeatedly addressing the believers directly and holding conciliatory conduct aloft as an external exposition of internal faith, whilst engendering an abhorrence of conduct leading to conflict through the damning term *fāsiq* (wilfully disobedient) and the metaphor of consuming the dead flesh of a brother. Twin metaphors, the positive image of the rope signifying unity and the negative image of a pit of fire signifying conflict, are also invoked in Group 1 in the seminal verse on unity, Q.3:103 mentioned above. In Group 3, Q.14:24 presents the image of a good word as a deep-rooted and flourishing tree. These metaphors invoke emotions and feelings such as abhorrence in the case of consuming human flesh, security in the case of the rope, danger in the case of a pit of fire, and satisfaction in the case of a flourishing tree. These emotions and feelings are employed as a means to encourage Conciliation and repel conflict, using the recurrent Qur'anic technique of *targhīb* (motivational appeal) and *tarhīb* (warning).

Amongst the literary techniques demonstrated in Groups 6 & 7, the embedding of Conciliation verses in the vivid descriptions of Paradise for motivational effect is particularly dramatic and effective, and employs the Qur'anic technique of *taṣwīr* (imagined scenes brought to life). In addition, the use of *kināya* (metonymy) to recurrently refer to 'feeding', whilst indicating various forms of social assistance, preserves the essential stylistic brevity and focus of this Qur'anic segment, without reducing the general scope of its social message. The combination of brevity and persistence provides a certain focus and impact to the Conciliation material in this concluding textual segment of the Qur'an, which is otherwise dominated by the over-arching theme of differentiated eschatological outcomes.

Reflecting on the above literary techniques, it can be seen that the Qur'an invokes commonality and mutuality to draw people together, channels their desire to please God and attain His reward towards good conduct in dealing with people, celebrates and lauds conciliatory models to inspire emulation, interrogates and appeals rationally and intuitively to engage and persuade its audience, and invokes an emotional response through antithesis and metaphor to influence human choices between Conciliation and conflict. Leveraging a diverse and powerful array of literary techniques, the Qur'an emphasises the concept of Conciliation and the values, choices and conduct which lead to it.

4 How Coherent Is the Exposition of Conciliation in the Qur'an?

The Groups 1–7 Summary Table illustrates that it has been possible to identify 14 sustained Conciliation themes in the Qur'anic discourse as a whole. The Conciliation themes identified do not themselves demonstrate an obvious linear coherence in their progression through the sequential Qur'anic discourse. However, a number of clearly identifiable Conciliation themes are, as discussed below, cohesively interwoven in a manner which provides a remarkable level of what I would term 'local' and 'global' coherence in light of the complex multi-dimensional nature of the Qur'an's thematic content.

It can be seen that some of the 14 Conciliation themes are sustained intra-Group demonstrating thematic cohesion of a sequential text segment, such as the protracted engagement with legal and quasi-legal processes in Group 1 and the pervasive notion of *iṣlāḥ* in Group 2. Despite a protracted alternation between a legislative and narrative style of exposition, the recurrent notion of *iṣlāḥ* in both styles maintains coherence in an exhaustive Conciliation discourse, providing a supporting concurrence of theory and practice similar to the supportive pairing of theory and practice in Q.48 and Q.49. The conflict management processes in Group 1 and the constituent notions within *iṣlāḥ* both correlate well with the *Maqāṣid Al-Sharīʿa* (underlying aims of Islamic Law), indicating the fundamental importance of Conciliation and its essential connection with both the letter and the spirit of Islamic Law.

Other themes are recurrent inter-Group such as good speech, disengagement and social justice, providing a sense of global coherence across the sura groups or through different over-arching contexts in the Qur'anic discourse. The theme of *iḥsān* is especially pervasive across the groups and becomes progressively more developed. It begins with a definition in Group 1, becomes prominently exemplified and enjoined in Group 3 and to a lesser extent Group

4 at the sequential centre of the Qur'anic discourse, and is then expounded in more theoretical detail in Group 5 where it connects to the real, historical, final reconciliation. Over-arching the group-level themes, both the Divine-Human and Social Conciliation contexts also demonstrate global cohesion in their consistent mutual focus on notions such as forgiveness, *iḥsān* and rational debate. As stated in the Introduction to this book, it is a well-known exegetical principle that different parts of the Qur'an *explain* each other: *al-Qur'ānu yufassiru baʿḍuhū baʿḍā*. I would argue, based on my research, that different parts of the Qur'an do more than this: they mutually support the multifarious development of ideas which are central to the *argument and exposition* of the Qur'an: ***al-Qur'ānu yu'ayyidu baʿḍuhū baʿḍā***. Thus, as the exposition of *iḥsān* is elucidated and developed through the different sura groups, so the message of Conciliation is itself defined, exemplified and detailed for the Prophet and through him his followers. This approach indicates that the greater existence of patterns of coherence within a Qur'anic theme may well provide an indication of its central importance within the global Qur'anic discourse.

More granular global coherence across sura groups is provided through the Qur'anic Conciliation discourse by its focus on a number of recurrent *keywords* mentioned previously. The recurrence of the specific linguistic terms: *iḥsān* (gracious conduct), *birr* (dutiful conduct) *iṣlāḥ* (order), *ṣabr* (patience) and *iʿrāḍ* (disengagement), provides both linguistic and thematic cohesion. In Group 4 and elsewhere in the Qur'an, the notion of *āyāt* (signs) also provides cohesion in the protracted enumeration of Qur'anic evidence in support of its argument, whilst recurrent rhetorical indicators, such as *alladhī* (who) six times in Q.25 and *amman* (who?) in Q.27, support the protracted extension of the Qur'anic argument, providing local coherence within a specific sura or passage. Recurrent terms of address also provide local coherence in protracted appeals, such as *yā ahl al-kitāb* (O People of the Book) six times in Q.3, *yā banī Adam* (O Children of Adam) four times in Q.7, and *yā ayyuha 'lladhīna āmanū* (O you who believe) five times in Q.49. These examples show the Qur'an's tendency to use recurrent linguistic terms to provide both global and local coherence and thus reinforce both the range and depth of its argument.

A number of structural hierarchies within the Qur'anic discourse provide coherence. In both Groups 1 and 2, Conciliation content can be divided into the personal, intra-societal and universal inter-societal social levels. In Group 4, a Matrix of Appeals progresses chronologically from the primordial to the eschatological, is based on intellect, intuition and emotion and reaches out to its audience at the personal, collective and universal levels. In Group 5, Q.49 presents a hierarchical paradigm commencing with obedience to God, then progressing to reverence for His Messenger and respect for leadership, and finally mutual reconciliation between groups and respect between individuals. These hierarchies provide a coherent range in the social levels at which the Qur'anic discourse pitches its Conciliation themes, apparently envisaging personal development, the establishment of intra-societal systems and the instillment of universal values.

The Qur'anic Conciliation narrative presents a sense of completeness, closing by return in Groups 6 & 7 with the notion of *birr* (dutiful conduct), which opens the Conciliation narrative at Q.2:177. This is particularly interesting because Q.2:177 contains both Divine-human and social duties and is summative yet comprehensive in its definition of the scope of religious obligations. Yet it is most immediately succeeded by issues of conflict management in social contexts such as homicide and testatory matters, before the sura goes on to deal with matters of worship but again highlighting issues of conflict management, such as the prohibition on in-fighting during the pilgrimage. This conciliatory emphasis on conflict management in the social context is both emphatically repeated and this time conclusively *foregrounded* in Chapter 6, where the notion of *birr* (dutiful conduct) is juxtaposed with social justice. At Q.60:6–8, *birr* (dutiful conduct) becomes absolutely central to the softening of relations and the attainment of a deep and lasting reconciliation between the Prophet and his followers and the Meccans, highlighting its fundamental importance as a Conciliation concept which both opens and closes the Qur'anic discourse. In numerous suras in this research, I have highlighted the strategic location of references to Conciliation at their commencement or conclusion, indicating the centrality of Conciliation to their central message. It appears that the same approach is adopted in the Qur'anic corpus as a whole, providing incremental levels of coherence.

5 What Is the Relative Importance of Conciliation in the Qur'an?

It has been argued above that Conciliation is pervasive at the intra-Group and inter-Group levels, both sequentially through its textual landscape, and hierarchically through its engagement with a range of social and societal contexts. Conciliation is also pervasive in both the Meccan and Medinan Qur'an, with the range of recurrence indicating its importance in the Meccan Qur'an and the depth of focus emphasising its importance in the Medinan Qur'an. At the same time, the Qur'anic discourse opens and closes with a key Conciliation theme, highlighting its strategic importance.

Amongst the range of aspects of Conciliation considered in this research, several indicate its particular importance. The binding nature of contractual peace treaties and financial agreements and the emphasis given to them, the systematic approach to integrating conflict management processes within the societal framework to prevent, manage and control conflicts, and the legislative language used to instil conciliatory conduct and values, are all clear indications of the utmost importance of Conciliation to the attainment of a prosperous society. The correlation in the Conciliation discourse to the *Maqāṣid Al-Sharī'a* (underlying aims of Islamic Law) also indicates its centrality within the aims of Islamic Law. The devotion of an entire sura to focus on the events at Ḥudaybiya and its aftermath at the Conquest of Mecca shows the importance of Conciliation in the historical context of the Qur'an, whilst the claiming of Divine credit for reconciling hearts and the determination of eschatological outcomes based on conciliatory conduct on earth provides yet further indications of its ultimate importance in the Qur'an's central discourse.

It has also been shown that the Qur'an employs an impressive array of linguistic techniques to persuade its audience of the merits of Conciliation and the hazards of conflict. It leverages emotions, intellect and intuition, and instructs, exemplifies and presents models of Conciliation. The invocation of the primordial Adam-Satan narrative, the term of address 'O Children of Adam', the stipulation of man's essential role as God's vicegerent maintaining the Divine order, and the reference to the *ṣirāṭ* as God's way and the Prophet's way are all central to this appeal. Whereas the Qur'an's *quantitative* engagement with its audience on the theme of Conciliation indicates its pervasive importance above, the literary techniques demonstrate the *qualitative* engagement with the audience and the maximal effort expended to appeal to and influence the audience to make choices and adopt values and behaviours consistent with a conciliatory approach. This indicates that Conciliation is central to the *aims* of the Qur'anic discourse.

The local and global coherence identified within the Conciliation discourse demonstrates how the Qur'an builds an interwoven tapestry of cross-referencing themes and linguistic terms to elucidate the importance of Conciliation. Although many writers have appreciated the rhetorical and stylistic effectiveness of the Qur'anic discourse, the perception of some writers that the Qur'an lacks coherence has clearly retracted from their ability to appreciate its semantic importance, such as Welch's perspective (2000, p.112, n.18) on the narratives employed in Q.7. For this reason, the above discussion on coherence should enable the semantic importance of the Conciliation discourse to be appreciated more fully. The coherent, sustained engagement with the theme of Conciliation indicates a deliberate, systematic and progressively developed theme which is of central importance within the structural arrangement and content of the Qur'anic text.

Finally on this subject, it is important to address and reconcile the position of conflict in the Qur'an with the conclusions reached above. I have argued on the basis of my research that a defensive response to transgression, rather than a difference of faith, is the criteria for conflict in the Qur'an, both against the Meccan disbelievers and between believers in Medina. This, to my mind, is a more historically and textually sound explanation of the role of conflict in the Qur'an than that argued by Iṣlāḥī or Cragg. As a principle, it also does not discriminate by faith and does not put conflict on a par with or above Conciliation in importance. Rather, conflict is a limited, anomalous situation which I have argued is delineated by multiple justifications and restrictive parameters in the Qur'an. The 'Sword Verse' itself, considered the most robust exposition of an injunction to enter into conflict in the entire Qur'an, is softened by references to Divine forgiveness and mercy, and is surrounded by restrictive parameters and conditions which clearly uphold peace treaties which have not been repudiated and refer to the granting of safe passage to those seeking refuge from conflict.

By clear contrast, the upholding of peace treaties is sacrosanct (Q.4:90, Q.8:72; Q.9:4, 7) and Conciliation verses such as Q.7:200 and Q.8:61 stress God's qualities of seeing and hearing which indicate accountability before God for failure to reconcile, through forgiveness and disengagement, or contractual agreement. Q.49:9 refers to Conciliation as *amri 'llāh* (God's command) showing its clear dominance in the Qur'an over conflict. Even normal legal principles are set aside for Conciliation, such as the binding nature of oaths at Q.2:224 and Q.24:22, the normally mandatory punishment in criminal law in the case of homicide at Q.2:178, and the binding nature of a legal will at Q.2:182. Both in military and civil conflicts, Conciliation remains of paramount importance in the Qur'an.

Critical Evaluation of Principal Research Sources

In general, I have found that Iṣlāḥī's sura groups provide a useful framework within which to marshal and analyse the vast Qur'anic corpus. Whilst my analysis is restricted to the Conciliation content and provides a limited basis for comment, the group-level themes he identifies appear to generally correlate with my analysis, most notably in Group 1 (Law) and Groups 6 & 7 (the Hereafter). A notable weakness in Iṣlāḥī's schema at the sura level, however, is that a number of his sura themes appear so generic as to provide little insight as to their individual content, for example 'warnings and good tidings', and some themes are recurrently applied to a significant number of suras, such as Q.10–34 and Q.25–32.

A strong pairing has been noted in some suras, providing some credibility to Iṣlāḥī's notion of sura pairing, although as mentioned my limited sample of

Conciliation material is not of course a sufficient basis for validating or undermining his general theory in this regard. Q.2 and Q.4 both display a notable emphasis on legislating for the prevention and management of disputes. It should be noted that this functional pairing based on Conciliation content is in fact distinct from Iṣlāḥī's *sequential* pairing of Q.2–3 and Q.4–5. At Q.12–Q.13, however, a strong sequential pairing is found in the maintenance of ties of kinship practically exemplified by Joseph in Q.12 and then explicitly enjoined at length by the Qur'anic discourse in Q.13, like Q.48–Q.49 below an example of practice and theory being closely coupled. Q.16–Q.17 also display a strong sequential pairing in their sustained engagement with the three Conciliation themes of Group 3, namely *iḥsān* (gracious conduct), kinship and good speech. Finally, Q.48–Q.49 display a notably strong pairing, with Q.48 providing a practical example of Conciliation and Q.49 providing a codified Conciliation paradigm. However, the strong pairing of Q.48–Q.49 identified in this research on Conciliation in fact addresses a notable *weakness* in the lack of formal pairing of these suras, and the lack in identification of thematic importance of Q.49, in Iṣlāḥī's schema.

I have mentioned in Chapter 3 that Iṣlāḥī misdirects two important references in Q.12 and Q.16 to *iḥsān* (gracious conduct) in social dealings towards excellence in worship. In these instances, a coherence-based analysis of the surrounding themes and context should have provided an important rectifying hermeneutic device. It should be mentioned, in fairness to Iṣlāḥī, that he employs this very approach in other instances, such as his global perspective of *birr* (dutiful conduct) at Q.2:177. This provides vital linkage in what might otherwise appear to be disparate passages dealing with teachings and rulings in a range of social and religious contexts. More generally, Iṣlāḥī's position on the Meccans' role as custodians of the *Ka'ba* provides a relatively coherent historical overlay to many of his interpretations of the verses around conflict, despite my ongoing disagreement with his position on the scope of conflict, particularly in Q.9 and Q.48. This entrenched position leads to ongoing difficulties for Iṣlāḥī, most notably in a passage dealing with forgiveness at Q.42:37–43 in Chapter 5 and another espousing reconciliation at Q.60:1–8 in Chapter 6, where his comments regarding ongoing hostilities with the Meccans appear very much at odds with the explicit wording of the verses, as well as demonstrating internal inconsistencies at different points within his own analysis. The issue here lies not in adopting a coherent stance in itself, but rather in the particular stance which Iṣlāḥī has subjectively chosen to adopt.

Al-Rāzī's linguistic insights and explanatory analysis in relation to key notions such as *iḥsān* (gracious conduct), *ṣabr* (patience), *mawaddata fī 'l-qurbā* (love amongst relatives) have been instrumental in enabling a full analysis of the subject matter both in its textual and historical context and in expounding and correlating that analysis to contemporary Conciliation theory. More particularly, Al-Rāzī's commentary regarding causation and the internal effects on the addressee of both contentious and honorific speech, and of gracious conduct in place of retaliation, have yielded profound insights into the Qurʾanic style and purpose of expression. His juxtaposition of the *qulūb* (hearts) of the polytheists in being prevented from *qubūl* (acceptance) of the faith at Q.6:108, shows a sensitivity to the Qur'anic style and semantic which, at Q.3:159, reflects a causative nexus between harshness and dispersal through acoustic resonance between ***faẓẓan*** and *(i)n**faḍḍ**ū*. Although Iṣlāḥī's coherence methodology has provided an analytical framework for this study, there is little doubt that Al-Rāzī's linguistic analysis has been an essential platform for the culmination of that research.

Al-Rāzī's methodology and perspective are quite different to Iṣlāḥī's. Where Iṣlāḥī argues from a subjective but generally consistent global vision of the Qur'an's central message and themes, running into difficulties in the consistency of his interpretation of proximate or otherwise related verses, Al-Rāzī does much the opposite. His *munāsaba* (chaining) methodology ensures consistency between locally proximate or otherwise related verses, such as in Q.16:125–128, Q.42:37–43 and Q.60:1–8, which actually sometimes provide more consistent and coherent explanations of Conciliation verses than those offered by Iṣlāḥī. Despite this local consistency, Al-Rāzī's global position on key issues such as conflict sometimes appears to fluctuate as he presents his own variations of emphasis alongside an encyclopaedic rendition of divergent positions from numerous commentaries.

Given the difference in their approach and outcomes, not to mention their language, culture and time, it is remarkable that the two exegetes concur so discernibly, most noticeably in Groups 6 & 7, on the recurrent and central importance of *iḥsān* (gracious conduct), and the dual tenets of maintaining social and Divine-human relations as the fundamental basis of Qurʾanic philosophy. In choosing these two complementary exegetes as the basis for my research, I had aimed to provide a balance of methodology and perspective which would provide a comparative reference-point to both identify weaknesses in their analysis and add credibility to any concurring conclusions. In this respect, the methodology does appear to have achieved these aims.

Limitations of Research

My own analysis is, of course, cast in the mould of my own subjective selection of Conciliation verses, structural segments of thematic importance, and passages from the exegesis which merit inclusion in the research. This is inherent in a task of this nature and I have attempted to provide some redress through transparency in my methodology, and by selecting Qur'anic material and exegesis on the basis of its relevance and its utility in examining the notion of Conciliation, irrespective of whether it supports or refutes my argument. Indeed, I have formed my argument in each chapter only after protracted reflection on my research findings.

It may be argued that a limitation to two exegetes represents a restricted analysis of the subject matter. I had commenced the research with a third exegete but decided that the depth of analysis I could offer was greater when restricted to the two I finally included, without loss of insight given that exegetes with similar methodologies tend to include similar material. I was also able to extend the range of exegetical insight somewhat on complex issues by reference to the diverse exegetical references provided by Nasr and the annotations of Yusuf Ali.

Finally, the innovative combination of coherence studies and a thematic study posed some risk of over-reliance on Iṣlāḥī's analysis in the examination of Conciliation. It should be apparent that I have used Iṣlāḥī's schema only as an organisational framework for marshalling a large volume of Qur'anic data, performing my own independent compilation and analysis of the Qur'anic data *before* examining, and therefore independently of, its exegesis. Furthermore, I have examined and presented Iṣlāḥī's commentary alongside that of Al-Rāzī, giving them equal voice. It should also be apparent from the above, that I have analysed Iṣlāḥī's exegesis critically.

Implications and Further Research

Although conflict in the Qur'an has attracted much interest, particularly in contemporary academic circles and the media, Conciliation in the Qur'an has hitherto remained a largely unexplored landscape in Western academia. This study demonstrates that in order to obtain a balanced and appropriately nuanced perspective on the relative importance of issues such as Conciliation and conflict, it is necessary to look beyond isolated, apparently sensational verses such as Q.9:5, and to conduct a detailed examination of the entire Qur'anic text in relation to the relevant subject matter. Furthermore, in compiling a balanced narrative, incoherence (for example, in Q.7) and disjuncts (for example, between Meccan and Medinan revelation) should not be assumed at face value. Instead, careful forensic analysis should be employed to consider whether themes or verses, which may appear disparate in isolation, are capable of being reconciled to provide a coherent and meaningful collective discourse.

The research shows that embarking upon a 'holistic' thematic study may entail an extension of the temporal, semantic and linguistic range of a subject.

Thus a study of Conciliation, for example, should include proactive conflict prevention and avoidance measures to obtain a proper understanding of the approach to the subject. In the same way, an understanding of what constitutes Conciliation should not be restricted to a particular manifestation, such as an Alternative Dispute Resolution process. In addition, such thematic studies should not focus merely on specific linguistic terms such as *ṣulḥ* (reconciliation, settlement) in a mechanical fashion, but should adopt an open, constructivist approach to exploring a concept using careful thought and deliberation to identify those terms which are most pertinent to the study of the subject, as well as manifestations of a theme which go beyond mere terminology.

The findings of this research should be highly relevant to the current emphasis on Community Cohesion in central and local Government policy,[18] particularly in positively influencing relations between Muslim and non-Muslim communities. This study has shown that the Qurʾan addresses the notion of Conciliation in the context of relations between believers, but often also between believers and other faith groups, and people in general. As such, the findings of this study provide a broad scope for understanding the Qurʾan's approach to Conciliation in different societal contexts. Furthermore, Conciliation discourse has often been found to align with contemporary Conciliation theories, indicating a contemporary application and relevance. This indicates useful synergies between classical and contemporary Conciliation theory, which can increase their mutual uptake across different cultures.

After the Qurʾan, the Ḥadīth collections are the most important source texts in Islamic Studies. As such, a study of Conciliation in the Ḥadīth would represent a natural progression from the current research. This study into Conciliation in the Qurʾan has touched on a number of *ḥadīth* mentioned in the exegesis reviewed. However, a more comprehensive and systematic study of Conciliation in the Ḥadīth by reference to one or more specific collections, and with regard to the level of authentication, would naturally be required for such a project. As with the exegesis-based research into the Qurʾan utilised in this study, authoritative commentaries on the selected Ḥadīth collections would provide valuable additional insights into the source texts. The findings of the two studies into Qurʾan and Ḥadīth could then be compared and contrasted providing additional insights into the study of Conciliation in these primary Islamic texts.

I have also, on several occasions in this study, made reference to the subject of *Maqāṣid Al-Sharīʿa* (underlying aims of Islamic Law). This is an important area of study in its own right and one on which much has been written by

18 See the Integrated Communities Strategy Green Paper (March 2018).

both classical and contemporary writers. The findings of the current research could be used to inform an evaluation of the importance of Conciliation in relation to the *Maqāṣid Al-Sharīʿa* (underlying aims of Islamic Law), and the implications for their future development. This in turn may have further implications for developments in Islamic Law.

Bibliography

ʿAbd al-Bāqī, M. 2001. *Al-Muʿjam Al-Mufahras Li-Alfāẓ Al-Qurʾan Al-Karīm*. Cairo: Dār al-Ḥadīth.
ʿAbd al-Quddūs, M. 1999. 'Al-Ṣulḥ Wal-Iṣlāḥ Fil-Qurʾan Al-Karīm – Vol.1'. Mecca: Jāmiʿat Umm ul-Qurā. https://quranpedia.net/ar/book/17257. <Accessed: 22 August 2021>.
Abdel Haleem, M. 1990. 'The Story of Joseph in the Qur'an and The Old Testament'. *Islam and Christian–Muslim Relations* 1(2), 171–191.
Abdel Haleem, M. 2001. *Understanding the Qurʾan: Themes and Style*. London: IB Tauris.
Abdel Haleem, M. 2005. *The Qurʾan*. Oxford: Oxford University Press.
Abdel Haleem, M. 2010. 'Qurʾanic Jihād: A Linguistic and Contextual Analysis'. *Journal of Qurʾanic Studies* 12, 147–166.
Abdel Haleem, M. 2012. 'The *Jizya* Verse (Q.9:29): Tax Enforcement on Non-Muslims in the First Muslim State'. *Journal of Qurʾanic Studies* 14(2), 72–89.
Abdel Haleem, M. 2017. *Exploring the Qurʾan: Context and Impact*. London: IB Tauris.
Abdel Haleem, M. and Badawi, E. 2013. *Dictionary of Qurʾanic Usage*. Leiden: Brill.
Abdul-Raof, H. 2003. 'Conceptual and Textual Chaining in Qur'anic Discourse'. *Journal of Qur'anic Studies* 5(2), 72–94.
Abu-Deeb, K. 2000. 'Studies in the *Majāz* and Metaphorical Language of the Qur'an: Abu ʿUbayda and al-Sharīf al-Rādī'. In: *Literary Structures of Religious Meaning in the Qurʾan*. Boullata, I. (ed.). Oxon: Routledge.
Abu-Nimer, M. 2003. *Nonviolence and Peace Building in Islam : Theory and Practice*. Gainesville, Florida : University Press of Florida.
Ahmad, N. 2009. 'Peace and Reconciliation, Its Significance and Role in the Mission of the Prophet (Peace Be on Him): The Case of Ṣulḥ Al-Ḥudaybiyah, a Qur'ānic View'. *Insights, Focused on Faith Studies* 2(ii–iii), 181–218.
Al-Baʿalbakī, R. 2000. *Al-Mawrid*. Beirut: Dar-El-Elm Lilmalayin.
Al-Ghazālī. 2011. *Al-Iḥyāʾ ʿUlūm Al-Dīn*. https://www.ghazali.org/site/ihya.htm. <Accessed: 22 August 2021>.
Al-Humaidhi, H. 2015. 'Ṣulḥ: Arbitration in the Arab-Islamic World'. *Arab Law Quarterly* 29(i), 92–99.
Al-Iṣfahānī, R. 2009. *Mufradāt Alfāẓ Al-Qurʿān*. Istanbul: Al-Dār Al-Shāmiya.
Al-Liḥyānī, H. 2007. 'Al-Maḍāmīn Al-Tarbawiyya Al-Mustanbiṭa Min Ṣulḥ Al-Ḥudaybia Wa Taṭbīqātihā Al-Tarbawiyya Fil Usra Wal-Madrasa'. Saudi Arabia: Umm Ul-Qurā. http://www.al-eman.com. <Accessed: 22 August 2021>.
Allred, K. 2005. 'Relationship Dynamics in Disputes'. In: *The Handbook of Dispute Resolution*. Moffitt, M., Bordone, R. (ed.). San Francisco: Jossey-Bass.
Al-Qurṭubī, A. 2006. *Al-Jāmiʿ li-Aḥkām il-Qurʾan*. 24 vols. Beirut: Al-Resalah.
Al-Ramahi, A. 2008. 'Sulh: A Crucial Part of Islamic Arbitration'. http://papers.ssrn.com/sol3/papers.cfm?abstract_id=1153659. <Accessed: 22 August 2021>.
Al-Rāzī, F. 1981. *Mafātīḥ Al-Ghayb*. Beirut: Dār al Fikr.
Al-Ṣabāḥī, Y. 2016. 'Mulāʾamat Al-Takālīf Al-Sharʿiyya Lil-Mukallaf Wa Awjah Al-Raḥma Fīhā'. *Journal of Social Studies* 48, 191–234.
Alsheikh, E. 2011. 'Distinction between the Concepts Mediation, Conciliation, *Ṣulḥ* and Arbitration in Sharīah Law'. *Arab Law Quarterly* 25(4), 367–400.
Al-Suyūṭī, J. 2013. *Tārīkh al-Khulafāʾ*. Beirut: Dār al-Minhāj.

https://doi.org/10.1515/9783110747348-011

Al-Zuhayli, W. 2007. *Financial Transactions in Islamic Jurisprudence*. Vol. 2, Damascus: Dar al Fikr.

Amadu, M. 2015. 'The Qur'ānic Concept of ʿAdl as a Significant Resource to the Qur'anic Concepts of Salām and Ṣulḥ'. British Library: EThOS Database.

Arkoun, M. n.d. 'Contemporary Critical Practices and the Qurʾān'. *Encyclopaedia of the Qurʾān*. Leiden: Brill.

Asad, M. 2003. *The Message of the Qurʾan*. Bristol: The Book Foundation.

Asfaruddin, A. 2010. 'Where Earth and Heaven Meet: Remembering Muḥammad as Head of State'. In: *The Cambridge Companion to Muḥammad*. Brockopp, J. (ed.). New York: Cambridge University Press.

Auda, J. 2011. 'A Maqāṣidī Approach to Contemporary Application of the Sharī'ah'. *Intellectual Discourse* 19(2), 193–217.

ʿAynī, B. 2000. *Al-Bināyah Sharḥ al-Hidāyah*. Vol. 10, Beirut: Manshūrāt Muḥammad ʿAlī Baydūn, Dār al-Kutub al-ʿIlmīyah.

Bauer, M. *et al.* (eds.). 2014. 'Textual Analysis'. In: *SAGE Benchmarks in Social Research Methods*. Vol. 1, xxi–xlvii, London: Sage. http://eprints.lse.ac.uk/57383. <Accessed: 22 August 2021>.

Berman, H. 1974. *The Interaction of Law and Religion*. Lowell Lectures. London: SCM Press.

Bin Salamah, A. 2002. 'Athar Al-Ṣulḥ ʿAlā Qaṭʿil Khuṣūmāt Al-Jināʾiyya'. Riyadh: Naif Arab Academy For Security Sciences. http://www.al-eman.com. <Accessed 22 August 2021>

Bouheraoua, S. 2010. 'Foundation of Mediation in Islamic Law and Its Contemporary Application'. International Islamic University Malaysia. http://www.asiapacificmediationforum.org/resources/2008/11-_Said.pdf. <Accessed: 22 August 2021>

Boullata, I. 2000. 'Sayyid Quṭb's Literary Appreciation of the Qurʾān'. In: *Literary Structures of Religious Meaning in the Qurʾan*. Boullata, I. (ed.). Oxon: Routledge.

Brown, C. 1998. 'Common-sense Ethics'. *Routledge Encyclopaedia of Philosophy*. Taylor and Francis. https://www.rep.routledge.com/articles/thematic/common-sense-ethics/v-1. <Accessed: 22 August 2021>.

Brown, J. 2019. *Slavery and Islam*. London: Oneworld Publications.

Burton, J. (ed.). 1990. *Conflict: Human Needs Theory*. Hampshire: The Macmillan Press Ltd.

Carlisle, J. 2007. 'Divorce Damascus Style: Court Mediation and Arbitration Strategies During Judicial Divorce Cases'. *Conference Papers – Law & Society* 1.

Chowdhury, S. 2015. *Introducing Arabic Rhetoric*. London: Dar al-Nicosia.

Cohen, R. 2001. 'Language and Conflict Resolution: The Limits of English'. *International Studies Review* 3(1), 25–51.

Cragg, K. 2001. *Muhammad in the Qur'an*. London: Melisende.

Davidson, E. *et al.* 2019. 'Big data, qualitative style: a breadth-and-depth method for working with large amounts of secondary qualitative data'. *Quality & Quantity* 53(1), 363–376.

Dayeh, I. 2010. 'Al-Ḥawāmīm: Intertextuality and Coherence in Meccan Surahs'. In: *The Qur'ān in Context: Historical and Literary Investigations into the Qur'ānic Milieu*. Neuwirth, A., Sinai, N., Marx, M. (ed.). Leiden & Boston: Brill, 461–498.

Denny, F. n.d. 'Community and Society in the Qurʾān'. *Encyclopaedia of the Qurʾān*. Leiden: Brill.

Derin, S. 2005. 'The Tradition Of Sulh Among The Sufis; With Special Reference To Ibn Arabi And Yunus Emre'. *Journal of Academic Studies* 7(27), 1–12.

Diab, R. 2016. *Shades of Sulh : The Rhetorics of Arab-Islamic Reconciliation*. Pittsburgh Series in Composition, Literacy, and Culture. Pittsburgh: University of Pittsburgh Press.

Draz, M. 2000. *Introduction to the Qur'an*. London: IB Tauris.
El-Ansary, W. and Linnan, D. (ed.). 2010. *Muslim and Christian Understanding: Theory and Application of a "Common Word"*. New York: Palgrave Macmillan.
El-Awa, S. 2006. *Textual Relations in the Qur'an : Relevance, Coherence and Structure*. Routledge Studies in the Quran, London: Routledge.
Ernst, C. 2010. 'Muḥammad as the Pole of Existence'. In: *The Cambridge Companion to Muḥammad*. Brockopp, J. (ed.). New York: Cambridge University Press.
Esposito, J. 2007. *Farahi, Hamiduddin*. Oxford University Press.
Fadl Allah, M. 1973. *Sulh Al-Imam Al-Hasan: Asbabuhu, Nata'ijuhu*. Beirut: Dar Al-Zahra Li Taba'ah Wa 'l-Nashr.
Faiq, S. 2011. 'Coherence'. *Encyclopedia of Arabic Language and Linguistics*. Leiden: Brill.
Farāhī, H. 1968. *Dalāil Al-Niẓām*. Azamgarh, India: al-Dāirah al-Ḥamīdīyah wa-Maktabatuhā.
Farrin, R. 2014. *Structure and Qur'anic Interpretation: A Study of Symmetry and Coherence in Islam's Holy Text*. Ashland: White Cloud Press.
Fayrūzuddin, M. n.d. *Fayrūz-ul-Lughāt*. Lahore: Fayrūz Sons ltd.
Fazaluddin, S. 2016. 'Conciliation Ethics in the Qurʾan'. *International Journal for the Semiotics of Law* 29(2), 333–358. doi: 10.1007/s11196-016-9455-z.
Gellman, M. and Vuinovich, M. 2008. 'From Sulha to Salaam: Connecting Local Knowledge with International Negotiations for Lasting Peace in Palestine/Israel'. *Conflict Resolution Quarterly* 26(2), 127–148.
Gopin, M. 2001. 'Forgiveness As An Element of Conflict Resolution in Religious Cultures'. In: *Reconciliation, Justice and Coexistence: Theory and Practice*. Abu-Nimer, M. (ed.). Maryland: Lexington Books.
Greenhouse, C. 1985. 'Mediation: A Comparative Approach'. *Man* Vol.20(1), 90–114.
Griffel, F. 2009. *Al-Ghazālī's Philosophical Theology*. New York: Oxford University Press.
Griffel, F. 2012. 'Al-Ghazālī's Use of "Original Human Disposition" (*Fiṭra*) and its Background'. *The Muslim World* 102, 1–32.
Gwynne, R. 2004. *Logic, Rhetoric and Legal Reasoning in the Qurʾan*. New York: Routledge.
Gwynne, R. 2007. 'Patterns of Address'. In: *The Blackwell Companion to the Qurʾan*. Rippin, A. (ed.) Blackwell Publishing Ltd.
Hallaq, W. 2005. *The Origins and Evolution of Islamic Law*. New York: Cambridge University Press.
Hallaq, W. 2009. *An Introduction to Islamic Law*. Cambridge: Cambridge University Press.
Hallaq, W. 2016. 'Law and the Qurʾān'. http://referenceworks.brillonline.com/entries/encyclopaedia-of-the-quran/law-and-the-quran-EQCOM_00106?s.num=2&s.f.s2_parent=s.f.book.encyclopaedia-of-the-quran&s.q=unity+of+the+text+of+the+quran.
Hamidullah, M. 1945. *Muslim Conduct of State*. Lahore: Sh. Muhammad Ashraf.
Harvey, R. 2018. *The Qurʾan and the Just Society*. Edinburgh: Edinburgh University Press.
Hāshmī, A. 2008. *Jawāhir Al-Balāgha*. Beirut: Muʾassa Al-Muʿārif.
Hassan, K. 2006. 'Employment Dispute Resolution Mechanism from the Islamic Perspective'. *Arab Law Quarterly* 20(2), 181.
Hidayatullah, A. 2014. *Intratextual Method*. Oxford University Press.
Ḥijāzī, S. 1986. *Manhaj al-Iʿlām al-Islāmī fī Ṣulḥ al-Ḥudaybia*. Jeddah: Dār al-Manāra.
Hossain, M. 2013. 'Arbitration in Islamic Law for the Treatment of Civil and Criminal Cases: An Analytical Overview'. *Journal of Philosophy, Culture and Religion* 1, 1–13.
Hoyland, R. 2001. *Arabia and the Arabs*. London; New York: Routledge.

Ibn Al-Ḥajjāj, M. 2006. *Ṣaḥīḥ Al-Muslim*. 2 vols. Riyadh: Dar Tayba.

Islam, M. 2012. 'Provision of Alternative Dispute Resolution Process in Islam'. *IOSR Journal of Business and Management (IOSR-JBM)* 6, 31–36.

Ibn Manẓūr, A. 2014. *Lisān Al-ʿArab*. Vol. 20, Saudi Arabia: Wizārat Al-Shuʾūn Al-Islāmiyya Wa 'l-Awqāf Wa 'l-Daʿwa Wa 'l-Irshād.

Iqbal, A. 1965. *Diplomacy in Islam*. Lahore: Institute of Islamic Culture.

Iṣlāhī, A. n.d. *Tadabbur-E-Qurʾān*. 9 vols. Delhi: World Islamic Publications. http://www.tadabbur-i-quran.org. <Accessed: 22 August 2021>.

Jaffer, T. 2013. 'Fakhr –al-Dīn al-Rāzī's System of Inquiry'. In: *Aims, Methods and Contexts of Qurʾanic Exegis*. Bauer, K. (ed.). New York: Oxford University Press.

Johns, A. 2000. 'Reflections on the Dynamics and Spirituality of Sūrat al-Furqān'. *Literary Structures of Religious Meaning*. Oxon: Routledge.

Juynboll, G. 1974. 'The Position of Qur'an Recitation in Early Islam'. *Journal of Semitic Studies* 19(2), 240–251.

Kamali, M. 2003. *Principles of Islamic Jurisprudence*. Cambridge: Islamic Texts Society.

Kāsānī, A. 1997. *Badāʾiʿ Al-Ṣanāʾiʿ Fī Tartīb Al-Sharāʾiʿ*. Al-Ṭabʿah 1. Vol. 7. Beirut: Manshūrāt Muḥammad ʿAlī Baydịn, Dār al-Kutub al-ʿIlmīyah.

Keshavjee, M. 2013. *Islam, Sharia and Alternative Dispute Resolution: Mechanisms for Legal Redress in the Muslim Community*. Library of Islamic Law. London: I.B.Tauris.

Khadduri, M. 2012. 'Ṣulḥ'. *Encyclopaedia of Islam, Second Edition*. Leiden: Brill.

Khan, I. 2002. 'Coherence in the Qur'ān: Principles and Applications'. *Intellectual Discourse* 10 (i), 47–60.

Khan, I. 2008. 'Amin Ahsan Islahi: An Introduction to His Tafsīr Methodology'. *American Journal of Islamic Social Sciences* 25(4), 21.

Lawson, T. 2008. 'Duality, Opposition and Typology in the Qurʾan: The Apocalyptic Substrate'. *Journal of Qurʾanic Studies* 10(2), 23–49.

Lecker, M. 2010. 'Glimpses of Muhammad's Medinan Decade'. In: *The Cambridge Companion to Muhammad*. Brockopp, J. (ed.). New York: Cambridge University Press.

Levy, R. 1969. *The Social Structure of Islam*. London: The Syndics of the Cambridge University Press.

Lings, M. 2005. *Muhammad – His Life Based on the Earliest Sources*. Cambridge: The Islamic Texts Society.

Locate-Timol, S. 2009. *Makkan and Madinan Revelations: A Comparative Study*. München: Lincom.

Lowry, J. 2010. 'The Prophet as Lawgiver and Legal Authority'. In: *The Cambridge Companion to Muhammad*. Brockopp, J. (ed.). New York: Cambridge University Press.

Lumbard, J. 2015. 'Covenant and Covenants in the Qur'an'. *Journal of Qur'anic Studies* 17(2), 1–23.

Malik, O. and Muda, F. 2015. 'The Concept of Reconciliation (Sulh) in Islamic Family Law and Matrimonial Dispute Settlement Practice in Nigeria'. http://www.academia.edu/download/37145547/PJSSH-14-022_Malik_et_al.pdf. <Accessed: 22 August 2021>.

Ministry of Housing, Communities and Local Government. 2018. 'Integrated Communities Strategy Green Paper'. https://assets.publishing.service.gov.uk/government/uploads/system/uploads/attachment_data/file/696993/Integrated_Communities_Strategy.pdf. <Accessed: 22 August 2021>.

Mir, M. 1983a. 'Unity of the Text of the Qurʾān'. *Encyclopaedia of the Qurʾān*. Leiden: Brill.

Mir, M. 1983b. 'Thematic and Structural Coherence in the Qur'an: A Study of Islahi's Concept of "Nazm" (India, Pakistan)'. Dissertation Abstracts International. Section A: *Humanities and Social Sciences* 44(02), 508–508.

Mir, M. 1986. *Coherence in the Qur'an: A Study of Islahi's Concept of Nazm in Tadabbur-I Qur'an*. Indianapolis: American Trust.

Mir, M. 2013. 'Continuity, Context, and Coherence in the Qur'ān: A Brief Review of the Idea of Naẓm in Tafsīr Literature'. *Al-Bayan: Journal of Qur'an and Hadith Studies* 11(ii), 15–29.

Muṣtafā, A. 2007. 'Al-Ṣulḥ Fī Al-Lugha Wa Al-Qurʾan Wa Al-Sunna Wa Aqwāl Al-ʿUlamāʾ Fī Dhālik'. https://vb.tafsir.net/forum. <Accessed: 22 August 2021>

Mutaf, A. 2004. 'Amicable Settlement in Ottoman Law: Sulh System'. *Turcica* 36, 125–140.

Nadeem, K. 1998. 'MAWLĀNĀ AMĪN AḤSAN IṢLĀḤĪ (1904–1997)'. *Islamic Studies* 37(1), 144–146.

Nadeem, N. 2015. 'A Call for a Collaborative Approach to Understanding Textual Coherence in Quran'. *Quranica – International Journal of Quranic Research* 7(i), 55–74.

Nasr, S. *et al.* (eds.). 2015. *The Study Quran*. New York: HarperCollins Publishers.

Neuwirth, A. 2000. 'A Pre-Canonical Reading of the Qurʾanic Creation Accounts (Part II)'. *Journal of Qurʾanic Studies* 2(2), 1–18.

Neuwirth, A. n.d. 'Form and Structure of the Qurʾān'. *Encyclopaedia of the Qurʾān*. Leiden: Brill.

Oseni, U. 2015. 'Sharī'ah Court-Annexed Dispute Resolution of Three Commonwealth Countries – a Literature Review'. *International Journal of Conflict Management (Emerald)* 26(2), 214.

Othman, A. 2007. '"And Amicable Settlement Is Best": Ṣulḥ and Dispute Resolution in Islamic Law'. *Arab Law Quarterly* 21(1), 64–90.

Quṭb, S. 1979. *In the Shade of the Qur'ān*. London: MWH.

Ramadan, S. 1961. *Islamic Law: Its Scope and Equity*. London : P. R. Macmillan.

Ramsey, C. 2015. 'Elucidating the Word: Sayyid Aḥmad Khān (1817–1898) : Revelation, and Coherence'. University of Birmingham. British Library: EthOS Database.

Rasyid, A. 2013. 'Relevance of Islamic Dispute Resolution Processes in Islamic Banking and Finance'. *Arab Law Quarterly* 27(4), 343.

Reinhart, K. 2016. 'Ethics and the Qurʾān'. http://referenceworks.brillonline.com/entries/encyclopaedia-of-the-quran/ethics-and-the-quran-EQCOM_00056?s.num=2&s.f.s2_parent=s.f.book.encyclopaedia-of-the-quran&s.q=salaha.

Rippin, A. 2013. 'Contemporary Scholarly Understandings of Qur'anic Coherence'. *Al-Bayan: Journal of Qur'an and Hadith Studies* 11(ii), 1–14.

Robinson, N. 2003. *Discovering the Qur'an*. London: SCM Press.

Rozmus, D. and Skoczek, M. 1997. 'Sulh'. *Folia Orientalia* 33, 113–118.

Saleh, W. 'The Arabian Context of Muḥammad's Life'. In: *The Cambridge Companion to Muḥammad*. Brockopp, J. (ed.). New York: Cambridge University Press, 2010.

Salem, F. 2014. 'Freewill, Qadar, and Kasb in the Epistle of Ḥasan al-Baṣrī to ʿAbd al-Malik'. *The Muslim World* 104(1/2), 198–219.

Samḥān, U. 2006. 'ʿAqd Al-Ṣulḥ Fīl Muʿāmalāt Al-Māliyya'. Nablus: Jamiat Al-Najāḥ Al-Waṭaniyya. http://www.al-eman.com. <22 August 2021>.

Sartori, P. 2011. 'The Evolution of Third-Party Mediation in Sharīa Courts in 19th- and Early 20th-Century Central Asia'. *Journal of the Economic & Social History of the Orient* 54(3), 311–352. doi: 10.1163/156852011X587416.

Sayen, G. 2003. 'Arbitration, Conciliation, and the Islamic Legal Tradition in Saudi Arabia'. *University of Pennsylvania Journal of International Law* 24, 905.

Shapiro, D. 2005. 'Enemies, Allies and Emotions'. In: *The Handbook of Dispute Resolution*. Moffitt, M., Bordone, R. (ed.). San Francisco: Jossey-Bass.

Shaybānī, M. 1966. *The Islamic Law of Nations: Shaybānī's Siyar*. Baltimore: John Hopkins Press.

Smith, A. 2018. 'Moses and Pharaoh's Magicians: A Discursive Analysis of the Qur'anic Narratives in the Light of Late Antique Texts and Traditions'. *Journal of Qur'anic Studies* 20(1), 67–104.

Ṭāhā, Ṭ. 2009. 'Al-Ṣulḥ Fī Ḍaw' al-Qur'an al-Karīm'. *Majalla al-Jāmi'a al-Islāmiyya bil-Madina al-Munawwara*. https://quranpedia.net/ar/book/22414. <Accessed: 22 August 2021>.

Tamdoğan, I. 2008. 'Sulh and the Eighteenth Century Ottoman Courts of Üsküdar and Adana'. *Islamic Law & Society* 15(1), 55–83. doi: 10.1163/156851908X287307.

Tolan, J. 2010. 'European Accounts of Muhammad's Life'. In: *The Cambridge Companion to Muḥammad*. Brockopp, J. (ed.), New York: Cambridge University Press.

'Umar, A. and Mukarram, A. 1983. *Mu'jama Al-Qirāāt Al-Qur'āniyya*. Kuwait: Dhāt al-Salāsil.

Watt, M. 1961. *Muhammad: Prophet and Statesman*. London: Oxford University Press.

Wehr, H. 1980. *A Dictionary of Modern Written Arabic*. Cowan, J., Beirut: Librairie Du Liban.

Welch, A. 2000. 'Formulaic Features of the Punishment Stories'. In: *Literary Structures of Religious Meaning in the Qur'an*. Boullata, I. (ed.). Oxon: Routledge.

Welchman, L. 2007. *Women and Muslim Family Laws in Arab States: A Comparative Overview of Textual Development and Advocacy*. ISIM Series on Contemporary Muslim Societies. Amsterdam: Amsterdam University Press.

Yusuf Ali, A. 2001. *The Meaning of the Holy Qur'an*. Maryland: Amana Corporation.

Zayla'ī, U. 2000. *Tabyīn Al-Ḥaqā'iq*. Vol. 5, Beirut : Dār al-Kutub al-Ilmīyah.

Zebiri, K. 2017. 'Argumentation'. In: *The Wiley Blackwell Companion to the Qur'ān*. Rippin, A., Mojaddedi, J. (ed.). New Jersey: John Wiley & Sons Ltd.

Index

https://doi.org/10.1515/9783110747348-012